MODERN ECONOMIC SYSTEMS
AND THEIR TRANSFORMATION

ST ANTONY'S SERIES
General Editors: Alex Pravda (1993–97), Eugene Rogan (1997–), both
Fellows of St Antony's College, Oxford

Recent titles include:

Mark Brzezinski
THE STRUGGLE FOR CONSTITUTIONALISM IN POLAND

Peter Carey (editor)
BURMA

Stephanie Po-yin Chung
CHINESE BUSINESS GROUPS IN HONG KONG AND POLITICAL
CHANGE IN SOUTH CHINA, 1900–25

Ralf Dahrendorf
AFTER 1989

Alex Danchev
ON SPECIALNESS

Roland Dannreuther
THE SOVIET UNION AND THE PLO

Noreena Hertz
RUSSIAN BUSINESS RELATIONSHIPS IN THE WAKE OF REFORM

Iftikhar H. Malik
STATE AND CIVIL SOCIETY IN PAKISTAN

Steven McGuire
AIRBUS INDUSTRIE

Yossi Shain and Aharon Klieman (editors)
DEMOCRACY

William J. Tompson
KHRUSHCHEV

Marguerite Wells
JAPANESE HUMOUR

Yongjin Zhang and Rouben Azizian (editors)
ETHNIC CHALLENGES BEYOND BORDERS

St Antony's Series
Series Standing Order ISBN 0–333–71109–2
(outside North America only)

You can receive future titles in this series as they are published by placing a standing order.
Please contact your bookseller or, in case of difficulty, write to us at the address below with
your name and address, the title of the series and the ISBN quoted above.

Customer Services Department, Macmillan Distribution Ltd
Houndmills, Basingstoke, Hampshire RG21 6XS, England

Modern Economic Systems and their Transformation

J. L. Porket

in association with
ST ANTONY'S COLLEGE, OXFORD

First published in Great Britain 1998 by
MACMILLAN PRESS LTD
Houndmills, Basingstoke, Hampshire RG21 6XS and London
Companies and representatives throughout the world

A catalogue record for this book is available from the British Library.

ISBN 0–333–72130–6

 First published in the United States of America 1998 by
ST. MARTIN'S PRESS, INC.,
Scholarly and Reference Division,
175 Fifth Avenue, New York, N.Y. 10010

ISBN 0–312–21324–7

Library of Congress Cataloging-in-Publication Data
Porket, J. L., 1926–
Modern economic systems and their transformation / J.L. Porket.
    p.   cm. — (St. Antony's series)
Includes bibliographical references (p.   ) and index.
ISBN 0–312–21324–7
1. Comparative economics.   2. Capitalism.   3. Free enterprise.
4. Economic policy.   I. Title.   II. Series.
HB90.P65 1997
330.1—dc21   97–47368
                                                              CIP

This book is printed on paper suitable for recycling and made from fully managed and
sustained forest sources.

10   9   8   7   6   5   4   3   2   1
07   06   05   04   03   02   01   00   99   98

Printed and bound in Great Britain by
Antony Rowe Ltd, Chippenham, Wiltshire

To my wife

Contents

List of Tables

List of Figures

Introduction

The collapse of communism in Eastern Europe and the Soviet Union fatally discredited the idea of totalist authoritarianism (conceived as authoritarian politics and political control over the economy and society) and boosted the idea of liberal democracy (conceived as democratic politics and free-market economics). It also seemed to have confirmed Francis Fukuyama's thesis, first formulated in the summer of 1989, that liberal democracy may constitute the end-point of mankind's ideological evolution and the final form of human government, and that as such it constituted the end of history.

Yet, although the collapse of communism undoubtedly boosted the idea of liberal democracy, it has not led to its triumph: in theory, the idea of liberal democracy continues to be widely challenged, albeit with the important proviso that among its challengers totalist authoritarianism is conspicuously absent; in practice, the future of liberal democracy is far from assured, even in Western societies. Expressed differently, the role of the state (the visible hand) in modern society has not ceased to be one of the crucial theoretical and political issues.

Since the role of the state in modern society has not ceased to be one of the crucial theoretical and political issues, also the multidimensional tension between economic individualism and economic collectivism, inherent in modern economies and revolving around the role of the state in the economy, has not disappeared. However, while between the end of the Second World War and the end of the 1980s the dominant tension was that between market capitalism and command socialism, currently the dominant tension is that between two variants of market capitalism, namely, the free-market variant and the interventionist variant.

Inasmuch as the tension between economic individualism and economic collectivism inheres in any modern economy irrespective of the established type of economic system, its examination requires an examination of modern economic systems and their transformation. This is the subject-matter of the present study, which has both a theoretical and an empirical dimension and which, despite its concentration on the present, does not neglect the past either. It opens with a brief overview of millennia-long economic development, based on the distinction between traditional and modern economies. The overview is followed by a typology of modern economic systems and a classification of their environment.

Market capitalism, market socialism, command socialism, and command capitalism are the four pure types of modern economic system distinguished in Part I. In some detail, they are discussed in Part II, bearing in mind that real modern economies are rarely (if ever) of a pure type. As a rule, they are variants of pure types, i.e., mixed economic systems, although the mix cannot be arbitrary. Having their own logic, economic systems are able to absorb contradictory elements within certain (rather narrow) limits only.

Whatever the established type of modern economic system, the three chapters making up Part III show, the government engages in various non-marketed economic activities, i.e., in the provision of specific services, transfer payments, and subsidies, financed through taxation and government borrowing. At the same time, though, governments face tax and spending constraints. Expressed differently, their extractive capabilities and their spending programmes are inevitably circumscribed.

An increasing or high level (share in GDP) of government spending is an unmistakable sign of an increasing or high degree of economic collectivism. Such a level of government spending has an adverse impact on economic growth and long-term prosperity. Yet, its reduction encounters considerable difficulties, particularly if it means cuts in state-provided welfare and in state bureaucracy.

In discussing types of modern economic system and the government economy, it should be added, attention is also paid to illegal and unrecorded second economy activities, which are a specific manifestation of non-observance of formal norms. The second or unofficial economy is a cross-system phenomenon, existing in any modern economy irrespective of the established type of economic system. The factors that contribute to its incidence include: in capitalist market economies, onerous regulation, punitive taxation, and the availability of social welfare benefits; in socialist command economies, chronic shortages and the bureaucratization of the economy.

Against this background, Part IV turns to the transformation of modern economic systems. It means that as a result of the ongoing tension between economic individualism and economic collectivism the established economic system loses ground and a new one comes into being. Of course, in practice tensions between economic individualism and economic collectivism need not (and do not) always lead to change *of* the system. Mostly, they lead only to change *within* the system.

In modern times, i.e., in the period since the year 1500, it is possible to find both the transformation of traditional economies into modern economies and, within modern economies, the transformation of one type of modern economic system into another. Concerning specifically the latter, during these five centuries variants of all four pure types of modern economic system have been tried. Of these four types, market capitalism has proved to be in the long run more successful and enduring than the others.

Consequently, the transformation in post-communist societies of command socialism into market capitalism is not the only case of economic transformation in modern history. However, it is unique in the sense that the economic system undergoing transformation is that of *command socialism*, characterized by the substitution of state co-ordination for market coordination and of public ownership of the means of production for private ownership of the means of production.

At the same time, this transformation is merely one dimension of the transformation of the communist system. Since prior to their sudden collapse the established communist systems were variants of totalist authoritarianism, their transformation has of necessity four interrelated dimensions, namely, the political, the economic, the social, and the cultural.

It would be wrong to assume, though, that change is confined exclusively to post-communist societies. As highlighted in Part V, in developed and developing countries economic liberalization has been in evidence since around 1980, amounting to privatization and deregulation. The factors contributing to it have included the worldwide resurgence of belief in market capitalism and the globalization of the world economy, brought about by the information revolution and improvements in transportation.

Naturally, markets can and do fail. But also governments can and do fail. However, while the former frequently find ways to correct their own failures, the latter frequently produce market distortions, some of which have long-lasting adverse consequences. Nevertheless, government intervention in the economy continues to abound, and explicit as well as implicit calls for more government intervention in the economy continue unabated, both during the contraction phase of the trade cycle and during its expansion phase.

Besides continuing government intervention in the economy and continuing calls for more government intervention in the economy, there are continuing calls for government intervention in the non-economic spheres of society, i.e., for social engineering. In this respect, a prominent role is played by those pressure groups that, fuelled by single-issue fanaticism, want to impose their values and standards on the population at large. Thus, although economic and political liberalization is taking place, reliance on the state and attempts to expand the scope of political power have not disappeared.

All in all, the present study argues that societies, whether traditional or modern, experience a tension between spontaneity (individual freedom) and control (regulation). Consequently, economies as a subsystem of society experience it too. More specifically, they experience a tension between economic individualism and economic collectivism, which in modern economies revolves around the role of the state in the economy.

Since the tension between spontaneity (individual freedom) and control (regulation) inheres in any society, in modern societies it manifests itself irrespective of whether they are politically organized in unitary or federal states, in nation-states or supranational states. For the same reason, although currently a trend towards liberal democracy (conceived as democratic politics and free-market economics) is visible, its final victory is not a foregone conclusion.

During the researching, writing, and revising of this book, the author benefited from seminars at St. Antony's College and the School of Slavonic and East European Studies, as well as from participation in various international conferences. He is indebted to many people, including Keith Bush (Washington, D.C.), John H. Goldthorpe (Oxford), Richard Hauser (Frankfurt), Michal Illner (Prague), Lubor Karlik (Vienna), Zdenek Pavlík (Prague), and Annemette Sørensen (Boston), and wishes to record his gratitude to the librarians of St. Antony's College, the School of Slavonic and East European Studies, the London School of Economics and Political Science, and the Royal Institute of International Affairs, as well as to the staff of the British Library and the Senate House Library. He would also like to express his thanks to the editor of this series, Dr Alex Pravda, Mr T.M. Farmiloe of Macmillan, and all those involved in the production of the volume, and to appreciate the unceasing support given him by his wife Barbara. Finally, he would like to acknowledge his debt to M.C. Kaser and the late Ernest Gellner.

Ruislip, June 1997   J.L. PORKET

Part I
Tensions

In the 1950s, when the Soviet bloc was still in existence and riding high, Daniel Bell and others announced the end of ideology. Since then, various authors have proclaimed, *inter alia*, the end of history, the end of work, the end of affluence, and the end of the nation-state, as well as (again *inter alia*) the death of competition, the death of money, the death of inflation, the death of the trade cycle, and the death of economics. However, all these 'ends' and 'deaths' must be taken *cum grano salis*, because reality is far more complicated and the future remains uncertain.

An inherent and, hence, universal feature of societies, whether traditional or modern, is a tension between spontaneity (individual freedom) and control (regulation). Consequently, Economies do not escape it either. That is to say, they experience a tension between economic individualism and economic collectivism, which in modern economies revolves around the role of the state (the visible hand) in the economy. At the same time, societies face a number of constraints, in particular the pervasive economic phenomenon of scarcity, due to which the basic economic problem is the allocation of scarce means (resources) among competing ends for the achievement of maximum results; the cost-benefit nexus, arising from the fact that there are no benefits without costs; and the risk factor, which means that no purposeful activity, whether economic or non-economic, is without a risk.

Bearing this in mind, Chapter 1 provides a historical background by offering a brief overview of millennia-long economic development, based on the distinction between traditional and modern economies. Chapter 2 then presents a typology of modern economic systems, discusses the so-called third way, and identifies the main interrelated dimensions of the tension between economic individualism and economic collectivism. Finally, Chapter 3 deals with the environment of modern economic systems, concentrating on one of its components, namely the political system, which gives rise to the tension between democracy and authoritarianism and to that between liberalism and totalism.

1 An Historical Overview

Although the subject-matter of the present study is modern economic systems and their transformation, it is deemed useful to begin with a brief overview of millennia-long economic development. The overview is based on the distinction between traditional and modern economies which, as types, are diametrically different.

1.1 TWO TYPES OF ECONOMY

As conceived here, traditional economies are self- sufficient, non-market, and non-monetized pre-agricultural or agricultural economies of small size. Since they are technologically undeveloped and limited in their productivity, they live close to the subsistence level and are unable to produce any substantial surplus to daily requirements. Since they live close to the subsistence level and are unable to produce any substantial surplus to daily requirements, they exhibit a low degree of economic inequality.

Being self-sufficient and non-market, these economies produce predominantly for their own consumption, for direct use. More precisely, they mostly consume what they produce and, simultaneously, mostly must produce what they consume. Consequently, they do not (and cannot) depend on trade. Nevertheless, there does exist some exchange, its forms being the giving and receiving of gifts and hospitality on the one hand and barter on the other.

The primary economic unit is the household, with a division of labour determined mainly by age and sex. However, the household is not exclusively an economic unit. In addition, it is the centre of a whole range of non-economic activities, including sexual, reproductive, social, recreational, educational, religious, and political. Hence, role differentiation is minimal, roles are functionally diffuse.

In contrast to traditional economies, dominated by custom and tradition, modern economies are complex non-agricultural economies which, due to advanced technology and high productivity, are able both to provide a standard of living far exceeding the subsistence level and to produce a substantial surplus, i.e., to accumulate capital. Since these economies are technologically developed, they have an elaborate

3

division of labour involving specialization.[1] As a result, producers are usually not identical with consumers, as is the case in traditional economies. That is to say, economic actors mostly consume what they do not directly produce and mostly need not directly produce what they consume. This, in turn, requires product and factor markets bringing together sellers and buyers of goods and services, and money as the main medium of market exchange.

Households are only one of several economic actors, the others being firms and financial institutions, central and local government, and voluntary organizations. Inasmuch as economic activity can be marketed or non-marketed, legal or illegal, and recorded or unrecorded, five sectors may be distinguished in modern economies, namely, the first or official economy, the second or unofficial economy, the government economy, the household economy, and the voluntary economy. Besides these five sectors, in modern economies it is possible to find what is sometimes termed the social economy[2] and what will be called here the mutual-help economy. It consists of non-market exchanges of goods and services (the giving and receiving of favours) among relatives, friends, and neighbours, avoiding the use of cash and barter.

Naturally, the two types of economy distinguished above conceal that in reality there exist differences between individual traditional economies as well as between individual modern economies, that both traditional and modern economies undergo changes over time, and that elements of the latter can appear in the former and elements of the former can survive in the latter. Therefore, the next section deals with stages of economic development prior to the sixteenth century and the subsequent section covers the emergence of national economies.

1.2 STAGES OF ECONOMIC DEVELOPMENT

Throughout most of the entire span of human existence, until approximately 7000 B.C., human beings lived by hunting and food-gathering. As a result, hunting-gathering societies[3] were inevitably nomadic and small. In these societies, characterized by subsistence technology, limited division of labour,[4] limited inequality, and limited contacts with other societies, the primary economic unit was the family. About half a dozen families made up a band, which was a kinship group. Kinship ties also linked bands together into tribes of fewer than one thousand people, spread out over a large area.

Gradually, some hunting-gathering societies evolved into pastoral societies engaged in nomadic shepherding, and others into horticultural societies engaged in the cultivation of plants by means of the digging stick or the hoe. Later, horticultural societies evolved into agricultural societies using the plough (first making its appearance in the great river valleys in the third or fourth millennium B.C.) as the basic tool in the cultivation of the land.

Farming, i.e., the growing of food, led to the establishment of permanent settlements. The early peasant villages consisted of from 10 to 50 families, with a total population of between 50 and 300 persons. Their social structure was relatively simple. Relations among members of the community were governed by custom and tradition, as interpreted by a council of elders.

Since farming made the supply of food more abundant, regular, and dependable, it encouraged population growth. And since it was able to produce a surplus to what was needed for immediate consumption, not everyone had to be constantly engaged in the production of food, and some individuals could devote all their time to the pursuit of non-agricultural activities, such as art, religion, administration, trade, and warfare.

Eventually, farming revolutionized the entire basis of human existence. The division of labour far exceeded that determined by age and sex. New crafts emerged, the examples being pottery and metallurgy. The professions of architecture, engineering, and medicine, among others, were born. An expansion of exchange in the form of barter and trade took place. Writing was invented, and coined money was introduced. Social stratification appeared, with priests, warriors, and bureaucrats ruling over peasants, artisans, and slaves.[5]

Towns were built, city-states were founded,[6] and empires rose, with the first civilizations established in Mesopotamia, Egypt, Crete, India, and China between about 3500 B.C. and 500 B.C.[7] In the millennium extending roughly from 800 B.C. to A.D. 200, then, the classical civilization of the Mediterranean world achieved a remarkable level of economic development. Given the absence of notable technological progress in the era, the explanation for this achievement should be sought in the extensive division of labour made possible by a highly developed network of trade and markets.[8]

Within the classical world, Greece consisted of a group of small city-states. In the middle of the eighth century B.C., the Greeks undertook massive organized ventures in colonization that resulted in the foundation of Greek cities throughout the Mediterranean and on the Black Sea coasts. However, by about 340 B.C. Greek independence was at an end, the Greek cities having exhausted themselves in internecine struggles.

Rome's greatest contribution to economic development was the *pax romana*, which lasted from the end of the first to the close of the second century of the Christian era. During those two centuries, the classical civilization reached its zenith, at least in its economic aspects. Afterwards, though, a decline set in: towns and cities were deserted, interregional trade decreased, and large self-sufficient estates grew. Finally, by A.D. 500 the Roman Empire in the West collapsed, but continued in the East, with its centre at Constantinople, for another thousand years.

After the collapse of the Roman Empire and its communications system, Western Europe relapsed into agrarianism. According to Rondo Cameron, '[f]rom the ancient city-states of Sumer to the Roman Empire, urban institutions determined the character of the economy and society, even though most of the population was engaged in agricultural labor. In medieval Europe, on the other hand, although the urban population grew in size and importance, especially in Italy and Flanders, agrarian and rural institutions set the tone.'[9]

Between the seventh and tenth century, the absence of effective central government capable of protecting the population against invaders and marauders gave rise to a system of military and political relationships which, subsequently, was labelled feudalism. Underlying it was the form of economic and social organization called in English manorialism. Manorialism began to take shape under the later Roman Empire, and in the eighth and ninth centuries it became the economic basis of the hierarchical feudal system, characterized by an exchange of obligations between superior and inferior.

The feudal hierarchy consisted of three 'orders', namely, the lords, the clergy, and the peasants. Each order had its assigned duty: the lords were expected to provide protection and maintain order, the clergy were expected to look after the spiritual welfare of society, and the peasants were expected to provide material sustenance for the two higher orders. At the same time, within each order there existed gradations of social status: within the peasantry, for instance, degrees of servility and freedom were to be found.

Rural self-sufficiency was the original purpose of the manorial system. However, under the pressure of market forces it began to disintegrate. As early as the tenth century a tendency appeared on the part of feudal lords to commute labour services into money rents and to lease or sell their demesne lands to commercial farmers.

Although the manorial system discouraged individual initiative and, hence, innovation, it did give rise to technological changes that increased productivity and stimulated population growth. The most important innovations in mediaeval agriculture were the substitution of a three-course crop rotation for the classical two-course one, the introduction of a heavy wheeled plough, and the use of horses as draft animals.

Within this feudal setting, the revival of urban life and the emergence of a merchant class took place. Already by the eleventh century the urban population constituted a sizeable category. Yet, despite its notable growth, it made up only a fraction of the total population. At the same time, towns and cities were hostile to their feudal setting, striving for autonomy or independence from territorial princes, some of whom tried to treat entire towns as vassals.

Besides providing markets for agricultural products, towns were trading and manufacturing centres. The volume of trade was gradually expanding. Intimately related to commerce were banking and credit, one of the reasons for the widespread dependence on credit being the multiplicity and confusion of coinage. Manufacturing industry, although greatly inferior to agriculture in terms of the numbers involved, was by no means a negligible sector of the economy. Moreover, its importance was steadily increasing with the passing centuries.

In the millenium after the collapse of the Roman Empire, population growth was slow. During this period there were two major declines in population with subsequent recoveries. The first population drop came in a wave of epidemic disease in the sixth and seventh centuries, and the other in the fourteenth century after the bubonic plague epidemic known as the Black Death. When population fell as a result of these demographic catastrophes, some evidence suggests, the standard of living rose temporarily.

1.3 NATIONAL ECONOMIES

The year 1500 is the date chosen by numerous scholars to mark the divide between modern and pre-modern times. Before the sixteenth century, Europe was only one of several more or less isolated regions of the world. However, from the sixteenth century to the middle of the twentieth century Europe (especially Western Europe) was the region that experienced the most dynamic growth and change. It was also largely responsible for creating the modern world economy.

Angus Maddison distinguished four epochs in the economic development of Europe between 500 and 1980, namely, that of agrarianism (500–1500), that of advancing agrarianism (1500–1700), that of merchant capitalism (1700–1820), and that of capitalism (1820–1980). Simultaneously, he compared the long-term trends of their economic performance in terms of population growth, per capita GDP growth, and GDP growth. The comparison is to be found in Table 1.1.

This categorization was meant by the author to be a rough description of the progressive evolution of the major material forces determining production potential. Yet, although it is set out in broadly chronological order of the evolution of production potential, 'all countries have not moved in steady succession through all these stages. Some have skipped an epoch; there have been cases of relapse; and there has sometimes been coexistence of countries whose economies were operating in different modes.'[10]

While advancing agrarianism was still predominantly rural and agricultural,[11] from about 1750 onward essential aspects of industrialization were taking shape in Western Europe in the form of population growth and the spread of new industrial technology. From this base, starting about 1820 (earlier in Britain), flowed industrialization proper. From about 1870 onward, in Britain again earlier, industrial society matured, an industrial society being regarded as mature when approximately half its population lives in towns and cities. By around 1950, then, the consumer (post-industrial, post-modern) society emerged, characterized by the expansion of the tertiary sector (i.e., services) at the expense of the secondary one (i.e., mining, manufacturing, and construction).[12]

Table 1.1 Performance Characteristics of Four Epochs

	Average annual compound growth rates		
	Population	GDP per capita	GDP
Agrarianism, 500–1500	0.1	0.0	0.1
Advancing agrarianism, 1500–1700	0.2	0.1	0.3
Merchant capitalism, 1700–1820	0.4	0.2	0.6
Capitalism, 1820–1980	0.9	1.6	2.5

Source: Angus Maddison, *Phases of Capitalist Development*, Oxford, Oxford University Press, 1982, p. 6, Table 1.2.

Of course, *per se* these stages of modern economic development say nothing about the role of the state in the economy. Yet, the question of the role of the state in the economy is of crucial importance due to the rise of nation-states (anxious to destroy both the particularism of feudal society and the universalism of the spiritual power of the Church) and the emergence of national economies towards the end of the fifteenth century.[13]

During the sixteenth and seventeenth centuries and most of the eighteenth century, the state in Western Europe pursued mercantilist policies, i.e., it extensively regulated both foreign trade and domestic economic activity.[14] The policies had a dual purpose: one was to build up economic power to strengthen the state; the other was to use the power of the state to promote economic growth, enrich the nation (conceived as a great commercial company), and further self-sufficiency.

Underlying mercantilist commercial policy was the striving for a trade surplus with a view to fostering the stock of precious metals (gold and silver). Therefore, exports were encouraged and imports discouraged, except that the import of domestically needed raw materials and products was facilitated by not being subject to import duties, while the export of important raw materials was hindered. Mercantilist commercial policy also favoured large merchant navies and, by means of navigation laws, tried to restrict the carriage of imports and exports to native ships. In addition, it regulated trade relations of the mother country's colonies, and conceded privileges and monopoly rights to the great national overseas trading companies.

In order to encourage domestic production, the state pursued industrial policy. Mercantilist industrial policy included grants of monopoly, state subsidies, tax exemptions, the importation of advanced technology, the acquisition of manufacturing secrets, the encouragement of the immigration of skilled workers, and even the creation of state factories. Simultaneously, though, every step in the technical process of manufacture was minutely prescribed. However, detailed instructions covered not only production, but consumption too. Sumptuary laws (i.e., laws governing private consumption) attempted to restrict the consumption of foreign merchandise and to promote that of domestic products. They also set standards for the apparel and the diet of the population.

All in all, mercantilist policies represented an application of the practices of mediaeval towns to the national level. It is not surprising, then, that E. Lipson described mercantilism as 'town economy writ large'.[15] Its most extreme case was colbertism in France, named after Jean-Baptiste Colbert, principal minister of Louis XIV between 1661 and 1683 and the founder of the French tradition of *étatisme* (statism) in economic affairs.

Besides encouraging evasion, mercantilist policies not infrequently had harmful consequences for the economy. Moreover, as early as the second half of the seventeenth century they began to be challenged by the advocates of economic freedom and competition. Finally, the principle of state regulation of economic activity gave way to the *laissez-faire* principle, to the doctrine of economic liberalism.

Economic liberalism reached its apex between the last quarter of the eighteenth century and the last quarter of the nineteenth century. It reduced – but did not eliminate altogether – the role of the state in the economy. Hence, it did not amount to unrestrained *laissez-faire*, to 'anarchy plus a constable', as satirized by Thomas Carlyle. At the same time, on the Continent the role of the state in the economy (including industrialization) continued to be greater than in Britain.

Nevertheless, already in the last quarter of the nineteenth century economic liberalism came under pressure. Protectionism was on the increase.[16] A trend towards monopolistically inclined corporations appeared. The foundations of the modern welfare state were laid. Socialist movements emerged, often bitterly disagreeing over the form of the envisaged socialist society and the means and timing for achieving it.[17]

Between 1914 and 1945, economic liberalism was weakened by the First World War, the Great Depression, the rise of totalitarian régimes, and the Second World War. These events or shocks usually resulted in greater government intervention in the operation of the market. However, in some cases they resulted in the substitution of state coordination for market coordination (e.g., in imperial Germany during the First World War, in Nazi Germany in the mid-1930s,[18] and in Britain during the Second World War), and in one case (the Soviet Union in the early 1930s) in the substitution of command socialism for market capitalism.

After the end of the Second World War, the retreat of economic liberalism intensified. In the West, socialist tendencies were strong. It was widely believed that sustained economic growth, full employment, and the provision of welfare were among the proper ends and responsibilities of government. Nationalization of the means of production came into fashion, as did Keynesian economics, indicative planning,[19] micro-economic regulation, and corporatism. Simultaneously, the welfare state expanded considerably.

Under the force of circumstances, though, reaction set in around the mid-1970s. Keynesian economics began to fall into disrepute, and neoclassical economics began to gain ground, to become most influential during the 1980s. The market, the private sector, and welfare pluralism were rediscovered. In order to roll back the frontiers of the state, free the market, and increase efficiency, privatization and deregulation were put onto the agenda.

Outside the West, the political and economic system established in the Soviet Union not only survived the Second World War, but was imposed on Eastern Europe.[20] As a result, in Eastern Europe state ownership of the means of production was substituted for private ownership of the means of production and state coordination was substituted for market coordination. Nevertheless, in both the Soviet Union and Eastern Europe the market mechanism was used to distribute the labour force among planned jobs and the planned supply of consumer goods among households; second economy activities, mostly (albeit not exclusively) illegal or semi-legal, abounded; and various economic reforms were attempted in the decades prior to the late 1980s, when communism collapsed.

The emerging countries of the Third World too fell under the sway of socialism. According to Anne O. Krueger, in developing countries '[t]hree important historical phenomena greatly influenced policy-makers' thinking and choices in the immediate postwar period. These were (1) the strong nationalistic and anticolonial sentiments that naturally accompanied the attainment of independence, (2) the legacy of the Great Depression and its impact on the economies of the developing countries, and on economic thought, and (3) the experience of the Soviet Union's apparently successful rapid industrialization under a command economy.'[21]

Indeed, many a developing country either followed the Soviet example and tried comprehensive and *dirigiste* planning, or practised indicative planning. Yet, by the end of the 1970s the attractiveness of the Soviet model of planned socialist development started to fade even in those Third World countries which in the preceding quarter of a century or so uncritically acclaimed it as a magic formula able to transform poverty and underdevelopment into a developed socialist economy.

CONCLUSION

Broadly speaking, economic development is characterized by a transition from a traditional economy to a modern economy. More specifically, it means a shift from a pre-agricultural society through an agricultural society to an industrial society and a consumer (post-industrial, post-modern) society.

Obviously, economic development in the sense of economic growth (i.e., a sustained increase in the total output of goods and services produced by a given society) accompanied by a substantial structural or organizational change in the economy (such as a shift from a local subsistence economy to markets and trade, or the growth of manufacturing and service outputs relative to agriculture) has far-reaching consequences. *Inter alia*, it has an impact on where people live (permanent settlements rather than nomadic bands, then towns and cities rather than rural communities and farms), where they work (work outside the home instead of production centred on the household),[22] how they work (by hand, operating machines, supervising automatic processes, processing information), the social structure,[23] the potential economic surplus available, and the numbers of people who can be supported around the world.[24]

Economic development in this sense is uneven and open-ended. At the same time, it entails a tension between spontaneity (economic freedom) and control (economic regulation) or, in other words, between economic individualism and economic collectivism. The tension inheres both in traditional economies dominated by custom and tradition, and in modern economies.

The multidimensional tension between economic individualism and economic collectivism inherent in modern economies revolves around the role of the state in the economy, which tends to oscillate between a limited one and an extensive one, and which has an impact not only on efficiency and welfare, but also on individual liberty and the nature of the political system. As a rule, any major change in the role the state plays in the economy is preceded by a shift in the intellectual climate, itself at least partly generated by the existing circumstances.

Despite the rediscovery of the market, the private sector, and welfare pluralism in the 1980s, the tension between free-market policies and interventionist policies has not disappeared.[25] In the late 1990s, government intervention in the economy continued to be very much alive all over the world, and calls for more regulation, more industrial policy, more trade policy, more redistribution, and more welfare statism did not cease.

Simultaneously, the tension between the market (the invisible hand) and the state (the visible hand) was not confined to individual countries, whether developed, developing, or post-communist. It was to be found in the European Union too. Although on 1 January 1993 it officially became a single market, this did not eradicate interventionist, corporatist, welfarist, and protectionist strivings within it. In the opinion of some of its critics, the single market was over-regulated, over-protected, and over-centralized.

2 Types of Modern Economic System

In practice, it follows from the brief overview of economic development presented in the preceding chapter that there exist differences between individual traditional economies as well as between individual modern economies. The differences existing between the latter arise partly from the degree of modernity attained by them, partly from the role the state (the visible hand) plays therein. Despite these differences, though, modern economies are of a limited number of types.

2.1 PURE TYPES

Modern economies differ in two respects.[1] First of all, they differ with respect to how economic activity is coordinated. Since there are two types of coordinating mechanism, one being the market (contract) and the other being command (directive), there are two corresponding types of modern economic system, namely, market economic systems dominated by the market and command economic systems dominated by command.

Modern economies also differ with respect to who owns the means of production (productive assets), i.e., has the right to acquire, keep, use, and dispose of them and of the products and/or income they generate. Since the means of production may be owned either privately or publicly, there are two corresponding types of modern economic system, namely, capitalist economic systems based on private ownership of the means of production and socialist economic systems based on public ownership of the means of production.

If the two types of coordinating mechanism and the two types of ownership of the means of production (property relations) are combined, four pure types of modern economic system are theoretically possible. They are, reading the boxes in Figure 2.1 clockwise, market capitalism, market socialism, command socialism, and command capitalism.

Since each pure type of modern economic system is characterized by one type of coordinating mechanism (the role of which is resource

14

OWNERSHIP OF THE MEANS OF PRODUCTION

		Private	Public
COORDINATING MECHANISM	Market	Market capitalism	Market socialism
	Command	Command capitalism	Command socialism

Figure 2.1 Pure types of modern economic system

allocation, income distribution, and dissemination of information) and one type of ownership of the means of production, the four pure types of modern economic system just distinguished differ with respect to the structure of economic power and economic decision-making, the direction of information flow, and the incentive system. In addition, they differ with respect to their origin and with respect to their openness.

Of the four pure types of modern economic system, market capitalism and command socialism are opposite, mutually exclusive systems.

Table 2.1 Systemic differences between Pure Market Capitalism and Pure Command Socialism

	Market capitalism	Command socialism
Coordinating mechanism	Market	Command
Ownership of the means of production	Private	Public
Economic power and economic decision-making	Dispersed	Concentrated
Information flow	Horizontal	Vertical
Incentives	Material	Identification with command
Origin	Spontaneously developed	Man-imposed
Interaction (exchange of goods, service, capital, and labour) with the international economic environment	Free	Controlled

With some exaggeration the former might be called an organic system, the latter a mechanistic one.[2] Their main features are contrasted in Table 2.1.[3] Of the remaining two pure types of modern economic system, market socialism contains a tension between public ownership of the means of production and the market, while command capitalism contains a tension between private ownership of the means of production and command.

2.2 MIXED SYSTEMS

Although pure types of modern economic system are possible in theory, actual modern economies are rarely (if ever) of a pure type. As a rule, they contain both types of coordinating mechanism (albeit in varying proportions and with one of them usually predominating) and both types of ownership of the means of production (albeit once again in varying proportions and with one of them usually predominating). Hence, as depicted in Figure 2.2, in actual capitalist market economies most (but not all) of the means of production are privately owned and economic activity is coordinated chiefly (but not exclusively) by the market, while in actual socialist command economies most (but not all) of the means of production are publicly owned and economic activity is coordinated chiefly (but not exclusively) by command.

The same applies to actual socialist market economies and actual capitalist command economies. Due to the inherent tension between the prevailing type of ownership of the means of production and the prevailing type of coordinating mechanism, though, these two types of actual modern economy are by their nature transitory, having a tendency to turn either into command socialism or into market capitalism.

At this juncture, the role of tradition in actual modern economies also deserves mentioning. Tradition, a set of procedures (rules of conduct) inherited from the past, is another (and the oldest) type of

Figure 2.2 Pure and actual market capitalism and command socialism

coordinating mechanism. As such, it too solves the problems of production and distribution. However, being inimical to change, its solution to the problems of production and distribution is a static one.[4]

While traditional economies are dominated by custom and tradition, with their modernization the role of tradition *as a coordinating mechanism* begins to decline in favour of the market or command. Nevertheless, in developing countries it continues to be of major importance, often impeding modernization, and even in modern economies it does not disappear completely.

In sum, actual modern economies are variants of pure types of modern economic system. They are mixed economic systems and may be perceived as being located on a continuum between two extremes, namely, pure market capitalism and pure command socialism. As Figure 2.3 shows, the continuum has two dimensions, one concerning the type of ownership of the means of production (private or public), the other concerning the type of coordinating mechanism (market or command, but leaving aside tradition).

Yet, although actual modern economies are mixed economic systems, types of ownership of the means of production and types of coordinating mechanism cannot be mixed in arbitrary proportions. The reason is that an economic system is an internally logical whole of compatible, interacting, mutually reinforcing, and integrated

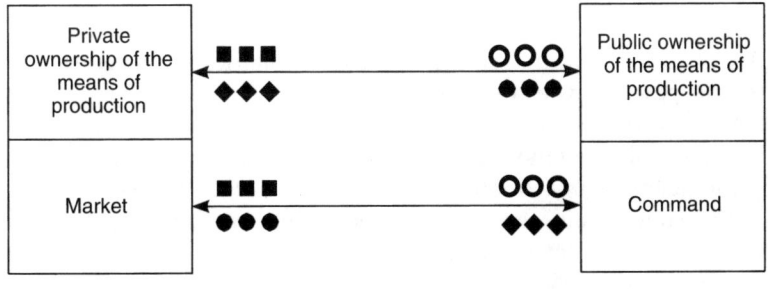

Figure 2.3 Continuum of actual modern economies

elements. Having its own logic, it resists those elements which are incompatible with it and, therefore, threaten it. That is to say, it is able to absorb contradictory elements within certain (rather narrow) limits only. If these limites are overstepped, penalties are to be paid and, unless retreat occurs, the nature of the established economic system begins to change.

The question of whether economic systems can be combined at will or whether there exist limits of the mixed economy was also raised by Karel Englis, a Czech economist. His answer, given in a book written during the last year of the Second World War, was that '[e]very economic system is made up of a number of congruous links, and it is clear that one cannot combine randomly an element of one system with an element of another, in the belief that one can thus create a new, or a mixed system.... The grafting of an alien element onto a particular economic system leads to its disintegration and transformation into one for which the grafted element is appropriate.... The forced inclusion of an alien element, which must necessarily lead to subversion of the existing system, is tantamount to a revolution. The revolution therefore need not immediately abolish the existing system and replace it with another. It can accomplish this as well through gradual transformation by means of such alien element.'[5]

2.3 THE THIRD WAY

Although both theoretical reasoning and empirical evidence suggest that in practice types of ownership of the means of production and types of coordinating mechanism cannot be mixed in arbitrary proportions, this limitation is sometimes forgotten. One example is the convergence theory. Another is the concept of the third way.

The convergence theory[6] found adherents beginning in the early 1950s, roughly after the death of J.V. Stalin, and was fashionable in the West in the 1960s. It posited that the differences between capitalist and communist societies were gradually diminishing and that both types of society were moving towards a similar type of economic, social, and political system. It was based on a technological-economic determinism that assumed a given technology causing a functionally corresponding social structure or system of social relations, and similar systems of social relations developing similar political systems.

What was to be the outcome of this process? According to one version of the convergence theory, the outcome was to be democratic socialism. That is to say, while communist societies were expected to undergo liberalization, albeit within a socialist framework, capitalist societies were expected to evolve towards socialism. According to a later version of the convergence theory, the outcome was to be an order modelled on bureaucratic organization, either in its corporate form or in the form of huge national governmental bureaucracies, civil or military.

Not surprisingly, the convergence theory (which was in vogue at a time when economic liberalism was out of favour and socialist tendencies were strong) had its Western critics, and Soviet scholars too championed the anti-convergence position, contending vehemently that there was no uniform type of industrial society, that capitalism and socialism were fundamentally dissimilar.

One component of the convergence theory was the prognosis that capitalist market economies and socialist command economies were moving towards a halfway house between market capitalism and command socialism, towards a third (middle) way. For example, John Kenneth Galbraith emphasized 'the convergent tendencies of industrial societies, however different their popular or ideological billing; the convergence being to a roughly similar design for organization and planning.'[7]

However, the concept of the third way (usually referred to as market socialism, a socialist market, or commodity socialism) was also advocated independently of the convergence theory, mostly (albeit not exclusively) as a recipe for socialist command economies. In the decades prior to the collapse of communism in the late 1980s, several communist countries (Yugoslavia, Hungary, China, Poland, and the Soviet Union) attempted a variant of market socialism, as a rule with unsatisfactory results. Nevertheless, the concept of the third way as a non-capitalist alternative to command socialism began to be discussed again in connection with the collapse of communism.

While at that time a third way in the sense of a mix of state and private property and state and market coordination continued to have some advocates, it was firmly rejected by most economists in both Western and post-communist societies. To give a few examples, Ralf Dahrendorf wrote about the mirage of a third way;[8] Jan S. Prybyla stressed that the only economically viable alternative to command socialism was the market system;[9] and János Kornai argued that '[t]he conception of a semideregulated economy is based on the premise that bureaucratic and market coordination can be combined in any proportion, let us say, in a ratio of fifty-fifty. Experience suggests this premise is mistaken. Lively operation of the market is compatible with a measure of state intervention, so long as it does not interpose too often in the processes taking place when the parties to the market reach free agreement. But bureaucratic intervention can attain a critical mass that destroys the market's vitality.'[10]

All in all, the discussion triggered off by the collapse of communism confirmed the drawbacks of a third way, of a halfway house between market capitalism and command socialism. Since it would lack system coherence, it would be unstable and, hence, transitory. Consequently, even if post-communist societies chose a third way as the alternative to command socialism, they still would not be able ultimately to avoid market capitalism, but the costs for the population of the detour would be much higher than those of a direct route.

2.4 THE INHERENT TENSION

As concluded in the preceding chapter, in modern economies there inheres a multidimensional tension between economic individualism and economic collectivism, which revolves around the role of the state in the economy. The tension has five main interrelated dimensions, concerning the coordinating mechanism, the ownership of the means of production, the criteria applied to economic activity, the perceived sources of the individual's welfare, and the distribution of income and wealth.[11] Since the first two dimensions (namely, the tension between the market and command and that between private and public ownership of the means of production) have just been discussed, it is possible to turn to the remaining three, beginning with the critera applied to economic activity.

Economic activity can be guided not only by economic criteria, but also by non-economic (political, ideological, social, ethical, and other) ones. This gives rise to a tension between them or, expressed differently, between efficiency and (*inter alia*) equity or social justice. Of these two criteria, efficiency denotes the ratio between the outcome attained by an effort and the costs incurred in producing it, and its importance stems from the fact that in any economy without exception the basic economic problem is the allocation of scarce means (resources) among competing ends for the achievement of maximum results. It requires competition and increases if the cost per unit of output decreases over time.

However, efficiency is of little or no interest to the idea of social justice, and so is the nexus between performance and provisions. As understood here, the concept of social justice gives priority to out-comes over costs, to distribution over production, to entitlements over obligations, and to needs-based provisions over performance-based provisions. Thus, social justice is the opposite of procedural justice,[12] and its critics (among whom is F.A. Hayek)[13] maintain, for instance, that in a free society no agreement exists about desirable distribution, that social justice is a demand by particular groups for a privileged position, that one source of the calls for it is pure envy, and that its pursuit would lead to a loss of personal freedom and the emergence of a totalitarian order.

In connection with the concept of social justice, a note on the question of economic and social rights is in place. Historically, West-ern societies have emphasized civil and political rights, i.e., the right to independence under the rule of law and the right to vote. The full significance of economic and social rights (i.e., the right to food, shelter, medical care, education, job, etc.) has become manifest only in the twentieth century, although some of these rights (e.g., the right to work and the right to education) were formulated already in the second half of the eighteenth century.[14]

A further dimension of the tension between economic individual-ism and economic collectivism concerns the perceived sources of the individual's welfare, and consists of a tension between self-reliance and dependency. Self-reliance means that able-bodied individuals are expected to provide for themselves and their families, as well as to make arrangements in the form of savings, investment, and private insurance that would support them and their families when, through no fault of their own, they are not able to do so because of illness, open unemployment, disability, old age, and the like. It encourages individual effort, initiative, risk-taking, and responsibility, and is encouraged by the market and the institution of private property.

Dependency is the opposite of self-reliance. It arises when indi-viduals, instead of looking after themselves and their families, are provided for by the state, irrespective of their previous contributions and their ability to provide for themselves and their families. Since they are supplied with a livelihood, it is not necessary for them to make an effort, show initiative, take risks, and assume responsibility. At the same time, though, inasmuch as they depend on the state economically, the state is in a position to exert control over them by unilaterally determining what they receive.

The last dimension of the tension between economic individualism and economic collectivism concerns the distribution of income and wealth, finding expression in a tension between economic inequality and economic equality.[15] The emphasis is on *economic* inequality and *economic* equality, because it is necessary to distinguish between equality before the law, political equality, equality of opportunity in the sense that no one should be prevented by arbitrary obstacles from using his or her capacities to pursue his or her own objectives, and equality of outcome (result, condition).

While the market and the institution of private property contribute to economic inequality, government intervention in the economy may aim at increasing either economic inequality or economic equality. Hence, economic inequality can appear and persist even without government intervention in the economy. In contrast, the pursuit of economic equality inevitably requires continuous government intervention in the economy and, at the same time, erodes individual liberty[16] and acts as a disincentive, i.e., weakens individual effort, initiative, risk-taking, and responsibility.

Nevertheless, at least some advocates of economic equality deny that its pursuit would adversely affect individual liberty and economic performance. According to Peter Self, for instance, '[t]here is plenty of historical and comparative evidence about different societies to show that moves towards greater economic equality are certainly possible without destroying the incentives to individual effort.... Moreover,... greater economic equality is in principle fully consistent with a wider spread of individual liberty, viewed as a given set of opportunities and constraints. Given the strong market bias towards inequality, a political bias towards greater equality is morally desirable.'[17] It should be noted, though, that in Self's argument the operative word is *greater* economic equality. This raises two important questions. First, how great is the economic inequality that is to be reduced? Secondly, how great would economic inequality remain if greater economic equality were achieved?

Note too that despite the market bias towards economic inequality competive markets keep it in check. As put by Norman Barry, '[t]he egalitarian aspects of markets had always been appreciated by liberal political economists. Perfectly competitive markets are in fact quite egalitarian: each factor of production is paid its marginal product, there is no "wasteful" profit, and the whole system is geared towards the satisfaction of the uncoerced wants of rational individuals. Even in the real world, as opposed to the texts of liberal economics, where there are (and, in some interpretations, must be) imperfections and excess profits, it is plausible to suppose that competition will be more effective than the state at eliminating them...'[18]

Although economic equality is usually advocated in the name of social justice or on some other magnanimous (albeit as a rule vague) grounds, in fact its advocacy often stems from pure envy. When envy is the real reason, the goal is economic equality for its own sake, even if no one else benefits.

In sum, as also depicted in Table 2.2, economic individualism is characterized by market as the coordinating mechanism, private ownership of the means of production, primacy of economic criteria, self-reliance, and a tendency towards economic inequality, whereas economic collectivism is characterized by command as the coordinating mechanism, public ownership of the means of production, primacy of non-economic criteria, dependency, and a tendency towards economic equality.

Since under economic individualism economic activity is coordinated by the market, economic individualism implies an open economy, i.e., a free flow of goods, services, capital, and labour across national borders. In contrast, since under economic collectivism economic activity is coordinated by command, economic collectivism implies a closed economy, i.e., a controlled flow of goods, services, capital, and labour across national borders.

It also follows from the aforesaid that under economic individualism the role of the state in the economy is diametrically different from that under economic collectivism. Under the former the state is means-orientated in the sense of being concerned with process or procedure; under the latter it is goal-orientated in the sense of being concerned with an end-state or final outcome.

Table 2.2 Pure Economic Individualism and Pure Economic Collectivism

Dimension	Pure economic individualism	Pure economic collectivism
Coordinating mechanism	Market	Command
Ownership of the means of production	Private	Public
Citeria applied to economic activity	Economic	Non-economic
Perceived sources of the individual's welfare	The individual	The state
Distribution of income and wealth	Unequal	Equal

Hence, in theory economic individualism and economic collectivism are mutually exclusive opposites. However, in practice neither
exists in its pure form. Although in any modern economy one of them
predominates, in varying proportions each contains elements of the
other, and their extent varies from one modern economy to another
and, within the same modern economy, undergoes changes over
time. At the same time, each has its own logic and, therefore,
resists those elements of the other which threaten it because they
are incompatible with it. That is to say, each is able to absorb
elements of the other within certain (rather narrow) limits only. If
these limits are overstepped, penalties are to be paid and, unless
retreat occurs, the nature of the established economic system begins
to change.

2.5   ECONOMICS AND POLITICAL ECONOMY

The multidimensional tension between economic individualism and
economic collectivism inherent in any modern economy irrespective
of the established type of economic system raises an important question: is there a valid core of economic theory, applicable to all types of
modern economic system? In other words, can market capitalism and
command socialism, as well as market socialism and command capitalism, be analyzed with the same set of conceptual tools?[19]

According to one view, the general principles of economics are the
same in all types of modern economic system in spite of different
institutional set-ups. According to another, different types of modern
economic system require different economic theories. For instance,
Igor Birman opined in 1989 that 'the Soviet economy can be properly
explained only with a special theory, which in some substantial points
should be very different from the Western theories because it has to
deal with a different subject.'[20]

Since scarcity is a pervasive economic phenomenon, in any economy (be it modern or traditional) the basic economic problem is the
allocation of scarce means (resources) among competing ends for the
achievement of maximum results. This suggests that universally valid
economic laws do exist and that universally applicable economic
theory is possible. However, when economics is subordinated to politics and the government tries to ignore, bypass, or eliminate economic laws, economics alone is not able to explain the functioning of
the economy, and another theory is needed.

If it is accepted that universally valid economic laws do exist, it follows that even in those cases when economics is subordinated to politics and the government tries to ignore, bypass, or eliminate them, these laws do not cease to operate. They merely manifest themselves in a different form. That is to say, governments cannot buck the market.

Against this background it is possible to turn to the distinction between economics and political economy,[21] bearing in mind that many economists deny that there is any difference between them. In classical Greek thought and, owing to the influence of Aristotle, in mediaeval philosophy, economics was considered to be the art of household management. In 1615, the term 'political economy' was coined by Antoine de Montchrétien who maintained that economics, the 'science of acquisition', was an important part of politics, and that it should concern itself not only with the household, but also with the state.

In the classical period of the eighteenth and nineteenth centuries, the term 'political economy' was generally used to describe the subject-matter of economic theory.[22] After 1870, though, the term 'economics' was introduced, at least in the Anglo-Saxon world, and its introduction coincided with the switch from classical economic thought to marginal analysis. By the middle of the twentieth century the term 'political economy' (never abandoned by Marxists) had become a rarity, to reappear in the 1960s.

To an extent, the difference between economics and political economy has already been indicated above. The subject-matter of economics is the allocation of scarce means (resources) among competing ends for the achievement of maximum results or, in brief, choice under scarcity. Economics, to quote Lionel Robbins, is 'the science which studies human behaviour as a relationship between ends and scarce means which have alternative uses.'[23] So defined, economics focuses not on a certain kind of human behaviour, but on a particular aspect of human behaviour, that determined by the presence of scarcity. At the same time, it disregards the impact of political, social, cultural, and other factors on economic activity, its aim being the formulation of universally valid economic generalizations (laws).

While economics studies economic processes in isolation from non-economic factors, political economy (which may be either a positive or a normative discipline) deals with the interaction of political and economic variables, with the relationship between the state and the economy. That is to say, it is concerned with government intervention in the economy on the one hand and with the limitations imposed on political power by the market on the other.

Not surprisingly, there is not just one political economy approach and one political economy. There are different political economy approaches and different political economies. Under the term 'new political economy', Ernesto Screpanti and Stefano Zamagni write, 'it is usual to include a mixed group of subdisciplines and areas of study, from public choice to new institutional economics and from behavioural economics to the economics of property rights.'[24]

One question arising in connection with the so-called new political economy or new political economics is that of whether political economy should be interdisciplinary or not. For example, Kurt W. Rothschild believes that political economy must be interdisciplinary and aim at formulating a unified theory of politico-economic processes, and contends that public choice cannot be counted as a branch of political economy proper, because this approach tries to extend the methods and axioms of neoclassical economics to the sphere of politics and sociology.[25] In contrast, Friedrich Schneider rejects the interdisciplinary approach and regards political economy to be identical with public choice.[26]

Another question arising in connection with the so-called new political economy or new political economics is that of the relation between economics and the other social sciences, *inter alia*, sociology. The question is of importance for two reasons. On the one hand, as just mentioned, in some cases the methods and axioms of neoclassical economics have been extended to the sphere of politics and sociology. On the other hand, no actual economy can be explained exclusively by neoclassical economics, and economists' analyses of actual economies tend to have a sociological dimension.

Concerning specifically the relation between economics and sociology, Richard Swedberg and Mark Granovetter have briefly summarized five main strategies for restructuring the relation between them:[27]

1. rational choice sociology: the basic idea is that the neoclassical model should be extended to topics that by tradition only sociologists have dealt with;
2. new economic sociology: the key notion is that many economic problems that by tradition belong to the economists' camp can be fruitfully analyzed with the help of sociology;

3. socio-economics: it is argued that neoclassical economics is not enough to solve economic problems, that a much broader perspective (which includes sociology, psychology, political science, and the other social sciences) must be used;[28]
4. PSA-Economics (Psycho-, Socio-, Anthropo-Economics): the idea is that by integrating certain findings from psychology, sociology, and anthropology directly into the economist's model, many problems, which for a long time have baffled economists, may be solved; and
5. transaction cost economics: many problems at the intersection of law, economics, and organization can be solved by assuming that institutions gravitate to forms that efficiently reduce transactions costs.

Focusing on the revival of economic sociology which started in the early 1980s, Swedberg and Granovetter argue that although the central tradition in economic sociology is rich and draws on many different sources, there is a common core of central propositions. In their view, there are three key propositions in economic sociology: economic action is a form of social action; economic action is socially situated; and economic institutions are social constructions.

CONCLUSION

Four pure types of modern economic system are theoretically possible, namely, market capitalism, market socialism, command socialism, and command capitalism. Each is based on certain values. Each has a distinct power and decision-making structure (who decides about what on the basis of what title), information structure (who collects and processes what information and to whom it is transmitted), and incentive structure (who gets what, when, how, and why, and who bears what risk). Each imposes distinct constraints on and provides distinct opportunities for economic actors.

However, in practice pure types of modern economic system are not to be found. Actual modern economies are variants of pure types of modern economic system: they are mixed economic systems. Yet, although actual modern economies are mixed economic systems, types of ownership of the means of production and types of coordinating mechanism cannot be mixed in arbitrary proportions. A half-way house between market capitalism and command socialism, a third way, would not be an economically viable alternative to either: lacking system coherence, it would be unstable and, hence, transitory.

Since actual modern economies are mixed economic systems, they experience a tension between economic individualism and economic collectivism. The tension is multidimensional, revolves around the role of the state in the economy, and has an impact not only on efficiency and welfare, but also on individual liberty and the nature of the political system.

3 Environment of Modern Economic Systems

Every economy, whether traditional or modern, makes decisions about what to produce as well as about how, where, when, by whom, and for whom to produce it, and engages in the production of goods and services and in the distribution of output among households. However, these decisions and the ensuing activities do not take place in a vacuum. They take place in an environment which affects them and which, in turn, is affected by them. This implies that modern economic systems function in an environment with which they interact.

3.1 COMPONENTS OF THE ENVIRONMENT

Following David Easton's classification of the environment of political systems,[1] it is possible to divide the environment of modern economic systems into two parts, namely, the intrasocietal or domestic environment and the extrasocietal or international environment. The former lies outside the boundaries of an economic system yet within the same society, and includes particularly the ecological system, biological systems, personality systems, the technological system, social structure, the cultural system, the political system, and the demographic system. The latter lies outside the society in which the economic system itself is a social subsystem, and includes particularly the international ecological system, the international technological system, the international social structure, the international cultural system, the international economic system, the international political system, and the international demographic system.

The environment of modern economic systems has an impact on their nature as well as on their performance. Consequently, their performance depends both on their nature and on their environment. And if the individuals who operate them are viewed not as a component of the environment but as a separate factor, then the performance of modern economic systems (SP) may be seen as being determined jointly by their nature (SN), the individuals who operate

them (I), and the environment in which they function (E):
$$SP = f\ (SN,\ I,\ E).$$
Of course, this still does not answer the question of what performance means. According to Karl W. Deutsch, for instance, '*[p]erformance* is the name we give to any outcome which is desired but improbable without an effort to produce it. Performance achieves some result which otherwise would not occur. If an outcome is certain, no one has to act to bring it about.... Any performance is measured by the outcome attained as against the costs and other adverse conditions which make its attainment unlikely. Performance thus includes two dimensions: *effectiveness* – making an unlikely outcome more likely to happen – and *efficiency* – the ratio between change in the probability of the outcome and the costs incurred in producing it.'[2]

The distinction between effectiveness and efficiency, recalled by Deutsch, is of crucial importance because an economic system can be effective without being efficient. The socialist command economies established in the former Soviet-bloc countries are a case in point: although effective in many respects, they had an inbuilt tendency towards inefficiency, i.e., towards underutilization and waste of employed resources.

While the environment of modern economic systems has an impact on their nature as well as on their performance, simultaneously the nature and performance of modern economic systems have an impact on their environment. *Inter alia*, each type of modern economic system has a distinct impact on the structure and values of society, the behaviour and attitudes of economic actors, the legal system, the political system, and the role the state plays in the economy.

As a result of the interaction between modern economic systems and their environment, both undergo change over time. Although a taxonomy of change will not be attempted here, the distinction between change *within* the system and that *of* the system deserves to be mentioned. The former refers to a change which does not alter the nature (structure) of the established system, the latter to a change which alters the nature (structure) of the established system.[3]

3.2 TYPES OF MODERN POLITICAL SYSTEM

Of the various components of the intrasocietal or domestic environment of modern economic systems identified above, the component that will now receive attention is the political system. This subsystem of society is a set of relationships concerned with the exercise of power at the societal level or, in other words, with the binding or authoritative allocation of values for the society as a whole.

Naturally, the exercise of power (the binding or authoritative allocation of values) takes place in families, extended kinship groups, firms, trade unions, political parties, churches, schools, clubs, and the like too. Yet, although these sets of relationships have similarities with the political ones, they also differ from them in important respects. In David Easton's terminology, they are parapolitical, not political.[4]

Modern political systems are either democratic[5] or authoritarian. In the former leadership is periodically elected in a public contest by the population on the basis of universal and equal adult suffrage.[6] This implies that the population has a number of political rights, such as freedom of expression, freedom of political association, the right to oppose, the right to compete for elective positions, and the right to vote in free and fair elections. In contrast, in the latter leadership is not elected by the population. The population has no political rights, political opposition is not tolerated, and leadership is not accountable to the population.

Expressed differently, while in authoritarian political systems the population is excluded from participation in politics, in democratic political systems it is able to participate in politics. The participation is not confined to voting in periodic elections. In the periods between elections, the population can in various ways let its views be known and articulate its demands with intent to influence the leadership and its policies. Yet, although the population is able to participate in politics and to influence political decision-making, it is not able directly to participate in political decision-making itself, the main exception being occasional referendums referring a specific political issue to the electorate for a direct decision by popular vote. As defined above, democratic poltical systems are not direct or participatory democracy in the sense of a political system in which all political decisions are made collectively by all citizens.

Democracies have been relatively rare in human history. If classical democracy is disregarded, democracies appeared only in the late eighteenth century, originally in North America and Western Europe.[7] In most of them, including those in England and the United States, expansion of the franchise was a gradual process: many contemporary democracies did not achieve universal adult franchise until fairly late in the twentieth century, and yet could meaningfully have been regarded as democracies even before that point.

Hence, modern societies experience a tension between democracy and authoritarianism. This tension inheres not only in authoritarian political systems, but also in democratic ones: while authoritarianism tends to give rise to calls for political liberalization, i.e., democratization, democracy can be manipulated, abused, intentionally or unintentionally undermined and, ultimately, transformed into authoritarianism.

Moreover, in democratic political systems there inheres a tension between leadership and direct participation in political decision-making, i.e., between representative democracy and direct or participatory democracy. Although it is generally accepted that the latter is hardly feasible in modern societies, given their size and complexity, there do exist proponents of and experiments with deliberative or semi-direct democracy, which would assume various forms (e.g., that of the so-called citizens' juries) and have an opinion-giving or consultative (albeit not a decision-making) role.[8]

3.3 THE SCOPE OF POLITICAL POWER

As argued above, modern political systems differ with respect to whether the population is or is not able to participate in politics, to engage openly in political activity: in the affirmative case they are democratic, in the negative case authoritarian. However, *per se* the distinction between democratic and authoritarian political systems discloses nothing about the scope of political power or government, i.e., about political control over non-political (economic and other) activity. In this respect, modern political systems can be either liberal or totalist. In the former the scope of political power is minimal, so that the autonomy of non-political actors is high. In the latter the scope of political power is all-embracing, so that the autonomy of non-political actors is low. Expressed differently, while liberal political systems do not control non-political activity, totalist political systems control all spheres thereof.

If democracy and authoritarianism are combined with liberalism and totalism, four pure types of modern political system are theoretically possible. They are, reading the boxes in Figure 3.1 clockwise, liberal democracy, totalist democracy, totalist authoritarianism, and liberal authoritarianism.[9] Of these four pure types of modern political

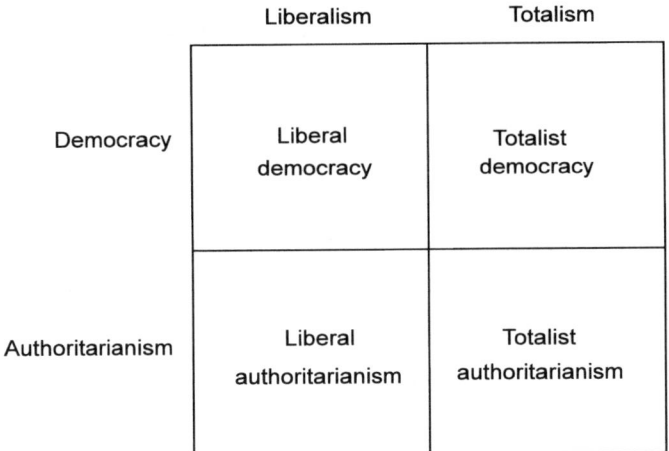

Figure 3.1   Pure types of modern political system

system, liberal democracy and totalist authoritarianism are opposite, mutually exclusive systems. The former is characterized by political and non-political pluralism and competition and by a means-orientated government operating under the rule of law. The latter is characterized by monism and the absence of political and non-political competition and by a goal-orientated government that is neither accountable to the population nor restrained by the law.

Although the rule of law is a *sine qua non* of liberal democracy, liberal democratic societies depend not only on legal norms, but also (and to a considerable degree) on custom and tradition. That is to say, they combine formal regulation with informal. In contrast, totalist authoritarianism is highly formalized, because it rejects autonomous activity, spontaneity. This implies that it is inimical to custom and tradition too.

Naturally, actual modern political systems are not of a pure type. They are variants of the pure types, and may be perceived as being located on a continuum between two extremes, namely, pure liberal democracy and pure totalist authoritarianism. The continuum has two dimensions, one concerning participation in politics, the other concerning the scope of political power. Hence, besides experiencing a tension between democracy and authoritarianism, modern societies experience a tension between liberalism and totalism as well. This tension inheres in both democratic and authoritarian political systems, and manifests itself by (calls for) liberalization on the one hand and by (calls for) an expansion of the scope of political power on the other.

In modern times, i.e., since the beginning of the sixteenth century, actual modern political systems have been predominantly variants either of totalist authoritarianism or of liberal authoritarianism. Liberal democracy is a relative newcomer, its appearance dating only from the late eighteenth century. Concerning specifically totalist authoritarianism, its variants existed, *inter alia*, in Western Europe during the sixteenth and seventeenth centuries and most of the eighteenth century, i.e., during the era of absolute monarchy and mercantilism; in Nazi Germany between about 1936 and 1945; and in the communist- ruled Soviet-bloc countries prior to 1989.

3.4 POLITICAL AND ECONOMIC SYSTEMS

Having presented a typology of modern political systems and, in the preceding chapter, a typology of modern economic systems, it is possible to turn to the important question of the relationship between the distinguished types of modern political system and the distinguished types of modern economic system.[10]

Since totalist authoritarianism is characterized by an all-embracing scope of political power exercised by unelected and unaccountable government, there exists an intrinsic linkage between it and command socialism, an economic system based on public ownership of the means of production and state coordination of economic activity. Hence, political and economic power and political and economic decision-making are concentrated in the hands of government.

In contrast, because liberal authoritarianism is characterized by a minimal scope of political power and, thus, by high autonomy of non-political (including economic) actors, it is incompatible with command socialism and makes market capitalism (an economic system based on private ownership of the means of production and market coordination of economic activity) possible. As a result, economic power and economic decision- making are separated from political power and political decision- making.

As a pluralistic and competitive political system, democracy is not compatible with command socialism, a non-pluralistic and non-competitive economic system. It is compatible exclusively with market capitalism, a pluralistic and competitive economic system. More precisely, modern democracy is dependent on market capitalism, the latter is a necessary (albeit not sufficient) condition for the former. This means that only liberal democracy is conceivable and that totalist democracy is a contradiction in terms.

What emerges from this brief account is the crucial importance of market capitalism for modern societies. Since market capitalism separates economic power and economic decision-making from political power and political decision-making, it acts as a check on the scope and arbitrariness of political power, whether authoritarian or democratic. Consequently, it provides economic freedom and, at the same time, promotes political freedom, in authoritarian political systems giving rise to pressures towards democracy.

It also follows from this account that democracy itself imposes limitations on the scope of political power, i.e., on the degree of totalism. In a democratic political system, the substitution by an elected government of command socialism for market capitalism would spell the end of democracy. A similar adverse effect on democracy would have the substitution in a democratic political system of command capitalism for market capitalism, unless adopted as a temporary measure in the event of a national emergency, e.g., in wartime.

Finally, this account suggests that an established socialist command economy could be transformed into market socialism or market capitalism either if totalist authoritarianism (a *sine qua non* of command socialism) gave way to liberal authoritarianism, or if it collapsed.

These propositions may be concluded by quoting Milton Friedman's view on the issue. He wrote in 1962 'that there is an intimate connection between economics and politics, that only certain combinations of political and economic arrangements are possible, and that in particular, a society which is socialist cannot also be democratic, in the sense of guaranteeing individual freedom.'[11]

Historically, it should be added, in modern societies command socialism has been introduced and maintained solely by totalist authoritarianism; market capitalism has originated under liberal authoritarianism, under conditions conducive to the pursuit of private economic activity; and modern democracy has arisen exclusively within market capitalism, and has been unable to survive except when coupled with it.

3.5 THE PARADOX OF DEMOCRACY

Although modern democracy is dependent on market capitalism, simultaneously it creates conditions for the emergence of the critics and opponents of market capitalism, who demand government intervention in the economy and, in extreme cases, advocate the introduction of market socialism, command capitalism, or even command socialism. Consequently, in democratic political systems the elected government can be pressed, *inter alia*, for more regulation, more industrial policy, more trade policy, and more social policy. Besides, the electorate can elect a government committed to the pursuit of interventionist or socialist policies.

In this clash over the role of the state in the economy, the main protagonists are the government, the opposition, the electorate, and pressure groups. The last-mentioned (which may be domestic and foreign private firms, public enterprises, public agencies,[12] trade unions, professional associations, voluntary organizations, and the like) defend the status quo or seek change by attempting to make the government bring about policy outcomes they desire. In other words, they try to persuade the government either to take a particular course of action (i.e., to intervene) or to refrain from taking a particular course of action (i.e., not to intervene). However, occasionally they also seek to acquire inclusion into the political decision-making process and, thus, to weaken the position of the government.

The intervention-demanding pressure groups may be divided into the gain-seeking ones and the norm-setting ones. The former confine themselves to demanding government intervention in the economy in order to protect their vested interests or gain an advantage for themselves and/or their clients. In contrast, the latter demand government intervention in the economy and society in order to impose their values and standards on the population at large, they want an activist government engaged in social engineering of the kind determined by them.

Pressure group activity raises the important question of the government's responsiveness to pressure group demands. In Robert A. Dahl's view, a key characteristic of a democracy is the continuing responsiveness of the government to the preferences of its citizens, considered as political equals.[13] Yet, responsiveness becomes a problem in those situations in which there exists a multiplicity of powerful pressure groups with diverse and conflicting demands for the allocation of resources, the distribution of income and wealth, the regulation of behaviour, access to information, direct participation in political decision-making, etc. It is plausible to assume that extensive and/or increasing government intervention in the economy will breed pressure group activity; that successful pressure group activity will encourage rather than discourage further pressure group activity, ultimately leading to demand overload; and that a highly responsive government, incessantly yielding to conflicting pressure group demands, would be a weak government, prone to frequent U-turns and unable to pursue any coherent policies, thus creating instability and putting both market capitalism and democracy at risk.

All in all, the role played by pressure groups in modern societies can be beneficial as well as harmful. On the one hand, they can act as mediating structures, standing between the individual and the state and protecting the former from the latter. Besides, since majority rule can operate at the expense of minority rights, they can temper the majoritarian failings of democracy. On the other hand, if determined and ruthless enough, they can exploit the majority, block its wishes, subvert the common interest, or undermine market capitalism as well as democratic order.[14]

However, modern democracy is vulnerable not only to pressure groups, but also to changes in the mood of the time. In the West, for instance, socialist tendencies were strong after the end of the Second World War, began to go out of fashion in the second half of the 1970s, and started to manifest themselves again in the early 1990s, albeit often in disguise.

To sum up, while market capitalism is not tied to democracy, modern democracy is dependent on market capitalism. Although dependent on market capitalism, modern democracy makes criticism of and opposition to market capitalism possible, and its critics and opponents either want to expand the role of the state in the capitalist market economy, or aim at substituting market socialism, command capitalism, or command socialism for market capitalism.

Of course, if there are market failures, there are government failures as well. Consequently, if the role the state plays in the economy is perceived as being too extensive and, simultaneously, detrimental to economic performance, voices are likely to appear demanding that the role of the state in the economy be curtailed. In turn, if the frontiers of the state are rolled back, calls for a greater role of the state in the economy are likely to be revived.

Hence, political democracy can stand in the way of economic development. However, it can not only retard economic development and undermine market capitalism. It can also undermine the fabric of society and itself, because it offers opportunity for the emergence of values, attitudes, and patterns of behaviour incompatible with social stability and political freedom. The factors which endanger the fabric of society and democracy include, *inter alia*, policy short-sightedness, a rights-without-responsibility culture,[15] dogmatic and intolerant single-issue fanaticism, tribalization and atomization of society,[16] and the dissolution of the family.

Accordingly, liberal democracy can be undermined both intentionally and (no less effectively) unintentionally. In connection with the former it should be recalled that its enemies can resort to semantic manipulation, to linguistic subversion. That is to say, instead of using the language of authoritarianism and totalism they use the language of democracy and liberalism, but engage in what George Orwell in his *Nineteen Eighty-Four* called Newspeak, i.e., they give a different meaning to commonly used words.[17] In connection with the latter it should be remembered that, just as people generally, democrats too can make wrong, foolish, and even wicked decisions.

CONCLUSION

Modern economic systems function in an environment which affects them and which, in turn, is affected by them. This environment has two dimensions, namely, the intrasocietal or domestic dimension and the extrasocietal or international dimension. Each consists of a number of components, one component of the former being the political system.

In theory, four pure types of modern political system may be distinguished. They are liberal democracy, totalist democracy, totalist authoritarianism, and liberal authoritarianism. However, actual modern political systems are merely variants of the pure types. Moreover, totalist democracy is a contradiction in terms, hardly possible in practice.

Since actual modern political systems are merely variants of the pure types, modern societies experience a tension between democracy and authoritarianism, as well as a tension between liberalism and totalism. Modern societies which have a democratic political system then experience yet another tension, that between representative democracy and direct or participatory democracy.

Each of these four types of modern political system is based on certain values and, in turn, has a distinct impact on the structure and scope of political and economic power and decision-making, the flow and nature of information, the character of institutions, the structure and values of society, and the behaviour and attitudes of political, economic, and other actors.

One of these four types of modern political system, liberal democracy, requires shared values and common rules of conduct, defined by law as well as by custom and tradition. In this connection, Michael Novak's concept of democratic capitalism deserves mentioning. He means under it 'three dynamic and converging systems functioning as one: a democratic polity, an economy based on markets and incentives, and a moral-cultural system which is pluralistic and, in the largest sense, liberal.' His argument is that 'political democracy is compatible in practice only with a market economy. In turn, both systems nourish and are best nourished by a pluralistic liberal culture.'[18]

Being dependent on market capitalism, political democracy might be expected to protect and promote it and, thus, to encourage economic development. Yet, although this possibility does exist,[19] the opposite cannot be excluded, because politics often prevails over economic logic. That is to say, political democracy can retard economic development and, in extreme cases, undermine market capitalism, the fabric of society, and itself. Expressed differently, in extreme cases it can develop a self-destructive tendency.

Part II
Systems

In modern economies, economic activity can be marketed or non-marketed, legal or illegal, and recorded or unrecorded. Consequently, five sectors may be distinguished in these economies. They are the first or official economy, the second or unofficial economy, the government economy, the household economy, and the voluntary economy. In addition, there is the so- called mutual-help economy.

The typology of modern economic systems presented in Chapter 2 refers to the first or official economy. According to this typology, four pure types of modern economic system are theoretically possible, namely, market capitalism, market socialism, command socialism, and command capitalism. However, in practice pure types of modern economic system are not to be found. Actual modern economies are merely variants of the pure types.

Each of these four types of modern economic system has a distinct impact on efficiency and welfare (prosperity), as well as on individual liberty and the nature of the political system. At the same time, the performance of each of them is determined jointly by its nature, the individuals who operate it, and the domestic and international environment in which it functions. Moreover, this environment has an impact on the nature of a modern society's economic system.

Although the chapters that make up Part II concentrate on the four types of modern economic system distinguished and, thus, on the first or official economy, they also draw attention to the second or unofficial economy, which is a cross-system phenomenon. That is to say, it exists in any modern economy, irrespective of the established type of economic system.

4 Market Capitalism

The first type of modern economic system to be examined in some detail is market capitalism. Since it is based on private ownership of the means of production and market coordination, it is a pluralistic, competitive, horizontally organized, spontaneous, and open economic system. This implies that economic power and economic decision-making are dispersed.

4.1 THE ECONOMY

Under market capitalism, private economic actors (i.e., private firms and households) enjoy a high degree of autonomy and are motivated by self-interest, with the former aiming at profit maximization and the latter at utility maximization. The pursuit of self-interest encourages individual effort, initiative, risk-taking, and responsibility. At the same time, being kept in check by the market which provides opportunities but imposes constraints as well, it contributes to the general welfare.

Private firms or, in other words, the producers of goods and services, assume various forms. The forms range from one-man businesses through sole-proprietor concerns, partnerships, and cooperatives to joint-stock companies with limited liability. The larger a private firm, the greater the probability of its experiencing the separation of the legal ownership title and management (the exercise of custody rights), thus giving rise to the question of corporate governance.

Since private firms operate on their own account and at their own risk, they must show profit if they want to survive (i.e., avoid bankruptcy) and expand. Being impelled by the profit motive, they are forced not only to satisfy effective demand (i.e., demand backed by purchasing power) in the face of domestic and foreign competition, but also to be flexible, innovative, and efficient, the last-mentioned meaning that they have to use as few resources as possible for a given output, i.e., to keep their costs down.

Crucial information for economic actors in their roles of sellers and buyers is provided by prices determined by the interplay of demand and supply in the market and, in turn, influencing both demand and supply, although their impact depends on the elasticity of demand and supply. Hence, they balance demand and supply, reflecting consumers' preferences and scarcity. According to F. A. Hayek, they are signals which inform people of what they ought to do in order to adjust themselves to the rest of the system, which bring about the unforeseen coordination of the efforts of thousands of individuals. False price signals misdirect human efforts.[1]

If in the interplay of demand and supply in the market no seller or buyer is large enough to affect the market price, perfect competition exists. It arises when the number of sellers and buyers in an industry is large, entry into and exit from the industry are free, and the products offered by sellers are homogeneous or indistinguishable, and leads to productive and allocative efficiency. However, in reality all markets need not be perfectly competitive. In some of them one firm or a group of firms acting together can establish a dominant position, so that price is able to deviate substantially and persistently from marginal cost. Consequently, the structure of consumption is distorted, the attainment of productive and allocative efficiency is prevented, and the firm or the group of firms enjoys excess profits.

Although prices provide crucial information both in product markets and in factor markets, economic actors do not normally possess complete knowledge and foresight with regard to the array of present and future prices as well as the characteristics, quality, availability, and location of goods and services. One reason is that it is costly to acquire information, that information cannot be obtained without expending time, effort, and money. Therefore, economic actors weigh the cost and benefit of acquiring information, and seek to acquire additional information only as long as its marginal benefit exceeds or equals its marginal cost.

To conclude, market capitalism with its private enterprise, consumer choice, voluntary and mutually beneficial exchange, free product and factor markets, and mobility of labour and capital separates economic power and economic decision-making from political power and political decision-making. Nevertheless, it fails in three respects: it gives rise to monopolies and anti-competitive practices, breeds externalities, and is unable to supply certain goods and services. Thus, its nature raises the question of the role of the state in capitalist market economies.

4.2 THE ROLE OF THE STATE

If market capitalism is to be preserved in a modern society, the role of the state in the economy must of necessity be limited. Extensive and expanding government intervention in the economy is likely to retard economic development and, ultimately, to undermine market capitalism as a pluralistic, competitive, horizontally organized, spontaneous, and open economic system.

Obviously, market capitalism requires a stable legal framework, established by the government. The framework lays down basic rules referring to general types of situation, to yet unknown cases. These rules define the rights and responsibilities of economic actors in the market process, especially in respect of property, contract, exchange, and tort; are general because they make no reference to particular economic actors and particular situations; and are prospective, not retrospective, in their effect, so that they allow predictability.

Although market capitalism is a competitive economic system, in reality it is not a perfectly competitive economic system, due to the existence of monopolies and anti-competitive practices. Their existence prevents the market (the invisible hand) from allocating resources efficiently, and calls for government intervention that would restore competition and improve allocative efficiency.

Government intervention is also called for when externalities occur. An externality arises when an economic activity affects uninvolved parties, when an economic actor's production, consumption, or investment imposes costs or confers benefits on others, other than through market prices. Hence, externalities (known as neighbourhood effects when they have a spatial dimension) can be either harmful (external diseconomies) or beneficial (external economies), two examples of the former being pollution and noise and an example of the latter being inoculation against infectious diseases.[2]

Finally, government intervention is called for in the case of pure public goods, because these would not be produced at all under market capitalism. The reason is that a pure public good is characterized by non-rival consumption (one person's consumption of the good does not reduce its availability to anyone else) and non-excludability (if the good is provided, the producer is unable to bar anyone from consuming it). Of course, pure public goods (such as national defence) are very rare. More common are impure public goods, where consumption is not completely non-rival (inasmuch as their availability is limited) or where exclusion is possible (i.e., their consumption can be made dependent on the willingness of consumers to pay for them).

Thus, under market capitalism government (the visible hand) has an important – albeit limited – role to play in the economy. The role consists of setting a stable legal framework defining economic actors' rights and responsibilities, and of correcting market failures like monopolies, anti-competitive practices, externalities, and lack of private initiative with a view to improving allocative efficiency. In connection with market failures it should be remembered, though, that markets often correct their own failures; that an apparent failure is not always harmful; and that government intervention in response to market failure is justified only if the failure is harmful and if governments are able to correct it.

Hitherto, the term 'market failure' has been used to denote exclusively those cases when the invisible hand fails to allocate scarce resources efficiently. However, the term may also be used in a different sense, namely, to denote those cases when the invisible hand fails to attain objectives other than allocative efficiency, such as stable economic growth, full employment, or a desired distribution of income. Naturally, if market failure is understood in the latter sense, government is expected to play in the economy a role exceeding that needed to improve allocative efficiency. As a result, limited (free-market, corrective) government is turned into big (interventionist, activist) government, intervening in property rights, the operation of the market, and/or the outcome of economic activity, thus inducing allocative distortions.

Government intervention in property rights may take various forms. Jan S. Prybyla mentioned seven of them, namely, nationalization, confiscation, expropriation, confiscatory death duties or inheritance taxes, discriminatory taxation against private producers and traders, input discrimination, and moral suasion. The last-mentioned meant 'the creation of a climate in which to be the private owner of productive assets and to be in business on one's own becomes socially unacceptable, unethical, and politically unwise.'[3]

Irrespective of whether governments intervene in property rights or not, they can intervene in the operation of the market. In order to regulate the aggregate level of economic activity, they resort to changes in taxation and government expenditure (i.e., in fiscal policy) and/or to changes in the supply of money, interest rates, and other conditions affecting the availability of credit (i.e., in monetary policy). The purpose of these changes is to influence the level of employment and prices, stimulate or dampen economic growth, and maintain or achieve balance in external payments.

However, government intervention in the operation of the market need not be confined to attempts to stabilize the aggregate level of economic activity through macroeconomic policies. It can also take the form of tax incentives, subsidies, and cheap loans to selected industries; export promotion and import barriers; controls on prices, wages, and profits; labour market regulation; licensing of entry; banning of certain goods and services; standards setting; and the like.

Finally, governments can intervene in the outcome of economic activity, i.e., in factor incomes (wages, rents, interest, and profits) earned by economic actors. Actually, to an extent at least they must intervene in the outcome of economic activity even if they do not intervene in property rights and the operation of the market, because they engage in non-marketed economic activity (*inter alia*, national defence and the maintenance of law and order) and because government spending on services, transfer payments, and subsidies requires government revenue, the main source of which is taxation.

4.3 VARIANTS OF MARKET CAPITALISM

Obviously, the role the state (the visible hand) plays in capitalist market economies varies from one country to another and, within the same country, over time. Nevertheless, the discussion conducted in the preceding section suggests that it is possible to distinguish three variants of market capitalism, namely, the *laissez-faire* variant, the free-market variant, and the interventionist variant.

It tends to be forgotten that the *laissez-faire* principle was formulated as a reaction to mercantilist policies, which the state in Western Europe pursued during the sixteenth and seventeenth centuries and most of the eighteenth century. Its proponents were the French physiocrats, writing in the third quarter of the eighteenth century, and the British classical economists.

The physiocrats[4] argued that the state should not regulate economic activity and that its role was simply that of upholding the natural order and safeguarding property rights. According to William Doyle, the physiocrats believed 'that there existed a natural, benevolent economic order which had been distorted by ill-judged and artificial human intervention. Economic wealth could only be unlocked by removing all unnatural burdens, particularly on agriculture, which was the only true productive activity.... Paradoxically, the economic freedom preached by the Physiocrats implied a powerful, interventionist role for governments, for only they had the strength to sweep away artificial impediments to the natural economic order.'[5]

Classical economics postulated an economic system based on the pursuit of self-interest, free competition, private property, inheritance, free contract, mobility of labour and capital, and the absence of private and public monopolies as well as of government intervention in economic activity. This automatically self-regulating economic system with its unconscious tendency towards equilibrium brought about by the operation of the law of supply and demand and the movement of market prices was seen as making for justice, prosperity, and progress, as ensuring a harmony between the interests of the individual and those of society.

Since classical economics rejected government intervention in economic activity, the role of the state was to be confined to that of a night-watchman, i.e., to national defence and the maintenance of law and order, including the protection of private property and the enforcement of contracts. To these two roles, Adam Smith added yet another one, namely, the erection and maintenance of those public institutions and public works which, although beneficial to the whole society, could not be expected to be erected or maintained by private enterprise due to their unprofitability. The public works in question comprised those facilitating the country's commerce (roads, bridges, canals, harbours, etc.). The public institutions in question comprised those for the education of the youth and those for the instruction (chiefly religious) of people of all ages.[6]

Thus, as conceived by Adam Smith and other classical economists, the *laissez-faire* variant of market capitalism did not mean that the state had no role to play in the economy. However, in playing a role in the economy, which included that of consumer and that of provider, the state was expected to preserve and expand economic freedom, understood as freedom under the law, not to impede it.

While the *laissez-faire* variant of market capitalism assumed perfect competition, the free-market variant of market capitalism recognizes that, due to the existence of monopolies and anti-competitive practices, competition need not be perfect. In order to foster competition and improve allocative efficiency, it contends, government intervention in the form of competition policy is necessary, aimed at breaking up monopolies, outlawing anti-competitive practices, and regulating natural monopolies, a natural monopoly being an industry in which the most efficient way of organizing production is through a single firm.

Not surprisingly, competition policy[7] requires a strong state, not a weak one. According to Wilhelm Röpke, for instance, 'the degeneration of competitive capitalism occasioned by the growth of *monopoly* and *interventionism* ... is largely the result of the disintegration of the state and of the exploitation of weak governments by sectional interests and pressure groups, for it has now become obvious that the working of competition presupposes a strong state which will with severity and impartiality provide the necessary legal and institutional framework of the competitive market.'[8]

Besides recognizing the existence of monopolies and anti-competitive practices, this variant of market capitalism recognizes the occurrence of externalities too. Consequently, under it the state is expected not only to provide national defence, to maintain law and order, and to step in when private initiative is lacking, as is the case under the *laissez-faire* variant. In addition, it is expected to foster competition and to deal with externalities.[9]

Hence, just as under the *laissez-faire* variant, also under the free-market variant the state plays an important role in the economy. Yet, and again just as under the *laissez-faire* variant, its role is of necessity limited. Expressed differently, under both variants the state is predominantly means-orientated in the sense of being concerned with process or procedure.

In contrast, under the interventionist variant of market capitalism the state is more or less goal-orientated in the sense of being concerned with an end-state or final outcome. Since market capitalism is seen as failing to attain specific economic or social objectives, such as stable economic growth, full employment, or a desired distribution of income, government intervenes in property rights, the operation of the free market, and/or the outcome of economic activity.

Government intervention in the economy exceeding that needed to improve allocative efficiency has been advocated and practised on various grounds. Also its objectives, instruments, and extent have varied from one country to another and, within the same country, over time. Irrespective of these differences, though, it contributes to a bureaucratization of the economy, which gives rise to a tension between bureaucracy and the market on the one hand and to that between bureaucracy and political leadership on the other.

When the advocacy of government intervention in the economy is discussed, the term *étatisme* should not be ignored. As used by French writers from the 1920s onwards, it referred to the direct intervention by the state in the economic life of a capitalist society – by nationalization, by the administering of prices and control of wages, and by social welfare legislation.[10]

In *The Affluent Society* first published in 1958, John Kenneth Galbraith cast doubts both on the adequacy of product information and on the wisdom of individuals, and suggested as a solution to shift a large portion of consumption decisions out of the hands of individuals and into the hands of government.[11] In his later publications he then called for state intervention systematically directed to redistributing income in favour of the poorest strata of society.[12]

An important cause of government intervention in the economy and of high government spending, high taxation, budget deficits, and government indebtedness has been Keynesian ideas. According to Peter A. Hall, the theories of John Maynard Keynes placed increasing responsibility for economic performance on the government's shoulders, and his attacks on the priority which classical economics attached to a balanced budget helped to loosen a fiscal constraint that stood in the way of more generous social programmes.[13]

From these examples of the advocacy of big (interventionist, activist) government it is possible to turn to two examples of the impact of such a government. Angus Maddison described the 1950–73 period in the advanced capitalist countries as the 'Golden Age', as a period of secular boom on an unparalleled scale.[14] Yet, this period was that of 'embedded liberalism', combining liberalism in foreign economic relations with activist, welfare-oriented policies at home.[15] However, after 1973 economic performance deteriorated significantly, the 'Golden Age' system broke down.[16]

Some economists attribute the remarkable economic success of the East Asian countries (Hong Kong, Indonesia, Japan, Malaysia, Singapore, South Korea, Taiwan, and Thailand) between 1965 and 1990 to interventionist policies. In fact, there was no single Asian economic model. The eight countries pursued a diverse mix of policies with varying degrees of intervention: while at one extreme Hong Kong followed the most free-market policies, at the other Japan (which by the end of 1993 was passing through a recession) and South Korea saw the most heavy-handed intervention. Moreover, these countries were changing their policies over time.[17]

To conclude, under the interventionist variant of market capitalism the state intervenes directly or indirectly in the economy with a view to attaining objectives other than allocative efficiency. At the same time, though, the extent of government intervention in the economy is constrained in two main respects: if market capitalism is to be preserved, government intervention in the economy must not lead to systemic change; and government intervention in the economy is not able to put out of operation universally valid economic laws.

Government intervention in the economy also raises the question of its costs and benefits as well as that of government failure. As recognized by public-choice theory pioneered by Joseph A. Schumpeter, not only the market, but government intervention too can fail, i.e., it need not attain its chosen economic or social objectives and can produce unintended consequences.

4.4 THE SECOND ECONOMY

Besides encouraging individual effort, initiative, risk-taking, and responsibility, the pursuit of self-interest under market capitalism encourages honesty, fairness, decency, and compassion.[18] Despite that, in economic transactions some economic actors occasionally, and others recurrently or persistently, lie, cheat, or break the law. And breaking the law in economic transactions means to engage in the second or unofficial economy, also known as the alternative, black, concealed, hidden, invisible, parallel, shadow, submerged, subterranean, underground, or unregistered economy.

As follows from Table 4.1, under market capitalism both the first or official economy and the second or unofficial economy consist of marketed economic activities. However, while first economy activities are legal (above-board) and recorded (i.e., included in gross domestic product), second economy activities are illegal and unrecorded.[19]

Second economy activities are illegal in the sense that they are undeclared for tax purposes, although *per se* they are legal; or in the

Table 4.1 Sectors of Capitalist Market Economies

	First (official)	Second (unofficial)	Government	Household	Voluntary
Economic activity			economy		
Marketed	+	+			
Non-marketed			+	+	+
Legal	+		+	+	+
Illegal		+			
Recorded	+		+		
Unrecorded		+		+	+

sense that they are intrinsically illegal; or in the sense that they deal in illegal goods and services. Expressed differently, in the first case it is the concealment of a legal economic activity that is illegal; in the second case it is the nature of an economic activity that is illegal and, therefore, must be concealed; and in the third case it is the nature of the product or service that is illegal and, therefore, must be concealed.

Examples of these activities on the part of private firms are business trading 'off the books', clandestine employment of workers, putting down private expenditures as company costs, and inter-company barter. Examples of these activities on the part of individuals are failing by design to declare for tax purposes income in cash and kind earned through moonlighting or received in the form of tips and gratuities, under-reporting of income from self-employment, benefit fraud (e.g., 'claiming and working'), pilfering and cheating on the job, production of illegal goods and services (such as drug-dealing or prostitution), and smuggling.

Participation in second economy activities arises, *inter alia*, from a low respect for law, lax moral standards, greed, envy, frustration, the need for survival, the wish to increase one's income or reduce one's costs, and the desire to get hold of illegal goods and services. At the same time, though, the environment in which economic actors operate can contribute to the incidence of second economy activities by, for instance, punitive taxation, minimum wage legislation, strict regulation of hiring and firing, open unemployment, pressures of domestic and foreign competition, and the availability of social welfare benefits.

One obvious and important consequence of the second economy is public revenue losses, caused by tax evasion and non-payment of social security contributions. Two further consequences are reallocation of resources and redistribution of income. Yet another consequence is increased risk: since second economy activities are illegal, not only are its participants not protected by law against unscrupulous or reckless behaviour of the party with whom they engage in a transaction, but are liable to punishment if detected.

Besides, the second economy has political consequences. If it cushions the adverse affects of restrictive or punitive economic policies, open unemployment, recession, and the like, it reduces its participants' dissatisfaction with their personal lot as well as with the operation of their economy and society, thus diffusing potential radicalism, militancy, and popular unrest. On the other hand, some second economy activities (e.g., drug-dealing) can lead to organized crime, violence, street riots, and looting.

According to Dieter Cassel and Ulrich Cichy, the second economy is a stabilizing factor, acting as an economic lubricant, a social mollifier, and a built-in stabilizer. It acts as an economic lubricant because it serves as a flexible reserve for the overall economy and has a considerable shock-absorbing potential with respect to political or economic shifts and shocks. It acts as a social mollifier because it provides additional opportunities for employment and production and, thus, reduces the social costs of anti-inflation policies and the political resistance against them. And it acts as a built-in stabilizer because the income derived from it is partly spent in the first economy.[20]

Since the second economy consists of illegal and unrecorded activities, measurements of its size face formidable obstacles. Nevertheless, the available (albeit often divergent) estimates do suggest that the size of the second economy varies from one country to another and, within the same country, over time, and that in some countries it is far from negligible. Between 1960 and 1978, it follows from one set of published figures, an expansion of the second economy took place. It nearly doubled its size in most of the seventeen OECD countries compared, trebled in Denmark, and increased fourfold in Ireland and Switzerland. For 1978, the estimates ranged from 4.1 per cent of official GDP in the case of Japan through 8.0 per cent in the case of the United Kingdom to 11.4 per cent in the case of Italy and 13.2 per cent in the case of Sweden.[21]

According to *The Economist*'s estimates, based on various studies and published in 1993 and again in 1994, the second economy amounted to 30 per cent of GDP in Greece, to 25 per cent in Spain, to 20 per cent in Italy and Portugal, to 13 per cent in Belgium and Sweden, to over seven per cent in Germany and France, to seven per cent in Britain, the United States, and Holland, and to four per cent in Japan and Switzerland. Large second economies, it was noted, were to be found in countries with high rates of self-employment (which offers ample opportunities to conceal income from the taxman) and registered unemployment. In contrast, countries with low rates of registered unemployment (Japan and Switzerland) had small second economies. It was noted too that '[m]ost studies suggest that recession tends to squeeze the black economy as much as the formal one' and that 'as a rule, the higher the level of taxation and the more onerous the employment regulations in the formal economy, the bigger the informal economy will be.'[22]

Faced with second economy activities, governments can respond in several ways. In principle, they can tolerate at least some of them;

engage in their deterrence, detection, and punishment; or try to reduce the incentive to act illegally, be it high taxation, restrictive regulation, a low respect for law, or lax moral standards. In practice, the response depends on a number of considerations, *inter alia*, on the nature, extent, and consequences of a particular second economy activity, and on the estimated costs and the assumed effectiveness of a particular response.

CONCLUSION

If market capitalism is to be preserved as a pluralistic, competitive, horizontally organized, spontaneous, and open economic system, the role of the state in the economy must of necessity be limited. Depending on the role the state plays in capitalist market economies, three variants of market capitalism may be distinguished, namely, the *laissez-faire* variant, the free-market variant, and the interventionist variant.

Under the *laissez-faire* variant, which assumes perfect competition, the role of the state is confined to providing national defence, maintaining law and order, and stepping in when private initiative is lacking. This variant is frequently misunderstood and/or misrepresented: there a is tendency to view and depict it as being identical with anarcho-capitalism, with a chaotic situation in which legal norms regulating private economic activity either do not exist at all or are widely ignored. Even then, though, private economic activity can be regulated by gradually and spontaneously developing informal rules (conventions).[23]

The free-market variant, which too is frequently misunderstood and/or misrepresented, recognizes that all markets need not be perfectly competitive and that externalities occur. Consequently, the role of the state widens somewhat, but remains limited. In addition to providing national defence, maintaining law and order, and stepping in when private initiative is lacking, the state is expected to foster competition and to deal with externalities.

While under both these variants the state is predominantly means-orientated in the sense of being concerned with process or procedure, under the interventionist variant it is more or less goal-orientated in the sense of being concerned with an end-state or final outcome. In order to achieve specific economic or social objectives other than allocative efficiency, such as stable economic growth, full employment, or a desired distribution of income, it intervenes in property rights, the operation of the free market, and/or the outcome of economic activity.

However, government intervention in the economy can fail, i.e., it need not attain its chosen economic or social objectives and can produce unintended consequences. One of its unintended consequences is the second economy, consisting of illegal and unrecorded economic activities. That is to say, interventionist policies are likely to encourage participation in the second economy if they adversely affect economic actors and if, simultaneously, economic actors resent them.

The existence of tax evasion, benefit fraud, and other second economy activities in capitalist market economies evinces that in these economies there are limits to effective interventionist policies, to the extractive, allocative, distributive, and regulative capabilities of government. Market forces cannot forever be denied, they can be defied only at one's peril.

5 Command Capitalism

Extensive and expanding government intervention in the economy, it has been argued in the preceding chapter, is likely to retard economic development and, ultimately, to undermine market capitalism as a pluralistic, competitive, horizontally organized, spontaneous, and open economic system. One alternative to market capitalism is command capitalism, which substitutes state coordination for market coordination.

5.1 THE PURE TYPE

As a pure type of modern economic system, command capitalism is characterized by private ownership of the means of production and state coordination of economic activity. Consequently, although nominally pluralistic, in fact it is a non-pluralistic, non- competitive, vertically organized, centrally directed, and closed economic system. This implies that private ownership of the means of production is an empty shell because economic power and economic decision-making are concentrated in the hands of government, that the economy is subordinated to and controlled by political power, and that the state is goal-orientated in the sense of being concerned with an end-state or final outcome.

Since command capitalism lacks a free market and, therefore, rational prices reflecting scarcity and consumers' preferences, in directing economic activity the government has to rely on non-market (i.e., bureaucratic) information, provided by subordinate units. Moreover, inasmuch as central direction of economic activity is all-embracing and detailed, in practice the government is overloaded with information. Despite that, it does not have at its disposal all relevant information (e.g., because certain information is concealed from it and other delayed), and at least some information received by it is insufficient, incomplete, unreliable, inaccurate, and distorted. As a result, the government is not only unable to process, analyze, and integrate the vast volume of collected information in time and in its entirety, but is also to a considerable degree out of touch with reality. Thus, its control over the economy is far from total.

All in all, command capitalism suppresses economic freedom, disregards consumers' preferences, and has an inbuilt tendency towards inflexibility, inefficiency (i.e., underutilization and waste of employed resources), chronic shortages, and repressed inflation. At the same time, it contains a tension between private ownership of the means of production and command, so that it is by its nature a transitory economic system, having a tendency to turn either into market capitalism or into command socialism. On top of that, its nature makes it incompatible with a democratic political system: the substitution by an elected government of command capitalism for market capitalism in a democratic political system would spell the end of democracy, unless adopted as a temporary measure in the event of a national emergency, e.g., in wartime.

Mercantilism, established in Western Europe during the sixteenth and seventeenth centuries and most of the eighteenth century, was a variant of command capitalism. In the twentieth century, variants of command capitalism were established in imperial Germany during the First World War (it was in imperial Germany during the First World War that central planning was originally conceived), in Nazi Germany between about 1936 and 1945,[1] and in Britain during the Second World War.

Before proceeding further, the concept of planner sovereignty market system deserves a brief mention. As formulated by Charles E. Lindblom, a planner sovereignty market system is an economic system in which government directs production not by commands, but by purchases of final products, including consumer goods. That is to say, government displaces the consumer as the 'sovereign'. While government planning is confined to the desired assortment of final outputs, all other production is subordinated to these final outputs through exchange. Consumer goods are either administratively allocated to consumers by government, as in wartime rationing, or sold to consumers by government at prices independent of those paid to producers for final products.[2]

Although Lindblom regards the planner sovereignty market system as one kind of market system, in its fully developed form it is a variant of command system. Since government is the sole buyer of final products, it determines both their assortment and how much it will pay for them. Since government is the sole provider or seller of consumer goods, it determines both what consumers will consume and what they will pay for consumer goods. Moreover, as the author admits, government could set wage rates and might even be forced to resort to the conscription of labour. In the final analysis, this system would have to be a closed economic system.

5.2 CORPORATISM

Command capitalism might be called corporatism on the condition that corporatism is defined as R.E. Pahl and J.T. Winkler do. In their view, the essence of corporatism as an economic system is private ownership and state control, corporatism attempts detailed control of economic activity and conscious direction of resources. Under it, the state intensively channels predominantly privately owned business towards four goals, namely, order (elimination of the 'anarchy' of the market in all its forms), unity (substitution of cooperation for competition), nationalism (the elevation of 'general welfare' to complete priority over self-interest or sectional advantage), and success (attainment of national objectives established by the state).[3]

However, in the literature corporatism is conceptualized in various ways.[4] *Inter alia*, while some writers conceive it as a comprehensive economic system, others regard it as a pattern of policy formation and still others as a mode of interest articulation. Dependent (state, authoritarian) corporatism is contrasted with pure (societal, liberal) corporatism. A distinction is made between different levels of corporatism, labelled macro-corporatism (corporatism at the national level), meso-corporatism (corporatism at the sectoral level), and micro-corporatism (corporatism at the plant level).[5]

Basically, corporatism is about government intervention in or government direction of economic activity and about direct participation by organized interest groups in political decision-making. As an economic system it is characterized by the rejection of pluralism, competition, horizontal integration, and industrial conflict, its major value being social harmony. One of its features is the existence of a limited number of national peak associations, organized according to the principle of economic function (i.e., sector of industry) and role in the economy (typically, that of employer and that of employee), and expected to mediate between the individual and the government in the manner of the mediaeval estates and guilds.

Concerning its origin, corporatism can be either imposed from above by the government or based on contract. In the case of imposed corporatism the national peak associations are created by and subordinated to the government, have compulsory membership, are hierarchically ordered, enjoy low autonomy, and are assigned the task of ensuring the implementation of governmental policies. Its variants existed in Fascist Italy, Nazi Germany, Vichy France, Franco's Spain, and Portugal under Salazar, as well as in some Latin American countries. Also in the case of contractual corporatism the national peak associations have compulsory membership and are hierarchically ordered. On the other hand, they develop spontaneously from below, enjoy autonomy, are recognized or licensed by the state, and are able to articulate their interests and to participate in the formation of governmental policies, although simultaneously expected to ensure the implementation of the agreed (negotiated) national policies. Thus, the core element of contractual corporatism is a tripartite structure made up of the state, the national peak associations representing employers (capital), and the national peak associations representing employees (labour). Since these associations take part in the formation of governmental policies, they are neither pressure groups nor mere advisory or consultative bodies, but have a public or quasi-public status.

While imposed corporatism is incompatible with a democratic political system, unless adopted as a temporary measure in the event of a national emergency, e.g., in wartime, contractual corporatism can arise in a democratic political system. Yet, it puts democracy at risk, because by concentrating the formation of governmental policies in the hands of the government and the leaders of the national peak associations it bypasses the parliament. On the other hand, it lacks stability if the leaders of the national peak associations are unwilling or unable to ensure the implementation of the decisions reached jointly by them and the government.

5.3 THE IDEOLOGY OF CORPORATISM

As an ideology, corporatism has a long history.[6] One of its sources was Roman Catholic social theory of the late nineteenth century and the early twentieth century. In the interwar period, corporatist ideas were widespread,[7] and even John Maynard Keynes is quoted as proposing in 1926 a return towards mediaeval conceptions of separate autonomies.[8] After the Second World War, corporatist ideas did not disappear, although the term itself was mostly out of favour, and corporatist tendencies were far from absent in practice. Under the impact of these tendencies, scholarly interest in corporatism re-emerged in the mid-1970s, concentrating mainly on contractual corporatism, usually called neo-corporatism.[9]

This renewed interest in corporatism induced some Western scholars to apply the concept also to communist countries with socialist command economies, in which private ownership of the means of production was practically absent, state coordination of economic activity was a rule, and the trade unions were a unified mass organization, subordinate to the ruling communist party. Thus, Valerie Bunce and John M. Echols contended in 1980 that in the Soviet Union the Brezhnev era could be understood best in terms of corporatist politics, although admitting that there were important differences between corporatist politics in advanced capitalist societies and the Soviet Union.[10] Six years later, Alex Pravda and Blair A. Ruble argued that 'the style of government and especially the system of national policymaking and interest intermediation in Hungary for the last twenty years has exhibited features which have a close affinity with state corporatism.'[11]

Not surprisingly, these four scholars quoted the most widely accepted contemporary definition of corporatism, namely, that proposed by Philippe C. Schmitter. They were aware, too, that Schmitter subdivided corporatism into state corporatism and societal corporatism. However, they ignored the fact that he distinguished four system-types of modern interest representation: he contrasted corporatism not only with pluralism, but with monism (based on the Soviet prototype) and syndicalism as well.[12]

5.4   THE DEGREE OF CORPORATISM

As an economic system, both imposed corporatism and contractual corporatism are identical with command capitalism. The main difference between them is that whereas in the former case economic activity is coordinated by the government, in the latter case it is coordinated jointly by the government, the leaders of the national peak associations representing employers (capital) and the leaders of the national peak associations representing employees (labour). Expressed differently, whereas in the former case there exists state coordination, in the latter case there exists corporatist (tripartite) coordination.

In practice, though, contractual corporatism need not constitute an economic system. It can be confined to a particular policy area (e.g., incomes policy) or to a particular sector of industry. Thus, there are degrees of contractual corporatism, and the extent of corporatization can vary from one country to another and, within the same country, over time. By the end of the 1970s, it follows from the available sources,[13] in the OECD area macro-corporatism was strong in Austria,[14] Norway, and Sweden, medium in Belgium, weak in Italy and the United Kingdom, and non-existent in Canada and the United States. Corporatism in Denmark, Finland, the Netherlands, Switzerland, and West Germany was regarded as strong by some scholars and as medium by others, while that in Ireland as either medium or weak. France and Japan were seen as having corporatism without labour.[15]

However, corporatism was to be found not only at the national level, but also at the supranational one. According to Gerhard Lehmbruch, for instance, the agricultural policy of the European Economic Community was 'an interesting case of sectoral corporatism on a supranational level.'[16] In the opinion of Philippe C. Schmitter, '[t]he notion of setting up a new neo-corporatist dynasty at the global-or meta-level is positively frightening, given the transaction costs involved and the potential decisional perversities. The Common Agricultural Policy of the European Community is the closest approximation we have to such a monstrosity...'[17]

5.5 THE PERFORMANCE OF CORPORATISM

In the heydays of contractual corporatism (neo-corporatism) its advocates asserted that corporatist economies tended to outperform less corporatist or non-corporatist economies. They believed that corporatism had a number of advantages because it contributed, *inter alia*, to wage restraint, lower levels of strike activity, and lower rates of open unemployment and open inflation.[18] Yet, in practice, moderation in wage bargaining and industrial peace can be traded for welfare provisions, fringe benefits, overmanning, subsidies, expansionary macroeconomic policies, and the like. Such trade-offs are prone to lead to inefficiency, low productivity, uncompetitiveness, reduced profitability of capital, and increased government spending. While these consequences may be sustainable in the short run, they adversely affect the long-term prospects of the economy.

The consequences of corporatism just mentioned are only one cause of its instability. Another is corporatism's inherent inflexibility, discouraging mobility of capital and labour. Still another is non-compliance with the decisions reached jointly by the government and the leaders of the national peak associations, if they do not command widespread or majority support.

Obviously, if the leaders of the national peak associations are unwilling or unable to ensure the implementation of the decisions reached jointly by them and the government, corporatism breaks down. It also breaks down, though, if some or all of the national peak associations involved in the formation of governmental policies pull out of participation in it, or if the government terminates participation by the national peak associations in policy formation.

At this juncture, a few examples are in place. To begin with Britain, in the 1970s it was widely believed that the British trade unions had excessive power[19] and that Britain was run by means of deals with them. However, after the Conservatives won the 1979 election, the trade unions were excluded from the policy process, incomes policies as a means of determining wage levels were explicitly rejected, and a monetarist macroeconomic strategy was substituted for a strategy based on Keynesian principles.

The Dutch case suggests that corporatism is a 'fair-weather phenomenon'. In the Netherlands, according to J. Wil Foppen, the 1959–73 period was an apparently happy and carefree period. These years of economic prosperity and social emancipation were marked by more or less unrestrained neo-corporatism and by a Keynesian strategy. Yet, under the impact of the subsequent economic crisis, a shift towards centralism and a monetarist strategy took place in the late 1970s and early 1980s.[20]

Swedish experience too suggests that corporatism is a 'fair-weather phenomenon'. For about four decades prior to the end of the 1980s, the Swedish economic system was regarded by many outsiders as a model to be emulated, and hailed as offering a third way between capitalism and communism. It was characterized by the incorporation of the trade unions and employers into the decision-making process, centralized wage bargaining, active labour market policies aiming at full employment at a high and rather equalized wage level, Keynesian demand management, and redistributive social policies.[21]

While the system functioned relatively well in the 1950s and 1960s, it functioned less well in the 1970s and even less so in the 1980s, leading to a rapid growth of the public sector, overmanning, sluggish productivity growth, rising unit labour costs, low GDP growth, a relatively high rate of open inflation, high taxes, high public spending, a recalcitrant budget deficit, and repeated devaluations.[22]

By the beginning of the 1990s, centralized wage bargaining broke down, the high-tax-for-high-spending policy was falling apart, and the government recognized that squeezing open inflation should take precedence over full employment. Faced with wage inflation, labour unrest, and a current-account deficit, in February 1990 the ruling Social Democrats attempted to introduce a drastic deflationary package, including a two-year freeze on wages, prices, rents, dividends, and local government taxes, and a ban on strikes. The package was defended as necessary to cool down an overheated economy, and resulted in the Social Democrats being voted out of office on 15 September 1991.

The recession that began in 1990 caused output to contract, registered unemployment to rise from 1.8 per cent in 1989 to 8.2 per cent in 1993, and open inflation to fall. However, registered unemployment went up also in other corporatist countries, such as Austria (from 3.1 per cent in 1989 to 4.8 per cent in 1993) and Switzerland (from 0.6 per cent in 1989 to 4.5 per cent in 1993).[23]

5.6 TRADE UNIONS

Under contractual corporatism, it follows from the aforesaid, one of the participants in policy formation and implementation is the national peak associations representing employees or, in other words, trade unions. Generally speaking, the position, role, behaviour, and power of trade unions depend on a number of factors, including the type of the established political system, the type of the established economic system, the legal system, the wage-setting system (centralized national collective bargaining versus decentralized local collective bargaining), union density, and the mood of the time. They vary from one country to another and, within the same country, over time.

During the 1960s and 1970s, trade union membership was rising in most OECD countries. By the end of the 1970s, the degree of unionization ranged from about 20 per cent in the United States and 23 per cent in France and Japan through 39 per cent in West Germany and 45–50 per cent in Great Britain to 58 per cent in Austria, 70 per cent in Belgium, and 80 per cent in Sweden.[24] During the 1980s, though, the degree of unionization fell in most OECD countries, the exceptions being Finland and Sweden. In 1990, the lowest trade union membership was to be found in France (10 per cent) and Spain (11 per cent).[25]

Not only trade union membership, but also trade union militancy (measured in terms of working days lost due to strikes per 1000 employees) declined during the 1980s. Everywhere, except Norway, there were fewer strikes in 1988–92 than in 1978–82. Britain, for instance, which used to be near the top of the strike league, lost only 20 working days per 1000 employees in 1992, the lowest since records began in 1891.[26]

Thus, the 1980s saw a decline in trade union power. The decline was caused partly, albeit not exclusively, by the rise in open unemployment. The other forces contributing to it included a contraction of highly unionized smokestack industries (coal, steel, and rail) and the public sector, an expansion of the service sector and the private sector, a fall in the plant size, and changes in the composition of the labour force and in the attitudes of economic and political actors.

Since trade union power declined during the 1980s, it may be assumed that trade union participation in policy formation declined too. The assumption is confirmed by the case of Britain. However, Hugh Compston argued that in Austria, Switzerland, the Netherlands, Belgium, and Ireland there had been no general decline in the level of trade union participation in economic decision-making between 1970 and 1992. 'Despite the liberal, free-market push, then, it seems clear that in these five countries at least, union movements as participants in economic policy-making are here to stay.'[27] In contrast, Andrei S. Markovits contended in 1996 that Austria's '[n]eutrality and corporatism are currently undergoing substantial changes to the point of suffering from serious erosion, though neither is in danger of disappearing completely.'[28]

CONCLUSION

Command capitalism is a transitory economic system, because it contains a tension between private ownership of the means of production on the one hand and state coordination on the other. State coordination also makes command capitalism incompatible with a democratic political system, unless adopted by an elected government as a temporary measure in the event of a national emergency, e.g., in wartime.

Since economic activity is coordinated by the government, the economy is bureaucratized, and its bureaucratization gives rise to covert non-compliance with those commands which impede economic actors' performance. In addition, since command capitalism has an inbuilt tendency towards chronic shortages affecting consumers and private firms alike, it gives rise to a second economy. As a matter of fact, non-compliance and a second economy are indispensable to the functioning of the official economy.

In order to run the economy and attain its goals, the government can organize employers and employees into a limited number of national peak associations with compulsory membership, expected to ensure the implementation of governmental policies. In this case, command capitalism assumes the form of imposed corporatism. However, command capitalism can also assume the form of contractual corporatism, in which case corporatist (tripartite) coordination is substituted for state coordination, i.e., economic activity is coordinated jointly by the government, the leaders of the national peak associations representing employers (capital), and the leaders of the national peak associations representing employees (labour).

Irrespective of whether it constitutes an economic system or is confined to a particular policy area or a particular sector of industry, contractual corporatism is not able to survive covert and overt non-compliance with the decisions reached jointly by the government and the leaders of the national peak associations. Moreover, it can be abandoned in favour of market coordination if it transpires that it adversely affects economic performance.

In the West, the retreat from contractual corporatism started around 1980, when economic liberalization in the sense of privatization and deregulation came onto the agenda. On top of that, contractual corporatism is being undermined by the globalization of the world economy, which puts a premium on competitiveness. Nevertheless, by the end of the 1990s corporatist arrangements continued to be in existence, and also the idea of corporatism was not dead, although the term itself tended to be avoided. Will Hutton's conception of the stakeholder economy and society, seen by him as escaping the polarities of collectivism and individualism, is a case in point: although he explicitly rejects any return to the failed British corporatism of the 1970s, in fact he proposes what might be called extended corporatism.[29]

6 Market Socialism

Command capitalism, which substitutes state coordination for market coordination while retaining private ownership of the means of production, is not the only alternative to market capitalism. Another is market socialism, which retains market coordination, but substitutes public ownership of the means of production for private ownership of the means of production.

6.1 THE CALCULATION DEBATE

The ideas of modern socialism originated in the first quarter of the nineteenth century. Between 1870 and 1914, then, socialism emerged as a major force in European history. Yet, before the socialist calculation debate of the 1920s and 1930s, very little atttention had been paid to the economics of socialism.

The socialist calculation debate was initiated by Ludwig von Mises who, in his German-written article published in 1920,[1] categorically denied the possibility of rational economic calculation under socialism, because the means of production were *res extra commercium* (i.e., could not become objects of market transactions) and, therefore, their prices could not be established. Without a free market, there was no pricing mechanism; without a pricing mechanism, there was no economic calculation.

Apart from von Mises, F.A. Hayek and Lionel Robbins argued that socialism was fundamentally flawed. In response, some academic advocates of socialism attempted to prove that rational economic calculation was possible even without private ownership of the means of production and the market. In this endeavour, they were able to resort to Enrico Barone's article of 1908,[2] in which he demonstrated the virtual equivalence between central planning and the free market in the efficient allocation of resources. In principle, the central planning board could determine prices by solving a set of simultaneous equations, much as this is done in practice by the market.

One of these academic advocates of socialism was Oskar Lange. In his model, devised in 1936,[3] the economy is guided by the decisions of households, the central planning board, and socialist managers.

Consumer preferences, expressed in a market for consumer goods, decide the goods to be produced. The central planning board, by trial and error,[4] sets the prices of capital goods so as to balance the supply and demand for each good. Given these parametric prices, the managers of socialist enterprises determine their inputs and outputs according to two broad rules: they must combine factors of production so as to minimize the average cost of production for any output; and they must fix output at the level where the marginal cost equals the price set by the central planning board. Together, these two rules secure the most economical production of the optimum output.

Besides setting the prices of capital goods and natural resources, the central planning board decides the aggregate rate of investment and then sets an interest rate on capital which equates the demand for capital, on the part of socialist managers, to the amount available. It also distributes a social dividend to households, the distribution being based on the principle that the social dividend paid to individuals must not affect their choice of occupation. Thus, the income of consumers is composed of the receipts for the labour services performed and a social dividend constituting the individual's share in the income derived from the capital and the natural resources owned by society.

Although Lange admitted that the real danger of socialism was that of a bureaucratization of economic life,[5] he claimed that the model of the competitive socialist economy had three advantages over its capitalist counterpart: a more just distribution of income owing to the elimination of private property incomes and, for the same reason, a more meaningful pattern of effective demand for consumer goods; more opportunity to take account of externalities; and the elimination of fluctuations in the level of economic activity, i.e., of trade cycles. Lange contended too that in a socialist economy 'the process of price determination is quite analogous to that in a competitive market. The Central Planning Board performs the functions of the market.... It follows that a substitution of planning for the functions of the market is quite possible and workable.'[6]

In 1944, then, Abba P. Lerner devised another model of market socialism, albeit eschewing to call it 'socialist'.[7] The basic operating principle of his model was the same as that of Lange's, namely, running the economy in the general social interest, technically defined by marginal-cost pricing and all the other conditions of optimality in allocation. However, his model differed from Lange's in at least two important respects: Lerner avoided price setting by a central planning board, leaving the process to the free market; and he stressed that private or state ownership of the means of production mattered little from the point of view of allocative efficiency.

While recognizing both private and state ownership of the means of production as perfectly legitimate, Lerner regarded private enterprise as preferable to its alternative of state enterprise because there was a closer identity of the interest of the manager with the social interest. He also acknowledged the significance of private enterprise as one of the guarantees of the freedom of the individual, saying 'that the liberty of the individual obtained its first start in modern times with the freeing of private enterprise and that the possibility for the individual of finding a means of livelihood outside of employment by the state can be a check on undue subservience to the employers who represent the state.'[8]

Not surprisingly, the concept of market socialism was mercilessly criticized. Its critics were not only the opponents of socialism, but also orthodox socialists. For most socialists of the time, it should be remembered, market socialism was an anathema. They abhorred the 'anarchy of the market', rejected consumer sovereignty, and identified socialism with state ownership of the means of production and central planning.

The calculation debate was re-examined by Don Lavoie in a book published in 1985. He was concerned exclusively with the microeconomic rather than macroeconomic aspects of central planning theory. The central focus of his reinterpretation of the debate was the notion of economic rivalry, meaning by it the clash of human purposes, a struggle of some members of society against others, a struggle in which one person's gain in some sense represents the other's loss.[9]

According to Don Lavoie, the cognitive function of markets may be interpreted in terms of computation, incentives, or discovery. The advocates of market socialism adopt either the computation approach (e.g., Oskar Lange) or the incentives approach (most later market socialists), but disregard F.A. Hayek's discovery approach which raises a challenge to the socialist condemnation of income from private property. That is to say, their view of the basic cognitive function markets are expected to provide tends to be narrow.[10]

Joseph E. Stiglitz concluded his discussion of the Lange-Lerner-Taylor theorem asserting the essential equivalency of market economies and market socialism by saying that 'there is more to a market economy than just the use of prices. My basic contention has been that by focusing on prices, the Lange-Lerner- Taylor theorem, as well as the Walrasian model on which it was based, badly mischaracterized the market economy. Neither the model of the market economy nor the model of the market socialist economy provided a good description of the economies they were supposedly characterizing... the fundamental difference between markets and market socialist economies lies not just in [their] institutions but in the broader array of mechanisms by which market economies handle information problems.'[11]

6.2 MARKET SOCIALISM UNDER COMMUNISM

Although the socialist calculation debate of the 1920s and 1930s took place in countries with capitalist market economies, the issue of market socialism existed in communist-ruled countries as well, having both a theoretical and a practical dimension. The brief account that follows begins with the Soviet Union where, between June 1918 and March 1921, a variant of command socialism was attempted. Known as War Communism, it seems to have been rather a product of the Bolshevik ideology than an emergency policy responding to events. Its main features were wholesale nationalization of industry, centralized economic decision-making, command, coercion, rationing, a decline in the role of money, and the requisition of peasants' produce.

War Communism was succeeded by the New Economic Policy (NEP), promulgated in March 1921. Under this variant of market socialism, the state retained control of heavy industry, foreign trade, banking, and transportation, but small-scale private enterprise in manufacturing, trade, and services was revived; requisitions in agriculture were replaced by a tax in kind; and market relations were restored. Yet, in the late 1920s NEP was discontinued. An industrialization drive was launched in October 1928. Forced mass collectivization of agriculture was officially announced in November 1929. Dekulakization was ordered in January 1930, and command socialism was introduced in the early 1930s.

After the Second World War, the Soviet Union imposed command socialism on Eastern Europe. However, Yugoslavia began to move towards a variant of market socialism at the beginning of the 1950s. According to Joze Mencinger, for instance, it passed through four distinct periods between 1945 and the collapse of socialism in the late 1980s, namely, that of administrative socialism (1945–52), that of administrative market socialism (1953–62), that of market socialism (1963–73), and that of contractual socialism (1974–88). In this periodization, which was closely related to changes in the formal allocation of decision-making in the economy, the starting years of the periods were the same as those in which new constitutions were adopted.[12]

For a number of years prior to the end of the 1970s, Yugoslavia's variant of market socialism (also known as the labour-managed market economy, because in 1950 the principle of workers' self-management was legally introduced) attracted considerable attention in the West, particularly among those critics of market capitalism who were reluctant to embrace command socialism. Yet, it produced a crisis of enormous proportions, dating from 1979.

Outside Yugoslavia, advocacy of market socialism appeared in some Soviet-bloc countries in the 1960s and again in the 1980s. Its proponents recognized the limits of central planning and management, and wanted a greater degree of autonomy for enterprises and an increased role for horizontal transactions at the expense of central controls. That is to say, they rejected the official tenet of the incompatibility of planning and the market, and called for a combination of plan and market.

While advocating an injection of market elements into the economy, the proponents of market socialism originally paid little or no attention to the politically and ideologically sensitive issue of ownership of the means of production. It was only later, especially in the 1980s, that calls emerged for an expansion of the role of legal small-scale private enterprise. Still later it began to be asked whether state ownership of the means of production was compatible with a thoroughgoing marketization of an economy. The issue was discussed by Gertrude E. Schroeder in 1988. As put by her, reformers in the socialist countries 'have discovered that property rights matter greatly and that markets for bundles of capital assets (not merely for individual capital goods) are essential... In Marxian terminology, socialist reformers are now tacitly admitting that socialist (state and collective) property has become a fetter on production.'[13]

In practice, a variant of market socialism was established in Hungary in 1968. However, over the next two decades this New Economic Mechanism (NEM) was not fully or consistently applied, underwent numerous modifications and zigzags, and did not put an end to government intervention in the microeconomic sphere.

Approximately ten years later, in the late 1970s, a variant of market socialism began to be introduced also in China, a communist-ruled country not belonging to the Soviet bloc. The reform proceeded in a piecemeal fashion and led to the creation of an economy that, at the end of the 1980s, was a disjointed mix of plan and market and of state-owned, collectively-owned, and private enterprises.

6.3 MARKET SOCIALISM IN THE WEST

Having discussed the issue of market socialism under communism, it is possible to turn again to the West. There, for several decades after the end of the Second World War, socialist tendencies were strong. However, reaction set in around the mid- 1970s, to become most pronounced during the 1980s. The market, the private sector, and welfare pluralism were rediscovered. In order to roll back the frontiers of the state, free the market, and increase efficiency, privatization and deregulation were put onto the agenda.

By the end of the 1980s, socialism was in retreat everywhere, and the notion of the inevitable 'march into socialism' in both its Marxist and Schumpeterian versions was discarded.[14] Yet, although socialism was in disarray, it was far from dead, as the advocacy of market socialism (which some of its socialist critics do not regard as socialism at all) evinces.

Numerous models of market socialism were proposed between the late 1980s and the mid-1990s. Their common denominator is that while they accept the market as desirable, they argue for democratization of the economy and/or the redistribution of wealth. There their similarities end and differences begin. For instance, Marc Fleurbaey's model of egalitarian democratic economy, despite being based mainly on market allocation (albeit supplemented by planning procedures) and private ownership, is characterized by workplace democracy, indirect finance, and wealth redistribution.[15] David Schweickart's thesis is that capitalism no longer has a valid justification, either economic or ethical, because there exists an alternative to it that is not merely viable but plainly superior, namely, his 'Economic Democracy', marked by the market, workplace democracy, and social control of investment.[16] John E. Roemer defines socialism as a kind of egalitarianism, as a system in which there are institutional guarantees that aggregate profits are distributed more or less equally in the population.[17]

Three further models will be described in a somewhat greater detail. According to David Miller,[18] market socialism has at least four aims: to obtain the efficiency advantages of markets in the production of most goods and services; to confine the economic role of the state in a way that makes democratic government feasible; to protect the autonomy of workers, both as individuals and as members of self-managed enterprises; and to bring about a much more equal distribution of primary income, rather than relying entirely on secondary redistribution.

The key idea underlying his pure model is that the market mechanism is retained as a means of providing most goods and services, while the ownership of capital is socialized. All productive enterprises are constituted as workers' cooperatives, with final control vested equally in all those who work in them. The cooperatives lease their operating capital from an outside investment agency.

Being the custodians of social capital, the investment agencies have to strike a balance between potentially conflicting demands. They must allocate capital efficiently but, at the same time, must take account of wider social factors. They must preserve the autonomy of workers' cooperatives but, in order to reach intelligent investment decisions, they need to know a good deal about the future production plans of each cooperative.

In sum, '[m]arket socialism has a composite institutional structure whose various components are intended to counter-balance one another....[Its] two main pillars are the market economy and the state. The market is relied on to produce most goods and services, but within a distributive framework established and enforced by the state. Moreover, government agencies are directly involved in provision in two areas at least: in the supply of public goods such as transport systems and environmental protection, and in guaranteeing rights to welfare (which in practice is sometimes likely to imply direct provision).'[19]

While Miller's model of market socialism puts the means of production into the hands of workers' cooperatives, other models are based on public ownership or its predominance. Thus, under James A. Yunker's pragmatic market socialism public ownership would apply only to large-scale, established corporations. Small firms and similarly entrepreneurial firms personally managed by their founder-owners would be exempted from public ownership. However, upon voluntarily departing from personal management of the firm, the founder-owner would realize its capitalized value by selling it either to an established publicly owned corporation, or directly to the public ownership agency.

Despite taking over the basic discretionary powers embodied in common stock, the public ownership agency would have absolutely nothing in common with a 'central planning agency' of any sort. That is to say, it would be statutorily prohibited from issuing any instructions whatsoever to the publicly owned firms regarding micro-economic firm decision variables, including investment projects.

The standard principle of operation for the typical, established, large-scale publicly owned firm would be profit maximization. The profit maximization incentive would be enforced upon corporation executives by competition from other firms and the threat of bankruptcy, by financial markets which would determine the prices of bonds and promissory notes issued by corporations, and by potential dismissal by the public ownership agency of chief executive officers of poorly performing corporations.

All publicly owned corporations would pay property return in the form of dividends to the public ownership agency. The agency would be allowed to retain a small fraction of this property return to cover its administrative expenses. The remainder would be paid out to private households in the form of a social dividend supplement to earned wage and salary income. Social dividend income would amount to an across-the-board, proportional wage and salary increase for all working members of the population.[20]

Finally, in their outline of a feasible economic mechanism of 'competitive socialism', Pranab Bardhan and John E. Roemer contend that public ownership in the narrow sense of state control of firms is not necessary to achieve one of socialism's goals, a relatively egalitarian distribution of the economy's surplus. They take public ownership, in a wider sense, to mean that the distribution of the profits of firms is decided by the political democratic process, yet the control of firms does not have to be in the hands of agents representing the state. They claim that competitive markets are necessary to achieve an efficient and vigorous economy, but that full-scale private ownership is not necessary for the successful operation of competition and markets.[21]

6.4 IMPLICATIONS

It follows from the discussion in this chapter that market socialism can be conceptualized in different ways. Nevertheless, most (albeit not all) of the proposed models can be subsumed under three variants:

1. Classical market socialism. The term denotes an economic system in which enterprises are publicly owned and run by managers

appointed by and accountable to the government, which appropriates their profits.

2. Labour-managed market socialism. Although enterprises are publicly owned, they are run by managers appointed by and accountable to their workers, but the distribution of their profits is decided by the government.

3. Collective market socialism. Enterprises are owned by their workers and run by managers appointed by and accountable to them. Since enterprises are labour-owned, the workforce has the right to the profits made by them.

The first two variants raise a number of questions. One of them is that of how in an established capitalist market economy the elected government would deprivatize, i.e., how in a democratic political system market capitalism would be transformed into market socialism. In any case, the substitution of public ownership of the means of production for private ownership of the means of production would considerably widen the scope of political power, generate bureaucratic tendencies in the economy, and discourage foreign investment.

Another question is that of the role of the state in the economy. Although market coordination would be retained, it would be confined to product markets and the labour market. Thus, there would be no capital market. Since there would be no capital market, the allocation of capital would be in the hands of the state. Inasmuch as the state would exercise control over the level and pattern of investment, it would be able to influence the quantity and assortment of the consumer goods and services produced.

Besides being able to influence by its investment policy the supply of consumer goods and services, the state would be able to influence the level and pattern of effective demand for them. This would be achieved partly by the elimination of income from private property, i.e., of private profit and rent, and partly by government intervention in the outcome of economic activity, i.e., in the earnings of individuals and the profits of firms, both these policies stemming from the striving for a more equal distribution of wealth and income.

Yet another question is that of the impact of public ownership of the means of production on efficiency and the motivation and behaviour of economic actors. It would make rational economic calculation and efficient resource allocation impossible, the reason being the absence of a capital market which is needed to place values on capital that in turn make it possible for the prices of goods to reflect the scarcity value of the resources used in producing them. Simultaneously, it would act as a disincentive, weakening individual effort, initiative, risk-taking, and responsibility, because nobody would have a personal stake in the market value of land and capital assets and because the threat of bankruptcy would be minimal or non-existent. It would also encourage enterprises to demand from the government excessive resource allocation.

Naturally, collective market socialism too raises a number of questions. One of them is that of how, in a democratic political system, privately owned firms would be transformed into labour-owned enterprises, in effect, into workers' cooperatives combining job-holding with capital ownership. Moreover, if such enterprises maintained a strict policy of self-financing, they would tend to be found in labour-intensive industries only, to have an incentive to limit entry of new labour to the enterprise, and to be biased against investment.

CONCLUSION

Market socialism can be advocated for countries with capitalist market economies as well as for countries with socialist command economies. In the former case it is conceived as an alternative to market capitalism, in the latter as an alternative to command socialism. In both cases it is designed as a halfway house between market capitalism and command socialism, as a third way.[22]

While the transformation of market capitalism into market socialism would considerably widen the scope of political power and lead to a more equal distribution of wealth and income, the transformation of command socialism into market socialism would contract the scope of political power and increase economic inequality. Yet, as argued in Chapter 2, market socialism is a transitory economic system, because it contains a tension between public or collective ownership of the means of production and market coordination. To quote John Gray, '[i]n world-historical terms, market socialism is in any case an anachronism.... Theoretically indefensible, market socialist institutions are in practice systemically unstable, tending to revert to central planning or to mutate into something resembling market capitalism. Wherever political democracy is instituted, the tendency to the latter is virtually irresistible.... it is high time that market socialism be struck off the agenda of policy.'[23]

The focus of the various models of market socialism is democratization of the economy and/or the redistribution of wealth. However, some proposals aiming at the redistribution of power and wealth in capitalist market economies do not envisage a *de jure* change in property rights, i.e., the abolition of private ownership of the means of production. Two such proposals are reported by John E. Roemer.[24] Under one of them, the composition of the boards of directors of private firms would be changed through legislation to consist of, for example, 35 per cent of employees, 35 per cent of asset holders, and 30 per cent of others, perhaps representing consumers or local citizens. Under the other, called associative democracy,[25] although *de jure* property rights in corporations might not change, *de facto* rights would, as active environmental associations and consumer associations, as well as trade unions, would force corporations to change their behaviour. Hence, the implicit economic model is a bargaining model, rather than a competitive one: the actions of firms and the wage structure, for instance, are set more by bargaining than by markets, and the outcome of bargaining depends on the relative bargaining power of the parties involved. This could give rise to 'factionalism', meaning that society would become partitioned into groups each concerned only with its own parochial interest.

Obviously, these two proposals do not put forward models of market socialism. They offer models of a stakeholder economy which, as noted in the previous chapter, might be called extended corporatism.

7 Command Socialism

Command capitalism and market socialism are not the only alternatives to market capitalism. Yet another is command socialism. It rejects both market coordination and private ownership of the means of production, and is intrinsically linked with totalist authoritarianism, of which it is a product. Thus, it is the opposite of market capitalism.

7.1 THE PURE TYPE

While market capitalism is a pluralistic, competitive, horizontally organized, spontaneous, and open economic system, command socialism is a non-pluralistic, non-competitive, vertically organized, centrally directed, and closed economic system, based on public ownership of the means of production and state coordination. This implies that economic power and economic decision-making are concentrated in the hands of government, that the economy is subordinated to and controlled by political power, and that the state is goal-orientated in the sense of being concerned with an end-state or final outcome.[1]

Pure command socialism substitutes central planning (and planner sovereignty) for the market (and consumer sovereignty), regarding the latter to be totally incompatible with the former. Since there is no market exchange, there is no need for money. Production is determined by the government, not by consumers' preferences, and planned in detail in terms of physical units. Consumer goods and services are distributed through physical rationing.

Not only capital and product markets, but also the labour market is absent. The supply of and demand for labour are balanced by means of command, so that if persons in need of placement appear, the government assigns them to the available or newly created jobs at predetermined rates of reward in kind. Besides, employed persons are not allowed to change jobs of their own accord, and only transfers exclusively arranged or approved by the government are possible.

All in all, as a pure type of modern economic system command socialism functions in a machine-like manner. The government has perfect knowledge of and complete control over the economy, although it is resource-constrained, i.e., cannot escape the pervasive economic phenomenon of scarcity. Its plans are comprehensive and detailed, as well as internally consistent. Subordinate economic actors show perfect compliance with commands. Conflicts of interest do not arise and bargaining does not exist. Consequently, by its very nature pure command socialism is incompatible with individual freedom, whether economic, political, or social.[2] *Inter alia*, private property is unknown, there is no consumers' choice, and labour is not free, the last-mentioned meaning that individuals are not able to choose their occupation and their job, or to choose between employment, self-employment and non-employment.

The ideological justification of command socialism is that it would do away not only with income from private property (i.e., private profit and rent) and the exploitation of wage labour by capital, but also with the 'anarchy of the market', and that the government is the best judge of what is good for society.

7.2 SOCIALIST COMMAND ECONOMIES

Although pure command socialism is possible in theory, in practice only its variants can be found. One, known as War Communism, was briefly attempted in Russia between June 1918 and March 1921. Another, of far greater importance, was introduced in the Soviet Union in the early 1930s, imposed on Eastern Europe after the end of the Second World War, and followed by a number of developing countries.

When established in practice, command socialism[3] does not function in a machine-like manner. Since it lacks a free market and, therefore, rational prices reflecting scarcity and consumers' preferences, in directing economic activity the government has to rely on non-market (i.e., bureaucratic) information, provided by subordinate units. Moreover, since central direction of economic activity is all-embracing and detailed, the government is overloaded with information. Despite that, it does not have at its disposal all requisite information (e.g., because certain information is concealed from it and other delayed), and at least some information received by it is insufficient, incomplete, unreliable, inaccurate, and distorted. As a result, the government is not only unable to process, analyze, and integrate the vast volume of collected information in time and in its entirety, but is also to a considerable degree out of touch with reality. Thus, its control over the economy is far from total.

Occupying a subordinate position in the vertically organized and centrally directed economy, state enterprises enjoy low autonomy, i.e., managerial latitude. Being expected to execute commands given them by superior organs, irrespective of whether these commands take the form of plan orders or non-plan orders, they shun initiative, are reluctant to innovate, and avoid risk-taking. On the other hand, they are not exposed to the pressure of market forces and are not threatened by bankruptcy, so that they have a soft budget constraint[4] and lack an incentive to economize on resources, including labour.

Despite the official emphasis on the primacy of societal interests as defined by the government, state enterprises pursue their own economic interests by persistently seeking a rent. One method employed by them to extract a rent is that instead of trying to minimize their inputs in relation to the output demanded from them and to maximize their output in relation to the inputs allocated to them, they strive for the opposite, namely, to maximize their inputs in relation to the output demanded from them and to minimize their output in relation to the inputs allocated to them. Therefore, in their dealings with superior organs they tend to overstate their needs and understate their capabilities. Further methods employed by them to extract a rent include manipulation of the product mix, sacrifice of quality for quantity, pseudo-innovation, violation of formal norms, and falsification of plan fulfilment reports.

Although economic activity is coordinated chiefly by command, the market mechanism is used to distribute the labour force among planned jobs and the planned supply of consumer goods and services among households. Consequently, job-seekers are to a considerable degree free to choose their place of employment at the officially set wage-rates and households exercise consumer choice in the expenditure of their money incomes on available goods and services at the officially set retail prices.

Thus, money is used, albeit merely in transactions involving households. Households receive money wages from state enterprises and transfer payments from social consumption funds, and use their incomes partly to buy consumer goods and services, partly to increase their savings deposits. State enterprises pay their money receipts from the sale of consumer goods and services into the bank, and draw money from the bank to pay wages. However, transactions among state enterprises are effected by the transfer of bank deposits.

Since central direction of economic activity is all-embracing, it covers not only domestic economic activity but also foreign trade. The latter means that the government controls the volume, composition, and destination of exports as well as the volume, composition, and provenance of imports, and that it is able to export at prices bearing no relation to production costs and to dispose of imports at prices bearing no relation to procurement costs. At the same time, it tries to minimize reliance on foreign suppliers, and views exports largely as a means of satisfying particular import needs and accomplishing specific political objectives.

While the state foreign-trade monopoly and the separation of domestic prices from world prices are incompatible with the principle of comparative advantage, they protect state enterprises against foreign-market competition, but do not make the economy as a whole immune against foreign-market fluctuations.

All in all, in practice command socialism severely circumscribes economic freedom, largely disregards consumers' preferences, and has an inbuilt tendency towards inflexibility, inefficiency (i.e., under-utilization and waste of employed resources),[5] chronic and general overmanning (i.e., the creation and preservation of excess jobs),[6] chronic shortages (including chronic labour shortage),[7] repressed inflation, and income levelling.

7.3 ECONOMIC REFORMS

Gregory Grossman characterized the *formal* Soviet-type command-economy system, the main variant of command socialism, in terms of the following institutional features: 'Party-run, state-owned and governed, "imperatively" planned, priority-driven, command-administered, money-using, with universal price and wage control, resorting to individual and group "material" (mostly money) incentives and with a limited but not negligible amount of household free choice in regard to jobs and the acquisition of consumer goods and semi-closed externally.'[8]

The failings of socialist command economies gave rise to attempts to reform the established economic system in order to improve its economic performance.[9] In the Soviet-bloc countries, there were three waves of economic reforms between the mid-1950s and the late 1980s: the first took place in the second half of the 1950s, the next for the most part in the second half of the 1960s, and the last in the 1980s. Outside the Soviet bloc, in China, a major economic reform was launched in the late 1970s.[10]

Reform blueprints varied from one communist-ruled country to another.[11] Nevertheless, in the Soviet bloc they had two features in common. One was their intention to retain public ownership of the means of production, i.e., their reluctance to put privatization of the means of production on the agenda. The other was their concentration on the coordinating mechanism, i.e., on the relationship between central planning and the market or, in brief, on economic management.

Originally, it follows from the foregoing, economic management was of a direct directive (centralized-administered) type, and the economy was managed as a single large unit. In theory, its alternatives were either indirect directive (decentralized-administered) economic management, a modified version of direct directive economic management, or non-directive (socialist market) economic management.

Under indirect directive economic management, the basic framework of central planning remains intact. Yet, although the principle of central planning primacy is retained and the central plan continues to handle all major macroeconomic issues, central planning becomes less detailed and more general. Simultaneously, state-parametric information is substituted for non-parametric information (command, binding administrative order): the government assigns to state enterprises aggregated targets, sets them limits to certain allocated resources, and determines the so-called economic instruments or levers. Consequently, economic decision-making is partially decentralized, with state enterprises having a greater degree of autonomy (managerial latitude) in micro-economic decisions, in their day-to-day operations. Besides, the role of horizontal transactions increases at the expense of vertical links, i.e., relations of superiority and subordination.

Non-directive economic management abandons central planning altogether, abolishes vertical links, and substitutes market information for both non-parametric information and state-parametric information. Economic decision-making is dispersed, and the autonomy of state enterprises (managerial latitude) is high. The role of the government is confined to the creation of legal and economic conditions for the pursuit of economic activity. Nevertheless, the economic system is not completely separated from political power, because public ownership of the means of production is retained. As a result, non-directive economic management contains a tension between public ownership of the means of production and the market: on the one hand, public ownership of the means of production constitutes a constraint for the market; on the other hand, the market constitutes a threat for public ownership of the means of production.

In practice, economic reforms in the Soviet bloc had both their advocates and their opponents,[12] and in none of the communist-ruled countries the political leadership wanted to lose control over the economy. As a result, non-directive economic management was rejected and reform blueprints tried to devise economic management based on a combination in various proportions of non-parametric, state-parametric, and market information. That is to say, prior to the end of the 1980s reform of the original direct directive economic management was to amount to change *within* the system, not *of* the system.

Since economic reforms faced not only opposition and resistance but also systemic constraints, they contained a tendency to fail. As put by János Kornai, 'the [socialist] system is incapable of stepping away from its own shadow. No partial alteration of the system can produce a lasting breakthrough. For that a change of system is required.'[13]

7.4 THE SECOND ECONOMY

In socialist command economies, the government does not (and cannot) have perfect knowledge of and total control over the economy. This means that in these economies there exists a second economy which, just as that in capitalist market economies, does not include the household economy. It consists of spontaneous gainful economic activities, of those gainful economic activities that escape central control because central control is either ineffectual or absent.

While under market capitalism second economy activities are defined in terms of illegality, under command socialism at least some second economy activities can be legal. However, in practice the demarcation line between legal and illegal second economy activities is frequently blurred, because a legal second economy activity can have an illegal dimension or serve as a front for an illegal second economy activity, and because a legal first economy activity can be intertwined with an illegal second economy activity.

Both illegal and legal second economy activities can take place either within the first economy (i.e., within the state sector) or outside it. Consequently, it is possible to make a distinction between illegal second economy activities within the first economy, illegal second economy activities outside the first economy, legal second economy activities within the first economy, and legal second economy activities outside the first economy. Two systemic factors contribute to participation in illegal second economy activities. One is chronic shortages affecting consumers and state enterprises alike: economic actors engage in these activities because the first economy fails to supply consumers with those consumer goods and services they need or desire and state enterprises with those inputs they need for plan fulfilment. The other is the bureaucratization of the economy: in order to achieve their output targets and protect their own economic interests, state enterprises (and, similarly, employed individuals) must often violate, evade, or ignore formal norms and administrative orders.

Naturally, the existence of illegal second economy activities suggests that economic actors are not constrained by considerations of legality and morality. Expressed differently, it indicates that the population's respect for formal norms, administrative orders, and public property is low, and that there is a tension between officially proclaimed moral standards and popular conceptions of right and wrong.

According to Dieter Cassel and Ulrich Cichy, while under market capitalism the second economy is a stabilizing factor, under command socialism it is a destabilizing one. Just as in capitalist market economies, it seems to be an economic lubricant and a social mollifier: on the one hand it compensates for shortages in the first economy, on the other it lifts the tolerance margin of individuals with respect to economic policies. However, it has no unambiguous function as a built-in stabilizer: it reduces the stability of the overall economy because it provides incentives to divert resources from the first economy; thereby, it aggravates shortages in the first economy; this, in turn, stimulates its further growth.[14]

7.5 THE LEGAL SECOND ECONOMY

The Soviet-bloc countries usually retained a small legal private sector. It was to be found both in agriculture and outside it, and its size varied from one country to another and, within the same country, over time.

In agriculture, the legal private sector consisted mainly of small private plots, as a rule not exceeding half a hectare in size, allotted to collective farmers, state farm workers, and white-collar and blue-collar workers. The only exception among the Soviet-bloc countries

Table 7.1 Share of the Private Sector in Arable Land and Total Agricultural
Output, Soviet-Controlled Eastern Europe, 1985 (per cent)

	Arable land	Total agricultural output
Bulgaria	13	25
Czechoslovakia	3	10*
East Germany	9	n.a.
Hungary	13	34
Poland	77	78
Romania	14	n.a.

* About 15 per cent according to Zdenek Lukas, *Der Privatsektor in der
tschechoslowakischen Landwirtschaft seit 1970*, Wien, Wiener Institut für
internationale Wirtschaftsvergleiche, 1986, p. i.

Source: Nancy J. Cochrane, 'The Private Sector in East European
Agriculture', *Problems of Communism*, vol. XXXVII, no. 2 (March–April
1988), p. 48, Table 1.

was Poland where, as Table 7.1 shows, in 1985 nearly four-fifths of the
arable land was privately owned and about four-fifths of total agricultural output came from private farms.

Although with the exception of Poland the legal agricultural private
sector was not large, its contribution to agricultural production was far
from negligible. The figures given in the table attest to it. Concerning
specifically the Soviet Union, not included in the table, in 1985 private
plots constituted a mere 2.7 per cent of the total sown area, yet their
share in total agricultural output hovered at 25 per cent.[15]

Official attitudes towards the legal agricultural private sector varied
from one Soviet-bloc country to another and, within the same country,
over time. Predominantly, they were a combination of toleration,
discouragement, and hostility. However, in the 1980s there appeared
a tendency in a number of these countries to encourage the production of food by the legal agricultural private sector, stemming from the
desire to improve the domestic supply of agricultural produce.[16]

In the 1980s there also appeared a tendency in a number of these
countries to encourage an expansion of the legal non-agricultural
private sector. The tendency was most pronounced in Poland and
Hungary. The Soviet Union passed a law on individual labour activity
in November 1986 and a law on cooperatives in May 1988, the underlying reasons being to alleviate shortages of consumer goods and
services, to tap unused labour reserves such as pensioners, house-
wives, and students, and to reduce illegal second economy activities.[17]

Despite experiencing some expansion, prior to the collapse of communism the legal non-agricultural private sector remained small everywhere. This applied even to Poland, where its share in gross material product went up from 2.3 per cent in 1980 to 5.4 per cent in 1988 and its share in the total labour force from 3.5 per cent in the former year to 7.0 per cent in the latter.[18]

Outside the Soviet-bloc countries, in China, persons working in the legal non-agricultural private sector numbered 0.33 million in 1978, 7.55 million in 1983, and 26.24 million (accounting for over 10 per cent of the non-agricultural labour force) in 1988. While one reason behind the official encouragement of private enterprise was shortages of consumer goods and services, another was the existence of open unemployment: despite severe overmanning, 26 million urbanites were openly unemployed in 1981. Although originally the private sector was intended to remain on an individual (one-person) scale, later up to seven employees were allowed, and in April 1988 companies with eight or more employees were officially recognized.[19]

7.6 THE ILLEGAL SECOND ECONOMY

Compared with the legal second economy, the illegal second economy was of far greater significance in the Soviet-bloc countries, because it evinced that in socialist command economies the government was not able to suppress the pursuit by economic actors of their own interests and, hence, was not omnipotent.

To a large extent, the illegal second economy depended on the diversion and unauthorized use of public property for private purposes and on the misappropriation of working time. Simultaneously, the diversion and unauthorized use of public property for private purposes amounted to its de facto privatization, giving rise to informal property rights in the sense of effective private control over formally public property.[20]

Of course, illegal second economy activities were not confined to the diversion (i.e., theft) of public property for private purposes and to the unauthorized use of public property (tools, machines, means of transport, and the like) for private purposes. They also included legally unsanctioned production, trade, and services for private gain; bribe-giving and bribe-taking; tax evasion on the part of legal private enterprises as well as on the part of persons engaged in moonlighting during and after working hours; and benefit fraud, particularly in the case of sickness benefits.

However, not every illegal second economy activity was motivated by private gain. Quite a few stemmed from state enterprises' search for ways to achieve their output targets and to protect their own economic interests. Therefore, they violated, evaded, or ignored formal norms and administrative orders, the examples being the falsification of plan fulfilment, price infringements, inter-enterprise barter, and the use of fixers (expediters).

As a rule, the available estimates of the size of the illegal second economy in the Soviet-bloc countries take into consideration exclusively those illegal second economy activities that were pursued for private gain. Bearing this in mind, it is possible to turn to at least some of them, beginning with those concerning the Soviet Union. In 1985, Peter Wiles estimated that the Soviet illegal second economy had risen from five per cent of official GNP in 1965 to 10 per cent in 1980.[21] According to T. Koryagina, the Soviet illegal second economy had an annual turnover of five thousand million roubles in the early 1960s and 90 thousand million roubles in the late 1980s, although simultaneously admitting that the figures for the late 1980s ranged from a low of 20–25 thousand million roubles to a high of 150 thousand million roubles.[22]

For Poland, one calculation put the income derived by the population from the illegal second economy at 3.8 per cent of that derived from the first economy in 1970, at 13.1 per cent in 1982, and at 8.9 per cent in 1984,[23] while another put the illegal second economy at 11.2 per cent of the national income in 1983, at 14 per cent in 1984, and at 18 per cent in 1985.[24] In this connection it should be noted that in 1989 the legal agricultural and non-agricultural private sector contributed 17.4 per cent to the gross material product (at constant 1984 prices) and 19.2 per cent to the domestic net material product at current prices.[25]

Discussing the second economy in Hungary, István R. Gábor defined it as the aggregate of all income-orientated economic activities performed, whether legally or not, by individuals and households. Towards the end of the 1980s, the second economy so defined produced about a quarter of the national income, with a labour input amounting to some 50 per cent of the total hours worked in the socialist sector. The total net personal income thus earned was equal to at least one-third of the wage fund in the socialist sector.[26]

As to Romania, in 1987 a Western source cautiously suggested that in the mid-1980s the share of illegal productive economic activities in the national income might have been approximately 10 per cent and that of legal private economic activities also approximately 10 per cent, so that the share of the second economy might have stood at over 20 per cent of the national income and at 35–40 per cent of the population's official income.[27]

Finally, in his estimate of the size of the illegal second economy in East Germany Horst Brezinski ignored those illegal second economy activities that had a predominantly redistributive effect, such as the theft of socialist property, tipping for under-the-counter sales, and tax fraud committed by the legalized private enterprises. Confining himself exclusively to second economy activities with a productive effect, he put the illegal second economy's contribution to the national income at approximately one per cent in the mid-1980s, and that of the entire second economy at six per cent.[28]

Naturally, these estimates (being mere estimates) must be taken with caution. Nevertheless, they do indicate that in the Soviet-bloc countries the size of the illegal second economy was not only far from negligible, but was also growing over time.

7.7 OFFICIAL RESPONSES

The existence in socialist command economies of an illegal second economy raises the question of what the government can do about it. The answer is that if the government wants to maintain command socialism, its options are limited to three main responses. One of them is to try to confine or suppress illegal second economy activities either by a stricter enforcement of formal norms and administrative orders, or by increasing the population's respect for formal norms, administrative orders, public property, and the officially proclaimed moral standards. However, because the causes of illegal second economy activities include systemic factors, namely, chronic shortages affecting consumers and state enterprises alike and the bureaucratization of the economy, this response is bound to fail.

Another possible official response is to tolerate illegal second economy activities as long as they act as an economic lubricant and a social mollifier, i.e., as long as they contribute to the functioning and maintenance of the first economy. It is based on the reluctant recognition that, due to their systemic causes, illegal second economy activities cannot be suppressed.

Yet another possible official response is to encourage an expansion of the legal private sector in the hope that it will lead to a contraction of illegal second economy activities. It would mean both an increase in the number of persons participating in it and an increase in its share in the national output, and could be achieved by making the entry into it easier, by widening the range of legal second economy activities, and/or by permitting new forms of legal private enterprise to emerge.

However, an expansion of the legal private sector would give rise to at least three problems, namely, that of how it would obtain materials, fuels, machinery, equipment, premises, and capital, that of how tightly it would be regulated, and that of how heavily it would be taxed. In all probability, if it faced difficulties in procuring its inputs, excessive regulation, and a high burden of taxation, it would be inclined or even forced to resort to illegal second economy activites.

Simultaneously, if the government wanted to maintain command socialism, the legal private sector (competing with the first economy for scarce resources) would have to remain marginal and supplementary even after its sanctioned expansion. Moreover, the government could try to tie it to the first economy, so that it would provide goods and services primarily for state enterprises, not directly for consumers.

CONCLUSION

Command socialism is a man-made economic system, based negatively on the rejection of economic pluralism, spontaneity (the 'anarchy of the market'), and the pursuit of self-interest, and positively on the belief in economic monism, central direction of economic activity, and the primacy of societal interests as defined by the government. That is to say, the economy is conceived as a single large unit functioning as a well-oiled machine.

Despite the official rejection of the pursuit of self-interest and the official emphasis on the primacy of societal interests as defined by the government, in practice both state enterprises and households do pursue their own interests, the former aiming at rent maximization and the latter at utility maximization. Thus, conflicts of interest come into existence, with state enterprises and households putting their own interests above the officially defined interests of society as a whole.

Underlying these conflicts are two systemic factors, namely, the pervasive bureaucratization of the economy and chronic shortages affecting producers and consumers alike. Bureaucratization gives rise to covert non-compliance with those formal norms and administrative orders which impede economic actors' activities and goal-attainment.[29]

Shortages give rise to illegal second economy activities which, obviously, are a specific manifestation of covert non-compliance. In sum, although command socialism is a highly formalized economic system, in practice it inevitably has an informal dimension too. This informal dimension is an unintended product of the formal system and deviates from it, in some respects complementing it, in others eroding it. Its examples are informal contacts, informal relationships, informal networks, informal exchanges, informal property rights, informal rules (conventions), and informal subcultures.[30] Expressed differently, under command socialism the government elicits on the part of economic actors in addition to conformist behaviour also deviant behaviour, which is both typical (i.e., chronic and general) and atypical (i.e., occasional and sporadic). Thus, the government experiences a tension between what it wants to do (i.e., its preferences) and what it can do (i.e., its constraints), and what it will do (i.e., its response) is frequently a compromise between the two.

Part III
Governments

Depending on the predominating type of coordinating mechanism and the predominating type of ownership of the means of production, in modern economies the first or official economy is always a variant of one of the four pure types of modern economic system, identified in Chapter 2. These types, discussed in some detail in the chapters making up Part II, are market capitalism, command capitalism, market socialism, and command socialism.

Irrespective of its economic system, in any modern economy there exists a second or unofficial economy too. Hence, the second or unofficial economy is a cross-system phenomenon. Yet, until the mid-1970s Western economists paid little attention to it, although they examined its individual dimensions in different economic systems. Their interest in it dates only from the second half of the 1970s. Soviet and East European economists began to talk about the second economy in the Soviet-bloc countries roughly a decade later, in the second half of the 1980s, usually calling it the shadow economy. Prior to the mid-1980s they, with the exception of Hungarian economists, ignored it. Nevertheless, they recognized its individual dimensions as early as the 1960s.

Besides a first or official economy and a second or unofficial economy, a government economy is to be found in any modern economy. It refers to what the government extracts from the economy and spends, i.e., to government revenue and expenditure, and its size is one (albeit not the only) indicator of the role the state plays in the economy. It is the subject-matter of the three chapters that constitute Part III.

8 The Government Economy

The government economy consists of economic activities that are non-marketed, legal, and recorded, and that require government revenue. Although it is to be found in any modern economy irrespective of its economic system, in the following exclusively that under market capitalism will be considered, unless stated otherwise.

8.1 GOVERNMENT SPENDING

In capitalist market economies, the size of the government economy depends on the role the state plays in the economy which, in turn, depends on the established variant of market capitalism. As argued in Chapter 4, under the *laissez-faire* variant the role of the state is confined to providing national defence, maintaining law and order, and stepping in when private initiative is lacking. Under the free-market variant the state is furthermore expected to foster competition and to deal with externalities. Finally, under the interventionist variant the state intervenes in property rights, the operation of the market, and/or the outcome of economic activity with a view to achieve specific economic or social objectives other than allocative efficiency, such as stable economic growth, full employment, or a desired distribution of income.

However, the role the state plays in the economy has an impact not only on the size of the government economy, on the level (share in GDP) of government spending, but also on the purpose of government spending. In principle, government spending can arise from the provision of certain services (national defence, the maintenance of law and order, the infrastructure, education, health care, and so on), transfer payments (*inter alia*, social security benefits and interest on government debt), and subsidies to public enterprises and private firms. It is divided into current spending (e.g., wages for government employees) and capital expenditure (e.g., new roads or schools), and is financed through taxation and government borrowing.

Besides having an impact on the level and purpose of government spending, the role the state plays in the economy has an impact on the number of persons directly or indirectly employed by the state in one capacity or another, as well as on the bureaucratization of the economy. Generally speaking, the greater the role the state plays in the economy, the greater the number of persons directly and indirectly employed by the state in one capacity or another, and the greater the bureaucratization of the economy.

Not surprisingly, government spending contributes to a tension in society. On the one hand, those individuals who benefit from it (because they are recipients of state-provided services, transfer payments, or subsidies, or because they are directly or indirectly employed by the state in one capacity or another) or expect to benefit from it in the future, are likely to have vested interests in its continuation and growth and to resist attempts to slim the state. On the other hand, those individuals who are adversely affected by it (because as taxpayers they have to finance it yet neither benefit from it nor expect to benefit from it in the future) are likely to be interested in its reduction and to favour measures intended to slim the state.

8.2 PUBLIC GOODS

Due to lack of private initiative, in capitalist market economies some beneficial goods (services) would not be produced (provided) by the market at all. When private initiative is lacking in such cases, the state must step in even under the *laissez-faire* variant of market capitalism. Thus, the question of public goods (as opposed to private ones) arises.[1] As noted in Chapter 4, it was already recognized by Adam Smith.[2]

To begin with private goods, a private good is characterized by rivalness in consumption (one person's consumption of the good reduces the quantity available to others) and the possibility of exclusion by both the producer (who can restrict the use of the good to those consumers who are willing to pay for it) and the consumer (who is not forced to consume the good). Where goods display these characteristics, free exchange is possible and the market can function. In contrast, a pure public good is characterized by non-rival consumption (one person's consumption of the good does not reduce its availability to anyone else) and non-excludability (if the good is provided, the producer is unable to bar anyone from consuming it, to ensure that the good is obtained only by those individuals who paid for it).[3] As a result, public goods give rise to the problem of free-riders who seek to escape payment while benefiting from the existence of the good, and prevent the market from functioning.[4]

Actually, pure public goods are relatively rare, their archetypal example being national defence. More common are impure public goods, those goods where consumption is not completely non-rival (because their availability is limited) or where exclusion is possible (i.e., their consumption can be made dependent on the willingness of consumers to pay for them). Therefore, they do not have to be supplied by government.

Thus, private enterprise is able to supply private goods. Since a price can be charged for them, there is no economic justification for the government to go into the business of supplying them. On the other hand, private enterprise is not able to supply pure public goods. Since a price cannot be charged for them, they must be supplied by government. As to impure public goods, these can be supplied by private enterprise if charging is both technically feasible and economic. If charging is technically feasible but uneconomic, it is sensible to supply them by government.

However, in practice impure public goods are frequently supplied by government on non-economic grounds, not on economic ones. Although they could be supplied by private enterprise, they are supplied by government because they are regarded as merit goods, as goods the consumption of which is deemed to be socially desirable, irrespective of consumers' preferences. In these cases, such as compulsory education and free health care, consumer sovereignty is suspended and consumers are encouraged and even compelled to use them.

In the opinion of at least some economists, the range of impure public goods supplied by government should and could be reduced. It should be reduced in order to reassert consumer sovereignty, improve quality, and increase efficiency. It could be reduced inasmuch as advances in technology make pricing possible where it was not before. As admitted by these economists, though, it is politically difficult to reduce the existing range of impure public goods supplied by government by transferring them to the market.[5]

Yet, even when political support for impure public goods supplied by government is widespread, there are limits to the range of pure and impure public goods so supplied: since these goods are financed

		Private	Public
FINANCE	Private	Goods financed privately and produced in the private sector	Goods financed privately but produced in the public sector
	Public	Goods financed publicly but produced in the private sector	Goods financed publicly and produced in the public sector

Figure 8.1 Private and public provision

through taxation, a tension inevitably arises between them and the consumption of private goods. Simultaneously, inasmuch as each public good makes demands on scarce resources, a tension arises between different public goods.

To sum up, it follows from the foregoing that a good can be financed either privately or publicly (i.e., through taxation) and produced either in the private sector or in the public one. Consequently, as Figure 8.1 shows, there are goods financed privately and produced in the private sector, goods financed privately but produced in the public sector, goods financed publicly but produced in the private sector, and goods financed publicly and produced in the public sector.

Although the figure distinguishes between spenders and producers, it does not reveal the source of spenders' income and whether the spender is identical with the consumer or not. This was taken into consideration by Milton and Rose Friedman, according to whom there are four categories of spenders, namely, individuals spending their own money on themselves, individuals spending their own money on someone else, individuals spending someone else's money on themselves, and individuals spending someone else's money on still another person.[6]

8.3 SUBSIDIES

Besides spending taxpayers' money on the provision of certain services, the government can spend taxpayers's money on transfer payments and on subsidies. Since the question of state-provided services has been discussed in the preceding section and because the question of transfer payments will be discussed in the next chapter, it is the question of subsidies that will now receive attention.

A subsidy (or, more precisely, a production subsidy) is a payment by government to public enterprises and private firms which forms a wedge between the price consumers pay and the costs incurred by producers, such that price is less than marginal cost. General subsidies (offered to all producers satisfying certain conditions) can be distinguished from specific subsidies (designed for a particular producer or project), and input subsidies (embracing factor inputs, i.e., capital, labour, and technology) can be distinguished from output subsidies. Besides, subsidies can have a geographic dimension, i.e., be intended for a designated area or region of the country.

One possible objective of production subsidies is to keep prices of selected goods down or stable and, thus, to encourage the consumption and output of goods deemed to be socially desirable, to prevent open inflation from rising, or to boost exports. Another possible objective of production subsidies is to maintain or raise producers' incomes and, thus, to reduce their losses, to prevent bankruptcies or closures, to support research and development, or to promote reorganization, re-equipment, and restructuring. Yet another possible objective of production subsidies is to maintain or increase employment and, thus, either to prevent open unemployment from going up or to bring it down.

Whatever their possible objectives, production subsidies affect the allocation and utilization of resources in the economy and, hence, are an instrument of government intervention in the operation of the market. As such, they are open to political pressures, and their advocacy is frequently justified on grounds of social benefits, in the name of the public or national interest, or as being required to correct a market failure. On the other hand, they distort prices and costs, can conceal or contribute to inefficiency, and can even be abused.

The degree of subsidization varies from one country to another and, within the same country, over time. In the OECD countries, for instance, the share of production subsidies in GDP ranged from 0.2 per cent to 4.5 per cent in 1960 and from 0.4 per cent to 8.4 per

cent in 1980. While these figures suggest that in the countries concerned the degree of subsidization increased over the two decades,
they may significantly underestimate the role of production subsidies.[7]

One type of production subsidy is agricultural subsidies. Overall
payments to OECD farmers through a combination of direct payments, cheap loans, and guaranteed prices, called producer subsidy
equivalents or PSEs, which averaged US$ 98 billion between 1979 and
1986, providing 34 per cent of farmers' total income, went up to US$
163 billion in 1993, providing 42 per cent of farmers' total income. As
to specifically the European Union, there the cost of the Common
Agricultural Policy reached US$ 79.6 billion in 1992, consuming over
50 per cent of the total EU budget for 1993.[8]

Besides production subsidies, the government can provide consumption and income subsidies. According to David W. Conklin,
they pursue some aspect of equality, i.e., are based upon the equality
objective of assisting low income groups, and include health care
subsidies, housing subsidies, education subsidies, and transfer payments.[9] In other words, they are a different name for state-provided
welfare.

In conclusion, two of the various consequences of production as
well as consumption and income subsidies deserve to be mentioned
specifically. They contribute to the bureaucratization of the economy
and to the creation of a subsidy culture, particularly if they are widespread and persistent.

8.4   TOTAL GOVERNMENT SPENDING

E.F. Schumacher listed five principles of orthodox public finance,
namely, to keep the budget small, to keep the budget balanced, to
tax consumption rather than saving, to issue long-term bonds if a
deficit cannot be avoided, and to borrow only for purposes of 'productive' investment. The principles followed logically from the original proposition of classical economic theory that private business
automatically maintains full employment.[10]

While classical economics argued that the budget should be both
small and balanced, in practice these two principles have often been
disregarded. One cause of high government spending, high taxation,
budget deficits, and government indebtedness has been Keynesian
ideas. According to Peter A. Hall, already quoted in Section 4.3, the
theories of John Maynard Keynes placed increasing responsibility for

economic performance on the government's shoulders, and his attacks on the priority which classical economics attached to a balanced budget helped to loosen a fiscal constraint that stood in the way of more generous social programmes.[11]

Between 1890 and 1990, the share in GDP of government spending increased sharply everywhere. By the end of the nineteenth century it was 7 per cent in the United States (1890), 9 per cent in Britain

Table 8.1 Total Government Expenditure as a percentage of GDP at Current Prices, 1913–86

	1913	1929	1938	1950	1973	1986
Average of six countries (France, Germany, Japan, the Netherlands, the United Kingdom, and the United States)	11.7	17.8	27.7	26.7	37.4	46.3

Source: Angus Maddison, *The World Economy in the 20th Century*, Paris, OECD, 1989, p. 71, Table 6.3.

Table 8.2 Total Government Expenditure as a percentage of GDP, OECD and EC, 1970–90

	1970	1975	1980	1985	1990
Total OECD	32.3	38.1	39.4	40.7	43.4
EC	36.9	44.7	46.0	49.8	48.7

Sources: *OECD Economic Outlook*, no. 50 (December 1991), p. 205, Table R 15, and *ibid.*, no. 52 (December 1992), p. 215, Table R 15.

Table 8.3 Total Government Expenditure as a Percentage of GDP, Selected OECD Countries, 1970–90

	1970	1975	1980	1985	1990
Low-spending countries					
United States	31.7	34.7	33.7	36.7	..
Japan	19.4	27.2	32.6	32.3	32.3
Switzerland	21.3	28.7	29.3	31.0	30.7
High-spending countries					
Sweden	43.3	48.9	61.6	64.7	61.4
Netherlands	43.9	52.8	57.5	59.7	55.6
Belgium	36.5	51.5	59.0	62.5	55.2
Denmark	40.2	48.2	56.2	59.3	58.4

Sources: *OECD Economic Outlook*, no. 50 (December 1991), p. 205, Table R 15, and *ibid.*, no. 52 (December 1992), p. 215, Table R 15.

(1890), and 13 per cent in Germany (1891).[12] In 1913 it still was no more than 8.0 per cent in the United States, 8.9 per cent in France, 13.3 per cent in the United Kingdom, 14.2 per cent in Japan, and 17.7 per cent in Germany.[13] The subsequent growth of government spending is shown in Table 8.1 (which covers the period from 1913 to 1986) and Table 8.2 (which covers the period from 1970 to 1990). Since these two tables do not show that the share in GDP of government spending varied considerably from one country to another, Table 8.3 offers examples of low-spending and high-spending OECD countries between 1970 and 1990.

As follows from the foregoing, an important cause of the growth of peacetime government spending has been a steady expansion of the welfare state financed through taxation. Generally speaking, the factors affecting the level of welfare spending include the range, scope, and generosity of welfare provisions, the age composition of the population, and the trade cycle (in recessions, welfare spending tends to be pushed up as unemployment benefits increase).

Obviously, government spending requires government revenue, the main source of which in modern economies is taxes on personal income, goods and services, corporate income, property, and the like. Historically, consumption taxes have been around since the ancient Greeks and Romans. In contrast, income tax dates back only to 1799, when it was first introduced in Britain.

Since between 1890 and 1990 the share in GDP of government spending increased sharply everywhere, also the tax burden (the ratio of tax revenues to GDP) rose,[14] although it continued to vary from one country to another: in 1990, for instance, tax revenues ranged from about 30 per cent of GDP in Australia, the United States, and Japan to 57 per cent in Sweden. At the same time, the relative importance of the individual sources of tax revenue varied from one country to another, with personal income taxes (including social security contributions) accounting in 1990 for over half of all the tax collected in the majority of OECD countries.

When government revenue does not cover government spending, budget deficits arise, requiring government borrowing and leading to government indebtedness and a decline in government saving.[15] While in the 1960s most OECD governments were net savers, in the 1980s they were dissavers.[16] As a result, gross public debt had an upward tendency, the two most conspicuous cases being Belgium (where it went up from 81.6 per cent of GDP in 1980 to 134.4 per cent in 1990) and Italy (where it went up from 59.0 per cent of GDP in 1980 to 100.5 per cent in 1990).[17]

8.5 COMMAND SOCIALISM

The provision by government of certain services, transfer payments, and subsidies is to be found in any modern economy irrespective of its economic system. Hence, it is to be found under command socialism as well. In contrast to market capitalism, though, under command socialism the government economy and the first economy are rolled into one.

At this juncture it should be noted that comparison of the performance of socialist command economies with that of capitalist market economies was hampered by four main factors: the socialist command economies established in the Soviet-bloc countries did not compute GDP,[18] had no convertible currency, relative prices in them differed to varying degrees but substantially from equilibrium ones, and their official statistics were defective. It should also be noted that in these socialist command economies government spending was financed through taxation and the profits of state enterprises producing both public and private goods, and that in the absence of a capital market investment was financed exclusively or predominantly from the state budget.

Bearing this in mind, it is possible to insert Table 8.4, giving the share in GDP of government spending in six Soviet-bloc countries at the beginning of the 1980s. As follows from the table, which does not include East Germany, the share ranged from 43.5 per cent in the case of Romania to 63.2 per cent in the case of Hungary. Of these six countries, the Table 8.5 singles out for consideration the case of the

Table 8.4 Government Expenditure as a Percentage of GDP, Soviet-Block Countries

Bulgaria	1980	47.0
Czechoslovakia	1980	53.1
Hungary	1981	63.2
Poland	1981	53.2
Romania	1981	43.5
Soviet Union	1981	47.1

Source: János Kornai, *The Socialist System*, Oxford, Clarendon Press, 1992, p. 135, Table 8.1.

Table 8.5   Government Expenditure, Budget Deficit, and Internal Debt as a
              percentage of GNP, Soviet Union, 1985–89

	1985	1986	1987	1988	1989
Government expenditure	49.7	52.2	52.2	52.5	52.2
Budget deficit	1.8	5.7	6.4	9.2	8.7
Internal debt	18.2	20.3	22.3	35.6	43.1

Source: Narodnoe khozyaistvo SSSR, 1989, pp. 11, 612, and 614.

Soviet Union between 1985 and 1989. Since it is confined to the
second half of the 1980s, it does not show that the share in GNP of
government spending had an increasing tendency already prior to the
mid-1980s, amounting to 41.1 per cent in 1960, to 41.7 per cent in
1970, and to 47.9 per cent in 1980.[19]

The budget deficits as presented in the table seem to be understated. According to a 1989 Soviet source, the budget deficit was 2.9
per cent of GNP in 1980, 2.7 per cent in 1985, 6.5 per cent in 1986, 8.0
per cent in 1987, and 9.1 per cent in 1988, and was expected to reach
13.0 per cent in 1989.[20] Its causes included a slump in the prices of oil
and petroproducts in the world market, lower budget revenue due to
the anti-alcohol campaign and deteriorating enterprise profits, run-
away investment expenditures, increased outlays for social programmes, soaring food subsidies,[21] and the costs resulting from the
Chernobyl' nuclear power plant catastrophe and the earthquake in
Armenia.

In the West, one widely discussed item of Soviet government spending was the cost of the Soviet empire in terms of trade subsidies, trade
credits, economic aid, military aid, and so on.[22] An even more widely
discussed item was defence spending. According to official Soviet
statistics, defence spending was equivalent to about 4.8 per cent of
GNP in 1970, 2.8 per cent in 1980, 2.5 per cent in 1985, and 2.3 per
cent in 1988. In contrast, the CIA put the Soviet defence burden at
12–14 per cent of GNP in the early 1970s and at 15–17 per cent in the
second half of the 1980s, although simultaneously both lower and
higher estimates were offered by other analysts, with at least one of
them putting the Soviet defence burden in the second half of the
1980s at 20–25 per cent of GNP, while the comparable figure for the
United States was less than six per cent.[23] It was only in 1989 that
the Soviet Union admitted that hitherto defence spending had been
understated, because it did not include procurement of weapons,
military research and development, military construction, pensions

for servicemen, and other expenditure. In that year, defence spending allegedly amounted to 8.1 per cent of GNP.[24] Nevertheless, the new Soviet figure still fell far short of Western estimates.

Not surprisingly, the East European defence burden was less heavy than the Soviet one. According to R.T. Maddock, in 1982 the countries of Soviet-controlled Eastern Europe spent on defence on average around 3.5 per cent of GNP measured in domestic currency.[25] According to Keith Crane, between 1962 and 1984 the reported defence budgets absorbed 2–6 per cent of utilized national income. In contrast to the Soviet defence budget, and with the possible exception of Czechoslovakia, defence expenditures reported by the East Europeans probably covered major expenditure categories except for military research and development and pensions for servicemen.[26]

As already mentioned above, in the Soviet-bloc countries all or nearly all investment was financed from the state budget. That part of investment which was not financed centrally was financed by state enterprises from their own resouces. In this connection, the case of China is of interest, because it shows the impact on the state budget of changes in the ways investment was financed. Prior to 1978, Mario I. Blejer and Gyorgy Szapary wrote in their article of 1990, in China 'enterprises remitted all their surplus funds to the budget and, in turn, the government undertook to provide finance for the enterprises' investment and working capital requirements. To improve efficiency, it was necessary to allow enterprises to retain a portion of their profits that could be used for investment and for incentive bonuses to management and labor. Therefore, in 1978 the Chinese authorities began to experiment with profit retention schemes and profit taxation for selected enterprises. In light of these experiences, in 1983 the authorities initiated a changeover, almost completed by 1986, for all enterprises from direct profit transfers to the government to income taxation.'

Due to these changes, government revenue declined from 34.4 per cent of GNP in 1978 to 20.4 per cent in 1988, and government expenditure from 34.1 per cent of GNP in 1978 to 22.9 per cent in 1988. Both in 1978 and in 1988, China's revenue and expenditure levels were substantially lower than in other socialist centrally planned economies. This reflected, in part, the absence of social security intermediation through the budget in China, where retirement benefits, as well as other welfare benefits such as education and health care, were still largely the responsibility of the enterprise sector.[27]

Obviously, in socialist command economies the level (share in GDP) of government spending is not an adequate indicator of the role the state plays in the economy, because in these economies economic activity is centrally directed. However, in capitalist market economies too the size of the government economy is not an adequate indicator of the role the state plays in the economy, because in these economies government intervention in the economy is not confined to taxation and government spending.

CONCLUSION

Although in capitalist market economies the size of the government economy is only one indicator of the role the state plays in the economy, it is an important indicator of the multidimensional tension between economic individualism and economic collectivism inherent in modern economies. The tension intensifies as the size of the government economy increases, as the tax-dependent (surplus-consuming) non-market sector grows at the expense of the surplus-producing market sector.[28]

By taxing the population and spending the money collected or borrowed, the government has an effect on resource allocation and income distribution and, thus, both on current consumption and on wealth creation. Somewhat more specifically, by taxing and spending it affects demand, the propensity to save, investment behaviour, growth, and the welfare of present and future generations.

The impact of taxation and government spending depends not only on the tax burden (i.e., the ratio of tax revenues to GDP) and the level and purpose of government spending, but also on the structure of taxes. The least harmful tax system is one that is fair, simple, and interferes as little as possible with private economic decision-making, with the operation of the market. This suggests that it is better to tax spending than to tax income, and that a broad tax base is needed if tax rates are to be kept low.

High marginal income tax rates, it should be noted, have a number of adverse consequences. They tend to encourage tax avoidance and tax evasion, to discourage hard work and risk-taking, and to influence the supply of labour. Since they reduce the taxpayers' disposable income, they depress saving and, hence, private investment and output, resulting in a welfare loss in the long run. At the same time, they may actually raise less government revenue than lower marginal income tax rates would do. It follows that the worst way to increase government revenue is to increase marginal income tax rates, and that it is desirable to shift the tax burden from income taxes to consumption taxes by trimming marginal income tax rates. Although the main argument against consumption taxes (such as VAT or a sales tax) is that they are regressive, during the 1980s a number of OECD countries trimmed marginal income tax rates, without necessarily cutting the total tax burden.

Consumption taxes are not identical with an expenditure tax, which is a form of income tax levied exclusively on the part of income that is spent, exempting the part that is saved. In other words, the tax base is the difference between receipts (salaries, wages, fees, investment income, the proceeds from asset sales, borrowing, etc.) and savings (bank deposits, equities, and the like). Thus, thrift is rewarded at the expense of profligacy, but there may arise problems of the definition of taxable expenditure.

Since government revenue need not cover government spending, budget deficits appear, and may be either occasional or permanent. The former occur irregularly and infrequently under the impact of recessions, natural catastrophes, armed hostilities, and other exigencies. The latter occur year by year, their cause being the structure of government spending, determined by long-standing commitments to particular programmes, such as state-provided welfare.

Budget deficits, especially permanent ones, lead to government indebtedness. However, an indefinitely rising ratio of public debt to GDP is unsustainable as well as dangerous: it can push up real interest rates and so crowd out private investment; it kindles a temptation to allow high open inflation to erode the real value of debt; it can restrict the ability of government to use fiscal policy to boost the economy in a recession; and it can create a vicious circle in which rising public debt requires higher interest payments, these in turn require extra borrowing, and so on.

All in all, in capitalist market economies the government faces tax and spending constraints. That is to say, there are limits to what it can extract from the population by way of taxation and borrowing and, consequently, to what it can spend. At the same time, its long-standing commitments to particular programmes, in the first place to state-provided welfare, make it difficult to slow down the rate of government spending's increase, and even more difficult to cut government spending's actual level.

In 1994, many governments continued to be big spenders. Leaving aside government borrowing, taxes were equivalent to 53 per cent of

GDP in Sweden, to over 50 per cent in Denmark, and to close to 50 per cent in Finland, Holland, Norway, Belgium, and Italy, while in Japan, Australia, and the United States they were below 30 per cent. Under these circumstances, a number of economists suggested that government spending should not exceed 30 per cent of GDP. Advocating this level, Robert Skidelsky added that '[t]he state as spender is the last bastion of collectivism. The collectivist age will not be over until state spending has been drastically pruned.'[29] It should be remembered, though, that the tax burden is only one indicator of the role the state plays in the economy.

9 The Welfare State

In capitalist market economies, the share in GDP of government spending increased sharply between 1890 and 1990, in the latter year averaging 43 per cent in the OECD countries and nearly 49 per cent in the European Community. An important cause of the growth of government spending has been the expansion of the welfare state financed through taxation, which has taken place especially since the end of the Second World War.

9.1 INDIVIDUAL WELFARE

Individual welfare denotes the range of needs and wants the individual is able to satisfy and the level at which he or she is able to satisfy them. The needs and wants concern, *inter alia*, food, clothing, shelter, safety, rest, sleep, activity, personal and social contacts, affection, love, appreciation, the esteem of others, self-respect, and self-realization. Their satisfaction depends both on the individual's resources (such as physical and mental health, knowledge, skills, possessions, and money) and effort, and on the economic, political, social, and cultural environment in which he or she lives.

Since the satisfaction of the individual's material and non-material needs and wants depends both on his or her resources and effort and on the environment in which he or she lives, individual welfare has multiple sources. One of them, albeit frequently disregarded, is the individual himself or herself. The others are the family (household), informal networks (relatives, friends, neighbours, colleagues), the market, voluntary organizations, and central and local government (the state). Hence, individual welfare is a result of welfare pluralism, not of welfare monism.[1]

Historically, the primary source of individual welfare has been the household, and even today the household economy remains of fundamental importance. At the same time, the size of the household has an impact on the efficiency of its operations. According to Alessandro Cigno, for instance, 'two non-identical individuals can, through division of labour, generate more goods jointly in a two-person household than they could separately in two one-person households.... Home-time being an amalgam of separate domestic tasks (shopping, cooking, cleaning, etc.), there may be further efficiency gains to be made by extending the principle of division of labour to the allocation of these specific tasks. . . . the potential for improving efficiency through division of labour increases with the size of the household.'[2]

The state[3] contributes to individual welfare indirectly by providing national defence and maintaining law and order, as well as by stepping in when private initiative is lacking, fostering competition, and dealing with externalities. Besides, it contributes to individual welfare directly by various welfare provisions, including welfare services (such as education, health care, and personal social services), social security transfer payments (pensions, unemployment benefits, child benefits, and so on), subsidies (e.g., housing subsidies and employment subsidies), and tax allowances and tax exemptions.

Prior to the emergence of the welfare state by the end of the nineteenth century, the sources of individual welfare were not confined to employment, self-employment, the household, and informal networks. They also included friendly societies (dating from the late eighteenth century), friendly society medical institutes, occupational welfare, church institutions, private charities, voluntary hospitals, free dispensaries, voluntary social services, local government, and the like. In the 1880s, state-sponsored social insurance was adopted in Bismarck's Germany, largely to damp down social unrest among workers and the appeal of socialism. It had spread considerably over the subsequent five decades, so that by the beginning of the Second World War some state-sponsored or state-provided social protection existed in most European countries. However, it was only after the end of the Second World War that a rapid and substantial expansion of the welfare state took place. This expansion lasted until the mid-1970s and was connected with a widely held belief that the provision of welfare was one of the proper ends and responsibilies of government. Simultaneously, an *étatiste* view assumed that the state was the sole source of welfare, that the household economy was irrelevant, and that the market was unable to provide welfare. Nevertheless, welfare pluralism has not disappeared, individual welfare continues to have multiple sources.

9.2 TYPES OF WELFARE STATE

The role the state plays in the provision of welfare varies from one country to another and, within the same country, over time. Despite this diversity, though, two basic welfare roles of the state may be distinguished, namely, that of a residual provider and that of a comprehensive provider.[4] The former is implied in economic individualism, the latter in economic collectivism.

As a residual provider, the state plays a limited (albeit important) role in the provision of welfare. The emphasis is put on self-reliance, i.e., able-bodied individuals are expected to provide for themselves and their families, as well as to make arrangements in the form of savings, investment, and private insurance that would support them and their families when, through no fault of their own, they are not able to do so because of illness, open unemployment, disability, old age, and the like. Since able-bodied individuals are responsible for their own welfare and that of their families, the state is regarded as the provider of last resort, which steps in only when the other sources of individual welfare fail, providing basic welfare services and cash benefits set at the subsistence level. Eligibility for these services and benefits is based on means tests.

In contrast, as a comprehensive provider the state is seen as the first-line provider, the responsibility of which is to secure the welfare of the entire population from the cradle to the grave. Coverage is universal, the range of state-provided benefits is comprehensive, state-provided welfare services are free at the point of entry, state-provided cash benefits are unrelated to previous contributions, and means tests are rejected. Consequently, the role of the other sources of individual welfare is vastly reduced, and redistributive policies are unavoidable.

Of course, the welfare states established in capitalist market economies are merely variants of the two pure types of welfare state just distinguished. Of the established welfare states, then, those established in the Scandinavian countries by the end of the 1980s came nearest to the comprehensive type.[5]

The established welfare states differ in a number of respects, particularly with respect to the range, scope, and generosity of welfare provisions, as well as with respect to their financing.[6] The range of welfare provisions may be narrower or wider. At one extreme, the state can provide only a minimal social safety net in the sense of providing means-tested social assistance exclusively to those individuals who are unable to subsist on the basis of private provision through market transactions and other private transfers. At the other extreme, the state can provide social protection against every possible contingency in the life of the individual. Historically, the range of welfare provisions has been widening, so that individuals have become protected against more and more risks.[7] Nevertheless, even in those capitalist market economies in which the range of welfare provisions is wide, means-tested social assistance usually continues to be available.

If there are differences in the range of welfare provisions, there are differences in their scope (i.e., in the persons covered) too. Coverage may be residual, employment-related, or universal. In the first case, means-tested social assistance is confined to those individuals who are without any private means of support. In the second case, benefits are conferred on the basis of the occupational status of the recipient. In the third case, benefits are defined as citizenship rights available to all members of society on the same terms.[8]

Obviously, this has an impact on the method of financing: while in the first and third cases financing is through general taxation, in the second case it is primarily through employer and employee contributions (in the sense of insurance premiums or contributory taxes), and only secondarily through general taxation. No less obviously, this has an impact on whether benefits in cash are differential or not: while in the first and third cases they tend to be flat rate, in the second case they tend to be proportional to contributions or previous earnings. Naturally, in practice flat-rate and differential benefits in cash can coexist.

Besides differences in the range and scope of welfare provisions, there are differences in their generosity, i.e., in the standard of living they make possible. The level of benefits in cash may be set between two extremes: at one extreme the benefit guarantees no more than the subsistence level, at the other it replaces the income lost as a result of a contingency. As follows from the aforesaid, in the case of residual and universal coverage benefits are apt to be set at or slightly above the subsistence level, whereas in the case of employment-related coverage they are apt to be proportional to contributions or previous earnings.

Irrespective of their initial level, benefits in cash (particularly the long-term ones) raise the question of their indexation in line with either open inflation or rising earnings. They also raise the question of their minimal level: should it be identical with the subsistence level, or should it allow the individual to lead a decent life in the community to which he (or she) belongs? It should be remembered, though, that the notion of decency is subjective, depending on changing social standards and expectations.

Finally, there are differences in the financing of welfare provisions. Generally speaking, benefits in cash are financed through taxation.

More precisely, they may be financed either exclusively through general taxation, or through a combination of employer and employee contributions and general taxation. When the latter mode of financing is used, it can vary from one capitalist market economy to another, with some relying less on contributions than others.[9]

Of course, the welfare states established in capitalist market economies provide not only social security transfer payments, such as retirement, invalidity, and widow's pensions, sick pay, unemployment benefits, child benefits, and social assistance. They further provide welfare services (education, health care, personal social services, and the like), subsidies (e.g., housing subsidies and employment subsidies), and tax allowances and tax exemptions. Of these welfare provisions, health care deserves to be mentioned explicitly.

Theoretically, two pure types of health care system may be distinguished: one, implied in the concept of the residual welfare state, is financed privately, with health care produced by private doctors and private hospitals, paid on the fee-for-service basis; the other, implied in the concept of the comprehensive welfare state, is financed through general taxation, with health care produced by publicly employed doctors and publicly owned hospitals. In practice, though, health care systems tend to be mixed (hybrid) systems, combining in varying proportions private and public health care.[10]

By the end of the 1980s, the health care system coming closest to the pure private system was that established in the United States of America. Health care was produced mostly by private doctors and private hospitals, and health insurance for workers and their dependants was private, usually paid for by employers. Nevertheless, besides private health insurance there existed federal programmes covering the old, the disabled, and the poor. In contrast, the British health care system (the National Health Service) was closest to the pure public system. It was financed predominantly through general taxation and covered the whole population. Health care was produced by salaried doctors and publicly owned hospitals and, with some exceptions, was free of charge. Despite that, private health care was available too.

Also the health care systems established in Canada and West Germany are of interest. For years, Canada had a health care system similar to the American one. However, in 1971 it switched to a national health insurance system, which covered the whole population, was financed through taxation, and banned nearly all private health insurance. Yet, most doctors and hospitals were private. West Germany continued to rely on its traditional sickness insurance system, under which coverage was basically employment-related and which operated through sickness funds with compulsory membership.

The health care systems established by the end of the 1980s in the remaining OECD countries were usually variants either of the (British) national health care system, or of the (Canadian) national health insurance system, or of the (West German) traditional sickness insurance system. Variants of the private health care system were rare.

In 1990, the share in total health spending of private health spending was about two per cent in Norway, 10 per cent in Sweden, 15 per cent in the United Kingdom, 21 per cent in Italy, 22 per cent in Germany, 25 per cent in France, 28 per cent in Canada, 30 per cent in Japan, 31 per cent in Spain, 35 per cent in Austria, and 60 per cent in the United States.[11]

9.3   WELFARE SPENDING

The welfare state financed through taxation underwent an expansion between its emergence in the late nineteenth century and the mid-1970s. The expansion was particularly pronounced during the first three decades after the end of the Second World War when, as Milton Friedman wrote in 1962, '[w]elfare rather than freedom became the dominant note in democratic countries.'[12] As a result, the share in GDP of government spending on state-provided welfare increased considerably in all capitalist market economies.

In the United Kingdom, for instance, the share of the nation's income that was taxed away or borrowed to finance education, housing, health, income maintenance, and social care services grew from about 2.6 per cent at the beginning of the century (when welfare provision consisted largely of poor-law provisions and elementary education) through about seven per cent in 1920, 11 per cent in the 1930s, 14 per cent in the 1950s, and 20 per cent in 1970 to about 25 per cent in the mid- 1970s.[13] Also the figures offered by Richard Rose and partly reproduced in Table 9.1 are relevant here, although they refer exclusively to sources of individual income. It follows from them that between 1851 and 1981 the role of the state as a source of individual income had increased sharply: while in the former year only 1.2 per cent of the British population received an income from the state, in the latter year 38.5 per cent did, either through income maintenance payments or through public employment.

Table 9.1   Sources of Individual Income, Britain, 1851–1981
(per cent)

Provision by:	1851	1911	1938	1951	1981
Market (private employment)	49.1	40.8	39.1	34.5	29.9
State					
Public employment	1.2	3.0	4.7	12.5	13.7
Income maintenance	0	2.5	8.9	12.5	24.8
Total state	1.2	5.5	13.6	25.0	38.5
Household transfers	49.7	54.8	47.3	40.5	31.6
Total population (millions)	20.8	42.1	47.5	50.2	55.8

Source: Richard Rose, 'The Dynamics of the Welfare Mix in Britain', in
Richard Rose and Rei Shiratori (eds), *The Welfare State East and West*,
Oxford, Oxford University Press, 1986, p. 83, Table 4.1.

Concerning specifically the postwar period, in OECD countries
expenditure on public social programmes (including education, health
care, transfer payments, and personal social services, but excluding
housing) accounted on average for 13.1 per cent of GDP in 1960, for
25.6 per cent in 1981, and for around 27 per cent in both 1985 and
1990. Obviously, these averages conceal that the share in GDP of
government spending on state-provided welfare varied widely from
one country to another: while in 1960 it ranged from 7.7 per cent
(Switzerland) to 20.5 per cent (West Germany), in 1981 it ranged
from 13.4 per cent (Greece) to 37.6 per cent (Belgium).[14]

It is not surprising, then, that towards the end of the 1970s and in
the early 1980s attempts appeared in a number of countries to restrain
welfare spending. However, attempts to control the growth of welfare
spending or to reduce welfare spending are hampered by those factors
that affect its level. The factors include the range, scope, and generosity of welfare provisions, the age composition of the population, and
the trade cycle. Of these factors, only the age composition of the
population and its impact on welfare spending will be singled out
here for a brief comment.

Early state pension schemes tended to follow the private insurance
practice of accumulating a fund that would be adequate to meet
future pension costs. Later, though, in most OECD countries state
pension schemes were put on a pay-as-you-go basis, which means that
pensions are paid out of current employer and employee contributions, the result being intergenerational transfers. Unfunded pay-
as-you-go state pension schemes can pay pensions immediately at their
inception even to generations which contributed little or nothing to

their funding. Moreover, as long as the aged dependency ratio (i.e., the ratio of pensioners to the population of working age) is low, they do not impose a high tax burden on employers and employees. On the other hand, they inevitably come under increasing pressure if, due to falling birth rates and rising life expectancy, the population is ageing.

A rapid ageing of the population is expected to take place in many industrial countries during the first half of the twenty-first century, because the postwar baby boom generation will start to retire by around 2010.[15] According to a study published in 1995 and covering Canada, France, Germany, Italy, Japan, the United Kingdom, and the United States, '[i]n all [these] major seven countries except the United Kingdom, elderly dependency ratios (the ratio of elderly to the "adjusted" working-age population) are projected almost to double by around 2030 to 2040 before stabilising or falling slightly. In Japan, Germany and France, elderly dependency ratios are projected to peak at around 0.6 and in Italy at over 0.7, while the peak for the United States, the United Kingdom and Canada is likely to be around 0.4 to 0.5.'[16]

Consequently, if the existing unfunded pay-as-you-go state pension schemes remained unchanged, the levels of public debt would be bound to rise, sometimes sharply. In order to prevent public debts from getting out of hand, the schemes would have to be modified, the options being to increase employer and employee contributions, to reduce the real value of state pensions, or to raise the retirement age. There is, however, yet another option, namely, to switch from state-provided pensions, paid for out of taxes, to private funded pensions, paid for out of personal savings. This option was advocated by a number of economists already prior to the mid-1990s,[17] when at least some governments finally began to concede the need to encourage the creation of private funded pension schemes to supplement rickety state-run ones.

Besides putting under pressure unfunded pay-as-you-go state pension schemes, the ageing of the population puts under pressure the established health care systems. It should be remembered, though, that other factors too push up spending on health care, including rising expectations and, particularly, advances in (typically expensive) medical technology and drugs.

Naturally, population ageing has an impact not only on welfare spending. It also has an impact on, *inter alia*, economic growth, labour force participation, labour adaptability and mobility, income distribution, consumption patterns, the propensity to save, investment, and voting behaviour.

According to a 1996 OECD publication, it should be added, the effects of rapid population ageing (most importantly perhaps in Japan and some European countries) on consumption, saving, and investment are one of the factors contributing to the possibility of world capital shortages over the coming years. The other factors are the long-term decline in saving rates in the industrialized countries in general, the persistence of the budget deficit in a number of OECD countries, in particular the United States, and the potential demand for capital to meet the investment needs of European transition economies and Russia, as well as those of the dynamic emerging economies in East and South-East Asia and Latin America. All in all, '[c]oncerns have been expressed that these factors could lead to worldwide demand for capital outstripping supply, and a subsequent rise in long-term interest rates.'[18]

9.4 CRITICISM OF THE WELFARE STATE

Although widely supported, the expansion of the welfare state financed through taxation has given rise to criticism of it. This criticism appeared already in the 1960s,[19] but intensified in the mid-1970s, when mounting welfare spending placed too large a burden on the less buoyant economies, one which they could not bear any more.

The welfare state has been accused, *inter alia*, of being centralized, bureaucratic, and inefficient; of creating monopoly welfare services and producing inflationary pressures; of giving priority to consumption and the redistribution of income and wealth over wealth creation; of neglecting obligations in favour of entitlements; of discouraging hard work and leading to its abuse by work-shirkers and welfare-chisellers; of having an adverse impact on self-reliance, consumer choice, and the propensity to save; of providing welfare services of low quality; and of not doing away with poverty. It also has been accused of making individuals economically dependent on the state; of helping to bring forth a social welfare ('free lunch') mentality or ethic (i.e., a dependency culture) on the part of welfare recipients and a welfare-producer mentality on the part of welfare producers; and of generating vested interests in its maintenance and uninterrupted expansion.

Consequently, the expansion of the welfare state financed through taxation has been seen as contributing to the multidimensional tension between economic individualism and economic collectivism inherent in modern economies, and as tilting the balance in the direction of the latter. Concerning specifically one dimension of this tension, namely, that between economic criteria (efficiency) and welfare criteria, Theodore Geiger opined that 'there is *no necessary conflict* between welfare criteria and efficiency criteria. The substitution of the former for the latter can and often does improve both welfare and efficiency. In other words, the two sets of decision criteria can be mutually reinforcing – in effect producing a positive-sum outcome, i.e., more of both.... Nonetheless, the substitution of welfare criteria for efficiency criteria can also be a negative-sum game..., that is, one in which not only efficiency but, sooner or later, welfare too would be reduced.... Thus, *too much or the wrong kinds of welfare can, by undermining efficiency, lead in time to a reduction of welfare as well.*'[20]

Geiger's proposition might be reformulated as follows: while the residual welfare state tends to contribute to efficiency and the wealth-creating process and, thus, to welfare, the comprehensive welfare state tends to hinder efficiency and inhibit the wealth-creating process and, thus, adversely affect welfare. This suggests that the former is preferable to the latter.

9.5   WELFARE TRIMMING AND REFORM

Although the welfare state financed through taxation has its critics, it has its staunch supporters too.[21] They hold the fallacious assumption that an increase in state-provided welfare inevitably means an increase in welfare in society, and that a reduction in state-provided welfare inevitably means a reduction in welfare in society. Therefore, they reject the provision of welfare by the market and voluntary organizations, and in extreme cases even dismiss as irrelevant the provision of welfare by the household.

Supporters of the welfare state financed through taxation are recruited from among welfare recipients (current, potential, and future), welfare producers (be they professionals or non-professionals), and welfare bureaucrats. Since they have vested (albeit not identical) interests in its maintenance and expansion, they vehemently resist its trimming or reform, intentionally exaggerate the gravity of welfare problems, loudly complain of underfunding, and unceasingly call for additional resources.

Hence, in democratic political systems the government faces pressure groups demanding higher welfare spending. However, in their competition for votes the government and the opposition too can contribute to higher welfare spending: the former by yielding to pressure group demands, the latter by promising to meet pressure group demands if elected. Thus, past governments can commit future governments to welfare spending that is one cause of high government spending, high taxation, budget deficits, and government indebtedness, and that is difficult to curb.

Yet, there are limits to welfare spending, to the expansion of the welfare state financed through taxation. These limits arise because the comprehensive welfare state has adverse effects on investment, allocative efficiency, and human performance. This also means that if there is free trade and markets are highly contested, it harms the country's international competitiveness by, *inter alia*, leading to high labour (wage and non-wage) costs.[22]

Under the impact of factors such as contraction of economic activity, low rates of economic growth, declining international competitiveness, and demographic changes, the point is reached when the economy is not able to bear the cost of state-provided welfare any more. As a result, the question of welfare cuts comes to the fore. The cuts can be achieved either by trimming welfare spending or by reforming the welfare state.

In the former case, i.e., in the case of welfare trimming, the established welfare state remains in existence. However, some measures are taken to restrain welfare spending, such as tightening eligibility criteria, freezing or reducing cash benefits and housing subsidies, subjecting cash benefits to taxation, and imposing user charges (e.g., requiring patients to pay for a portion of the health care they actually receive). Besides, measures can be taken to improve the performance of state-provided welfare services. One possibility is that instead of providing welfare services via the public sector, the government buys them on behalf of the users from competing independent producers. Another possibility is to introduce vouchers in education and health care to give users the choice between alternative producers, thus creating competition.[23] Expressed differently, the flow of funds would change from $G \rightarrow MP \rightarrow U$ to $G \rightarrow CP \rightarrow U$ or to $G \rightarrow U \rightarrow CP$, where G stands for government as funder, MP for monopoly public sector welfare producers, CP for competing welfare producers, and U for users.

While in the case of welfare trimming the established welfare state remains in existence, in the case of its reform it is either substantially scaled down or dismantled. That is to say, private provision through self-insurance and individual savings is substituted for public provision paid for out of taxes. A system of individual welfare funds (of personal lifetime accounts) is created, into which people pay their premiums and out of which they draw benefits in the event of open unemployment, sickness, disability, retirement, and the like.

Although self-insurance could be voluntary or compulsory, the disadvantage of the former is that left to themselves, some individuals might fail to insure themselves adequately or at all against future contingencies. Although the system could be run privately or by the state, there are three objections against state-run funded schemes: they tend to be monopolies, their investment performance may suffer from lack of competition between fund managers, and they can be raided too easily by governments inclined to guide investment or to carry out back-door nationalization. It seems, then, that private provision through self-insurance would best be served by a system that is funded, privately run and, as to basic insurance, compulsory. It would restore the nexus between contributions and benefits, reduce taxation, free funds for investment, and weaken the dependency culture.

Naturally, the substitution of private provision for public provision would considerably reduce the welfare role of the state and, hence, welfare spending as well. The state would cease to be the first-line provider. Its welfare role would be confined to regulating the privately run system, maintaining the minimum income below which nobody should fall, encouraging the work of voluntary organizations, and stepping in when something goes wrong.

While considerably reducing the welfare role of the state, the substitution of private provision for public provision need not spell the end of company-run schemes. However, the drawback of such schemes is that they frequently penalize those employees who change their jobs. Thus, they discourage labour mobility which, in turn, can hinder economic growth.

In practice, as noted above, attempts to restrain welfare spending appeared in a number of countries already towards the end of the 1970s and in the early 1980s. Some examples of welfare trimming were given by a 1990 OECD publication. According to it, '[i]ndexation of benefits has been abandoned (Italy), or limited (Canada, Netherlands), while arrangements for social provision have become increasingly income-tested (Australia); [i]n income transfer programmes, tighter links between income and work have been established (France, Germany, Netherlands, Spain, United Kingdom); [i]n the health sector there have been attempts to introduce market forces as well as capacity constraints (on hospitals) in order to induce a more efficient use of resources (Germany, Italy, Netherlands, Portugal, United Kingdom, United States).'[24]

Although welfare trimming continued during the first half of the 1990s,[25] governments were reluctant to embark upon a fundamental reform of the established welfare state, mainly because there was almost no public support for it. Nevertheless, some economists and politicians did recognize that the established welfare state could not be afforded any more, that welfare trimming did not do away with the problems created by it,[26] and that at least a partial substitution of private provision for public provision was unavoidable.

CONCLUSION

Two pure types of welfare state may be distinguished, namely, the residual welfare state (implied in economic individualism) and the comprehensive welfare state (implied in economic collectivism). The former is the provider of last resort, which steps in only when private provision through market transactions and other private transfers fails. The latter is the first-line provider, which protects the entire population against every possible contingency from the cradle to the grave.

Each of these two pure types of welfare state is based on certain values and, in turn, has a distinct impact on the values of society and the attitudes and behaviour of economic, political, and other actors. While the central value of the residual welfare state is self-reliance, that of the comprehensive welfare state is the right of the individual qua citizen to state-provided welfare. By emphasizing self-reliance, the former encourages individual effort, initiative, risk-taking, and responsibility. In contrast, by emphasizing welfare rights the latter weakens individual effort, initiative, risk-taking, and responsibility, contributes to the creation of a dependency culture, and makes the individual economically dependent on the state.

Concerning specifically the comprehensive welfare state, since it protects the entire population against every possible contingency from the cradle to the grave, it generates vested interests in its maintenance and expansion on the part of welfare recipients as well as welfare producers and welfare bureaucrats. Since it is seen as being responsible for individual welfare, people put the blame on it when their welfare expectations are not met. Since it is financed through taxation, it adversely affects the propensity to save and, thus, private investment and economic growth, the final outcome being a reduction in the welfare of present and future generations. This means that there are limits to welfare spending, to the expansion of state-provided welfare.

Despite these limits, in democratic political systems the comprehensive welfare state gives rise to demands by the opposition, pressure groups, and the electorate for higher welfare spending. The articulation of such demands (and, similarly, the occurrence of benefit fraud) suggests that in its functioning the comprehensive welfare state is subject to the famous Say's Law, according to which supply creates its own demand.

In practice, only variants of the comprehensive welfare state as a pure type are to be found in capitalist market economies. The established variants may be criticized in two ways: on the one hand for failing to relieve poverty, emancipate the underclass, improve welfare services, and the like; on the other hand for having adverse economic and non-economic effects, such as blunting the work ethic, inhibiting wealth creation, turning people into wards of the state, and encouraging the breakup of families.

As the expansion of the welfare state continues, the point is reached when the economy is not able to bear the cost of state-provided welfare any more. Thus, the question of welfare cuts comes to the fore. The cuts can be achieved either by trimming welfare spending while maintaining the established welfare state, or by reforming the established welfare state, i.e., by substituting private provision for public provision.

The substitution of private provision for public provision would considerably reduce the welfare role of the state and, hence, the share in GDP of government spending and taxation. It would also free funds for investment, restore the nexus between contributions and benefits, and weaken the dependency culture. Ultimately, it would increase welfare in society. Yet, when a variant of the comprehensive welfare state is established, attempts to substitute private provision for public provision are likely to lack public support, because the welfare state financed through taxation is seen as providing welfare without requiring individual responsibility. This avoidance of responsibility on the part of individuals stems from their fear of responsibility which, in turn, means a fear of freedom.

10 Welfare Under Command Socialism

Naturally, the provision of welfare by the state is not confined to capitalist market economies. It can be found in any modern economy irrespective of its economic system. Consequently, it can be found in socialist command economies as well. Therefore, the present chapter will concentrate on the welfare role of the state in these economies.

10.1 INDIVIDUAL WELFARE

In capitalist market economies, it has been argued in Section 9.1, individual welfare has multiple sources. One of them is the individual himself or herself. The others are the family (household), informal networks (relatives, friends, neighbours, colleagues), the market, voluntary organizations, and central and local government (the state). Hence, individual welfare is a result of welfare pluralism, not of welfare monism.

However, also in socialist command economies individual welfare has multiple sources. They include on the one hand the individual himself or herself, the family (household), informal networks, and the second (legal and illegal) economy. On the other hand they include the first economy, the so-called social or mass organizations, and the government economy. Thus, in these economies too, individual welfare is a result of welfare pluralism, not of welfare monism.

Despite this similarity, though, socialist command economies differ from capitalist market economies in two major respects. A far from negligible source of individual welfare, namely, voluntary organizations, is missing. In their stead, the so-called social or mass organizations, particularly the official trade unions, are a source of individual welfare.[1] Secondly, the first economy is based on public (not private) ownership of the means of production and state (not market) coordination.

Since state coordination (central direction of economic activity) is substituted for market coordination, the state affects individual welfare by determining the share of consumption in national income; the volume and composition of consumer goods and services; retail

prices; the global wage-fund at the macroeconomic level and its distribution among economic sectors and occupational groups; the wage-
rates for the whole economy; the wage-bill and personnel size of
individual state enterprises; and the provision of welfare services,
social security transfer payments, and subsidies.

Besides, the state affects individual welfare by using the market
mechanism to distribute the labour force among planned jobs and the
planned supply of consumer goods and services among households.
Consequently, job-seekers are to a considerable degree free to choose
their place of employment, albeit at the officially set wage-rates, and
although consumer sovereignty is suppressed, households are able to
exercise consumer choice in the expenditure of their money incomes
on available goods and services at the officially set retail prices.

Finally, the state affects individual welfare by rejecting privately run
insurance schemes, because such schemes are incompatible with public ownership of the means of production and state coordination.
Hence, if state-provided welfare did not exist, in case of a contingency
individuals would have to rely on their savings, their families, informal
networks, and the second economy. Therefore, in contrast to capitalist
market economies, in established socialist command economies the
state must of necessity be a comprehensive welfare state financed
through taxation and protecting the entire population against every
possible contingency from the cradle to the grave.

10.2   HISTORICAL BACKGROUND

Unless stated otherwise, the examination that follows will be confined
to the seven communist-ruled European countries that for about four
decades prior to the end of the 1980s constituted the Soviet bloc,
namely, the Soviet Union, Bulgaria, Czechoslovakia, East Germany
(the GDR), Hungary, Poland, and Romania. Their economic systems
were variants of command socialism, introduced in the Soviet Union
in the early 1930s and in the remaining six countries within a few years
after the end of the Second World War. In all these seven countries,
more or less developed social insurance predated the introduction of
command socialism.

In Tsarist Russia, social insurance for the non-agricultural labour
force was in existence, but its coverage was restricted and the range of
benefits limited.[2] After the October Revolution,[3] the Bolsheviks
promised comprehensive social insurance (renamed social security in

1918) for all wage-earners. Its implementation encountered difficulties, though, one reason being resource constraints. For example, old-age pensions for some blue-collar workers were brought in only in 1928 and those for white-collar workers in 1937. Despite that, pensioners tended to be neglected until 1956 when, as a result of a pension revision, an improvement in their lot took place.

For a long time, Soviet collective farmers were expected to provide their own income maintenance through mutual assistance programmes. Finally, social security for them and the members of their families was introduced in 1964. Yet, it was less comprehensive than that for workers, and provided lower cash benefits. While subsequently it began to be equalized with that for workers, the process still was not finished by the mid-1970s.

Of the countries of Soviet-controlled Eastern Europe,[4] four (namely, Czechoslovakia,[5] East Germany, Hungary,[6] and Poland) had a well-developed social insurance system already before the Second World War, and also Romania and Bulgaria had a tradition of social insurance. Yet, within a few years after the communist takeover of power the existing social insurance systems were transformed according to the Soviet model, although elements of the previous national systems were retained in some cases, particularly in East Germany and, to a smaller extent, in Poland.

All in all, the available evidence suggests that the development of social security in the Soviet-bloc countries had both common and country-specific features. Concerning the former, originally priority was given to social security for workers and the members of their families over that for collective farmers. Simultaneously, emphasis was put on equalization of the social security status of blue-collar workers with that of white-collar ones.

Originally, too, social security was used to help liquidate private artisans, tradesmen, and farmers, as well as to punish people labelled as the enemies of the state. *Inter alia*, in the late 1950s the countries of Soviet-controlled Eastern Europe still continued either to deny old-age pensions to the so-called class aliens and to anyone considered to be opposed to the communist régime, or to pay reduced old-age pensions to prominent representatives of the former political and economic order; and as late as the 1970s the Polish régime tried to persuade private farmers to transfer their land to the state in exchange for an old-age pension.[7]

Finally, from its very beginning social security was viewed not only as a protection against officially recognized contingencies, but also as an important means of the state for the control over the labour force. It did not lose this latter function throughout the communist era, although over the decades it was expanding in terms of coverage and the range of benefits.[8]

10.3   IDEOLOGY

Since the Soviet-bloc countries provided social security, they pursued a social policy. Nevertheless, until the 1970s the term 'social policy' was officially out of favour. Following the Soviet example, between the late 1940s and the mid-1960s the countries of Soviet-controlled Eastern Europe too avoided using the term, for two reasons: social policy was perceived as an attempt to alleviate the contradictions of capitalism, as a means of integrating the working class into the structure of an exploitative economic system and of buying off potential working-class resistance; and it was believed that under socialism social policy was no longer needed because concern for human beings lay at the very core of socialism.[9]

The term 'social policy' reappeared in Soviet-controlled Eastern Europe in the second half of the 1960s and in the Soviet Union in the 1970s. Once it reappeared, emphasis was put on the unity of economic and social policy,[10] in East Germany as early as 1971.[11] It was also stressed that social policy was a component of the uniform policy of the working class, without being an autonomous sphere.[12]

While after years of being in abeyance the term 'social policy' finally gained recognition, the term 'welfare state' remained a pejorative word until the collapse of communism. According to a 1972 Soviet source, for instance, the theory of the welfare state was 'a contemporary bourgeois-reformist apologist theory about the nature of capitalist society and the bourgeois state that portrays the state as a force eliminating the injustices of the capitalist system and guaranteeing the growth of the well-being of the broad masses of the population.... In reality, the theory of the "welfare state" represents a veiled form of defence of state-monopoly capitalism ...'[13]

A similar view was to be found in a Soviet reference book originally published as late as 1986. It contended that the welfare state was 'a bourgeois theory saying that *capitalism* can develop into "people's capitalism" under which a bourgeois state conducting a welfare policy can presumably eliminate social contradictions.' However, there 'is evidence that the welfare state theory is ineffective and that the social and economic policy of the modern bourgeois state is in essence directed against the people.'[14]

Despite this rhetoric, in the Soviet-bloc countries the state was a welfare state because, *inter alia*, it provided education, health care, social security transfer payments, and housing subsidies. Social consumption funds[15] were devoted to these purposes, with the state determining besides the composition, size, allocation, and financing of centralized social consumption funds, also the formation and use of decentralized social consumption funds by state enterprises, state and collective farms, and the so-called social organizations.

It should be remembered too that in the Soviet-bloc countries citizens nominally enjoyed a number of economic and social rights. According to the Soviet constitution of 1977, for instance, they included the right to work, i.e., to guaranteed employment and pay in accordance with the quantity and quality of work, and not below the state-established minimum; the right to rest and leisure; the right to health protection; the right to maintenance in old age, in sickness, and in the event of complete or partial disability or loss of the breadwinner; the right to housing; and the right to education. With the exception of the right to housing, Soviet citizens enjoyed similar rights already under the previous constitution of 1936.

10.4 SOCIAL POLICY

In the Soviet-bloc countries, the provision by the state of education, health care, social security transfer payments, and housing subsidies constituted only one dimension of social policy. The other dimensions of social policy were the creation and preservation of excess jobs (i.e., overmanning), retail price subsidies, and egalitarian strivings, particularly the narrowing of wage differentials between individual occupational groups and the achievement of social homogeneity.

Overmanning[16] was brought about and maintained by three sets of factors, of which exclusively political and ideological factors fell under social policy. The official ideology contended that socialism abolished unemployment entirely and once and for all, guaranteed the right to work, and ensured full employment. On top of that, able-bodied individuals of working age had to be provided with a paid job because participation in social production was both a constitutional right and a constitutional duty, because avoidance without good cause of socially useful work could be prosecuted and punished, and because the legitimate sources of the individual's income were confined to earnings from officially recognized economic activity and to social security benefits (albeit with unemployment benefits unavailable).

Another set of factors contributing to overmanning was cultural factors, i.e., the vested interests of managers, the non-managerial personnel, and party and trade union functionaries in state enterprises. Besides being expected to achieve their output targets, state enterprises had to cope with (and tried to minimize) the disruptive effect of extraordinary demands and the defects in the official supply system. Therefore, to protect their own economic interests, they hoarded resources, including labour, and when bargaining over their plans, overstated their needs and understated their capabilities.

Yet another set of factors contributing to overmanning was systemic factors, i.e., the nature of command socialism. This type of economic system is characterized by extensive (resources-based) rather than intensive (productivity-based) economic development. Under it, state enterprises are not exposed to the pressure of market forces and are not threatened by bankruptcy, so that they have a soft budget constraint and lack an incentive to economize on resources, including labour. Thus, overmanning is an endemic feature of command socialism, having a lasting impact on the behaviour of both political and economic actors.

Since overmanning ranged from 10 to 20 or more per cent of the total labour force, it was a mass phenomenon. While it kept open unemployment down, it had a number of harmful consequences, helping to bring about – *inter alia* – low labour productivity, low average wages, repressed inflation, shortages of consumer goods and services, slow and undemanding work rhythms, slack work discipline, a weak work ethic, relaxation and moonlighting during working hours, egalitarian tendencies, and the divorce of rewards from performance. At the same time, inasmuch as earnings were insufficiently linked to performance, they contained a concealed social (unearned) element which was not identical with any of the legally recognized social security benefits and which violated the official principle of payment in accordance with the quantity and quality of work. Expressed differently, wages partly assumed the function of unemployment benefits.

Obviously, an insufficient link between earnings and performance arose not only as a result of chronic and general overmanning, but also as a result of the minimum wage. After all, its purpose was not to reward performance, but to guarantee a certain (albeit low) standard of living.

Retail price subsidies were another prominent dimension of social policy. Since they kept the prices of selected consumer goods and services low and stable, they increased demand for the subsidized goods and services, contributed to shortages, queuing, and a surplus of purchasing power, encouraged waste in consumption, and were a source of inefficiency. In addition, they put a strain on budgetary expenditure: in the Soviet Union, for instance, food subsidies alone went up from 8.9 per cent of total budgetary expenditure in 1975 to 13.7 per cent in 1986;[17] in East Germany, state subsidies for private consumption, without housing subsidies, amounted to 10.8 per cent of total budgetary expenditure in 1971, to 9.8 per cent in 1975, to 10.5 per cent in 1980, and to 11.4 per cent in 1983;[18] in Czechoslovakia, subsidies for food, industrial products, and services were equivalent to about 15.4 per cent of state and local government budgetary expenditure in 1985.[19]

10.5 FUNCTIONS OF SOCIAL POLICY

According to many Western scholars, under capitalism social policy fulfils a number of functions, including protection (particularly of earning capacity, income, and employment) and compensation and redistribution (e.g., in the case of housing policies, family policies, educational policies, and special groups policies). Simultaneously, income redistribution is said to be of three different kinds, namely, that by contingency groups (e.g., from the employed to the openly unemployed), that over the life-span (e.g., from the employed to children and the retired), and that by income group (e.g., from those with high income to those with low income).

Besides, at least some Western scholars contend that under capitalism the basic function of social policy is integration and stabilization, i.e., the preservation of existing structures. As already mentioned in Section 10.3, this view was held by Soviet-bloc scholars too. To give yet another example, a 1976 Czech publication described the contemporary bourgeois social policy as part of the internal imperialistic policy, aiming at weakening the class struggle and increasing exploitation of the working people.[20]

Concerning social policy under socialism, the official Soviet-bloc ideology repeatedly stressed that under socialism social policy was not only entirely different from that under capitalism, but also in all respects superior to it, and that the constantly increasing expenditure on it reflected the state's concern for man and evinced the humanity of the socialist system. More specifically, social policy was explicitly or implicitly expected to fulfil the following nine functions:

1. demographic investment, intended to ensure the reproduction of the population and, thus, of the labour force;
2. development and maintenance of physical and mental capabilities, with emphasis on preparation for full-time continuous participation in social production;
3. manipulation of the labour force, i.e., to regulate labour supply, allocate labour, strengthen work discipline, raise labour productivity, and reduce labour turnover;
4. creation of job opportunities and of conditions guaranteeing employment and even job security;
5. income maintenance in case of involuntary loss of earnings, i.e., protection against such contingencies as maternity, illness, accident, disability, old age, and death of the breadwinner, albeit not against open unemployment;
6. stabilization of retail prices;
7. satisfaction of specific individual and group needs and interests in the sense of a provision of facilities for cultural, recreational, sport, and other leisure activities;
8. lessening of economic and social inequalities; and
9. achievement, sustainment, and enhancement of the régime's legitimacy.

These functions suggest that in the Soviet-bloc countries social policy could hardly be accounted for on purely humanitarian grounds. It had a predominantly instrumental character, i.e., was an important device of the régime for the control over the masses and the attainment of desired objectives. As such, its primary purpose was partly to encourage that which was officially wanted and to deter that which was officially unwanted, partly to reward that which was officially regarded as proper behaviour and to punish that which was officially regarded as misbehaviour.

10.6 FINANCING AND SPENDING

As already noted in Section 8.5, in the socialist command economies established in the Soviet-bloc countries government spending was financed through taxation and the profits of state enterprises producing

Table 10.1 Sources of Revenue for Social Security Programmes,* Soviet-Bloc Countries, 1979–80

| | | Contributory taxes | | |
Country	Government revenues	Insured persons	Employers	Other (including interest)
		per cent		
Soviet Union	96.7	–	–	3.3
Czechoslovakia	95.1	–	3.7	1.2
East Germany	49.7	21.9	28.3	0.1
Romania	45.6	–	54.4	–
Hungary	43.6	14.6	41.1	0.7
Poland	32.3	2.2	54.3	11.3

* Sources of revenue for public employee and veterans' benefit programmes are excluded.

Source: Margaret S. Gordon, *Social Security Policies in Industrial Countries*, Cambridge, Cambridge University Press, 1988, p. 32, Table 2.4.

both public and private goods. This implies that in these economies welfare spending too was so financed.

Concerning specifically social security as one dimension of state-provided welfare, it was financed predominantly through a combination of general taxation, employer contributions (i.e., contributory taxes on state enterprises), and the profits of state enterprises, although the relative importance of these sources of social security revenue varied widely from one country to another. Employee contributions as a source of social security revenue were usually absent, the two major exceptions being East Germany and Hungary. The figures for 1979–80 are given in Table 10.1 which, however, does not include Bulgaria.

Table 10.2 compares the mean levels of social security expenditure in the Soviet-bloc countries (albeit without Romania) with those in twenty-one capitalist countries. It shows that while in terms of the share of GDP devoted to social security no great differences existed between the two groups of countries either in 1965 or in 1980, in terms of per capita expenditure the differences not only were considerable, but in fact widened from 1965 to 1980.

In Table 10.3, which compares social expenditure in the Soviet Union and Poland with social expenditure in Austria, social expenditure includes social expenditure in cash (pensions, allowances from social security funds, scholarships, and other benefits), social expenditure in kind (education, health, and social welfare), and housing subsidies. It follows from the table that in 1985 the share of social expenditure in GDP as well as in total consumption of the population was noticeably higher in Austria than in Poland and the Soviet Union.

Before leaving this table it should be added that according to official Soviet statistics the share in Soviet GNP of social expenditure

Table 10.2   Mean Levels of Social Security Expenditure* in Soviet-Bloc and Capitalist Countries, 1965 and 1980

	Mean levels of social security expenditure			
	as per cent of GDP		*per capita in US dollars*	
	1965	*1980*	*1965*	*1980*
Twenty-one capitalist countries	11.0	18.5	432	1 121
Soviet-bloc countries (Bulgaria, Czechoslovakia, East Germany, Hungary, Poland, the Soviet Union)	12.1	16.5	348	698

* Benefits under the rubric of social security include health care and sickness, unemployment, old-age, employment injury, family, maternity, invalidity, and survivors' benefits.
Source: Francis G. Castles, 'Whatever Happened to the Communist Welfare State?' *Studies in Comparative Communism*, vol. XIX, nos. 3–4 (Autumn-Winter 1986), pp. 213–226.

Table 10.3   Ratios of Social Expenditure to GDP and TCP in Austria, Poland, and the Societ Union, 1985

	Austria	*Poland*	*USSR*
Social expenditure, expressed in national currency, in per cent of			
- gross domestic product (GDP)	29.1	19.0	16.9
- total consumption of the population (TCP)	43.1	30.8	28.8
Social expenditure, expressed in common currency (Polish zlotys), in per cent of			
- gross domestic product (GDP)	25.0	19.0	15.5
- total consumption of the population (TCP)	37.0	30.8	30.3

Source: Austrian Central Statistical Office, *Comparative Analysis of Social Expenditure and its Finance: Austria, Poland and USSR*, Moscow, Vienna, and Warsaw, 1990, pp. 33–34.

(of the so-called social consumption funds) increased only very slighly between 1980 and 1989. It was 18.9 per cent in 1980 and 1985, 19.4 per cent in 1986, 19.7 per cent in 1987, 20.0 per cent in 1988, and 20.2 per cent in 1989.[21]

Obviously, these three tables offer a far from complete picture of welfare financing and spending in the Soviet-bloc countries, partly because they do not cover all dimensions of state-provided welfare. In this respect, the last table is more comprehensive than the other two, inasmuch as it takes into consideration, besides social security, education and housing subsidies.

No less obviously, these three tables reveal nothing about the achievements, shortcomings, and consequences of state-provided welfare, about its impact on individual welfare, the behaviour and attitudes of economic and other actors, the functioning of the established economic sytem, and so on. This question cannot be ignored, though, and will therefore receive at least some attention in the section that follows.

10.7 PERFORMANCE AND CONSEQUENCIES

In the Soviet-bloc countries, a comprehensive welfare state financed through taxation and the profits of state enterprises had developed only gradually. Once it was established, it protected practically the entire population against officially recognized contingencies from the cradle to the grave. Nevertheless, it had a number of serious shortcomings and adverse consequences.

Since the consequences of overmanning and retail price subsidies have already been discussed above, it is possible to turn to old-age pensions.[22] They were employment-related, and entitlement to them depended on reaching the retirement age (which for women was lower than for men) and on having the required employment record. With a partial exception of East Germany, they were tied to previous (in the sense of recent, not lifetime) earnings, but the principle of earnings-related old-age pensions was violated by the existence of minimum and maximum old-age pensions.

Just as wages, old-age pensions too were designed to provide a livelihood exclusively for one person. Once awarded, they were not automatically adjusted to the rising wage level, so that the recipients of old-age pensions awarded earlier were on the average worse off than the recipients of old-age pensions awarded later. On top of that,

Table 10.4 Average Monthly Old-age Pension in Payment, Soviet Union, 1970–88

	1970	1980	1985	1988
White-collar and blue-collar workers				
A. Average monthly gross wage (roubles)	122.0	168.9	190.1	219.8
B. Average monthly old-age pension (roubles)	53.4	71.6	87.2	93.9
B as a percentage of A	43.8	42.4	45.9	42.7
Collective farmers				
A. Average monthly gross wage (roubles)	74.9	118.5	153.4	181.8
B. Average monthly old-age pension (roubles)	14.0	35.2	47.2	54.5
B as a percentage of A	18.7	29.7	30.8	30.0

Source: Narodnoe khozyaistvo SSSR, 1988, pp. 77, 83 and 88.

old-age pensions were frequently inadequate, even by local standards, and some persons of retirement age were without an old-age pension.

The economic status (the relative economic position) of old-age pensioners varied from one country to another and, within the same country, over time. It also varied from one category of old-age pensioners to another: thus, there were differences between the average old-age pension for white-collar and blue-collar workers and that for collective farmers, as well as between ordinary old-age pensions and special (more generous) old-age pensions for élite groups and privileged occupational categories. Generally speaking, although in the 1960s and the 1970s the average nominal old-age pension was rising everywhere, the gap between the average old-age pension and the average wage did not diminish everywhere.[23] For illustration, Table 10.4 presents the case of Soviet retired workers and collective farmers between 1970 and 1988.

Of particular interest is Table 10.5, which shows the sources of total income in the families of Soviet pensioners without employed members in 1988. It is of particular interest because it makes clear that state-provided pensions were not the only source of pensioners' income, that pensioners derived their income from other sources too, the two most important ones being private plots (especially in the case of collective farmers) and informal networks.

Health care was usually produced by a national health care system, an exception being East Germany, which had a national health insurance system. Since legal private health care was practically non-existent, the established health care systems were of a nearly pure public type and, hence, centralized and bureaucratized.

Table 10.5 Sources of total Income in the Families of Pensioners Without employed Members, Soviet Union, 1988

	Pensioners under the pension scheme for	
	white-collar and blue-collar workers	collective farmers
Total income per family member per month (roubles)	102	112
of which (in per cent)		
pensions	75.5	49.1
wages	1.1	3.7
income from the private plot	11.5	40.9
receipts from relatives, friends, etc.	11.9	6.3

Source: *Vestnik statistiki*, no. 11 (1989), p. 26.

Free health care was originally far from universal. Yet, even when it finally did become universal (which took place between the mid-1960s and the mid-1970s, depending upon the country) and the entire population was entitled to a full range of health services free of charge, some officially imposed direct charging was to be found. Moreover, although in principle free of charge at the point of delivery, in practice health care was riddled with illegal second economy activities. Unofficial cash payments (gratuities, bribes) and gifts in kind by patients or their relatives to doctors and the nursing personnel were widespread and in many instances expected, and also unofficial private consultations and treatments paid on the fee-for-service basis were not unknown.

These illegal second economy activities stemmed from the patients' striving to elicit a better or faster treatment than they would receive otherwise. After all, the established health care systems had severe shortcomings.[24] *Inter alia*, they were inefficient; provided low-quality services; offered insufficient financial incentives to their employees; suffered from shortages of medical supplies, equipment, and technology; and failed to ensure equal access to health care, as evinced by the existence of separate (closed) health care facilities for élite groups and privileged occupational categories. Moreover, the professional standards of quite a few doctors and nurses were low, and a number of hospitals did not meet the necessary sanitary and hygiene standards.

Before leaving health care, a brief note should be made on life expectancy and infant mortality, which are two important indicators of a nation's health. By the end of the 1980s, the Soviet-bloc countries trailed behind the OECD countries in both respects: relative to them, they had lower life expectancy at birth for men as well as women and higher infant mortality rates.[25] *En passant*, this raises the question of whether health care has an impact on life expectancy. A Western view holds that life expectancy is only marginally, if at all, affected by health care. According to it, there is a strong relationship between GDP per capita and life expectancy at birth. The effects of diet, lifestyle, personal habits, education, housing, and poverty are generally far greater than the influence of health care.

Everywhere in the Soviet bloc, housing was a major problem.[26] There was a housing shortage, waiting lists for flats were long, living space per capita was small, and overcrowding with its concomitant lack of privacy was widespread, particularly in urban areas. The quality of housing was low, maintenance and repairs were neglected, and in many a case amenities were absent. At the same time, rents in the public housing sector were subsidized, considerable social and regional housing inequalities persisted, and the housing situation was one of the factors inducing second economy activities.

Although the existence of low-income households was officially admitted, the existence of poverty was officially denied. Nevertheless, poverty (as measured in terms of the national social and subsistence minima) was not eradicated, the potentially vulnerable groups being families with children, old-age and other pensioners, and those outside the state sector.[27]

Just as the welfare states established in capitalist market economies, also those established in the Soviet-bloc countries contributed to the emergence of a social welfare ('free lunch') mentality or ethic, i.e., a dependency culture. Under the impact of the official ideology and social policies, the individuals' sense of responsibility for their own welfare and that of their families was weakened: they came to believe that their entitlements had priority over their obligations, and expected the state to provide job opportunities, employment and even job security, rising real wages, stable retail prices, desired consumer goods, inexpensive housing, cheap public transport, free welfare services, and social security transfer payments.

CONCLUSION

In the Soviet-bloc countries, a comprehensive welfare state financed through taxation and the profits of state enterprises had evolved only gradually. Once it was established, it protected practically the entire population against officially recognized contingencies from the cradle to the grave, albeit in a modest way. Moreover, unemployment benefits were absent, means-tested social assistance was incompletely developed or non-existent, and the same applied to personal social services.

Since these countries had an authoritarian political system, their governments were not exposed to the pressures of democratic politics or, expressed differently, to demands by the opposition, pressure groups, and the electorate for higher welfare spending. Consequently, they had considerable freedom to determine the range, scope, and generosity of welfare provisions, the methods of financing them, the share in GDP of welfare spending, and the like.

Nevertheless, the governments were not absolutely free in this respect. On the one hand, they had to contend with resource constraints. On the other hand, they had to meet at least some popular expectations in order to elicit overt compliance and defuse potential popular unrest and socio-political destabilization. Thus, a kind of tacit social contract was struck: people agreed to accept the established political and economic system and to refrain from revolting against it; in return, the governments promised to tolerate certain non-political freedoms and to provide economic security.

The contract contributed to the creation and reinforcement of an entitlement mentality, so that the image of an entitlement society became an important and deeply entrenched trait of popular culture. However, the contract also indicated that the régimes' legitimacy was based more on utilitarianism (material gratification) than on normative principles, which implied that if their ability to gratify materially declined noticeably, they were left naked and troubles were likely to ensue.

Although the state was an important source of individual welfare, it was not the only one. The other sources of individual welfare included the individual himself or herself, the family (household), informal networks (relatives, friends, neighbours, colleagues), and the second (legal and illegal) economy, as well as the first economy (i.e., state enterprises and state and collective farms) and the so-called social or mass organizations (particularly the official trade unions).

Compared with the Soviet-bloc countries, in communist-ruled China[28] state enterprises played a far greater role in the provision of welfare. As already mentioned in Section 8.5, Chinese state enterprises were largely reponsible for housing, education, health care, and benefits in cash, including sick pay and pensions. Their welfare expenditure was treated as part of production costs, and this was one reason why government spending was substantially lower than in the Soviet-bloc countries.

In the countryside, prior to the 1978 economic reform, an important source of welfare was the commune system, which provided education, health care, and other welfare benefits. Its demise in the early 1980s increased the role of rural households and the market in the provision of welfare.

Under the impact of marketization and privatization, the Chinese government began to face the question of how individuals should be protected against various contingencies, in other words, of defining the welfare role of the state, the market, households, and voluntary organizations. Yet, by the mid-1990s this question still remained unanswered.[29]

Part IV
Transformation

Throughout the preceding three parts of the present study, emphasis has been put on the multidimensional tension between economic individualism and economic collectivism, inherent in modern (as well as traditional) economies. Part I provided a brief overview of economic development, presented a typology of modern economic systems, identified the main interrelated dimensions of the tension between economic individualism and economic collectivism, and dealt with the environment of modern economic systems, particularly with one of its components, namely, the political system. Part II examined in some detail the individual types of modern economic system, simultaneously drawing attention to the second or unofficial economy, which is a cross-system phenomenon. Finally, Part III discussed the government economy, including the so-called welfare state and its consequences.

Against this background, Part IV turns to the transformation of modern economic systems. It means that as a result of the ongoing tension between economic individualism and economic collectivism, the established economic system loses ground and a new one comes into being. Of course, in practice tensions between economic individualism and economic collectivism need not always lead to change of the system. Mostly, they lead only to change within the system.

With the exception of Chapter 11, which discusses economic transformation in general terms, the chapters that make up this part concentrate on economic transformation in post-communist societies, triggered off by the unexpected collapse of communism in the Soviet-bloc countries towards the end of the 1980s.

11 Economic Transformation

Economies, whether traditional or modern, experience change within the system as well as change of the system. In contrast to the former which does not alter the nature (structure) of the established system, the latter alters the nature (structure) of the established system. Compared with the latter, the former is far more frequent and, if unchecked, its cumulative effect can result in systemic change.

11.1 ECONOMIC DEVELOPMENT

Economic development in the sense of economic growth accompanied by a substantial structural or organizational change in the economy is characterized by the decline of traditional economies and the emergence and diffusion of modern ones. In this development, a crucial role was played by the agricultural revolution (which started in the third or fourth millenium B.C.) and the industrial revolution (which started in the late eighteenth century). A third revolution, no less crucial, namely, the information revolution, is currently under way.

The transformation of traditional economies into modern economies is a protracted process. It begins with the appearance in the former of elements of the latter, until under the impact of industrialization it gives rise to what development economics (dating from the Second World War to deal with the problem of growth in the Third World countries) calls dual economies. As conceived by the various dual economy models, a dual economy consists of a traditional (agricultural) sector and a modern (industrial) sector.[1]

Being a protracted process, the transformation of traditional economies into modern economies may be divided into a number of stages. For example, Angus Maddison (already quoted in Section 1.3) distinguished four epochs in the economic development of Europe between 500 and 1980, namely, that of agrarianism (500–1500), that of advancing agrarianism (1500–1700), that of merchant capitalism (1700–1820), and that of capitalism (1820–1980). This categorization of

1982 was meant to be a rough description of the progressive evolution of the major material forces determining production potential.[2]

W.W. Rostow argued in 1960 that is was possible to identify all societies, in their economic dimensions, as lying within one of five categories, namely, the traditional society, the preconditions for take-off, the take-off, the drive to maturity, and the age of high mass-consumption. Simultaneously he emphasized that while it was true that economic change had political and social consequences, economic change itself was the consequence of political and social as well as narrowly economic forces.[3]

Although in this 'non-communist manifesto' Rostow concentrated on the uniformities in the sequence of economic modernization, he did not deny the uniqueness of each nation's experience. He also discussed the similarities and differences between his stages-of-growth analysis and Karl Marx's economic interpretation of history.

Marx[4] distinguished four stages of human history, the basis for the distinction being the dominant mode of production, defined as a specific combination of forces of production and relations of production. These modes of production were the Asiatic (characterized by the subordination of all to the state), the ancient (characterized by slavery), the feudal (characterized by serfdom), and the bourgeois or capitalist (characterized by wage labour). Of these modes of production, the last three constituted the three stages of Western history as well as the three distinct modes of man's exploitation by man.

The bourgeois or capitalist mode of production was the last antagonistic social formation, which was expected to give rise to socialism, under which private ownership of the means of production was abolished and production was planned by associated producers. It was to have two phases: in the first, generally called 'socialism', relative scarcity continued to exist and incentives to induce people to work were still needed; in the second, generally called 'communism', there was plenty, the principle of full needs satisfaction covering all different needs of all different individuals prevailed, and no incentives to induce people to work were needed any more.

If the Asiatic mode of production is disregarded and the primitive commune is taken into consideration, the Marxian view of mankind's development may plausibly be reinterpreted as using three basic stages. In this reinterpretation, mankind's development leads:

1. from a classless society (the primitive commune) through a sequence of class-divided societies (slavery, feudalism, capitalism) to a classless society (communism);
2. from societies without a surplus and exploitation (the primitive commune) through societies with a surplus and exploitation (slavery, feudalism, capitalism) to a society with a surplus but no exploitation (communism); and
3. from production for direct use (the primitive commune, slavery, feudalism) through the commodity mode of production (capitalism) to a non-commodity mode of production (communism).

While Marx contended that political, social, and cultural factors were the function of economic factors and that economic change was the prime mover of social change, Stephen K. Sanderson argued that the principal causal factors in social evolution were the material conditions of human existence, i.e., the demographic, ecological, technological, and economic forces at work in social life. However, these causal factors operated probabilistically: non-material factors played a role in evolutionary processes, even if ordinarily in a highly secondary way.[5]

Sanderson distinguished three great evolutionary transformations in world history: the first was the Neolithic Revolution, which ushered in agriculture and settled village life; the second was the origin of civilization and the state; and the third was the rise of modern capitalism after the sixteenth century. The most appropriate path for the future, he believed, lay in a combination of the best elements of the plan and the market, which would simultaneously eliminate or neutralize their worst elements.[6]

Finally, a note on development economics. As already mentioned above, it dates from the Second World War and deals with the growth problems of poor countries. According to Angus Maddison, '[f]ive main types of explanation for the lower income and productivity of "developing" countries emerge from this literature: (1) the institutional setting was or is less favourable to capitalist development than that of western Europe and its offshoots; (2) various kinds of colonialism retarded development; (3) demographic growth has been much greater than was ever the case in the advanced capitalist countries; (4) their levels of investment in human and physical capital are very much lower than in the advanced countries; (5) inflationary and dirigiste policies have lowered efficiency.'[7]

Of these five main types of explanation, the second is known as dependency theory. Originally formulated by a group of Latin American scholars in the 1960s, it contends in essence that underdevelopment is caused by external factors, by economic dependence on developed countries, not by internal deficiencies.[8] In contrast, modernization theory maintains that underdevelopment is a result of internal factors, such as traditional values, outdated working practices, illiteracy, and the lack of skills, not of external ones.

Keith Griffin identified six distinct strategies of economic development, namely, the monetarist strategy, the open economy strategy, the industrialization strategy, the green revolution strategy, the redistributive strategy, and the socialist strategy. He argued that each imposed different demands upon the state, and concluded that there was no best path to development as well as no close correspondence between development policy or development strategy on the one hand and the resulting political system on the other.[9]

The relationship between economic policies (and the ability to change them) and the type of government was examined by Anne O. Krueger. She discussed the benevolent social guardian model of the state and its alternatives, and pointed out that while the 'typical' developing country witnessed its initial economic policies being put in place by a 'benevolent social guardian' state, whether that state was democratic or authoritarian under a charismatic nationalist leader, soon afterwards the benevolent social guardian state in many cases was transformed into a bureaucratic-authoritarian state.[10]

Concerning the impact of economic policies on developing countries' economic performance, the available evidence indicates that government intervention in the economy and protectionism were mostly detrimental to these countries' economic development. Particularly during the 1960s and 1970s, it should be added, the pursuit of interventionist and protectionist policies was influenced by development economics with its statist bias, with its belief that the state had to play a big role in fostering modernization.

All in all, the transformation of traditional economies into modern economies is a protracted process, which started long before the Second World War and which was once experienced even by those countries that nowadays are developed. Since it is affected both by intrasocietal or domestic factors and by extrasocietal or international factors, it varies from one transforming economy to another, and so does its outcome.

11.2 MODERN ECONOMIES

Differences exist not only between traditional economies and modern economies, but also between individual traditional economies and between individual modern economies. At the same time, though, the economic systems of modern economies are variants of a limited number of pure types only. As Figure 2.1 shows, these pure types of modern economic system are market capitalism, market socialism, command socialism, and command capitalism.

Each type of modern economic system is based on certain values. In turn, it has a distinct impact on the structure of economic power and economic decision-making, the flow and nature of information, the character of economic institutions, the structure and values of society, the behaviour and attitudes of economic actors, the legal system, the political system, and the role the state plays in the economy. Consequently, the transformation of an established modern economic system into another implies not only change of property relations and/or the coordinating mechanism, but also change of values, norms, economic institutions, behaviour, and attitudes. Of these, values are basic principles or standards.[11] Norms are formal or informal rules regulating economic activity, the examples of the former being laws and directives and the examples of the latter being custom, tradition, and convention. Economic institutions are sets of normatively prescribed interdependent and integrated positions and roles. Behaviour refers to observed patterns of behaviour and interaction on the part of economic actors. And attitudes are economic actors' learned and more or less generalized and affective (or evaluative) tendencies to respond in a particular manner to ideas, individuals, groups, institutions, objects, events, processes, and situations.

One of the questions raised by the transformation of an established modern economic system into another is that of the rejected system's successor. In principle, because there are four pure types of modern economic system, the substitution of a new modern economic system for the old one means chosing from among three alternatives. In practice, though, the choice is complicated by the fact that variants of each pure type are possible.

As argued in Section 2.2, market socialism and command capitalism contain a tension between the prevailing type of ownership of the means of production and the prevailing type of coordinating mechanism. Due to this inherent tension, these two types of modern economic system are by their nature transitory, having a tendency to turn either into command socialism or into market capitalism. However, also command socialism is a transitory type of modern economic system. Although as a pure type it is characterized by system coherence, when it is established in practice it is permeated by covert noncompliance and illegal second economy activities. Their occurrence evinces that the government does not (and cannot) have perfect knowledge of and complete control over the economy, i.e., that it is neither omniscient nor omnipotent.

It seems, then, that the only economically viable type of modern economic system is market capitalism, a pluralistic, competitive, horizontally organized, spontaneous, and open economic system, based on private ownership of the means of production and market co-ordination. In contrast to the other types of modern economic system, it enhances individual liberty, encourages individual effort, initiative, risk-taking, and responsibility, and has an inbuilt tendency towards flexibility, efficiency, and the satisfaction of effective demand.

Although under market capitalism government has an important role to play in the economy, it is of necessity a limited one. Yet, governments need not confine themselves to the pursuit of *laissez-faire* policies or free-market policies. They can engage in the pursuit of highly interventionist policies, i.e., intervene directly or indirectly in property rights, the operation of the free market, and the outcome of economic activity with a view to attain specific economic or social objectives other than allocative efficiency.

Obviously, government intervention in the economy can fail, i.e., be unsuccessful in attaining its chosen objectives and produce unintended consequences. It can also harm the economy, particularly in the long run, if it adversely affects the propensity to save, private investment, productivity, efficiency, competitiveness, economic growth, and the general welfare.

In any case, government intervention in the economy is constrained in three main respects: it depends on the government's extractive, allocative, distributive, and regulative capabilities; on the condition that market capitalism is not to be undermined, it must not lead to systemic change; and it is not able forever to defy the laws of economics, which amounts to saying that market forces cannot forever be denied.

Since around the mid-1980s, two further factors began to impose additional constraints on government intervention in the economy. One is the new computer and information technology, which contributes to the dispersion of information, economic power, and economic decision-making.[12] The other is the increasing globalization of the world economy, which according to its critics erodes national economic sovereignty and leaves governments powerless to defend their countries' economic interests.[13]

Besides raising the question of the rejected system's successor, the transformation of an established modern economic system into another raises the question of support for and opposition and resistance to it. Broadly speaking, underlying the former is dissatisfaction with the established system and belief in superior economic performance of the chosen alternative. The latter stems from vested interests, reluctance to discard old routines, unwillingness to learn and adapt, uncertainty about the outcome of transformation, and the expected costs of transformation.

In modern times, i.e., in the period since the year 1500, it is possible to find both the transformation of traditional economies into modern economies and, within modern economies, the transformation of one modern economic system into another. Concerning specifically the latter, during these five centuries variants of all four pure types of modern economic system have been tried in practice. Of these four types, market capitalism has proved to be in the long run more successful and enduring than the others.

11.3 ECONOMIC AND POLITICAL SYSTEMS

Modern economic systems function in an environment which affects both their nature and their performance and which, in turn, is affected by them. This environment has two dimensions, namely, the intrasocietal or domestic one and the extrasocietal or international one. Each consists of a number of components, one component of the former being the political system.

As discussed in Chapter 3, modern political systems differ with respect to the structure of political power, i.e., with respect to whether the population is or is not able to participate in politics: in the affirmative case they are democratic, in the negative case authoritarian. Besides, modern political systems differ with respect to the scope of political power, i.e., with respect to political control over non-political (economic and other) activity: they are liberal if the scope of political power is minimal and totalist if it is all-embracing.

If these two criteria are combined, four pure types of modern political system are theoretically possible: liberal democracy, totalist democracy, totalist authoritarianism, and liberal authoritarianism.

However, actual modern political systems are merely variants of the pure types, so that modern societies experience a tension between democracy and authoritarianism as well as a tension between liberalism and totalism. Modern societies which have a democratic political system then experience yet another tension, that between representative democracy and direct or participatory democracy.

Thus, modern political systems undergo change. At a particular point of time, the ongoing change (be it within the system or of the system) can concern either the structure of political power, or the scope of political power, or both simultaneously. This implies that systemic change amounts either to the transformation of authoritarianism into democracy (or vice versa), or to the transformation of totalism into liberalism (or vice versa), or to the transformation of totalist authoritarianism into liberal democracy (or vice versa).

As to specifically the relationship between the distinguished types of modern political system and the distinguished types of modern economic system,[14] the following three relationships are of crucial importance:

1. there exists an intrinsic linkage between totalist authoritarianism and command socialism, i.e., neither can exist without the other;
2. liberal authoritarianism, while incompatible with command socialism, makes market capitalism possible; and
3. democracy is incompatible with command socialism; it is compatible exclusively with and dependent on market capitalism, the latter being a necessary (albeit not sufficient) condition for the former.

Consequently, the transformation of market capitalism into command socialism requires transformation of liberal democracy or liberal authoritarianism into totalist authoritarianism. Conversely, the transformation of command socialism into market capitalism requires transformation of totalist authoritarianism either into liberal authoritarianism or into liberal democracy.

The relationship between the distinguished types of modern political system and the remaining two types of modern economic system (i.e., command capitalism and market socialism) is affected by the latter's transitory nature. Since these two types of modern economic system contain a tension between the prevailing type of ownership of the means of production and the prevailing type of coordinating mechanism, they have a tendency to turn either into command socialism or into market capitalism. Hence, if in a democratic political system an elected government transformed market capitalism into command capitalism, democracy would be put at risk, unless the transformation were meant only as a temporary measure in the event of a national emergency, e.g., in wartime. Similarly, democracy would also be put at risk if in a democratic political system an elected government transformed market capitalism into market socialism.

While the transformation of market capitalism into market socialism would be likely ultimately to lead to command socialism and, thus, to totalist authoritarianism, the transformation of command socialism into market socialism would require transformation of totalist authoritarianism (a *sine qua non* of command socialism) into liberal authoritarianism, or its collapse. At the same time, this transformation would pave way for market capitalism and for democracy.

To wind up with a brief historical note, in modern societies market capitalism has originated under liberal authoritarianism, not under democracy. In contrast, modern democracy has arisen exclusively within market capitalism and has been unable to survive except when coupled with it.

An early variant of command capitalism was mercantilism, which was maintained by the state in Western Europe during the sixteenth and seventeenth centuries and most of the eighteenth century. In the twentieth century, variants of command capitalism have been adopted by both authoritarian and democratic political systems, usually in connection with (preparations for) war, the examples being imperial Germany during the First World War, Nazi Germany between about 1936 and 1945, and Britain during the Second World War.

Variants of command socialism came into being only in the twentieth century, invariably introduced and kept in existence by totalist authoritarianism. One of its variants, known as War Communism, was briefly attempted in Russia between June 1918 and March 1921. However, its most important variant was introduced in the Soviet Union in the early 1930s, imposed on Eastern Europe after the end of the Second World War, and followed by a number of developing countries.

Finally, variants of market socialism were tried by totalist authoritarianism, seeking to reform the established variants of command socialism. Thus, in Russia War Communism was succeeded by the New Economic Policy (NEP), promulgated in March 1921. Yugoslavia began to move towards a variant of market socialism at the beginning of the 1950s, Hungary in 1968, and China in the late 1970s.

CONCLUSION

Modern economic systems undergo change within the system as well as change of the system. These changes are a result of the interaction between the nature of the established systems, the individuals who operate them, and the environment in which they function. Expressed differently, these changes are a result of the interaction between the nature of the established systems and the relevant ecological, biological, psychological, demographic, technological, social, cultural, economic, and political factors.

In the process of change, an important role is played by non-material factors, such as ideas, theories, ideologies, knowledge, values, norms, attitudes, and expectations, because they can both induce and hinder change. To give an example, while technological progress depends on human creativity, the adoption of a new technology can be impeded by, *inter alia*, tradition or vested interests. In the opinion of Felipe Fernández-Armesto, '[t]here are lots of instances in history ... of technological novelties which have helped to reshape societies; generally, however, societies only get the technologies they want or need.'[15]

Besides both inducing and hindering change, the nature of the established systems and the relevant material and non-material factors on the one hand provide opportunities, on the other constitute constraints. This implies that economic, political, and other actors are neither absolutely free nor capable of total control over events, situations, and developments. This further implies that no purposeful activity is without a risk, inasmuch as it need not produce intended consequences.

When systemic change takes place, the established system is transformed into another. Of the four theoretically possible types of modern economic system, market capitalism has proved to be in the long run more successful and enduring than the others. It provides economic freedom and, at the same time, promotes political freedom, in authoritarian political systems giving rise to pressures towards democracy. Yet, although modern democracy is dependent on market capitalism, simultaneously it creates conditions for the emergence of the critics and opponents of market capitalism who either want to expand the role of the state in the economy, or aim at transforming market capitalism into command capitalism, market socialism, or command socialism. Hence, political democracy can retard economic development and, in extreme cases, undermine market capitalism, the fabric of society, and itself.

The transformation of an established economic system into another can be a result either of a protracted process, extending over a long period of time, or of a sudden event (shock). If the shock means the collapse of the established totalist authoritarian political system, a temporary systemic vacuum is likely to appear, giving rise to anarcho-capitalism, i.e., to a chaotic situation in which legal norms regulating private economic activity either do not exist at all or are widely ignored. Even then, though, private economic activity can be regulated by gradually and spontaneously developing informal norms (conventions).

12 Post-Communist Transformation

In the euphoria produced by the unexpected breach of the Berlin Wall in late 1989, the complexity of the transformation of the communist system tended to be underestimated. Only gradually it began to be realized that the transformation would raise a number of political, economic, social, and cultural problems; that it would face obstacles and cause hardships; and that it would have an impact on Western societies too.

12.1 THE LEGACY

The communist systems established in the Soviet-bloc countries were variants of totalist authoritarianism, conceived as authoritarian politics and political control over the economy and society. More specifically, the communist political system was a one-party political system, basing itself on Marxism-Leninism as its official ideology. Political power and political decision-making were highly concentrated, ultimately resting with the party leadership. The party leadership was neither periodically elected in a public contest by the population nor restrained by the law, and ensured its position by the application of the principle of democratic centralism and the ban on factionalism and groupism within the party and by the ban on political opposition outside it.

Besides exerting tight control over the political sphere, the unaccountable party leadership exerted wide-ranging control over all spheres of non-political behaviour and opinion as well, including the economy, the trade unions, the mass media, the judiciary, education, research, the arts, and religion. This control, which stemmed from the party leadership's totalist orientation, was justified by the application of the principle of the leading role of the party.

Simultaneously, the system had a distinct impact on the values of society and the behaviour and attitudes of political, economic, and other actors. On the one hand, it discouraged individual effort, initiative, risk-taking, and responsibility, and contributed to the emergence of a social welfare ('free-lunch') mentality or ethic, i.e., a dependency culture. On the other hand, it gave rise to covert non-compliance with formal norms and administrative orders and to illegal second economy activities.

Despite all the systemic similarities, the Soviet-bloc countries differed considerably from each other in many respects. *Inter alia*, they differed in respect of the size of their territory, their geographical location, the size and nationality composition of their population, their culture, and their history. Moreover, they differed in respect of their per capita national income, the rate of economic growth, the share of the agricultural labour force in the total labour force, the size of the legal private sector, dependence on foreign trade, the level of hard currency debt, the standard of living, and so on.

Against this background it is possible to turn in some detail to the important question of these countries' economic performance, bearing in mind that the economic performance of each of them was determined jointly by the nature of the established economic system, which was a variant of command socialism; the individuals who operated it; and the domestic and international environment in which it functioned.

12.2 ECONOMIC PERFORMANCE

The official ideology of the Soviet-bloc countries contended that socialism was not only completely different from capitalism, but also in all respects (i.e., socially, economically, politically, culturally, and morally) superior to it. In order to substantiate this contention, the ideology claimed among other things that socialism put an end to the exploitation of man by man, abolished unemployment, and was devoid of poverty, inflation, and economic crises. However, the available evidence suggests that the officially alleged superiority of socialism over capitalism was merely a mirage.[1] While in the short run the advantage of socialist command economies over capitalist market economies was their capability to mobilize resources for the pursuit of a limited range of objectives, in the long run the performance of the former was inferior to that of the latter.[2]

As follows from Table 12.1, in 1980 per capita GDP varied widely from one Soviet-bloc country to another, with East Germany and Czechoslovakia being (just as in the preceding three decades) the two most economically developed Soviet-bloc countries. Even so, their per capita GDP was no more than about two-fifths of that of

Table 12.1   Per Capita GDP, Soviet-Bloc Countries, 1980

| | As a percentage of per capita GDP in | |
	USA	Austria
Bulgaria	29.9	49.5
Czechoslovakia	42.3	70.1
East Germany	45.9	76.0
Hungary	31.7	52.4
Poland	27.3	45.2
Romania	21.3	35.2
Soviet Union	34.1	56.4

Source: Eva Ehrlich, 'Contest between Countries: 1937–1986', *Soviet Studies*, vol. 43, no. 5 (1991), pp. 875–896. The figures are taken from Table 1 on p. 878.

Table 12.2   Changes in Net Material Product, Soviet- Bloc Countries, 1986–89

	1986	1987	1988	1989
	per cent			
Bulgaria	5.3	5.1	2.4	−0.4
Czechoslovakia	2.6	2.1	2.4	1.3
East Germany	4.3	3.3	2.8	1.0
Hungary	0.9	4.1	0.3	−2.0
Poland	4.9	1.9	4.9	0.0
Romania	7.3	4.8	3.2	n.a.
Soviet Union	2.3	1.6	4.4	2.4

Source: Saul Estrin, 'The Inheritance', in Nicholas Barr (ed.), *Labor Markets and Social Policy in Central and Eastern Europe*, New York, Oxford University Press, 1994, p. 67, Table 3.3, and NATO Economic Committee, *The State of the Soviet Economy*, Brussels, March 1991, p. 27, Table 2.

the United States (which amounted to US$ 11 850) and approximately seven-tenths of that of Austria (which was 60.4 per cent of that of the United States).[3]

In all of these countries, economic growth was slowing down between the early 1950s and the late 1980s.[4] One cause of this slowdown was the near exhaustion, by the mid-1970s at the latest, of the previously available non-employed resources. Changes in net material product during the last four years of the 1980s are given in Table 12.2. The table does not show, though, that in the Soviet Union net material product fell by four per cent in 1990 and by eleven per cent in 1991.

According to the official retail price indices, open inflation (i.e., a sustained rise in the general price level) was either low or non-existent. However, official retail price indices understated the actual rate of inflation, because they disregarded both hidden inflation and repressed inflation. The former occurred through increases in retail prices not reflected in the official retail price index, the latter signified an excess of purchasing power, a monetary overhang caused by central control (the state) preventing retail prices from increasing despite shortages of consumer goods and services. To give an example, for Czechoslovakia the annual rate of total (open, hidden, and repressed) inflation in the 1970–89 period was put at between four and eight per cent, of which roughly half was attributed to repressed inflation.[5]

During the 1980s, the Soviet-bloc country with the highest rate of open inflation was Poland where, in 1989, the annual rate was 251.1 per cent and the end-year rate 639.5 per cent.[6] A much lower, albeit still far from negligible, rate of open inflation was to be found in Hungary, where the annual rate went up from 7 per cent in 1985 to 17 per cent in 1989.

Registered unemployment was not officially recognized as a separate risk, and unregistered unemployment was low. This situation in the labour market concealed, though, that the employed labour force was considerably underutilized, with overmanning (i.e., unemployment on the job) being chronic and general and reaching mass proportions. Expressed differently, open unemployment was kept down by hidden unemployment and wages partly assumed the function of unemployment benefits.

Labour force participation rates for men and women alike were high. At the same time, participation in social production was predominantly on a full-time basis and, in addition, was expected to be continuous and lifelong. That is to say, opportunities for part-time employment, temporary employment, and casual employment were limited, and the same applied to self-employment.

Household income was increasing over the decades. Despite that, households faced a limited range, low quality, and outdated design of consumer goods and services available in the first economy at the officially set prices. They also had to cope with chronic shortages, which gave rise to queuing, searching, tipping, bribery, the use of personal connections and second economy suppliers, hoarding, forced substitution, and forced saving; made shopping time-consuming; and adversely affected the performance of persons employed in the first economy.

By the end of the 1980s, the standard of living continued to vary widely from one Soviet-bloc country to another. It also continued to be noticeably lower than that in the developed capitalist market economies, even in the case of East Germany and Czechoslovakia, the two most prosperous Soviet-bloc countries. More precisely, from approximately the mid-1960s to the late 1980s the gap between the standard of living in the Soviet-bloc countries and that in the developed capitalist market economies increased substantially to the detriment of the former.[7]

12.3   THE COLLAPSE OF COMMUNISM

Chronologically, communism collapsed first in Soviet-controlled Eastern Europe, and its collapse therein in 1989 meant the breakup of the Soviet empire. Two years later, in 1991, it collapsed in the Soviet Union too, and the Soviet Union disintegrated. Outside the former Soviet bloc, Yugoslavia fell apart in 1991, and Albania's communist era came to its end in 1992.

Of course, *per se* these dates say nothing about why communism collapsed in the countries mentioned. To answer this question in general terms, the collapse of the established communist systems may be seen as a result of the interaction between their nature, the individuals who operated them, and the domestic and international environment in which they functioned.

Despite the fact that chronologically communism collapsed first in Soviet-controlled Eastern Europe, the examination has to begin with the Soviet case. Alexander Dallin suggested that there was 'a cluster of interrelated developments that together, and in their interaction, formed the essential preconditions – necessary but not sufficient – for what occurred in the 1990s. In brief, they are: (1) the loosening of controls; (2) the spread of corruption; (3) the erosion of ideology; (4) the impact of social change on values and social pathologies; (5) the growing impact of the external environment on Soviet society and politics; and (6) the consequences of economic constraints. Against these background conditions, certain decisions of the Gorbachev regime, in turn, appear decisive as catalysts for collapse.'[8]

Of these background conditions, the external factors included the rearmament programme of Ronald Reagan's administration, the Strategic Defence Initiative (SDI), the United States' support for anti-communist guerillas throughout the world, the sharp decline in world oil prices, the inclusion of 'Basket 3' (on human rights) in the 1975 Helsinki accords, the costs of and the defeat in the Afghan war, and the economic progress made by the OECD countries and the newly industrialized countries.[9]

As to the Gorbachev factor, Mikhail Gorbachev contributed to the collapse of Soviet communism by his misconceived policies, his preference for half measures, and his perpetual vacillation. *Inter alia*, the 1987 economic reform (which undermined the old command system but refrained from dismantling it and creating a viable alternative to it) and the party leadership's economic policies produced chaos and led to an economic crisis. By the end of 1990, the ongoing economic crisis was complicated by a strife between the republics (which adopted declarations of 'economic sovereignty') and the recentralizing all-union government.

In addition to contributing to the collapse of Soviet communism, Gorbachev contributed to the collapse of the Soviet empire (which was based on coercion and constituted a drain on Soviet resources) by repudiating the Brezhnev doctrine, i.e., by signalling that the Soviet Union would not intervene militarily in Eastern Europe in order to preserve the communist systems established there.[10]

By that time, although the communist systems established in Soviet-controlled Eastern Europe still had some supporters, most sections of the population perceived a gap between their expectations (material and non-material, political and non-political) and reality, and attributed it largely to the communist system and the visible hand of the party leadership. Indeed, many of the people's expectations were not met because the party leadership was neither willing (due to its reluctance to lose control over society) nor able (due to its limited resources) to meet them.

To erupt, the bottled up popular dissatisfaction with the status quo needed only an effective stimulus. The stimulus was provided by the decision of the East German party leadership, announced on 9 November 1989, that all East German citizens were free to travel to the West. The decision was made after Hungary opened its frontier with Austria for East German citizens, who started fleeing to the West in considerable numbers. Hence, the fall of the Berlin Wall triggered off the collapse of communism in the countries of Soviet-controlled Eastern Europe. Having acquired independence, these countries were able to embark on the transformation of the communist system, the main objective of which was the achievement of greater individual freedom and higher living standards.

All in all, the collapse of communism was caused by the interaction between a number of factors, which may be divided into systemic, policy, and environmental. Of the various issues raised in the discussion about these causes,[11] at least two deserve a brief mention: that of the reformability of command socialism, and that of its viability.

Without doubt, reforms in the sense of deliberate changes within the system can take place in socialist command economies. However, as argued in Section 2.2, these changes face systemic constraints: having its own logic, command socialism resists those elements which are incompatible with it and, therefore, endanger its existence. That is to say, it is able to absorb contradictory elements within certain (rather narrow) limits only.

In fact, as suggested by the present author elsewhere, command socialism might be called a system of perpetual change. The changes are introduced by the party leadership with intent to do away with perceived problems. Yet, they tend to be ineffective or ephemeral if they tackle the problems' symptoms rather than causes, if they are of a piecemeal character, if they are internally inconsistent, or if they contradict the logic of the system.[12] Expressed differently, in socialist command economies reforms in the sense of deliberate changes within the system need not necessarily improve the system's economic performance. Actually, they can lead to its deterioration. Moreover, they can reduce the system's coherence and make it unstable.

Despite the shortcomings of command socialism and the failure of introduced reforms to improve its economic performance, the party leadership may continue to be reluctant to lose control over the economy. Nevertheless, it faces a tension between what it wants to do (the question of preferences) and what it can do (the question of constraints). In the long run, for two main reasons, command socialism is an economically unviable (and, hence, transitory) type of modern economic system. First, it is being undermined by its inbuilt tendency towards inefficiency, i.e., towards underutilization and waste of employed resources, because it is not able to escape the pervasive economic phenomenon of scarcity, due to which the basic economic problem is the allocation of scarce means (resources) among competing ends for the achievement of maximum results. Secondly, it is being undermined by the existence of an informal dimension consisting of covert non-compliance and illegal second economy activities, to which it gives rise and which permeate it.

Although in the long run command socialism is an economically unviable (and, hence, transitory) type of modern economic system, it is difficult to predict when the demise of an established variant of command socialism will take place. Only some assumptions are possible, such as that the lifetime of an established variant of command socialism depends on the party leadership's will to maintain it and on its capability to elicit compliance with command and to keep popular expectations in check. Another assumption is that the less a socialist command economy depends on foreign trade, the longer it is likely to survive.

12.4 DIMENSIONS OF THE TRANSFORMATION

As already mentioned in Section 12.1, the communist systems established in the Soviet-bloc countries were variants of totalist authoritarianism, conceived as authoritarian politics and political control over the economy and society. It follows from its nature that its transformation has four interrelated dimensions, namely, the political, the economic, the social, and the cultural.

In principle, the transformation of the political system means the substitution of liberal authoritarianism or liberal democracy for totalist authoritarianism and, in either case, includes the substitution of the rule of law for the arbitrariness of political power. While the substitution of liberal authoritarianism for totalist authoritarianism would affect the scope of political power but not its structure, the substitution of liberal democracy for totalist authoritarianism would affect both.

The transformation of the economic system signifies a deliberate retreat from command socialism as the extreme manifestation of economic collectivism or, to use Marie Lavigne's characterization, from a one-party, one-property, one-plan system.[13] Hence, it amounts to a redefinition of the scope of political power or, more precisely, of the role in the economy of the state and, implicitly, of that of the market and private ownership of the means of production.

Obviously, these systemic changes would have a distinct impact on the structure of society. *Inter alia*, they would lead to the demise of the unified and politicized bureaucracy needed for the operation and maintenance of totalist authoritarianism, and give rise to private owners of property, entrepreneurs (who both own and manage a business enterprise), the self-employed, and the like. Besides, they would enlarge the freedom of action of the so-called mediating structures or intermediate institutions (such as churches, interest groups, professional associations, trade unions, and voluntary organizations) standing between the individual and the family on the one hand and the state on the other.

No less obviously, these systemic changes would have a distinct impact on the values of society and the behaviour and attitudes of political, economic, and other actors. Since each type of modern political as well as economic system is based on certain values, the substitution of liberal authoritarianism or liberal democracy for total-ist authoritarianism would require to root out those values, attitudes, and patterns of behaviour that are incompatible with liberal author-itarianism or liberal democracy and to develop those values, attitudes, and patterns of behaviour that are compatible with and indispensable for liberal authoritarianism or liberal democracy.

All in all, totalist authoritarianism can be transformed either into liberal authoritarianism or into liberal democracy. Post-communist societies chose the latter alternative, i.e., their professed goals were democratic politics and free-market economics. Initially, though, these goals were only loosely defined and the ways of achieving them had not been worked out.

Since the collapse of communism gave rise to political pluralism and competition for power, the extent and pace of transformation were destined to depend on the interaction between the government, the opposition, pressure groups, and the electorate, as well as on changes in the mood of the time. This implies that democratization on the one hand paved the way for the transformation of command socialism into market capitalism, on the other hand made opposition and resistance to it possible.

Despite the fact that the professed goals of post-communist societ-ies were democratic politics and free-market economics, when com-munism collapsed these societies had no direct and intimate experience of political democracy and market capitalism. That is to say, they were not familiar with the rules of the game prevailing under liberal democracy, their meaning, and their rationale. Thus, the trans-formation required considerable learning capacity on the part of politicians, bureaucrats, professionals, emerging entrepreneurs, and ordinary citizens.

Besides giving rise to political pluralism and competition for power, the collapse of communism triggered off an explosion of unrealistic expectations, which failed to take into account that the transformation could face obstacles and bring about hardships. Consequently, it was highly likely that many of these expectations would not be met; that the unmet expectations would lead to disillusionment and mood swings; and that disillusionment and mood swings would be a breeding ground for the emergence of populist, nationalist, and other demagogues.

CONCLUSION

According to Zbigniew Brzezinski, '[c]ommunism's domination of much of the history of the twentieth century was largely rooted in its role as the timely "grand oversimplification". Locating the origins of all evil in the institution of private property, it postulated that the abolition of property would permit the attainment of true justice and of the perfection of human nature.' However, by August 1988, when his book *The Grand Failure* was completed, communism was 'in a state of general crisis, both ideologically and systemically.'[14]

Four dimensions of this crisis may be distinguished, namely, an economic crisis (the economic system did not produce the requisite quantity of consumable values), a rationality crisis (the administrative system did not produce the requisite quantity of rational decisions, the state apparatus could not adequately steer the economic system), a legitimation crisis (the legitimation system did not provide the requisite quantity of generalized motivations), and a motivation crisis (the socio-cultural system did not generate the requisite quantity of action-motivating meaning).[15]

The unexpected collapse of communism gave rise to a temporary systemic vacuum, sometimes also called the noisy phase of transformation,[16] characterized by political, legal, economic, and social uncertainty. In at least two cases, though, signs of a systemic vacuum were noticeable already prior to the collapse of communism. These two cases were Poland and the Soviet Union.

Not surprisingly, the collapse of communism raised the question of whether it was a revolution or not. In trying to answer this question it should be remembered that the term 'revolution' has two basic meanings. In its narrow (political) sense it refers to a sudden, illegal, and usually violent change of the established political system, an example being the French Revolution. In its broad sense it refers to any fundamental change, whether or not sudden, illegal, or violent, the examples being the agricultural revolution, the industrial revolution, and the information revolution. Hence, because the collapse of communism was to lead to systemic change and to have a distinct impact on the structure and values of society and the behaviour and attitudes of political, economic, and other actors, it is justified to regard it as a revolution in the broad sense.

Secondly, the collapse of communism raised the question of whether the changes triggered off by it constituted a transition or a transformation. Some scholars reject the former term (inasmuch as it implies emphasis on a specific outcome) and prefer the latter (inasmuch as it implies emphasis on actual processes), arguing that in post-communist societies there is no simple and guaranteed transition to political democracy and market capitalism.[17] According to others, the term 'transition' makes sense despite tremendous uncertainty about the future, despite the possibility that the transition could stall or be blocked, could create a prolonged period of instability, or could lead to a system different from the proclaimed target and possibly undesirable.[18] On balance, when dealing with the changes triggered off by the collapse of communism, the term 'transformation' seems to be more suitable than the term 'transition'.

Finally, the collapse of communism raised the question of the obstacles that transformation would face. One of them is opposition and resistance to transformation on the part of those actors who see it as threatening their vested interests and thwarting their expectations. Another is transformation costs which are likely to be higher the larger the post-communist country, the more heterogeneous the populace, the stronger the population's opposition and resistance to transformation, the more isolated from the outside world the population used to be under communism, and the greater the need for creative destruction due to the economy's misdevelopment.[19] Yet another is the path-dependent nature of transformation, path-dependency meaning not only that transformation will be affected by the initial state and, therefore, by the history of the system and country undergoing transformation, but also that steps taken earlier will influence the direction and speed of later policy choices.

13 Models for Transformation

As argued in Section 12.4, the transformation of the communist system has four interrelated dimensions, namely, the political, the economic, the social, and the cultural. However, in the following chapter, exclusively the transformation of the communist economic system will be examined. This does not mean, though, that it will be possible to disregard non-economic factors completely.

13.1 BASIC OPTIONS

The collapse of communism in Eastern Europe and the Soviet Union fatally discredited the idea of totalist authoritarianism (conceived as authoritarian politics and political control over the economy and society) and boosted the idea of liberal democracy (conceived as democratic politics and free-market economics). It also seemed to have confirmed Francis Fukuyama's thesis, first formulated in the summer of 1989, that liberal democracy may constitute the end-point of mankind's ideological evolution and the final form of human government, and as such constituted the end of history.[1]

Fukuyama recognized that the emergence of stable democracy could be hindered by culture. The cultural obstacles to the emergence of stable democracy identified by him were nationalism and ethnicity; religion; the existence of a highly unequal social structure and of the habits of mind that arise from it; and a society's inability autonomously to create a healthy civil society.[2] On the other hand, he failed to recognize that there were variants of market capitalism.

Yet, although the collapse of communism boosted the idea of liberal democracy, it has not led to its triumph: in theory, the idea of liberal democracy continues to be widely challenged, albeit with the proviso that among its challengers totalist authoritarianism is conspicuously absent; in practice, the future of liberal democracy is far from assured, even in Western societies. Expressed differently, the role of the state (the visible hand) in modern society has not ceased to be one of the crucial theoretical and political issues.

It is not surprising, then, that for post-communist societies free-market capitalism is not regarded as the only alternative to command socialism. Pat Devine, for instance, distinguished four broad alternatives to command socialism, namely, casino capitalism (characterized by *laissez-faire* and minimal state), social market capitalism (characterized by corporatist consensus and social solidarity), regulated market socialism (characterized by worker self-management and indicative planning), and democratic planning (characterized by social ownership and negotiated coordination). Of these four alternatives, the author contended, the first was a real danger, the second was the most desirable and probably the most likely alternative in the short-to-medium term, the third appeared to be a non-starter for the foreseeable future, and the last was the most desirable alternative in the longer term.[3]

Democratic planning deserves a separate note, because it is seen by Devine as offering an alternative perspective for both post-communist and Western societies. It means self-government in the economic sphere which 'requires democratic control over the use of society's assets by the people who are affected by that use [i.e., by an enterprise's workers, customers, the community in which the enterprise is located, competing enterprises, environmental groups, and so on]. The planning of major investment decisions through a process of negotiated co-ordination, combined with self-government at the level of the enterprise, would enable production to take place within a framework that had been shaped consciously in accordance with socially agreed priorities.'[4] In other words, Devine advocates a stakeholder economy which, as observed in Chapter 5, might be called extended corporatism.

Hans van Zon constructed five basic scenarios for post-communist Central Europe, called the *laissez-faire* capitalist scenario, the populist-authoritarian scenario, the leaning-upon-the-West scenario, the sustainable development scenario, and the muddling on scenario. In the sustainable development scenario, which he considered as the most desirable but improbable scenario, 'government has a firm commitment to democracy, the introduction of a market economy and the dismantling of the suffocating state bureaucracy, but nevertheless acknowledges the important role the state has to play in the bringing about of economic progress and social and political cohesion.'[5]

In all these five scenarios, the author concluded, 'the first phase is characterized by a deterioration of living standards and political instability, which may vary in intensity between the countries of the region. The first phase is also decisive for developments in subsequent phases. Faults made in the first phase will be difficult to repair.'[6]

A different picture emerges if the question of alternatives to command socialism is approached from the point of view of the typology of modern economic systems, adopted in Section 2.1. According to it, there are four pure types of modern economic system, namely, market capitalism, market socialism, command socialism, and command capitalism. Since command socialism is based on public ownership of the means of production and state coordination, it can hardly be transformed into command capitalism. It can only be transformed either into market socialism or into market capitalism. Of these two alternatives, exclusively market capitalism is an economically viable type of modern economic system, whereas market socialism is a transitory type of modern economic system.

Consequently, post-communist societies should aim at transforming command socialism into market capitalism, not into market socialism. However, even if post-communist societies choose to transform command socialism into market capitalism, they will experience a temporary systemic vacuum, giving rise to anarcho-capitalism, i.e., to a chaotic situation in which legal norms regulating private economic activity either do not exist at all or are widely ignored. Besides, as long as most of the means of production continue to be publicly owned but state coordination is not operative any more, they will experience a variant of market socialism. Finally, they will face a choice between three variants of market capitalism, identified in Section 4.3 as the *laissez-faire* variant, the free-market variant, and the interventionist variant.

13.2 FREE-MARKET APPROACH

By 1989, there existed a considerable number of theories predicting the imminent downfall of capitalism and the inevitable rise of socialism, i.e., theories based on the principle of socio-economic determinism and a linear definition of history. In contrast, there was no theory dealing with (and, hence, providing guidance to) the transformation of command socialism into market capitalism. After all, the collapse of communism was not expected and, on top of that, the transformation of command socialism into market capitalism had no historical precedent. Thus, post-communist societies travelled into uncharted waters.[7]

In these circumstances, post-communist societies initially chose as one of their professed goals free-market economics. In the then prevailing view, market capitalism (a pluralistic and competitive economic system) separated the economy from arbitrary political power, was the only economically viable alternative to command socialism (a non-pluralistic and non-competitive economic system), and had a vastly superior economic performance. Moreover, communism collapsed at a time when in the West the role of the state in the economy was under scrutiny. Around the mid- 1970s, Keynesian economics began to fall into disrepute, and neoclassical economics began to gain ground, to become most influential during the 1980s. The market, the private sector, and welfare pluralism were rediscovered. In order to roll back the frontiers of the state, free the market, and increase efficiency, privatization and deregulation were put onto the agenda.

Expressed differently, the 1980s were a decade of Thatcherism in Britain,[8] Reaganomics in the United States,[9] and Rogernomics in New Zealand. Concerning specifically the last-mentioned, prior to 1984 New Zealand had a highly regulated, protected, and distorted economy. However, in 1984 the newly elected Labour government launched a comprehensive free-market reform programme, named Rogernomics after Roger Douglas, Labour's finance minister until 1988: prices, wages, the exchange rate, and interest rates were set free, the financial system was deregulated, tax rates were slashed, government subsidies eliminated, state firms privatized, and monetary and fiscal policies tightened to squeeze out inflation.[10]

The mood of the time manifested itself in electoral results too: between 1979 and the end of the 1980s, conservative parties in many parts of the world won a series of elections.[11] Socialism was on the defensive, although socialist parties continued to exist and in some cases were in office or formed part of the ruling coalition, and socialist values did not disappear.

All this helps explain why after the collapse of communism neoclassical economics became fashionable in post-communist societies. As perceived by them, its advantage lay in demonstrating that an economy can function (and efficiently at that) without public ownership of the means of production and state coordination. Yet, as recalled by Barbara Krug, traditional textbook economics does not contribute to an explanation of the transformation process, because it restricts itself to an explanation of the functioning of markets and because it is outcome-oriented.[12]

13.3   SOCIAL MARKET ECONOMY

Naturally, free-market economics is not the only alternative to command socialism. Other alternatives are possible, and have not been ignored in discussions about models for the transformation of the communist economic system. One of them is the so-called social market economy.

The concept of the social market economy[13] was developed during and after the Second World War by a group of German economists, dubbed 'Ordo-Liberals'. According to them, the social market economy was to be based upon the market, but was to have a social dimension. That is to say, it was to combine the principle of freedom in the market-place with the principle of social harmonization and, in this way, to bring about a novel synthesis of freedom and security.

More specifically, the social market economy was to be characterized by private property, free prices, open markets, free competition, freedom of contract, and monetary stability. The state was expected to create a legal and institutional framework protecting an order of liberty, not just individual choice; to regulate the money supply in order to prevent inflation and deflation, albeit not for countercyclical purposes; to pursue competition policy, i.e., to check monopolistic and oligopolistic tendencies; and to refrain from interfering with or suspending the free market.

As to the welfare role of the state, two strands existed among the original social market economists, differing in their views on state-provided welfare, the redistribution of income and wealth through taxation, and welfare provisions paid for along conventional insurance lines. Yet, whatever welfare role they assigned to the state, these economists rejected the welfare state and emphasized that social welfare policies and spending should not inhibit the functioning of the free market, that social objectives should be pursued through the free market. This implied, *inter alia*, that they preferred subsidies (e.g., rent subsidies) to price controls (e.g., rent restrictions).

Hence, the social market economy was to be different from both the planned economy and the *laissez-faire* economy in that it was to be characterized by the concurrence of freedom, efficiency, and equity. In contrast, the planned economy might go some way towards the promotion of equity, but at the sacrifice of individual freedom and economic efficiency, while the pure *laissez-faire* economy would fail adequately to promote equity, would permit freedom to be curtailed (by, for example, neglecting to regulate monopoly), and would not be fully satisfactory even in promoting efficiency (due to the inadequacy of the political infrastructure).

In practice,[14] a variant of the social market economy was imposed on West Germany between 1948 and 1952. The transformation started in mid-1948 with a currency reform accompanied by the abolition of most of the regulations, price controls, and rationing that had been left over from the Nazi variant of command capitalism or established by Allied Occupation Powers. It was helped by the fact that the first postwar general election took place in late 1949, after the introduction of the market and when its benefits were just beginning to show.

Commitment to the free market lasted for approximately a decade and half. After the Social Democrats came to power in December 1966, though, this commitment weakened. There was a shift to Keynesian demand management,[15] and the principles of global guidance and concerted action had their day. Simultaneously, and especially during the first half of the 1970s, the welfare state was expanding substantially and welfare spending rising.

While between the late 1960s and the late 1970s the role played by the state in the economy increased, during the 1980s it declined somewhat. A turn away from Keynesianism took place, and some deregulation and welfare trimming occurred. Nevertheless, by the end of the 1980s West Germany continued to have a bureaucratized, high-cost, and high-subsidy economy, a lavish welfare state, and a leisure society. Moreover, neither the postwar tradition of industry-wide collective bargaining and contracts nor the institution of co-determination disappeared from the scene.[16]

Consequently, the economic system established in West Germany by the end of the 1980s differed considerably from the original concept of the social market economy. This suggests that as an alternative to command socialism the social market economy could be offered either in its original sense or in its degenerate form.

As a term, the social market economy is a pleonasm: since all market relationships (just as all command relationships) are necessarily social, the addition of the word 'social' to the noun 'market' is merely an adjectival frill. As a concept, the social market economy contains a tension between economic and social criteria, which both in theory and in practice may culminate in the subordination of the former to the latter. All in all, it has no unambiguous meaning and allows different interpretations.

During the first half of the 1990s, it should be added, the social market economy of unified Germany continued to experience a number of problems. They included high labour costs, overregulated labour and product markets, rising registered unemployment, a falling rate of GDP growth, high taxes, high government expenditure, bulging budget deficit, a strong currency, and declining competitiveness. At the same time, in 1994 the average real net income of employees in former West Germany was only three per cent higher than in 1980.[17]

13.4 THE SWEDISH WELFARE STATE

Another alternative to command socialism, considered in discussions about models for the transformation of the communist economic system, has been the Swedish welfare state which, by the end of the 1980s, was characterized by private ownership of the means of production, powerful trade unions, centralized wage bargaining, narrow wage differentials, commitment to full employment, high government spending, high taxes, a bloated public sector, and generous cradle-to-grave welfare provisions in the form of transfer payments, welfare services, and subsidies (see also Section 5.5).

The size of the government economy was increasing throughout the postwar period. Thus, the share in GDP of total tax revenue went up from 20.9 per cent in 1950 through 28.7 per cent in 1960, 40.0 per cent in 1970, and 52.0 per cent in 1979 to 56 per cent in 1989;[18] the share in GDP of government spending went up from 31 per cent in 1960 through 43.3 per cent in 1970 and 61.6 per cent in 1980 to 64.7 per cent in 1985 (see Table 8.3); and the share in the labour force of public sector employment went up from about 12 per cent in 1960 to about 32 per cent in 1988.[19]

Owing to the pursued policies, in the early 1970s relative economic performance began to deteriorate.[20] The problems experienced by the economy during the subsequent two decades included wage inflation, rising unit labour costs, sluggish productivity growth, high absenteeism, low GDP growth, retail price inflation, budget deficits, and a huge public debt. Moreover, in order to improve the country's international competitiveness, a series of devaluations had to take place.

While until the end of the 1960s the government confined itself mostly to intervention in the outcome of economic activity, i.e., to the redistribution of income, afterwards it increasingly intervened in the operation of the free market and in property rights as well. *Inter alia*, it considerably strengthened job security, and advanced industrial democracy by widening trade union participation in company decision-making and by requiring companies to seat trade union representatives on their boards of directors.

All in all, for some time prior to the collapse of communism in Eastern Europe and the Soviet Union the Swedish economy was showing signs of progressive arteriosclerosis and the Swedish model was becoming an anachronism. Finally, by the beginning of the 1990s centralized wage bargaining broke down, the high-taxes-for-high-spending policy was falling apart, and the government recognized that squeezing open inflation should take precedence over full employment.

During the 1970s and the 1980s, it should be recalled, the actual practice of the Swedish welfare state and that of the German social market economy began to resemble each other in significant ways. Therefore, a brief note on the so-called Rhine model of capitalism is in place. According to Michel Albert,[21] this model is associated mainly with countries such as Germany, Switzerland, and the Netherlands, but its elements are to be found in Scandinavia and Japan too. It is an alternative to the neo-American model of capitalism, the homeland of which is the United States, although to some extent it also exists in other Anglo-Saxon countries, including Britain.

Of these two differing and opposing models of capitalism, the neo-American model is based on individual success and short-term financial gain, and gives pride of place to negotiable goods (i.e., commodities and services that can always be exchanged), whereas the Rhine model emphasizes collective success, consensus, and long-term concerns, and has a preponderance of mixed goods (those which are partly negotiable on the open market and partly dependent on public sector initiative). At the same time, the latter is seen by the author as being both more efficient and more equitable than the former. On the other hand, compared with the former the latter is less open and more rigid, and is characterized by a tendency to social conformity and uniformity, thus leavening individual self-interest, discouraging individual autonomy, and distrusting individual diversity.

Yet, although the Rhine model is outperforming the neo-American model, Albert recognizes (albeit with deep regret) that it is the latter which is in the ascendant, for there are signs in Germany, Japan, and elsewhere that company structures are changing, that the welfare consensus is under strain, and that the traditional role of the banks in financing investment is being challenged by increasing reliance on stock market funding. One reason for these changes lies in the globalization of the financial markets.

There are, however, at least two other reasons why the Rhine model is under threat. Rhine model countries are high-cost countries, which adversely affects their international competitiveness. Moreover, these countries are culturally less tolerant of individual diversity and freedom than neo-American model countries.

13.5 TWO OTHER MODELS

Besides the alternatives to command socialism considered hitherto, various other models for the transformation of the communist economic system have been advanced in discussions triggered off by the collapse of communism. Of these, only two will receive attention, namely, the Chinese model and the East Asian model.

As its adjective indicates, the Chinese model[22] refers to the economic reform launched in 1978 in China, a communist-ruled and predominantly rural country of more than one thousand million inhabitants. The reform started in the countryside, to be extended to urban industry in 1984. Its distinctive feature was the gradually increasing marketization of the economy without the privatization of state enterprises, leading to the emergence of a dual production and price system, to a disjointed mix of plan and market and of state-owned, collectively-owned, and private enterprises.

During the 1980s, the reform on the one hand produced a rapid (albeit uneven) growth, boosted the proportion of goods and services traded at market prices, and reduced state enterprises' share of industrial output, on the other unleashed open inflation. State enterprises continued to be heavily overmanned and to have a soft budget constraint. Bankruptcies were rare if any, despite the adoption of a bankruptcy law.

Consequently, at the beginning of the 1990s the reform was far from complete. Not only the state sector, but also the tax system, the banking system, and the legal system were in need of change. Moreover, neither the tension between market and state coordination nor that between private and public ownership of the means of production disappeared. Expressed differently, China did not cease to experience a tension between totalism and liberalism, as well as a tension between authoritarianism and democracy.

According to Joseph S. Berliner, the Chinese model was adopted by the Soviet Union under Gorbachev. The programme of *perestroika* mirrored the four components of the Chinese model, namely, an expansion of the private sector, the free sale of overplan output by state enterprises, a dual price system, and an open door policy. In contrast to the remarkable improvement that occurred in China, though, between 1988 and 1991 economic performance deteriorated rapidly in the Soviet Union, because the Soviet version of the Chinese model unfolded under conditions much less favourable than those in China.[23]

Despite its shortcomings and the failure of its Soviet version, the adoption of the Chinese model by post-communist societies has had some advocates in the West. They emphasize China's economic success and attribute it to the gradualist approach which, in their view, reduces the costs of economic transformation. For example, Patrick Bolton wrote that '[t]he Chinese experience shows that it is not necessary to privatize a state-owned firm in order to improve its efficiency, and that it is possible to avoid the huge (short-run) disruptions in the economy caused by "shock therapy" reforms',[24] and Louis Emmerij opined that '[t]he "two-track" approach ("governing the market"), as for instance pursued in China, seems to be a more effective policy than moving directly from one extreme (central planning) to the other (a capitalist market economy)'.[25]

However, the adoption of the Chinese model by post-communist societies has had its opponents too. They argue that the model, which implies the continuous existence of an authoritarian political system, is not transferable because of differences in initial conditions. They maintain that 'China's reintegration into the world economy and rapid growth have been facilitated by the large overseas Chinese community (not only in Hong Kong, Taiwan and Southeast Asia, but also in North America, England and Australia).'[26]

While the Chinese model refers to one country only,[27] the East Asian model refers to eight countries, namely, Hong Kong, Indonesia, Japan, Malaysia, Singapore, South Korea, Taiwan, and Thailand. Between 1960 and 1990, these eight high-performing East Asian economies experienced astounding economic growth, considerably exceeding that achieved elsewhere, including the OECD economies. They also enjoyed low open inflation, low taxes, and low government spending, and had high levels of domestic saving and private domestic investment, as well as relatively low income inequality.

The foundation of East Asia's economic success, the World Bank concluded in its 1993 report, was a market-friendly strategy.[28] Yet, apart from Hong Kong, the governments pursued interventionist (not free-market) policies. *Inter alia*, subsidies, cheap credit, and tax incentives to selected industries were widespread, export was promoted, and import barriers were erected to protect domestic industries in their early stages of development. At the same time, though, the governments tried to keep the implicit or explicit costs of interventions within well-defined bounds.

Besides strong, activist, and usually authoritarian governments with a more or less single, overriding objective, namely, economic growth, other factors contributed to East Asia's economic success. They included the competence and relative lack of corruptibility of civil servants; flexible labour markets; openness to foreign ideas and technology; focus on universal primary and secondary education; willingness to defer gratification, i.e., to sacrifice current satisfaction for future gains; the continuing importance of the extended family; and aversion to the comprehensive welfare state.

Not surprisingly, the extent of government intervention in the economy varied from one East Asian country to another and, within the same East Asian country, over time. Consequently, there was in fact no single East Asian model.

According to Paul Krugman, popular enthusiasm about East Asia's boom deserves to have some cold water thrown on it. Just as in the Soviet-bloc countries in the 1950s, in East Asia too rapid economic growth was based in large part on an astonishing mobilization of resources, on rapid growth in inputs. That is to say, it was not based on increases in efficiency, on increases in the output per unit of input. Only in Japan it seems to have been achieved both through high rates of input growth and through high rates of efficiency growth.[29]

Since input-driven economic growth is inevitably limited and since raising efficiency is much harder than increasing inputs, it is likely that economic growth in East Asia will slow down in the future. Nevertheless, as Krugman concluded, it may be expected to continue to outpace economic growth in the West.

In this connection, a brief separate note on Japan is in place. Japan's economic system was called 'government-controlled capitalism' by Kyoko Sheridan[30] and characterized by Brian Reading as 'a half-way house between capitalism and communism, democracy and dictatorship. It is corporatist, with big business run for the benefit of stakeholders, management, employees and customers, not shareholders. It is a controlled economy, by bureaucratic regulation, designed to eliminate competition for the benefit of powerful producer interests. It is virtually a one-party state, corrupt, paternalistic and nepotistic, a neo-feudal system operated for the benefit of powerful and wealthy political and industrial dynasties,...'[31]

While prior to 1990 Japan experienced four decades of remarkable (albeit decelerating) economic growth, in the first half of the 1990s it was passing through a severe recession. The recession started in 1991, turned budget surplus into budget deficit, pushed up gross public debt, and increased registered unemployment. Although signs of a recovery began to manifest themselves in the second half of 1994, Japanese economists generally believed that the sustainable rate of economic growth was no more than three per cent.

To sum up, East Asia's economic success has evoked two principal responses in the West: one has been to view East Asian economies as a model for imitation or at least inspiration and, hence, to advocate extensive government intervention in the economy, including protectionism; the other has been attempts to gain greater access to East Asian markets. However, none of the eight East Asian economies is a suitable model for the West and, similarly, for post-communist societies, the reason being considerable differences in political, economic, social, and cultural conditions.

Although East Asian economies are unsuitable as a model both for the West and for post-communist societies, some lessons may be learned from their experience. The same applies to Latin America where, in the late 1970s or the early 1980s, many countries started deliberately to dismantle government intervention in the economy.[32]

CONCLUSION

The establishment of command socialism first in the Soviet Union and then in Soviet-controlled Eastern Europe did not put an end to the multidimensional tension between economic individualism and economic collectivism, inherent in modern economies. This was indicated by the persistent existence of covert non-compliance with formal norms and administrative orders and of illegal second economy activities, as well as by the various attempted and usually unsuccessful economic reforms.

It was only after the collapse of communism, though, that the tension could come fully into the open. Since it revolves around the role of the state (the visible hand) in the economy, the rejection of command socialism by post-communist societies inevitably raised two basic questions, namely, that of the role the state should play *during* economic transformation and that of the role the state should play *after* the completion of economic transformation.

Despite the fact that initially one of the professed goals of post-communist societies was free-market economics, there was no theory dealing with (and, hence, providing guidance to) the transformation of command socialism into market capitalism. This was not surprising, because the collapse of communism was unexpected and because the transformation of command socialism into market capitalism had no historical precedent.

While initially one of the professed goals of post-communist societies was free-market economics, gradually other alternatives to command socialism began to be discussed, such as the social market economy, the Swedish welfare state, the Chinese economic reform, and East Asian economies. However, adopting a particular economy as a model for the transformation of command socialism requires extreme caution, for two main reasons: due to differences in political, economic, social, and cultural conditions, the reference economy need not be suitable for post-communist societies; due to problems facing it, the reference economy may be undergoing change which is not taken into account by post-communist societies, so that in fact an outdated model is chosen for imitation or inspiration.

In the West, it should be added, discussions about how to transform command socialism have not been dominated by the so-called sovietologists, specializing in the study of communist economies and societies. They have been dominated by standard economists, specializing in market economies and having little interest in and limited knowledge of communist economies and societies.

14 Components and Dynamics of Economic Transformation

The economic systems established in the Soviet-bloc countries were variants of command socialism. That is to say, in these countries most of the means of production were publicly owned and economic activity was coordinated chiefly by command. At the same time, these countries had a comprehensive welfare state financed through taxation and the profits of state enterprises. Bearing this in mind, it is possible to turn to the main dimensions of economic transformation in post-communist societies.

14.1 COMPONENTS

Economists in both Western and post-communist societies broadly agreed that the core components of economic transformation in post-communist societies were macroeconomic stabilization, liberalization, privatization, and institution- building.[1] Of these four components of economic transformation,

1. macroeconomic stabilization entailed pursuing a tight monetary policy and maintaining a responsible fiscal policy, supported (if necessary) by a temporary incomes policy for the state sector, its aim being to bring inflation, the state budget deficit, and the balance of payments deficit under control;
2. liberalization meant the substitution of market coordination of economic activity for state coordination of economic activity, and involved freeing prices, including interest rates; devaluing the currency to a realistic level; making the currency convertible for international transactions of goods and services; eliminating barriers to cross-border movements of goods, services, capital, technology, and ideas; and deregulating financial, labour, and other markets;
3. privatization referred to changes in the ownership of productive assets, land, and housing, and comprised liquidation, restructuring,

and commercialization of the existing state enterprises; transfer of productive assets, land, and housing from the state to private hands; and spontaneous formation of new private firms; and
4. institution-building entailed building the institutions necessary to sustain a capitalist market economy, such as a legal system defining the rights and responsibilities of economic actors in the market process, especially in respect of property, contract, exchange, competition, and tort; a tax system based on rules and formulas rather than on arbitrary retention of income by the state; a system of autonomous financial intermediaries; and statistical, accounting, and other economic information systems.

Besides broadly agreeing on the core components of economic transformation, economists in both Western and post-communist societies agreed that economic transformation required an adequate social safety net, and argued that its creation should be an integral part of the transformation design,[2] inasmuch as it was needed to cushion the most vulnerable groups of the population from the impact of economic transformation, as well as to ensure political support for economic transformation. As conceived by these economists, the social safety net was to be confined to measures intended to protect exclusively those individuals who were hit particularly hard by economic transformation, either because they became openly unemployed, or because they depended on low and relatively fixed incomes. Simultaneously, though, they empasized the necessity of trying to minimize the drain on the state budget.

More specifically, the transformation of command socialism into market capitalism implies the transformation of chronic and general overmanning (i.e., unemployment on the job) of mass proportions into open unemployment. Consequently, one of the early tasks of post-communist governments is to recognize open unemployment as a separate risk, introduce registered unemployment, establish an unemployment benefit system, and set up a network of state employment offices. In addition, the transformation of command socialism into market capitalism implies the transformation of repressed inflation into open inflation, which requires prices to be allowed to rise to market-determined levels. Consequently, another early task of post-communist governments is to adjust low and relatively fixed incomes (e.g., pensions) both to the initial jump in retail prices and to the subsequent retail price increases.

To sum up, among economists in both Western and post-communist societies there existed a broad consensus on the core components of economic transformation in post-communist societies. This consensus notwithstanding, these economists were far from unanimous when it came to the important question of the dynamics of its implementation, to the issues of its speed, comprehensiveness, sequencing, sectoralism (the extent to which the state interferes with market forces to promote 'winners' and suppress 'losers' at the level of sectors, industries, and enterprises), and intensity (i.e., how vigorously a policy is implemented).

14.2   SPEED

Concerning the speed of economic transformation, economists were divided into radicals and gradualists. The former, who were of the neoclassical persuasion, advocated what was termed the shock therapy, i.e., a quick break with the old economic system by adopting a rapid, simultaneous, and comprehensive transformation strategy. The role of the state during the transformation was to be limited, the market was to be not only the end goal of the transformation, but also the mechanism for effecting the transformation. In contrast, the gradualists advocated a step-by-step transformation, proceeding at a slow pace and spread over a long period of time. Thus, there was to be no quick break with the old economic system, with the economic institutions and policies inherited from the communist era. The state was expected to exert control over the transformation, and the end goal of the transformation was to be the interventionist variant of market capitalism.

Not surprisingly, the pros and cons of these two transformation strategies were widely and hotly discussed.[3] Shock therapy, its proponents argued, would signal that the government meant business, i.e., was determined to transform command socialism into market capitalism; would compress transformation costs into a short period of time, when the population was willing to tolerate them and opposition and resistance to the transformation were weak; would quickly break inertia and change expectations; and would strengthen the irreversibility of the transformation.

While the radicals believed that shock therapy would be endurable because it would be of short duration and would be followed by slow but steady improvements in the economic situation, the gradualists disagreed. In their view, shock therapy would provoke intolerable social costs, and so erode popular support for the transformation. They emphasized that gradualism would spread transformation costs over a long period of time, which would make the transformation more acceptable politically and, hence, more achievable.

However, gradualism too was severely criticized. According to its critics, although it would minimize transformation costs in the short run, it would increase them in the long run and, simultaneously, fail to generate perceptible benefits. It would create uncertainty, fuel dissatisfaction, give rise to opposition and resistance to the transformation, and encourage zigzagging on the part of the government. In the final analysis, it could lead to the abandonment of the transformation.

For post-communist societies, shock therapy was advocated on the basis of experience gained in Latin America in the 1970s and 1980s. It was initially applied in Poland and eastern Germany in 1990. Shortly afterwards, in 1992, Andreas Pickel opined that 'the radical strategy in East Germany has failed in crucial respects.... The East German experience suggests that there are some fundamental weaknesses in the radical strategy.'[4]

While eastern Germany was generally regarded as the only example of genuine shock therapy,[5] Hungary was generally regarded as a clear example of gradualism. Gabor Bakos argued, though, that 'the transition in Hungary was not gradual because earlier reforms failed to resolve the basic problems. Therefore it was in fact a hidden shock therapy.' As a result, 'what we have to do with is not a "transformational crisis", a crisis necessarily appearing with the transition from socialism to capitalism, but the disastrous consequences of a one-sided, naively liberal marketisation approach.'[6]

Be that as it may, it was primarily the economic reform launched in 1978 in China by an authoritarian political system that was used in support of gradualism by its proponents. Yet, China's experience did not prove conclusively that in post-communist societies gradualism would work and shock therapy would not.[7]

14.3   COMPREHENSIVENESS

As argued in Section 2.2, modern economies are variants of pure types of modern economic system. Expressed differently, they are mixed economic systems. Despite that, types of ownership of the means of production and types of coordinating mechanism cannot be mixed in arbitrary proportions. The reason is that an economic system is an internally logical whole of compatible, interacting, mutually reinforcing, and integrated elements. Having its own logic, it resists those elements which are incompatible with it and, therefore, threaten it. That is to say, it is able to absorb contradictory elements within certain (rather narrow) limits only. If these limits are over-stepped, penalties are to be paid and, unless retreat occurs, the nature of the established economic system begins to change.

Thus, economic phenomena are interdependent. Since in economic life everything depends on everything else, economic logic dictates that in post-communist societies economic transformation should be comprehensive, that all the measures necessary to effect it, or at least preparations for them, should be launched quickly and simultane-ously. This does not mean, though, that all these measures can be implemented at the same instant, because the duration of both pre-paration and implementation varies from one measure to another.[8]

In contrast to shock therapy, gradualism assumes that the post-communist government inherited a functioning variant of command socialism, and requires a high degree of central controls. Con-sequently, a step-by-step (piecemeal) transformation would continue to experience many of the old inconsistencies, as well as give rise to new ones. Besides, because it would generate perceptible benefits in the long run only, the government would face a credibility problem.

Yet, although economic logic dictates that in post-communist societ-ies economic transformation should be comprehensive, in practice it is not possible to prepare and implement everything at once. Hence, the issue of sequencing comes to the fore. According to Louis Haddad, '[t]he process of transition to a functioning market economy is essen-tially about the logical and chronological sequencing of the required reform measures. Sequencing is not merely a major problem of transi-tion but is synonymous with it: it permeates the entire process.'[9]

14.4 SEQUENCING

The concept of sequencing suggests that in order to effect economic transformation, some measures should precede others and that to reverse the order of succession would be harmful. As put by Jozef M. van Brabant, '[t]ransforming the PETs [planned economies in transition] into market economies is fraught with hazards and uncer-tainty, ... Nevertheless, the transition needs to be comprehensive and carried out quickly. But the order in which the various reform components are introduced is not, of course, a random matter.'[10]

While the importance of sequencing was recognized and the issue was widely discussed, there was no general agreement on the appropriate sequence of individual measures. Concerning the sequencing of the four core components of economic transformation, the radicals argued that economic transformation should start with macroeconomic stabilization and liberalization, closely followed by privatization. According to Jeffrey Sachs, [s]hock therapy presupposes that rapid privatization will be initiated at the time of stabilization and liberalization, so that after a few years, the economy will be not only market-oriented, but predominantly privately owned. Privatization proceeds from two directions: "top-down privatization" signifies the transfer of ownership of state assets to private owners, while "bottom-up privatization" signifies the formation of new enterprises by private entrepreneurs.'[11]

In contrast, due to their direct concern with *ex ante* constraints, the gradualists contended that economic transformation should start with institution-building and restructuring. In Peter Murrell's view, for instance, '[c]omprehensive economic reform means first and foremost a radical change in the economic environment.'[12]

The radicals' advocacy of the primacy of macroeconomic stabilization and liberalization was understandable: a sound currency is a necessary condition for maintaining a capitalist market economy and, ultimately, a stable government and a stable society; free prices, determined by the interplay of supply and demand in the market and, in turn. influencing both supply and demand, provide crucial information for economic actors in their roles of sellers and buyers. Expressed differently, macroeconomic stabilization and liberalization were expected rapidly to change the behaviour and attitudes of economic actors, be they households, state enterprises, new private firms, or the government.

Of course, the question of the sequencing of the four core components of economic transformation did not exhaust the issue of sequencing. The dispute was also about sequencing within each of the four core components of economic transformation, about – *inter alia* – whether domestic liberalization should precede or follow foreign trade liberalization; whether demonopolization should precede or follow privatization; and whether restructuring (i.e., changes in the relative importance of individual industries) should precede or follow privatization.

Besides, attempts were made to formulate general principles of sequencing. Three such principles were put forward by Gerard Roland: it is better to start first with reforms having a higher expected outcome than with reforms having a lower expected outcome; under a democratic framework, it is always better to start first with reforms that are advantageous for a majority; and where two reforms have an equivalent expected outcome, it is better to start first with the more risky reform. The application of these principles would mean, for example, the following: if restructuring is considered to hurt more than price liberalization, then it is better, from the political economy point of view, to start with price liberalization before restructuring begins; if political constraints impose gradual privatization, it is better to start privatizing the best enterprises rather than the bad enterprises.[13]

Not surprisingly, the concept of sequencing might give an impression that sequencing means proceeding in a linear sequence, that it is identical with (and confined to) the step-by-step approach. This is not the case. Irrespective of the adopted transformation strategy, sequencing cannot be avoided. Moreover, it does not exclude concurrence of several transformation measures.

14.5   THE ROLE OF THE STATE

As already mentioned, one of the differences between shock therapy and gradualism concerns the role the state should play in post-communist societies during economic transformation and after its completion. The former postulates a limited role for the state during the transformation, the market is to be not only the end goal of the transformation, but also the mechanism for effecting the transformation. The latter expects the state to exert control over the transformation, and the end goal of the transformation is to be the interventionist variant of market capitalism.

Although shock therapy postulates a limited role for the state during the transformation, its role would of necessity be an important one. This clearly follows from the four core components of economic transformation in post-communist societies. In addition, this follows from the need to create an adequate social safety net: for obvious reasons, a quick break with the old economic system envisaged by shock therapy requires an adequate social safety net more urgently than gradualism.

Compared with shock therapy, gradualism relies less on the market (as both the means and the end of the transformation) and more on the state. That is to say, it prefers big government to limited government: public ownership of the means of production would not be totally out of favour; the state would engage in macroeconomic as well as microeconomic management and perhaps even in social engineering; and welfare statism would continue to meet with approval. It is not surprising, then, that there appeared a number of calls for expansionary demand management and for industrial policies. It was maintained, *inter alia*, that restructuring and demonopolization should occur before privatization and be carried out by the state, because they could not be entrusted to the market.

One of the advocates of industrial policies during the transformation was Michael A. Landesmann. He argued that in the West the case for industrial policies was made on the basis of what the market could not achieve due to externalities, economies of scale, information problems, or capital market imperfections. However, in post-communist societies during a period of transition 'the case for industrial policies... is not simply the one based on market failure, but one based on the non-existence of markets, or the only rudimentary existence of markets and market responses. In such conditions, the vital question is not whether the state should or should not intervene but rather, what are the types of state intervention able to increase the response rate of agents (firms, households, workers) to a newly emerging market environment and equip them with "capabilities" that allow them to respond more flexibly to market signals.' In a word, 'the transition process cannot occur without a relatively high degree of state involvement.'[14]

A more balanced position was taken by Janos Fath. In his opinion, the fate of industry in East-Central Europe will be shaped, in varied proportions, by the free-market institutional approach and the industrial-activist (interventionist) influences. At the same time, though, national ambitions will be constrained by world markets and international institutions. Moreover, industrial policies should take into consideration that the behaviour of state enterprises can be either defensive-conservative, i.e., resisting or at least not promoting changes, or dynamic-innovative, i.e., responsive to changing environment.[15]

Hence, there existed diverse views on the role of the state during economic transformation.[16] In this connection it is worth recalling once again that any government without exception experiences a tension between what it wants to do and what it can do, i.e., between its preferences and its constraints. Since governments generally face numerous constraints, including imperfect knowledge on their part, their extractive, allocative, distributive, and regulative capabilities are constrained too. This means that they are neither omniscient nor omnipotent (*inter alia*, they are not able forever to defy the laws of economics). Consequently, government intervention in the economy can fail, i.e., be unsuccessful in attaining its chosen objectives and produce unintended consequences. It can also harm the economy, particularly in the long run, one reason being that policies and reforms once introduced may be difficult to undo.

Concerning specifically post-communist societies, in these societies economic transformation requires a government that has a clear idea of what it wants to achieve, that is committed to the economic transformation programme, and that has the political will to see the programme through. Yet, whatever its orientation, commitment, and resolve, it faces political, economic, social, and cultural constraints, both intrasocietal (domestic) and extrasocietal (international), which affect policy choices as well as policy implementation.

Inasmuch as economic transformation aims at the transformation of command socialism into market capitalism, it inevitably involves interaction between the government and the market. The former is expected to play an important, albeit limited role, namely, to introduce market-oriented measures and, thus, to create an environment conducive to private ownership of the means of production and market coordination, while simultaneously refraining from pursuing market-distorting policies.

Although government involvement is a necessary condition for economic transformation, it is not a sufficient one. The government can create opportunities for private economic activities, i.e., enlarge economic freedom. However, if market capitalism is to be established, private economic actors must take advantage of these opportunities and, in their own interest, accept the need for individual effort, initiative, risk-taking, and responsibility.

CONCLUSION

Economists in both Western and post-communist societies broadly agreed on the core components of economic transformation in post-communist societies. According to them, the transformation of command socialism into market capitalism and, implicitly, the integration of post-communist economies into the world economy, required macroeconomic stabilization, liberalization, privatization, and institution-building.

Despite this consensus, though, these economists were far from unanimous when it came to the question of the dynamics of implementation of the transformation strategy. They were divided into radicals and gradualists, differing with respect to the speed, comprehensiveness, sequencing, sectoralism, and intensity of economic transformation. As to the sequencing of the core components of economic transformation, the former gave priority to macroeconomic stabilization and liberalization, closely followed by privatization,[17] while the latter gave priority to institution-building and restructuring.

Consequently, radicals and gradualists also differed with respect to the role the state should play during economic transformation as well as after its completion. Basically, the former favoured limited government, the latter big government. Yet, in either case economic transformation needs a strong government, i.e., a government that has a clear idea of what it wants to achieve, that is committed to the economic transformation programme, and that has the political will to see the programme through. A weak and/or frequently changing (in other words, unstable) government would prolong economic transformation and increase its costs for the population.

Of course, a strong government does not mean an omniscient and omnipotent government. Nevertheless, belief in the omniscient and omnipotent government seems to survive, at least in some quarters. As to economic transformation, gradualists are more likely than radicals to believe in the omniscience and omnipotence of the state because, compared with the latter, they rely less on the market (as both the means and the end of economic transformation) and more on the state.

In connection with the differences between radicals and gradualists it may be asked to what extent these differences are associated with different academic disciplines, and how different academic disciplines assess the prospects for economic transformation in post-communist societies. The answer given by Robert Skidelsky is that economists and economic historians tend to be optimists, whereas sociologists and general historians gravitate towards pessimism. Sociologists typically fear the disruptive impact of the market on civil society, and for historians the only future they can imagine is the past.[18]

15 Economic Transformation in Practice

Having in the two preceding chapters discussed at some length economic transformation in post-communist societies from a theoretical point of view, it is possible to turn to an examination of the transformation process itself. Of necessity, though, this examination will be highly selective and far from exhaustive, as well as mostly confined to the first half of the 1990s.

15.1 THE STARTING-POINT

As already noted in Section 12.3, communism collapsed first in Soviet-controlled Eastern Europe, and its collapse therein in 1989 meant the breakup of the Soviet empire. Two years later, in 1991, it collapsed in the Soviet Union too, and the Soviet Union disintegrated. Outside the former Soviet bloc, Yugoslavia fell apart in 1991, and Albania's communist era came to its end in 1992.

One consequence of the collapse of communism was a considerable increase in the number of independent countries. In the late 1980s, nine communist countries existed in Europe, of which seven (Bulgaria, Czechoslovakia, East Germany, Hungary, Poland, Romania, and the Soviet Union) were members of the Soviet bloc. By the mid-1990s, as many as twenty-eight post-communist countries were to be found, namely, eighteen Central and Eastern European ones, Russia, eight non-European states of the former Soviet Union, and Mongolia.[1]

Economic transformation started in Poland on 1 January 1990, in East Germany on 1 July 1990, in Romania on 1 September 1990, in Czechoslovakia on 1 January 1991, in Bulgaria on 1 February 1991, and in the Russian Federation (Russia in brief) on 2 January 1992. Only in Hungary it had no distinct beginning, because post-communist Hungary continued many of the systemic reforms and economic policies of the previous régime.[2]

For most of these countries, despite some foreign advisory and financial assistance, economic transformation was primarily a domestic affair. The only exception was East Germany: as a result of German unification,[3] economic transformation was imposed on East Germany from the outside by West Germany, and was to lead to a merger of the two economies by the substitution of the West German variant of market capitalism for the East German variant of command socialism.

Concerning the transformation strategy, a number of countries adopted shock therapy. In its extreme form, not repeatable elsewhere, it was applied in eastern Germany, formerly known as East Germany or the German Democratic Republic (GDR).[4] The strategy initially applied in Poland[5] served as a model especially for Bulgaria and Russia. In contrast, gradualism was adopted by Hungary and Romania.

Hence, both the beginning of economic transformation and the design of the economic transformation programme varied from one post-communist country to another. However, the same was true of the implementation of the economic transformation programme as well: for various reasons, the transformation process tended more or less to deviate from the original design, an eminent example being Russia.

Below, only some post-communist countries will be considered. Of those considered, it should be noted, Czechoslovakia split into the Czech Republic and the Slovak Republic on 1 January 1993. Until then, it was a federal state.

15.2 OPEN INFLATION

When economic transformation started in post-communist countries, one of the first steps taken was the liberalization of prices, so that they could reflect consumers' preferences and scarcity, influence the behaviour and attitudes of economic actors (be they households, state enterprises, new private firms, or the government) in their roles of sellers and buyers, and balance demand and supply.

Hungary began to liberalize prices before the collapse of communism, the share of consumer prices freed going up from 35 per cent in 1985 through 62 per cent in 1989 to 77 per cent in 1990 and 90 per cent in 1991.[6] Poland too began partially to liberalize prices before the collapse of communism. Of the remaining countries, where price liberalization had to wait until after the collapse of communism, Bulgaria and Romania adopted gradual price liberalization, while others adopted instant liberalization of between 80 and 90 per cent of prices.

At the start of economic transformation, the monetary overhang (the surplus of purchasing power) varied considerably from one post-communist country to another: it was large in Russia, Bulgaria, and Poland, small in Romania and Czechoslovakia, and practically non-existent in Hungary. When price liberalization took place, this obviously had an impact on the size of the initial jump in the price level.

During the first half of the 1990s, Table 15.1 shows, post- communist countries continued to face inflationary pressures. Although in most of them after the initial jump in the price level inflation was on a downward trend, its reduction to low digit levels was proving difficult. According to a 1995 United Nations publication, 'there are limits to the degree of price stabilization that can be achieved with purely macroeconomic measures....Further progress in curbing inflation seems to require addressing more closely the microeconomic and structural issues such as market imperfections, competition, enterprise behaviour, structure of public spending, and expectations of economic agents and the general public.'[7]

Some consequences of inflation were mentioned by a 1994 IMF publication. The experience of post-communist countries confirms, it stated, 'that higher inflation does not deliver increased ouput in the medium term. If anything, higher inflation is associated with lower growth. In the very short run, there may appear to be a positive relationship to the extent that higher inflation postpones output

Table 15.1   Consumer price Inflation, Selected Post-Communist Countries, 1989–95 (per cent)

	1989	1990	1991	1992	1993	1994	1995
Bulgaria	6.4	23.9	333.5	82.0	72.8	96.0	62.1
Czechoslovakia	1.4	10.8	59.0	11.0	...	...	...
Czech Republic	...	...	...	...	20.8	10.0	9.1
Slovak Republic	...	...	...	...	23.0	13.4	9.9
Eastern Germany	...	...	12.8	11.1	8.4	3.7	...
Hungary	16.9	29.0	34.2	23.0	22.5	18.8	28.2
Poland	251.1	585.8	70.3	43.0	35.3	32.2	27.8
Romania	0.9	4.7	161.1	210.3	256.0	136.8	32.3
Russia	2.4	5.6	92.7	1 353.0	896.0	302.0	190.2

Sources: IMF, *World Economic Outlook*, May 1996, p. 133, Table A13; DIW, *Wochenbericht*, various issues.

declines. But higher inflation also jeopardizes the limited reserves of goodwill and credibility existing at the beginning of the transition process, creates an even more uncertain investment climate, and ultimately exacerbates a largely inevitable output drop.'[8]

In many of the post-communist countries not included in Table 15.1, it should be noted, average annual inflation rates were considerably higher that those in Russia, and in some of them continued to exceed those in Russia even in 1995.

15.3 OUTPUT

In the Soviet-bloc countries, it was noted in Section 12.2, economic growth was slowing down between the early 1950s and the late 1980s. When communism collapsed and economic transformation started, post-communist countries experienced a sharp fall in output, i.e., in the level of recorded economic activity. However, in Poland and eastern Germany economic growth had already resumed in 1992, and in some other post-communist countries not long afterwards, in 1993 or 1994.

For the 1989–95 period, changes in GDP are to be found in Table 15.2 and those in industrial output in Table 15.3. In addition, Table 15.4 presents indices of GDP and gross industrial output. It shows that in 1994 the level of recorded economic activity continued to be below that in 1989, in a number of cases considerably, and that with the exception of Russia the fall in gross industrial output was steeper than the fall in GDP.

Table 15.2 Changes in GDP, Selected Post-Communist Countries, 1989–95 (per cent change over previous year)

	1989	1990	1991	1992	1993	1994	1995
Bulgaria	−0.5	−9.1	−11.7	−7.3	−1.5	1.8	2.6
Czechoslovakia	4.5	−0.4	−15.9	−8.5	...	...	...
Czech Republic	...	...	...	...	−0.9	2.6	4.8
Slovak Republic	...	...	...	...	−3.7	4.9	7.4
Eastern Germany	...	...	−28.4	9.7	5.8	8.5	...
Hungary	0.7	−3.5	−11.9	−3.1	−0.6	2.9	1.5
Poland	0.2	−11.6	−7.0	2.6	3.8	6.0	6.5
Romania	−5.8	−5.6	−12.9	−8.8	1.3	3.9	6.9
Russia	...	...	−13.0	−19.0	−12.0	−15.0	−4.0

Sources: IMF, *World Economic Outlook*, May 1996, p. 125, Table A7; ibid., October 1996, p. 177, Table A7; DIW, *Wochenbericht*, various issues.

Transformation

Table 15.3 Changes in Industrial Output, Selected Post-Communist
Countries, 1989–95 (per cent change over previous year)

	1989	1990	1991	1992	1993	1994	1995
Bulgaria	2.2	−16.8	−27.8	−15.0	−6.9	4.1	5.2
Czechoslovakia	0.8	−3.7	−23.0	−7.9	...	...	...
Czech Republic	...	...	...	...	−5.1	2.3	9.5
Slovak Republic	...	...	...	...	−10.6	6.4	8.7
Hungary	−1.0	−9.6	−18.2	−9.7	4.0	9.5	4.8
Poland	−0.5	−24.2	−11.9	3.9	5.6	13.0	6.9
Romania	−5.3	−23.7	−22.8	−21.9	1.3	3.3	8.9
Russia	1.4	−0.1	−8.0	−18.8	−16.2	−22.8	−3.0

Sources: United Nations, *World Economic and Social Survey 1996*, New York,
1996, p. 314, Table A.10; *Russian Economic Trends*, vol. 4, no. 4 (1995), p. 113,
Table A.2.

Table 15.4 Indices of GDP (A) and Gross Industrial Output (B) Selected
Post-Communist Countries, 1989–94 (1989 = 100)

	1990	1991	1992	1993	1994
Bulgaria	A 90.9	80.2	75.7	74.5	74.7
	B 83.2	64.7	54.4	49.0	50.0
Czechoslovakia	A 98.5	84.4	78.8	...	...
	B 96.5	75.2	67.6	...	...
Czech Republic	A 98.8	84.7	79.2	78.4	80.5
	B 96.5	73.0	67.2	63.6	65.1
Slovak Republic	A 97.5	83.3	77.5	75.0	78.6
	B 95.5	78.7	67.6	60.5	64.3
Eastern Germany	A 84.5	68.2	73.6	77.8	84.8
	B 72.7	37.0	34.7	36.7	42.2
Hungary	A 96.5	85.0	81.4	79.5	81.1
	B 95.5	77.3	69.7	72.4	79.0
Poland	A 88.4	82.2	84.4	87.5	91.9
	B 75.8	66.8	69.4	74.4	84.1
Romania	A 94.4	82.2	74.0	75.0	77.5
	B 81.9	63.3	49.4	50.1	51.6
Russia	A 97.0	84.6	68.3	60.1	51.1
	B 99.9	91.9	75.3	64.7	51.2

Source: Economic Commission for Europe, *Economic Survey of Europe in
1994–1995*, New York, United Nations, 1995, p. 249, Appendix Table B.1 and
p. 250, Appendix Table B.2.

Neither Table 15.2 nor Table 15.4 takes into consideration, though,
that in the autumn of 1995 the figures for Russia's GDP were revised
by the State Statistical Committee (Goskomstat) in collaboration with

the World Bank. According to the revised figures, between 1990 and 1994 Russia's GDP declined by about a third only, not by almost a half as previously reported.[9]

Almost certainly, all the figures given in the three tables exaggerate the magnitude of the fall in output in the early years of economic transformation, partly because communist statistics tended to over-state output,[10] but mainly because the level of unrecorded economic activity increased after the collapse of communism. Consequently, the fall in output was somewhat less sharp than official statistics portray. Nevertheless, output did fall, and was caused by both demand-side factors and supply-side factors.

The demand-side factors discussed by John Williamson[11] are a fall in external demand due to the dismantling of the Council for Mutual Economic Assistance (CMEA) and recession in the West, overvalued currency, Keynesian demand deficiency (restrictive macroeconomic policy), a shortage of foreign exchange, and demand-shift, a special case of which occurs when goods that were formerly produced are no longer wanted. The supply-side factors discussed by him are exogen-ous shocks (Russian oil), uneconomic output (production of goods with negative value-added), input dislocation, a credict squeeze, and monopoly pricing.

In connection with this taxonomy of possible causes of output collapse in post-communist countries, Williamson emphasized that some output losses were positively desirable, others were unavoidable, and still others were in the nature of an investment. The output losses that constituted a benefit and not a cost were the production of fewer unwanted goods and the ending of the production of goods with negative value-added.

All in all, economic transformation initially resulted in a sharp fall in output. This fall in output, also called 'transformation recession', was caused by a combination of various factors,[12] the weights of which varied from one post-communist country to another. If deficiencies of official statistics are left aside, these factors may be divided into external and internal, and the latter then into systemic change and the behaviour and attitudes of economic as well as political actors, thus including, *inter alia*, the existence and duration of a temporary systemic vacuum, the design and implementation of the economic transformation programme, and political and social stability or instability.

However, the fall in output in the early years of economic transform-ation did not necessarily have an adverse impact on the welfare of the population. To the extent to which output contraction meant a reduction in or the elimination of the production of unwanted goods and goods with negative value-added, it actually contributed to the general welfare.

15.4   OPEN UNEMPLOYMENT

In the Soviet-bloc countries, as already noted in Section 12.2, labour force participation rates for men and women alike were high; participation in social production was predominantly on a full-time basis and was expected to be continuous and lifelong; registered unemployment did not exist because open unemployment was not officially regarded as a separate risk; and unregistered unemployment was low. However, this situation in the labour market concealed that the employed labour force was considerably underutilized, with overmanning (i.e., unemployment on the job) being chronic and general and reaching mass proportions. Expressed differently, open unemployment was kept down by hidden unemployment and wages partly assumed the function of unemployment benefits.

Hence, although these economies were high-employment ones, simultaneously they were low-productivity and low-incentive ones. It is not surprising, then, that economic transformation had a noticeable impact on the labour market: temporary and permanent withdrawals from the labour force took place, absolute levels of employment declined,[13] and registered unemployment came into being. At the same time, as Table 15.5 shows, the rates of registered unemployment varied greatly from one post-communist country to another.

A combination of factors contributed to low rates of registered unemployment in the Czech Republic. They included a fall in labour force participation, employment and self- employment opportunities in the rapidly expanding private sector, wage moderation, commuting to work abroad (West Germany, Austria), work for foreign subcontractors, creation of the so-called socially useful jobs, a stringent unemployment compensation scheme, and a reluctance on the part of state enterprises to sack excess workers.

In Russia, according to the conducted labour force surveys using the ILO definition of unemployment, the rates of unemployment were significantly higher that those of registered unemployment given in Table 15.5, namely, 4.8 per cent in 1992, 5.5 per cent in 1993, 7.1 per cent in 1994, and 8.2 per cent in 1995.[14] In addition, under the impact

Table 15.5   Registered Unemployment, Selected Post-Communist Countries, 1989–95 (as per cent of the labour force, end of the year)

	1989	1990	1991	1992	1993	1994	1995
Bulgaria	0.0	1.6	11.7	13.3	16.4	12.8	10.5
Czech Republic	0.0	0.8	4.1	2.6	3.5	3.2	3.0
Slovak Republic	0.0	1.5	11.8	10.4	14.4	14.8	13.1
Eastern Germany	0.0	8.6*	11.6	14.8	15.6	15.3	14.0
Hungary	0.5	1.6	7.5	12.3	12.1	10.4	10.4
Poland	0.3	6.3	11.8	13.6	15.7	16.0	14.9
Romania	n.a.	1.3	2.7	8.4	10.2	10.9	8.9
Russia	0.0	0.0	0.1	0.8	1.1	2.1	2.6
Memorandum item							
EC (annual averages)	8.9	8.3	8.9	9.7	10.9	11.3	10.7

* JANUARY 1991.

Sources: J.L. Porket, *Unemployment in Capitalist, Communist and Post-Communist Economies*, Basingstoke, Macmillan, 1995, p. 99, Table 11.1; EIU, *Country Reports*, various issues; DIW, *Wochenbericht*, various issues.

of falling demand, supply difficulties, and financial problems, state enterprises put some workers on short-time working and sent others on paid, partially paid, or unpaid leave.

There were several reasons why workers were willing to accept lower or no wages, if this saved their jobs. *Inter alia*, they did not lose their social standing; retained access to important non-cash benefits, especially housing and health care; and could continue to use the enterprise's tools and equipment for second economy activities. However, state enterprises also had reasons for not resorting to compulsory redundancies. One of them was financial considerations, i.e., to avoid paying severance pay.[15]

Besides high rates of registered unemployment, eastern Germany had short-time working and participation in state subsidized job-creation schemes, training programmes, and early retirement schemes. If these labour market policies had not been implemented, the unemployment rate would have been about 38 per cent in July 1992, and if the strain on the labour market had not been alleviated by daily commuting to western Germany, it would have reached 45 per cent. In early 1995, on the same assumptions, the unemployment rate would have been 25 and 32 per cent, respectively.[16]

Generally, in post-communist countries industrial employment declined at a slower rate than industrial output did. Consequently, also labour productivity in industry also declined substantially. To give an example, from 1988 to 1992, in Hungarian industry output fell by 42.2 per cent, employment by 30.9 per cent, and labour productivity (measured as the ratio of real output to employment) by 16.4 per cent.[17] In Polish industry, average output per employee was only about 75 per cent of the 1989 level in 1991, but reached 88 per cent of the 1989 level in 1992, met that level in 1993, and exceeded it by almost 15 per cent in 1994.[18]

Since employment declined at a slower rate than output did, over-manning in the state sector was not eliminated.[19] Underlying its persistence were two factors. One was budgetary considerations: because it kept registered unemployment down, it eased the pressure on the state budget. The other was the belief that, by keeping regis-tered unemployment down, it reduced the danger of social unrest and socio-political instability.

Naturally, the persistence of overmanning perpetuated an ineffi-cient allocation of labour. At the same time, the establishment of unemployment compensation schemes gave rise to welfare scroun-gers, who assumed the role of registered unemployed (claimant) with-out being genuinely interested in getting a paid job. In Hungary, János Köllo wrote in 1995, 'many unemployed workers do casual work or are employed illegally. An unknown but not negligible part of the [unemployment] benefits in fact serves as wage subsidies for illegal businesses.'[20]

15.5 THE GOVERNMENT ECONOMY

Economic transformation in the sense of the transformation of com-mand socialism into market capitalism requires not only a tight monetary policy, but also a responsible fiscal policy. That is to say, fiscal policy[21] is critical for the success of macroeconomic stabiliza-tion. At the same time, the transformation process itself has important implications for government budgets, and the fiscal balance is an important signal about the government's commitment to macroeco-nomic stabilization. In the absence of well-established government securities markets, budget deficits tend to be financed largely through money creation.

The collapse of communism had an adverse impact on government revenues. Between 1989 and 1993, government revenues as a percen-tage of GDP fell by about 20 percentage points in Bulgaria, the Czech Republic, Slovakia, and Romania, but remained fairly stable in

Table 15.6 Subsidies, Selected Post-Communist Countries, 1989–93, (as per cent of GDP)

	1989	1990	1991	1992	1993	1994
Bulgaria	15.5	14.9	4.1	1.8	2.2	1.3
Czechoslovakia	25.0	16.2	7.7	...	...	...
Czech Republic	...	...	...	5.0	3.9	3.4
Slovak Republic	...	...	...	5.4	4.8	...
Hungary	12.1	9.5	7.4	5.5	4.3	4.5
Poland	12.9	7.3	5.1	3.2	2.2	2.2
Romania	5.7	7.9	8.1	12.9	5.5	3.8
Russia	...	...	...	14.2	7.3	...

Source: IMF, *World Economic Outlook*, October 1994, pp. 82–83, and *ibid.*, May 1996, p. 81, Table 20.

Hungary and Poland. This was a result of the fall in the level of recorded economic activity, price liberalization, privatization, tax arrears, tax evasion, and the overhaul of the inherited tax system.[22]

Government spending too was affected by the collapse of communism. On the one hand, government spending as a percentage of GDP fell between 1989 and 1993 by about ten or more percentage points in Bulgaria, the Czech Republic, Slovakia, and Romania, albeit not in Hungary and Poland. The reduction was due mainly to cuts in subsidies, shown in Table 15.6. On the other hand, government spending was boosted by the inevitable creation of social safety nets.

As discussed in Section 14.1, economic transformation needs an adequate social safety net that cushions the most vulnerable groups of the population from its impact and, simultaneously, ensures political support for it. However, economic transformation also needs an overhaul of the inherited cradle-to-grave welfare state financed through taxation and the profits of state enterprises.[23] This implies, *inter alia*, that it is necessary to divest state enterprises of their social role, consisting of the provision of housing, health care, crèches, job security, etc. If state enterprises were not divested of their social role, economic transformation would be delayed or even undermined.

Faced with a fall in government revenues and pressure on government spending, most post-communist countries were not able to balance government budgets. As the figures presented in Table 15.7 indicate, budget deficits were often substantial. In the case of Russia, it should be added in this connection, some Western estimates put the overall budget deficit at 31.2 per cent of GDP in 1992 and at 14.1 per cent in 1993.[24]

Table 15.7   Budget Deficits, Selected Post-Communist Countries, 1989–95,
(as per cent of GDP)

	1989	1990	1991	1992	1993	1994	1995
Bulgaria	−1.4	−12.8	−14.7	−15.0	−15.7	−7.0	−6.0
Czech Republic	...	...	...	−2.2	0.6	−1.3	−1.6
Slovak Republic	...	...	...	−11.9	−7.1	−1.3	−0.4
Hungary	−1.3	0.9	−3.0	−6.8	−6.7	−8.6	−6.7
Poland	−8.0	3.3	−6.7	−8.0	−4.0	−2.0	−2.7
Romania	8.4	1.1	−1.7	−4.6	−0.1	−1.0	−2.5
Russia	...	...	...	−18.9	−7.6	−10.1	−4.8

Source: IMF, *World Economic Outlook*, May 1996, p. 78, Table 18.

Eastern Germany, not included in the table, deserves a separate note. German unification was financed by western Germany. Gross public sector transfers from western Germany to eastern Germany amounted to 75.6 per cent of eastern German GDP in 1991, to 74.0 per cent in 1992, to 69.6 per cent in 1993, to 61.1 per cent in 1994, and to 56.2 per cent in 1995. Of these transfers, about two-thirds went on consumption (wage subsidies, unemployment pay, and other social security benefits) and only about one-third was earmarked for investment.[25]

The costs of unification were financed partly by tax increases levied on the western German population, partly (and mainly) by public sector borrowing. Consequently, the budget deficit grew sharply. The bulging budget deficit together with a fear of rising open inflation then pushed German interest rates up and these, in turn, contributed to rising open unemployment in Europe and put the exchange rate mechanism (ERM) – which had become a means of exporting the costs of unification – under strain, until it effectively collapsed in mid-1993.

CONCLUSION

One of the professed goals of post-communist societies was the transformation of command socialism into market capitalism and, thus, the achievement of higher living standards and greater economic freedom (conceived as being concerned with property rights and choice). Nevertheless, these societies differed both in respect of the beginning of economic transformation and in respect of the design and implementation of the economic transformation programme. At the same time, the transformation process tended to deviate more or less from the original design.

From the outset, an important difference to emerge between individual post-communist societies was about the dynamics of implementation of the transformation strategy, about the speed, comprehensiveness, sequencing, sectoralism, and intensity of economic transformation. Judging by the available evidence, radical economic transformation (giving priority to macroeconomic stabilization and liberalization, closely followed by privatization) worked better than a gradualist approach, which usually complicated and prolonged economic transformation due to its vacillation. The harmful consequences of gradualist policies in Russia (where shock therapy was initially intended but, in fact, was not applied consistently), Ukraine, and Belarus may serve as eminent examples.

Irrespective of the adopted transformation strategy and the actual progress of economic transformation, deficiencies of official statistics were a problem everywhere. They stemmed from changes and weaknesses in data gathering and the statistical methods used, distorted reality, inhibited meaningful comparisons over time as well as across countries, and misled both politicians and the public. Of course, as noted by Salvatore Zecchini, some of the statistical problems faced by post-communist countries were somewhat similar to those encountered by OECD countries, e.g., the measurement of the second economy.[26]

16 Privatization

After the collapse of communism and the start of economic transformation, post-communist societies began to experience price liberalization, a fall in output, a fall in labour force participation, the emergence of registered unemployment, a fall in government revenues, pressure on government spending, and budget deficits. Simultaneously, though, they faced a number of other problems, one of them being privatization, i.e., change in the ownership of productive assets, land, and housing.

16.1 PRIVATIZATION IN THE WEST

Market capitalism is based on private ownership of the means of production and market coordination. Nevertheless, in capitalist market economies there always exists a smaller or larger public sector too. It means that part of the economy which is publicly owned, and includes non-marketed production of goods and services by the government as well as marketed production of goods and services by public enterprises.

Public ownership of the means of production and, hence, also nationalization of private firms, has been advocated and brought about on fiscal, economic, social, ideological, political, and military grounds. More specifically, the reason for it has been, *inter alia*, to raise government revenue through state-owned monopolies on the sale of tobacco, salt, alcohol, and other products; to correct market failures such as natural monopolies, externalities, and lack of private initiative; to rationalize production, sustain or accelerate economic growth, and stimulate regional development; to preserve and create jobs and keep open unemployment down; to eliminate incomes from property (profit and rent) and the exploitation of wage labour by capital; to promote social justice; to enable the state to assume a dominant position in the economy, and to facilitate the introduction of central planning; and to change the nature of the economic system.[1]

Besides, national security and the conduct of war have been factors leading to permanent or at least temporary nationalization. According to John Keegan, for instance, '[s]o important to national defence were

196

the railways held by the Prussian, later Imperial German, government that by 1860 half had been taken into public ownership, and the whole twenty years later.'[2] The examples of temporary nationalization are French railways 1914–21, US rail 1917–20, and UK rail 1914–21.[3]

Nationalization was in fashion particularly after the end of the Second World War, and frequently took place under the impact of circumstances the war brought into existence. It did not cease during the following three decades or so, with governments passing nationalization acts especially between the mid-1960s and the mid-1970s. Around 1980, in Western economies the share in total value added (or output) of state enterprises and public corporations was on average slightly over nine per cent, ranging from 1.3 per cent in the case of the United States to 16.5 per cent in the case of France.[4] In connection with these figures it deserves to be noted that, in contrast to continental Europe, in the United States private and profit-seeking utilities have always been the rule rather than the exception.

By the end of the 1970s, though, nationalization was going out of fashion and privatization was coming into vogue. Its pioneer was Britain, where the first step towards it was the sale of council houses, which began in 1979. It spread during the 1980s and continued in the the first half of the 1990s, with governments throughout the world (in Britain, Western Europe, Asia, Latin America, and elsewhere)[5] selling off state-owned firms. Between 1985 and 1992, these governments raised through privatization some \$328 billion.[6] And while in 1990 the global value of privatization totalled almost \$30 billion, in 1996 it totalled \$88 billion.[7]

Consequently, privatization was a source of revenue, a means to finance budget deficits and pay for social security costs run up by open unemployment and ageing populations. However, this was not the only reason for it. The other reasons were to widen share ownership, promote economic efficiency, encourage competition, attract foreign investment and, sometimes, to break the power of public-sector trade unions. In any case, it was expected to reduce the role of the state in the economy, to roll back its frontiers.

Yet, privatization was not confined to denationalization, i.e., to the sale of public sector assets to the private sector, but took the form of deregulation (the opening of state activities to private sector competition) and tendering (the contracting-out of public provision to private firms) as well. Be that as it may, by the end of 1996 it still was not completed and, at the same time, in some countries the political commitment to it continued not to be excessively strong.

16.2 POST-COMMUNIST PRIVATIZATION

In contrast to capitalist market economies, in the Soviet- bloc countries with their variants of command socialism most of the means of production were publicly owned. By the end of the 1980s, i.e., shortly before the collapse of communism, the share of the public sector usually amounted to over 95 per cent. Lower shares were to be found exclusively in Hungary (92.9 per cent) and Poland (81.2 per cent).[8] On top of that, in terms of the number of employed persons, state enterprises were on average noticeably larger than Western firms, so that the concentration of production was much higher than that in capitalist market economies.[9]

Since most of the means of production were publicly owned and since state enterprises tended to be of considerable size, privatization in post-communist societies was likely to be more complicated than privatization in capitalist market economies. Besides, it was likely to face various other obstacles, such as uncertainty over property rights, the difficulty of correctly pricing the assets, the problem of finding domestic and foreign buyers, vested interests, and hostile attitudes. Yet, inasmuch as one of the professed goals of post-communist societies was the transformation of command socialism into market capitalism and, thus, the achievement of higher living standards and greater economic freedom, privatization was inevitable. After all, private ownership motivates economic actors, whereas public ownership acts as a disincentive. As a result, private firms tend to be more efficient and more responsive to effective demand than state enterprises. No less significantly, private ownership puts a check on political power, whereas public ownership increases its scope and, hence, constitutes a constraint for the market.

Private firms tend to be more efficient than state enterprises because, operating on their own account and at their own risk, they must show profit if they want to survive (i.e., avoid bankruptcy) and expand. Their efficiency is enhanced by the existence of competition and reduced by its absence and/or undue government intervention. In contrast, state enterprises tend to be less efficient than private firms because they need not fear bankruptcy and because they are not able to escape government intervention. In addition, the absence of competition contributes to their inefficiency. However, exposure to competition or threat of privatization might induce greater efficiency on their part.

It follows that efficiency is affected on the one hand by whether the means of production are privately or publicly owned, and on the other hand by whether private firms and state enterprises face competition or not. This applies to both productive efficiency (which is achieved when a given output is produced with minimum costs) and allocative efficiency (which is achieved when the economy's resources and output are allocated in such a way that no reallocation can make anyone better off without making at least one other person worse off). Consequently, there are four possibilities, namely, private ownership combined with a competitive market, private ownership combined with the absence of a competitive market, public ownership combined with the absence of a competitive market, and public ownership combined with a competitive market. Of these four possibilities, private ownership combined with a competitive market and public ownership combined with the absence of a competitive market are polar cases: the former induces productive as well as allocative efficiency, the latter induces productive as well as allocative inefficiency.

All in all, in the interest of achieving higher living standards and greater economic freedom, in post-communist societies economic transformation requires not only the substitution of market coordination for state coordination, but also the substitution of private ownership of the means of production for public ownership of the means of production. As put by Peter L. Berger, '[t]here can be no effective market economy without private ownership of the means of production.'[10]

Expressed differently, in post-communist societies economic transformation means the transformation of command socialism into market capitalism. So conceived, economic transformation implies the substitution of a demand-constrained system for the resource-constrained (supply-constrained) system, the substitution of a buyers' market for the sellers' market, and the substitution of hard budget constraint (and, hence, productive efficiency) for soft budget constraint (and, hence, productive inefficiency).

However, the reasons for the transformation in post-communist societies of command socialism into market capitalism are not exclusively economic, i.e., the achievement of higher living standards and greater economic freedom. They are political too, because democracy is dependent on market capitalism. That is to say, market capitalism (which is the only economically viable type of modern economic system) is a necessary (albeit not sufficient) condition for democracy.

16.3 METHODS OF PRIVATIZATION

Since in the Soviet-bloc countries most of the means of production were publicly owned, post-communist societies inevitably faced the difficult problem of their privatization, of their transfer to private hands.[11] Yet, as Joseph E. Stiglitz recalled, 'privatization itself is only one means of achieving a market economy. Establishing new enterprises is the other.'[12]

The proponents of gradualism went considerably further, though. According to Peter Murrell, for instance, the appropriate goal of economic transformation was the creation of a new private sector, not privatization of the state enterprise system, because the latter was bound to be a long and costly process, using resources that might be more profitably employed in facilitating the former.[13] A similar view was expressed by L. Haddad, who argued that 'a minimalist approach to reforming SOEs [state-owned enterprises] combined with a maximalist strategy for developing the private sector, through the "organic" growth of small and medium-size firms, would prove less disruptive and less costly [than a privatization rush]. It would also, in the long run, achieve the objectives of reform more quickly. With the growth of the private sector the state sector would diminish until a balanced blend of the two sectors was reached.'[14]

Hence, the gradualist or evolutionary approach preferred the creation and growth of a new private sector to privatization of state enterprises. If this approach were adopted in practice, a large public sector would continue to exist and predominate for a very long time. The private sector might be expanding over time, but would not cease to be relatively small and fragile. On top of that, there would be no guarantee that, ultimately, it would succeed in crowding out the public sector.

It follows that although in post-communist societies spontaneous formation of new private firms (sometimes called bottom-up transformation) is an important part of economic transformation, it does not remove the need for privatization of state enterprises, for the so-called top-down transformation.[15] As suggested by the present author elsewhere,[16] privatization of state enterprises has by its nature four interdependent dimensions, concerned with *who* gets *what*, *when*, and *how*.

The *who*, i.e., the recipients of property rights, may be either insiders or outsiders. The former, who could also be labelled as squatters, consist of current employees (including managers) of the state enterprises to be privatized, collective farmers cultivating the land to be privatized, and occupiers of apartments. The latter are other private individuals (be they citizens or not) and domestic and foreign institutions (banks, companies, pension funds, etc.) Thus, privatization is inherently a process of property distribution.

Small, medium-sized, and large state enterprises, land, and housing constitute the *what*, which must precisely define the property that is to be privatized. In the case of state enterprises this means their corporatization (commercialization), denoting a process of turning them into joint-stock or limited liability companies still wholly owned by the state and of establishing in them Western-type managerial structures (corporate governance). As part of the process, some state enterprises (especially large ones) may be broken up into separate, smaller units.

While the *what* is about the extent (comprehensiveness) of privatization, the *when* is about its speed. In essence, the speed of privatization depends on whether it is launched quickly or put off to a later time, and on whether it proceeds case-by-case or cluster-by-cluster or occurs all at once. The reasons for delays in its implementation include technical problems, political bickering, grass roots resistance, and the adoption of the principle of restitution (i.e., return of property to original private owners).

Finally, the *how* is the question of privatization methods. If restitution is disregarded, the main ones are leasing, sales to outsiders, management and worker buy-outs, management and worker transfers, and voucher schemes. Since these methods are not mutually exclusive, their combination is possible. At the same time, most of them require the establishment of privatization agencies, either independent (such as holding companies or mutual funds) or governmental.

Each method has its advantages and disadvantages. For instance, free hand-over of state-owned assets to their current users would speed up privatization, but would deprive the state of revenue.[17] The same applies to free distribution of vouchers which, on top of that, would disperse ownership widely.[18] Sales to domestic and foreign outsiders would generate revenue for the state but, in the event of lack of capital or interest, would slow down privatization.

Irrespective of *who* gets *what*, *when*, and *how*, privatization of state enterprises inevitably gives rise to the need for developing capital markets (absent in socialist command economies) and creating private commercial banks. So does, of course, spontaneous formation of new private firms. After all, capitalism cannot exist without well-functioning capital markets which, in turn, cannot do without commercial banks that are repositories of financial information on existing firms as well as institutions primarily responsible for payment settlements.[19]

The reason why capitalism cannot exist without well-functioning capital markets follows from the functions these markets fulfil. Joseph E. Stiglitz mentioned eight central ones:

1. transferring capital from those who have it (savers) to those who can make use of it (borrowers or investors), because in any capitalist economy there is never a perfect coincidence between those who have funds and those who can make use of them;
2. agglomerating capital, because many projects require more capital than is available to any single saver or to any small set of savers;
3. selecting projects, because there are always more individuals who claim that they have good uses for resources than there are funds available;
4. monitoring, because it ensures that funds are used in the way promised;
5. enforcing contracts, because those who have borrowed must be made to repay the funds;
6. transferring, sharing, and pooling risk, because capital markets not only raise funds, but the rules that determine repayment determine who bears what risk;
7. diversifying risk, because by pooling a large number of investment projects together, the total risk is reduced; and
8. recording transactions, because especially banks can be thought of as running as the medium of exchange, including activities such as cheque clearing.[20]

16.4   PRIVATIZATION IN PRACTICE

As a result of German unification, it was noted in Section 15.1, economic transformation in eastern Germany differed – and considerably at that – from that in the other post- communist countries. This applied to privatization too. A voucher scheme was rejected in favour of restitution, direct sales to outsiders, and management buy-outs. The process, which proved to be swift and successful albeit extremely costly, was in the hands of the Treuhandanstalt (Treuhand in brief), a government trustee agency wound up on schedule at the end of 1994 with a sizeable deficit of some DM 250–270 billion, a sum equal to the total GDP of eastern Germany in 1994.[21]

Since in eastern Germany economic transformation was financed by western Germany, Treuhand-type privatization was not appropriate elsewhere, and was not adopted by any of the other post-communist countries, perhaps with the exception of Estonia which attempted to emulate it. Consequently, outside eastern Germany the extent, speed, and methods of privatization varied widely from one post-communist country to another. Nevertheless, voucher privatization was used in a number of cases, including Mongolia.[22]

In general, small-scale privatization focusing on retail trade, catering, and consumer services proceeded faster than large-scale privatization of state enterprises did.[23] In mid-1996, according to a rough EBRD estimate covering 25 post-communist countries, the share in GDP of the private sector reached 75 per cent in Albania and the Czech Republic, 70 per cent in Estonia, Hungary, and Slovakia, 65 per cent in Lithuania, 60 per cent in Latvia, Poland, Romania, and Russia, 50 per cent in Armenia, Croatia, Georgia, Kyrgyzstan, and Macedonia, 45 per cent in Bulgaria and Slovenia, 40 per cent in Kazakhstan, Moldova, Ukraine, and Uzbekistan, and less in the remaining four countries.[24]

Hence, although the share in GDP (as well as employment) of the private sector had been growing steadily over the years, in mid-1996 privatization still was not completed in post-communist countries, including the most advanced ones such as the Czech Republic, Hungary, and Poland. Moreover, besides being mere rough estimates, the figures just quoted conceal various (and far from insignificant) problems connected with privatization.

The collapse of communism created opportunities for unofficial or wild privatization, one form of which was the establishment by state enterprise managers (usually in cahoots with trusted outsiders) of parallel private firms. In some cases, a portion of the state enterprise's income was channelled to such a private firm by contracting out to it some of the state enterprise's supplies or sales and manipulating price differentials. In other cases, some of the state enterprise's productive assets were transferred or leased to such a private firm.[25]

It has to be remembered, though, that in socialist command economies too informal (de facto) privatization was not totally absent. As already noted in Section 7.6, in these economies the persons employed in state enterprises (be they managers or workers) engaged in illegal appropriation of public property, i.e., in its diversion (theft) and unauthorized use for private purposes. Collective farmers, it should be added, were no exception.

Besides creating opportunities for unofficial or wild privatization, the collapse of communism created opportunities for opposition and resistance to privatization, stemming from vested interests, reluctance to discard old routines, unwillingness to learn and adapt, uncertainty about the outcome of privatization, and the expected costs of privatization. After all, state enterprises had much to lose in the event of their privatization: while command socialism discouraged individual effort, initiative, risk-taking, and responsibility, state enterprises were not exposed to the pressure of market forces and were not threatened by bankruptcy, so that they had a soft budget constraint and lacked an incentive to economize on resources, including labour; while under command socialism the pursuit of self-interest was officially rejected and the primacy of societal interests as defined by the government was officially stressed, in practice state enterprises were able to pursue their own economic interests by persistently seeking a rent and its maximization.

An inevitable consequence of the collapse of communism was the appearance of a temporary systemic vacuum, characterized by political, legal, economic, and social uncertainty. In these circumstances, state enterprises became survival orientated, i.e., tried to ensure their continuing existence. Therefore, they placed more emphasis on current cash flow than on the long-run value of their assets and, to keep afloat in face of falling demand, began financing their operations by running up debts to each other as well as by tax arrears and bank loans.[26]

State enterprises' survival-orientated behaviour with its clear bias towards realizing income and its no less clear bias against both employment-reducing restructuring and investing for the future was quite often condoned by post-communist governments. This follows from these governments' adverse attitudes towards bankruptcies of state enterprises.[27] Indeed, bankruptcies of state enterprises were rare during the first half of the 1990s, despite the fact that, at world-market prices, some of the state enterprises were not only making a loss (i.e., their revenues were less than the total sum of their costs of labour, capital, and material inputs), but subtracting value (i.e., their revenues failed to cover even the cost of material inputs).

If the appearance of a temporary systemic vacuum was one inevitable consequence of the collapse of communism, the appearance of a temporary power vacuum within state enterprises was another. Expressed differently, corporate governance of state enterprises was loosened and, in extreme cases, lacking altogether. Thus, the behaviour of managers and workers underwent a noticeable change, and so did relations between them.

However, also the privatization of state enterprises raised the question of effective corporate governance. In particular, this is implied in the nature of voucher privatization: its advantage is not only that it is likely to be popular, but that it can be implemented without undue delay in a relatively short time, because it renders *ex ante* pricing unnecessary as long as there is no foreign participation; its disadvange is that it may result in ownership being spread too thinly, so that individual shareholders would not be able effectively to control the managers of privatized firms.

CONCLUSION

Private ownership of the means of production motivates economic actors, encourages efficiency and responsiveness to effective demand, and puts a check on political power. These motivational, economic, and political consequences of private ownership of the means of production contrast diametrically with the motivational, economic, and political consequences of public ownership of the means of production.

While without private ownership of the means of production no market economy can function effectively, without market coordination private ownership of the means of production loses its *raison d'être*. In the long run, neither is able to exist without the other. Together, they constitute market capitalism which, besides being the only economically viable type of modern economic system, is a necessary (albeit not sufficient) condition for democracy.

Hence, in post-communist societies economic transformation requires not only the substitution of market coordination for state coordination, but also the substitution of private ownership of the means of production for public ownership of the means of production. The latter then entails not only privatization of the established state enterprises, but also creation of conditions for spontaneous formation of new private firms.

In practice, privatization in post-communist societies of state enterprises faces a number of political, economic, social, and cultural obstacles. Simultaneously, it gives rise to a number of problems, including enterprise restructuring, enterprise behaviour, unofficial or wild privatization, the definition and protection of property rights, effective corporate governance, and the building of supportive institutions such as capital markets and private commercial banks.

Despite these obstacles and problems, during the first half of the 1990s privatization of state enterprises was taking place in post-communist countries. However, its extent, speed, and methods varied widely from one post-communist country to another. In mid-1996, if eastern Germany is disregarded, it still was not completed anywhere, not excluding the most advanced post-communist countries. At the same time, everywhere it continued to bc in need of further support-ive institution-building.

17 Households

One of the professed goals of post-communist societies was the achievement of higher living standards and greater economic freedom. Initially, though, the obstacles facing economic transformation and the hardships caused by it tended to be underestimated. That it to say, it tended to be forgotten that economic transformation would involve both costs and benefits, that these costs and benefits must be weighed against each other, and that short-term costs were necessary in the interest of long-term benefits.

17.1 HOUSEHOLD INCOME

In the Soviet-bloc countries, households enjoyed a regular (albeit modest) income. However, when shopping in the first economy at the officially set retail prices, they were able to choose exclusively from a limited range of consumer goods and services of low quality and outdated design, yet quite often relatively expensive. On top of that, they had to cope with chronic shortages, i.e., with unsatisfied effective demand.

Although household income was increasing over the decades, it was increasing noticeably more slowly than that in the developed capitalist market economies. Consequently, as concluded in Section 12.2, from approximately the mid-1960s to the late 1980s the gap between the standard of living in the Soviet-bloc countries and that in the developed capitalist market economies widened substantially to the detriment of the former.[1]

Economic transformation had a profound impact on households. On the one hand, it eliminated the existing monetary overhang and chronic shortages, because retail prices began to reflect consumers' preferences and scarcity, and improved product composition as well as households' access to foreign goods. On the other hand, it resulted in withdrawals from the labour force, open unemployment, a fall in real wages, and greater income disparities.

Changes in real wages are given in Table 17.1 which shows that between 1989 and 1994 real wage fall and growth varied considerably from one post-communist country to another. In Russia, not included

Table 17.1   Changes in Real Wages, Selected Post-Communist Countries,
              1989–95 (per cent change over previous year)

	1989	1990	1991	1992	1993	1994
Bulgaria	3.0	6.2	−42.3	18.6	1.1	−20.3
Czech Republic	0.8	−5.5	−26.3	10.3	3.6	6.5
Hungary	0.8	−0.2	−3.7	1.7	−0.4	5.0
Poland	11.6	−27.4	0.2	−2.9	−3.0	0.5
Romania	2.4	4.5	−20.6	−13.0	−23.3	−19.9
Slovak Republic	1.2	−5.4	−28.7	9.4	−3.9	3.2

Source: Employment Observatory: Central & Eastern Europe, no. 8 (November
1995), pp. 41–42.

in the table, the average real wage index (1985 = 100) was 132 in
1990, 123 in 1991, 73 in 1992, 83 in 1993, 76 in 1994, and 55 in 1995.[2]
However, all these figures must be taken with extreme caution: the
official wage statistics usually disregarded at least some private firms,
especially small ones; and some employers might have understated
the actual level of wages in order to reduce the amount of contributory taxes.

Despite a fall in real wages, gross monthly wages expressed in US
dollars tended to increase. Nevertheless, everywhere the average
monthly dollar wage (i.e., the average gross monthly wage in domestic
currency divided by the dollar exchange rate) remained very modest in
comparison with the wage levels prevailing in Western Europe, Japan,
and the United States. For example, in the Czech Republic the average
monthly dollar wage went up from US$ 128 in 1991 to US$ 240 in
1994, and in Russia from US$ 28 in 1992 to US$ 96 in 1994.[3]

In eastern Germany, it should be added, gross monthly wages rose
from 48.3 per cent of the western German wage level in 1991 through
62.7 per cent in 1992 and 70.1 per cent in 1993 to 72.9 per cent in
1994. Simultaneously, productivity per employee rose, but only from
31.0 per cent of the western German productivity level in 1991
through 43.1 per cent in 1992 and 50.7 per cent in 1993 to 53.0 per
cent in 1994.[4]

Before presenting some data on GDP per capita, a brief (albeit
important) note on its measurement is necessary. GDP per capita can
be measured either at current exchange rates or at purchasing power
parity (PPP) exchange rates. In contrast to the former, which disregards differences in relative price levels, the latter takes differences in
relative price levels into account. Consequently, the two magnitudes
are not identical.

Table 17.2   PPP-GNP Per Capita,* Selected Post-Communist
Countries, 1993 AND 1994 (in US dollars)

	1993	1994
Czech Republic	7 550	8 173
Slovak Republic	6 290	6 671
Hungary	6 050	6 211
Russia	5 050	4 294
Poland	5 000	6 364
Bulgaria	4 100	5 132
Romania	2 800	3 542
Memorandum items		
China	2 330	...
High-income non-communist countries	18 682	...

* PPP stands for purchasing power parity, defined as the number
of units of the country's currency required to buy the same
amount of goods and services in the domestic market as one US
dollar would buy in the United States.
Source: EBRD, *Transition Report 1995*, p. 21, Table 2.2, and IMF,
World Economic Outlook, October 1996. p. 88, Table 23.

In the case of post-communist countries, GDP per capita measured
at PPP exchange rates was markedly higher than GDP per capita
measured at current exchange rates.[5] Even then, though, as the
estimates presented in Table 17.2 show, in 1993 and 1994 these
countries were considerably poorer than the developed capitalist
market economies.[6] According to another estimate, in 1994 GDP
per capita measured at PPP exchange rates was 45 per cent of the
EU average in the Czech Republic, less in Slovakia, Hungary, Poland,
and Bulgaria, and below 20 per cent in Romania.[7]

17.2   POVERTY

Although officially denied, poverty did exist in the Soviet-bloc countries, and calculations of subsistence and social minima were under-
taken.[8] As as result of economic transformation, the standard of living
of many households declined and, at least in the short run, an increase
in poverty took place. Simultaneously, poverty became more visible.

In 1992, for instance, 18.2 per cent of Czech households, 21.3 per
cent of the Hungarian population, 30.2 per cent of Slovak households,
42.5 per cent of the Polish population, 51.1 per cent of Romanian
households, and 53.6 per cent of Bulgarian households were allegedly

living in poverty. These figures were arrived at by identifying poverty with income below 35 per cent of the 1989 average wage in the Czech Republic, below 40 per cent in the Slovak Republic, and below 45 per cent in the remaining countries.[9]

The percentage of the Russian population falling below the poverty line, calculated on the basis of a minimum subsistence basket of goods, was 31.5 per cent in 1992, 30.9 per cent in 1993, 23.1 per cent in 1994, 26.2 per cent in 1995, and 21.4 per cent in 1996. However, partly due to changes in inflation, the poverty rates varied not only from one year to another, but also from one quarter (and month) to another.[10]

Generally, the groups at risk of poverty included especially children, young adults, and the unemployed. Besides, quite a few employed persons experienced poverty. On the other hand, the incidence of poverty among pensioners was relatively low: according to the United Nations Children's Fund, UNICEF, if official statistics are to be believed, 'pensions have kept ahead of the average wage in ten [post-communist] countries since 1989 and fallen only slightly in another four.'[11]

It is also worth recalling some of the findings of Branko Milanovic, based on his analysis of poverty in Central and Eastern Europe during the early years of economic transformation. One is that the poverty rates go up as household size increases and the level of education decreases, but decline with age. Another is that hitherto poverty has been shallow and transient, i.e., people may go in and out of poverty relatively easily and frequently. Still another is that statistics on the ownership of consumer durables show that poverty has not yet been reflected in a significant deterioration in asset ownership by the poor.[12]

17.3   THE CONTROVERSY

Just as the official post-communist wage statistics, the official post-communist poverty statistics too must be taken with extreme caution. At the same time, the problem of poverty is not confined to post-communist societies, but is a worldwide problem. Yet, as the brief account presented below suggests, the definition, measurement, and incidence of poverty are highly controversial.

To begin with definitions, a distinction is commonly made between absolute poverty and relative poverty. The former is defined in relation to the subsistence level, i.e., in relation to the minimal economic resources necessary in given circumstances for survival. The latter is defined in relation to the economic situation of others. Consequently, absolute poverty means living below the subsistence level, whereas relative poverty means having fewer economic resources than the reference group.

In the developed capitalist market economies, where absolute poverty is practically non-existent, attention is paid primarily to relative poverty. Its concept on the one hand implies that as long as economic differences are to be found in a society, the incidence of relative poverty cannot be avoided, so that relative poverty is a permanent feature of that society, and on the other hand does not exclude the possibility of improvements over time in the standard of living of those regarded as poor.

Quite a few advocates of the concept of relative poverty have recourse to Adam Smith who wrote in 1776 that '[b]y necessaries I understand not only the commodities which are indispensably necessary for the support of life, but whatever the custom of the country renders it indecent for creditable people, even of the lowest order, to be without.... Under necessaries, therefore, I comprehend not only those things which nature, but those things which the established rules of decency have rendered necessary to the lowest rank of people. All other things I call luxuries.'[13] Yet, these advocates of the concept of relative poverty tend to overlook one point: although for Adam Smith necessaries were partly determined by the *established* rules of *decency*, the examples given by him to demonstrate the role of custom in the determination of necessaries suggest that he still conceived the necessaries as being close to the subsistence level.

Another distinction commonly made is that between objective poverty and subjective poverty. The former denotes a gap between people's economic lot and the officially (politically) defined poverty line which, being so defined, is inevitably more or less arbitrary, particularly in the case of relative poverty. The latter denotes a gap between people's economic lot and their expectations and perceptions, a feeling (not a fact) of poverty. Of course, the two need not coincide: on the one hand, people objectively regarded as poor need not regard themselves as poor; on the other hand, people regarding themselves as poor need not be regarded as poor objectively.[14]

Objective poverty, whether absolute or relative, can be measured in various ways. Four indicators of objective poverty will be considered here, namely, income, expenditure, consumption, and assets. Of these four indicators, income will receive attention first.

In the case of absolute poverty, the poverty line is equal to the income providing the subsistence level. In contrast, in the case of relative poverty the poverty line is equal to the income amounting to an officially (politically) specified percentage of the national average. This percentage, which is purely a matter of judgement, has an impact on the poverty rate (the share of the poor) in a country: a higher percentage increases the poverty rate, and vice versa. Hence, if this percentage is changed, the poverty rate too is automatically changed, although no change in economic circumstances has taken place.

Naturally, using income as an indicator of poverty requires its definition. Basically, the income used as an indicator of poverty may be either original income consisting of earnings from employment and self-employment *plus* private pensions *plus* annuities *plus* investment income *plus* other income; or disposable income consisting of the original income *plus* cash benefits *minus* income tax *minus* contributory taxes; or final income consisting of the disposable income *minus* indirect taxes *plus* benefits in kind (education, health care, and the like).

However, the measurement of poverty is also affected by using as an indicator of poverty income after deduction of housing costs: the poverty rate is likely to increase if poverty is measured on the basis of income net of housing costs. Moreover, the measurement of poverty using income as an indicator of poverty is affected by undeclared transfers between family members, proceeds from second economy activities, dissaving, or borrowing: the poverty rate is likely to increase if reported income is understated.

Since income can be understated, people may in fact spend more (and quite often considerably more) than the income admitted by them suggests. Consequently, expenditure is a more accurate indicator of poverty than income is. An even more accurate indicator of poverty is total consumption, which takes into account not only expenditure, but household production and benefits in kind as well. Hence, the poverty count based on expenditure or total consumption may be lower than that based on income.

The last indicator of objective poverty is economic assets, financial and material. Their importance lies in that they have an impact on people's standard of living and make life easier for them when their current income is low. More specifically, if people have economic assets and their current income is low, they are able to draw on their savings and to use or sell the things they own. Thus, low current income does not necessarily mean lack of capital, property, household articles, valuables, and the like.

Before leaving the indicators of objective poverty it should be noted that sometimes the poor are identified with those at the bottom of the income distribution. However, income inequality does not inevitably imply poverty, unless poverty is defined in strictly relative terms. As the available evidence suggests, in the developed capitalist market economies the income of the lowest twenty per cent of households tends to increase over time, and so do housing standards and rates of ownership of such items as television, refrigerator, deep freezer, washing machine, telephone, car, video cassette recorder, and home computer.[15]

When measuring poverty, the unit of analysis is undeniably of importance. In principle, it may be either the individual or the household, the latter consisting of a married or unmarried couple, a nuclear family, an incomplete (single-parent) family, or an extended family. In thus defining the household, the criteria used include common residence, common spending, blood or marital relationship, and dependence.[16]

If the unit of analysis is not the individual but the household, the equivalence scales to be applied to households of different size and composition need to be considered. An equivalence scale gives the relation between the poverty line for a household composed of two or more persons and that for a single person. For example, the 1982 OECD equivalence scale recommended 1 for the first adult in the household, 0.7 for each additional adult, and 0.5 for each child under 14 years, while the modified OECD equivalence scale recommended 1 for the first adult, 0.5 for each additional adult, and 0.3 for each child.

One of the questions that inevitably arise in connection with poverty is that of its duration. That is to say, do the poor experience permanent or temporary poverty? More specifically, are the poor a permanent discrete socio-economic group with unchanging membership? Or are they a social category (a collection of individuals and households) the ranks of which are constantly changing due to inflows and outflows, with people becoming poor and the poor rising out of poverty?

To answer this question it is necessary to take into consideration the difference between intergenerational and intragenerational mobility and that between upward and downward mobility. Intergenerational mobility implies that people coming from poor families can become affluent and people coming from affluent families can become poor.

Intragenerational mobility implies that during their lifetime poor people can escape from poverty and affluent people can fall into poverty.

Whether people experience upward or downward mobility during their lifetime or not, their economic lot is affected by the family life cycle proceeding from childhood through early adulthood, a child-bearing and child-raising period, and a period of economically independent grown-up children to old age. Moreover, well-to-do people can experience spells of poverty in the sense that their current income falls temporarily below the officially (politically) defined poverty line.

In sum, poverty rates conceal the duration of poverty, i.e., for how long the poor remain poor. At the same time, if poverty is conceived as relative poverty and measured exclusively in terms of current income, its duration *per se* does not convey an accurate picture of poor people's standard of living and assets.

Another of the questions that inevitably arise in connection with poverty is that of the poverty gap, which refers to the extent to which the incomes of the poor fall short of the officially (politically) defined poverty line, and which is an attempt to measure the intensity of poverty. Hence, the intensity of poverty is high if the poverty gap is large and low if the poverty gap is small. However, neither a high (rising) poverty rate nor long-term poverty necessarily means a large (widening) poverty gap, and vice versa.

Yet another of the questions that inevitably arise in connection with poverty is that of its causes. According to one view, poverty is a result of external factors, the poor are poor through no fault of their own, they are the victims of circumstances. Without doubt, factors outside people's control can contribute to poverty, the examples being recessions, involuntary unemployment, the tax system, the welfare state, the officially (politically) defined poverty line, poor upbringing and schooling, chronic illness, disability, and age. In addition, though, people themselves can contribute to their poverty by their attitudes and behaviour, such as unwillingness to learn and acquire marketable qualifications and skills; avoidance of gainful employment; lack of effort, initiative, risk-taking, and responsibility; divorce; and out-of-wedlock childbearing.

The perceived causes of poverty have an impact on recommendations about how poverty should be relieved. If it is believed that poverty is a result of external factors and that people are entitled to a certain income or standard of living irrespective of what they do, it follows that the state has the duty to provide the poor with the necessary economic resources. If it is believed that poverty is a result of economic and other policies, it follows that such policies should be modified or dropped altogether. If it is believed that poverty is a result of people's attitudes and behaviour, it follows that these attitudes and this behaviour need to be changed.

All in all, in the developed capitalist market economies poverty became a fashionable topic in the 1980s, when privatization and deregulation were put onto the agenda. While scholars admitted that its definition, measurement, and incidence were highly controversial, the poverty lobby (industry) that came into being dramatized the issue by trying hard to prove that the poor were rising in number as well as getting poorer, that immiseration was taking place.

Obviously, the issue of poverty can be dramatized in various ways. They include concentrating on relative poverty measured in terms of money income only; creating an impression that relative poverty means in fact absolute poverty; avoiding making a clear distinction between people living *at* the officially (politically) defined poverty line and those living *below* it; ignoring the duration of poverty, i.e., whether the poor are poor permanently or temporarily; disregarding the poverty gap; labelling the trickle-down effect as a myth; simplifying the causes of poverty by subscribing to the no-fault explanation which portrays the poor as the victims of circumstances; and using compassionate language.

No less obviously, governments and sample survey respondents too can contribute to a misleading picture of poverty. The former do so by setting a high level of the poverty line: according to the definition of poverty favoured by the European Commission, for instance, a household is considered poor if its income (or expenditure) is less than half the national average. The latter do so by intentionally or unintentionally understating their income.

Moreover, poverty research itself confuses the issue of poverty, the issue of its incidence and severity. This is because the use of different indicators of objective poverty (income, expenditure, consumption, and assets) and of different data sources (e.g., interviews and income statistics) tends to produce different (and sometimes considerably different) poverty rates.[17]

It goes without saying that also the estimated incidence and severity of poverty in post-communist societies must be taken with caution, especially if poverty is measured exclusively in terms of money income. Thus, the World Bank identifies poverty with a monthly per capita income below a certain level expressed in US dollars. UNICEF makes a distinction between low income and poverty, defining the low income line as 35, 40, or 45 per cent of the average wage, with the percentage depending on the country in question, and the poverty line as 60 per cent of the low income line.[18]

Such estimates suggest that in post-communist societies the incidence of poverty increased between 1989 and 1994, and that in 1994 the incidence of poverty varied considerably from one post-communist country to another, being lowest in the Czech Republic, Hungary, Slovakia, and Slovenia. They do not reveal, though, what standard of living poor people actually enjoyed in those years, because they are based on income statistics that leave much to be desired.

17.4 THE SECOND ECONOMY

Economic statistics must be taken *cum grano salis*, because they tend to obscure the true level of economic activity. The reason is that some economic activity (whether legal or illegal, marketed or non-marketed) is not recorded. This applies especially to second or unofficial economy activity and to household production, both of which are to be found in any modern economy irrespective of the established type of economic system.

In post-communist societies, second economy activity as well as household production underwent an expansion as a result of the collapse of communism and economic transformation. After all, the collapse of communism created a temporary systemic vacuum, characterized by political, legal, economic, and social uncertainty; anarcho-capitalism or at least its elements came into being, meaning a chaotic situation in which legal norms regulating private economic activity either do not exist at all or are widely ignored; and households had to cope with open inflation, withdrawals from the labour force, open unemployment, a fall in real wages, and changes in state-provided and enterprise-provided welfare.

As the available estimates suggest, during the first half of the 1990s the size of the second economy was far from negligible. For example, in Estonia it was put at about 13 per cent of GDP in 1993,[19] in the Czech Republic at (at least) 5–6 per cent in 1990–93 and at 10–15 per cent in 1994,[20] in Poland at approximately 20 per cent in 1993,[21] in Hungary at between 25 and 33 per cent in 1992–94,[22] and in Russia at between 20 and 40 per cent in 1994.[23] As to household production, some sample surveys revealed, *inter alia*, the important role played by the growing of one's own food.

Since official post-communist statistics recorded neither second economy activity nor household production, they understated the true level of GDP and the true standard of living of the population, and overstated the true level of open unemployment and the true incidence and severity of poverty. Thus, they presented a more or less distorted and misleading picture of post-communist economies.

Two consequences of second economy activity and household production deserve mentioning. On the one hand, they resulted in public revenue losses, arising from tax evasion in the case of the former and reduced participation in market transactions in the case of the latter. Simultaneously, though, they lessened the risk of social unrest and socio-political destabilization by significantly contributing to the total of goods and services produced.

Despite its undoubted importance, household production will from now on be disregarded and attention will be paid exclusively to the second economy. More precisely, the discussion will focus on one category of its participants, namely, the so-called mafia, which term denotes organized crime.

A number of factors contributes to participation in the second economy, *inter alia*, the environment in which economic actors operate. In capitalist market economies the causes of second economic activity include punitive taxation, restrictive regulation, the existence of the welfare state financed through taxation, and open unemployment (see Section 4.4). In socialist command economies as well as in capitalist command economies the systemic causes of second economy activity are chronic shortages and the bureaucratization of the economy (see Section 7.4). In any economy, second economy activity is encouraged by the illegal character of some goods and services that are in demand, an historical example being alcohol[24] and a contemporary example being drugs.

Obviously, second economy activity is to be found not only in established economic systems, where its existence evinces the limits of government control over the economy. As might be expected, it is also to be found in conditions of a systemic vacuum, which is a result of the collapse of the hitherto established political and economic system and which gives rise to anarcho-capitalism. Since mafia organizations are part of the second economy, they too can operate either in established economic systems or in conditions of a systemic vacuum. At the same time, it is possible as well as useful to distinguish two types of mafia organization, namely, the mafia as a profit-maximizing firm and the mafia as a government.[25]

Illegal firms, because they are illegal, cannot rely on external legal enforcement of employment contracts. They themselves must strictly monitor the activities of their employees to be able credibly to punish them for their misbehaviour. Thus, they incur monitoring and enforcement costs, which tend to increase more than proportionally with the number of their employees. Consequently, they face a constraint on their size: inasmuch as there is a disadvantage in becoming too big, they are likely to be smaller rather than bigger both in a geographical and in a functional sense.

Competition is another constraint that illegal firms frequently face, particularly if they operate in markets that have low barriers to entry and where economies of scale are not great. In order to minimize competition and protect their market share, they can either try to deter the entry of rival firms or conclude collusive agreements with one another. However, deterring the entry of rival firms is apt to result in violence, and so is the breakdown of collusive agreements among illegal firms.

Yet another constraint that illegal firms operating in established economic systems face is the legal government in its role of law-maker and law-enforcer, because their simultaneous existence inevitably gives rise to conflictual relations between them. Despite that, though, mutually advantageous collusive relations can develop between illegal firms on the one hand and politicians and bureaucrats on the other.

Having discussed the mafia as a profit-maximizing firm, albeit illegal, it is possible to turn to the mafia as a government. This type of mafia organization does not directly engage in or control the production and distribution of goods and services. It plays a rule-making role in a given territory, be it geographically or functionally defined, and imposes regulations on legal and/or illegal firms. Thus, it provides a rule of law of a sort and a system of dispute settlement, i.e., a relatively stable framework for economic activity.

In order to be able to play a rule-making role in a given territory, the mafia must first and foremost acquire a monopoly of coercion therein. Once it succeeds, it can extract a rent from (levy taxes on) illegal as well as legal firms, set the rules of the game, define property rights, act as an adjudicator in case of complaints and conflicts, and regulate private actors through non-fiscal tools. Consequently, it substitutes for or competes with the legal government, and when necessary or beneficial reaches collusive agreements with it.

Since its main objective is to maximize its revenue, the mafia as a government has to protect the capital and profitability of the firms in its domain. That is to say, there is a limit to what it can extract from economic actors. Hence, it is a stationary bandit, not a roving bandit who is a predator appropriating everything available, even if it means a complete breakdown of production. According to Mancur Olson, '[a] stationary bandit will take only a part of income in taxes, because he will be able to exact more tax from his subjects if he leaves them with an incentive to generate more income. . . . In a world of roving banditry there is little or no incentive for anyone to produce or accumulate anything that may be stolen and thus little for bandits to steal.'[26]

All in all, second economy activity is to be found both in established economic systems and in conditions of a systemic vacuum. One category of second economy participants is organized crime, the so-called mafia. At the same time, two types of mafia organization may be distinguished, namely, the mafia as a profit- maximizing firm and the mafia as a government.

In post-communist societies, an expansion of second economy activity took place as a result of the collapse of communism and economic transformation. Since a temporary systemic vacuum appeared, giving rise to anarcho-capitalism, a situation conducive to the emergence and growth of mafia organizations of both types was created. One of the post-communist countries where mafia activity was flourishing during the first half of the 1990s was Russia, because there was no effective rule of law. According to some reports, by 1995 the Russian mafia consisted of some 5000 gangs and three million people who worked for or with them, and extorted from firms protection money averaging 10–20 per cent of their profits.

CONCLUSION

The welfare of individuals and households has multiple sources. In the case of individual welfare, its sources are the individual himself or herself, the family (household), informal networks (relatives, friends, neighbours, colleagues), the market, voluntary organizations, and central and local government (the state). In the case of household welfare, its sources are the ability, effort, and contribution of household members, informal networks, the market, voluntary organizations, and central and local government (the state).

Since individual and household welfare has multiple sources and since many an economic activity is unrecorded, official statistics tend to understate the true standard of living of the population. Obviously, the same applies to post-communist official statistics too. Yet, whatever their inaccuracies, they are not able to conceal that in the mid-1990s post-communist societies continued to be considerably less affluent than the developed capitalist market economies.

Not only are some countries less affluent than other countries, but in any country some individuals and households are less affluent than other individuals and households. Thus, the problem of poverty comes into being. However, its definition, measurement, and incidence are highly controversial. There is absolute and relative poverty, as well as objective and subjective poverty.[27] To measure objective poverty, four indicators may be used, namely, income, expenditure, consumption, and assets.

Poverty also raises the question of its duration, that of its gap (and, thus, that of its intensity), that of its causes, and that of its alleviation. Concerning the nexus between the two last-mentioned, the perceived causes of poverty have an impact on recommendations about how poverty should be relieved. The recommendations put forward have included a minimum wage, a negative income tax,[28] a basic (or citizen's) income,[29] and others.[30]

In the mid-1990s, the main role in the alleviation of poverty continued to be played by the welfare state financed through taxation, with charities playing a minor (albeit not negligible) role. At the same time, though, attempts were being made to make people self-reliant, which could be achieved by a combination of reduced public provision, increased private provision, and informal social control (such as reassertion of traditional values, contempt for unconventional lifestyles, and stigmatization of those who bring poverty upon themselves).

While on the one hand the poverty lobby (industry) did not cease to dramatize the issue of poverty, on the other hand governments in the developed capitalist market economies tended to minimize its importance, because it was politically sensitive as well as embarassing. In any case, it was very much alive and, in the European Union at least, compounded by the issue of social exclusion.[31] The concept was introduced by the European Commission and the Council of Ministers towards the end of the 1980s. Social exclusion was seen as a broader, more comprehensive, concept than poverty. The latter denoted insufficient material resources. In contrast, the former denoted the denial of citizenship rights, the failure of civic, economic, social, and interpersonal integration.

Nevertheless, in the mid-1990s social exclusion continued to be a vague term: there was no agreement on the differences between poverty and social exclusion, and in EU circles poverty and social exclusion were used interchangeably. At the same time, however social exclusion is defined, it raises a number of questions. For example, is social exclusion exclusively involuntary? To what extent do individuals and groups contribute to their social exlusion? Does integration as the opposite of social exclusion always inevitably need government intervention, or can it also be achieved spontaneously?

18 Attitudes and Politics

Economic transformation, which means systemic change, i.e., the substitution of one type of economic system for another, inevitably raises the question of support for and opposition and resistance to it. If it takes place in conditions in which public opinion polls and free elections are conducted, this support and this opposition and resistance manifest themselves in public opinion and voting behaviour, without excluding the possibility of other manifestations of support and opposition and resistance, such as strikes and demonstrations.

18.1 EXPECTATIONS

A discussion of the level of support for and opposition and resistance to economic transformation, including that in post-communist societies, cannot disregard people's expectations. The reason is simple: economic transformation implies a tension between expectations and reality. It has to be remembered, though, that objective reality and people's perception of it need not coincide.

Expectations, in the sense of goal-attainment expectations, refer to what people believe they are entitled to be, do, achieve, receive, and possess, and to how they are entitled to live. Expressed differently, they refer to the status, roles, power, influence, resources (such as money, wealth, knowledge, and skills), opportunities, and the political, economic, social, and cultural conditions people think they rightfully deserve. In contrast, reality refers to what people actually are, do, achieve, receive, and possess, and to how they actually live. In other words, it refers to their actual status, roles, power, influence, resources, and opportunities, and to the political, economic, social, and cultural conditions they face.

If people's expectations were fully realized, they would have no incentive to make effort, show initiative, take risks, and assume responsibility. Thus, a gap perceived by people between their expectations and reality can stimulate them to make effort, show initiative, take risks, and assume responsibility. However, it can also lead to crime, aggressiveness, strikes, popular unrest, or terrorism on the one

222

hand and to a lowering of expectations, withdrawal, escapism, or apathy on the other.

Although a subjectively perceived gap between expectations and reality gives rise to relative deprivation, i.e., to frustration or feelings of dissatisfaction, people who are subjectively deprived with reference to their expectations need not be regarded as being deprived (in want) by an objective observer. Conversely, people who are regarded as being deprived (in want) by an objective observer need not regard themselves as being deprived, they need not be discontented or resentful.[1]

Moreover, since people's expectations tend to undergo change over time and since realized expectations tend to generate new expectations, improvements in reality need not necessarily reduce the subjectively perceived gap between expectations and reality. Actually, they may widen it. That is to say, a rising standard of living, an expansion of free public services, increased participation in decision-making, and the like may in fact intensify relative deprivation.

To sum up, people have expectations that are material as well as non-material, political as well as non-political. These expectations may expand or contract, and be specific or vague, realistic or unrealistic, and complementary or contradictory. Their realization may be seen as being either one's own responsibility or somebody else's responsibility.

Concerning the impact of the collapse of communism on people's expectations, it met some of them (namely those the realization of which had been hindered by the communist system) and thwarted others (namely those the realization of which had been tied to the continued existence of the communist system). At the same time, though, it triggered off an explosion of unrealistic expectations, which failed to take into account that post-communist transformation was likely to face obstacles and bring about hardships. Consequently, it was highly probable that many of these expectations would not be met, at least in the short run; that the unmet expectations would lead to disillusionment and mood swings; and that the disillusionment and mood swings would be a breeding ground for the emergence of populist, nationalist, and other demagogues.

Besides goal-attainment expectations, discussed hitherto, there are predictive expectations. Economists define them as the beliefs or views held by economic actors about the future behaviour of economic variables, and distinguish between adaptive expectations and rational expectations. Expectations are said to be adaptive if economic actors form their expectations about the future value of an economic variable on the basis of its past value only, i.e., in a rather mechanical way by extrapolating from past experience. In contrast, rational expectations are said to be formed on the basis of all available information. They do not suffer from systematic errors, although random errors may occur. Thus, on average, the forecasts based on rational expectations are correct and unbiased.

The rational-expectations proposition has had a profound impact both on macroeconomic theory and on the way economists think about the effects of economic policies. It implies that governments are not able to use fiscal and monetary policy systematically to fool people, that fiscal and monetary policy would be futile because it would be frustrated by the actions of economic actors. In a word, it provides a foundation for a theory of non-interventionist macroeconomic policy.

All in all, economic transformation (including that in post-communist societies) cannot avoid taking into consideration people's goal-attainment and predictive expectations. The former concern the possibility of a tension between people's goal-attainment expectations and reality arising, *inter alia*, from unwillingness to defer gratification, i.e., to sacrifice current satisfaction for future gains. The latter, if conceived as rational expectations, concern the limits of political power and the issue of the government's credibility.

18.2 THE VISIBLE VERSUS THE INVISIBLE HAND

Post-communist economic transformation inevitably raises the important question of the role the state should play in the economy both during economic transformation and after its completion. Hence, post-communist economic transformation is characterized by a tension between the state (the visible hand) and the market (the invisible hand),[2] and this tension is reflected in public opinion as ascertained by sample surveys.

During the first half of the 1990s, Table 18.1 shows, support for the market economy (defined as one largely free from state control) varied considerably from one post-communist country to another, being lowest in Belarus, Russia, and Ukraine, where the supporters of the market economy were outnumbered by its opponents. Within the same post-communist country, then, support for the market economy varied considerably from one year to another.

Table 18.1   Support for Market Economy, Selected Post-Communist
Countries, 1990–95 (per cent of positive minus per cent of negative responses)

	1990	1991	1992	1993	1994	1995
Albania	–	45	51	52	41	59
Bulgaria	22	45	36	18	−2	6
Czech Republic	54	39	24	15	11	6
Hungary	47	52	39	21	20	5
Poland	47	28	33	29	26	46
Romania	–	−5	41	29	50	38
Slovakia	28	29	15	−4	0	0
Estonia	–	32	19	26	14	20
Latvia	–	43	−12	2	−5	1
Lithuania	–	55	44	33	9	16
Belarus	–	–	−24	−25	−27	−13
Russia	–	8	−7	−22	−41	−46
Ukraine	–	–	−12	−19	−18	−27

Source: European Commission, *Central and Eastern Eurobarometer*, no. 6
(March 1996), Text figures 1–23.

However, these figures must be taken with caution. The reason is that they disregard those who did not answer, who did not say whether the creation of a market economy was right or wrong for their country's future. Yet, the percentage of such respondents fluctuated widely. In 1995, for instance, they amounted to 7 per cent in Albania, 10 per cent in Estonia and Romania, 16 per cent in Russia, 19 per cent in Latvia, 22 per cent in the Czech Republic, Poland, and Slovakia, 24 per cent in Lithuania, 25 per cent in Belarus and Ukraine, 28 per cent in Bulgaria, and 29 per cent in Hungary.[3]

Another survey, conducted in ten post-communist countries in the autumn of 1995, shows support for the old (communist) economic system, the current economic system, and the future economic system (defined as one expected in five years' time). As follows from Table 18.2, in most cases the current system was viewed less favourably than the old system, and in the case of Hungary, Russia, Bulgaria, Belarus, and Ukraine also the future system was viewed less favourably than the old system. Despite that, everywhere at least some respondents expected the future system to be an improvement on the current system.

One further finding of this survey deserves mentioning. With the exception of the Czech Republic and Romania, in each of the remaining eight countries (including Poland) the majority of respondents believed that the state should be responsible for everyone's economic

Table 18.2   Approval of Economic Systems, Post-Communist Countries,
Autumn 1995 (per cent)

	Old system	Current system	Future system
Poland	38	68	86
Czech Republic	42	69	85
Slovenia	47	55	75
Romania	50	37	61
Hungary	69	27	54
Slovakia	71	43	72
Russia	72	22	40
Bulgaria	75	23	72
Belarus	88	16	57
Ukraine	90	15	41

Source: Richard Rose and Christian Haerpfer, *New Democracies Barometer IV: A 10-Nation Survey*, Centre for the Study of Public Policy, University of Strathclyde, Studies in Public Policy No. 262 (1996), pp. 29 and 44, Table 3.2.

security, whereas merely a minority believed that individuals should be responsible for their own welfare. That is to say, for many people the nanny state (state paternalism) did not lose its attractiveness. As put by Jirí Vecerník, 'there is a considerable reliance on state protection within post-communist nations.'[4]

Not only these two surveys, but various other surveys too indicate that by the end of 1995 post-communist societies continued to be divided as to the preferred type of economic system and the expected role of the state in the economy. Basically, the division was between

1. the supporters of a free-market economy;
2. the supporters of a social market economy, a mixed economy, a third way, and neo-corporatism;[5]
3. the supporters of a socialist command economy; and
4. those who could not make up their minds.

Underlying support for either an interventionist and paternalistic government or a socialist command economy were a number of factors. Three of them were the thwarting of expectations tied to the existence of command socialism; disillusionment with the progress of economic transformation, because it had not met people's expectations; and the doggedly surviving dependency culture developed under communism.

Concerning eastern Germans, not included in the account given above, in 1993 slightly over a third (36 per cent) of them rated the old (communist) economic system positively and three-quarters rated the current social market system positively. At the same time, nearly two-thirds (62 per cent) believed that the state should be responsible for everyone's material well-being.[6]

18.3   HOUSEHOLD ECONOMIC SITUATION

As discussed in the preceding chapter, economic transformation resulted in open inflation, withdrawals from the labour force, open unemployment, a fall in real wages, greater income disparities, and changes in state-provided and enterprise-provided welfare. In a word, it adversely affected the standard of living of many a household. This implies that it frequently increased the share of expenditure on food in household expenditure.[7]

By the end of 1995, in post-communist societies merely a minority of employed persons reported that they were earning enough from a regular job to get by: in Ukraine, for instance, as few as 12 per cent. If eastern Germany is disregarded, the only exception was the Czech Republic, where 53 per cent of employed persons were able to live on earnings from their regular job.[8] However, when pensions, unemployment benefits, growing their own food, and proceeds from second economy activity were also taken into consideration, then most households could cope, i.e., make ends meet without dissaving or borrowing money from friends. To give a few examples, in the Czech Republic 79 per cent of all households could cope, in Hungary and Russia 68 per cent, in Poland 64 per cent, and in Bulgaria 51 per cent.[9]

Many households rated their current economic situation either as not very satisfactory or as very unsatisfactory: 46 per cent in the Czech Republic, 65 per cent in Poland and Slovakia, 79 per cent in Hungary, and 90 per cent in Ukraine. Moreover, many households viewed their economic situation before the start of economic transformation as much or at least a little better than their current economic situation: 41 per cent in the Czech Republic, 50 per cent in Poland, 59 per cent in Slovakia, 72 per cent in Hungary, and 78 per cent in Ukraine. Simultaneously, though, a considerable number of households expected their economic situation to improve within the next five years.[10]

Obviously, statements about satisfaction or dissatisfaction with one's economic situation reveal nothing about what people regard as a satisfactory economic situation. Similarly, admissions of one's participation in second economic activity reveal nothing about how people judge second economic activity on the part of others. In this connection, two findings are of interest: in November 1994, four-fifths of Czech respondents opined that in their country people became rich mainly by acting dishonestly;[11] and in January 1996 two-thirds of Russian respondents blamed the mafia for the country's economic problems.[12]

Since economic transformation adversely affected the standard of living of many a household, it could also be asked how it affected the number of marriages, birth rates, divorce rates, death rates, infant mortality rates, and life expectancy at birth. Concerning the last-mentioned two, the World Bank's data suggest that, compared with the 1981–90 period, in 1994 infant mortality rates were lower in most of the 26 post-communist countries surveyed. In contrast, life expectancy at birth was higher only in about two-thirds of them, and in Russia it was lower by nearly five years.[13]

18.4   AUTHORITARIANISM VERSUS DEMOCRACY

The collapse of communism gave rise to political pluralism and competition for power. That is to say, it created conditions for the transformation of the hitherto established authoritarian political system maintained by coercion into a democratic political system, which implied change of values, norms, political institutions, behaviour, and attitudes.

During the first half of the 1990s, Table 18.3 shows, satisfaction with the way democracy was developing varied considerably from one post-communist country to another and, within the same country, from one year to another. In most cases, those who were dissatisfied outnumbered (often quite heavily) those who were satisfied. At the same time, in 1995 at least, those who did not express their satisfaction or dissatisfaction usually amounted to less than 9 per cent, the exceptions being Poland (12 per cent), Ukraine (15 per cent), and Belarus (19 per cent).[14]

Naturally, these figures leave some questions unanswered. In particular, when the respondents expressed their satisfaction or dissatisfaction with the way democracy was developing, were they referring to democracy as a type of modern political system, or to the political system actually existing at the moment of the survey, or to the behaviour of post-communist politicians and the policies pursued by them? Moreover, what were the preferred alternatives of those who rejected democracy as a type of modern political system?

Table 18.3 Satisfaction with Development of Democracy, Selected Post-Communist Countries, 1990–95
(per cent of positive minus per cent of negative responses)

	1990	1991	1992	1993	1994	1995
Albania	–	−17	−10	−17	−33	18
Bulgaria	−23	−6	−17	−49	−87	−67
Czech Republic	−16	−25	−19	0	−9	−4
Hungary	−54	−29	−50	−54	−43	−57
Poland	1	−21	−24	−14	−40	12
Romania	–	−11	−40	−26	−36	−21
Slovakia	−42	−55	−53	−59	−62	−40
Estonia	–	−21	−35	−15	−26	−20
Latvia	–	−9	−58	−31	−42	−38
Lithuania	–	23	5	−20	−31	−40
Belarus	–	–	−66	−55	−62	−53
Russia	–	−51	−64	−56	−75	−79
Ukraine	–	–	−54	−57	−53	−55

Source: European Commission, *Central and Eastern Eurobarometer*, no. 6 (March 1996), Text figures 1–23.

Another survey, conducted in Russia in January 1996 but elsewhere in the autumn of 1995, shows support for the old political system, the current political system, and the future political system (defined as one expected in five years' time). As follows from Table 18.4, in four

Table 18.4 Approval of Political Systems, Post-Communist Countries, Autumn 1995 (per cent)

	Old system	Current system	Future system
Poland	25	76	90
Czech Republic	27	76	86
Romania	28	60	73
Slovenia	36	66	75
Slovakia	52	61	78
Hungary	56	50	68
Bulgaria	58	66	83
Russia	59	28	43
Ukraine	75	33	52
Belarus	77	35	66

Sources: Richard Rose and Christian Haerpfer, *New Democracies Barometer IV: A 10-Nation Survey*, Centre for the Study of Public Policy, University of Strathclyde, Studies in Public Policy No. 262 (1996), pp. 19 and 72–76, and Richard Rose, *New Russia Barometer V: Between Two Elections*, Centre for the Study of Public Policy, University of Strathclyde, Studies in Public Policy No. 260 (1996), pp. 47–50.

Table 18.5 Reactions to Regime Change, Post-Communist Countries, Autumn 1995 (per cent)

	Democrats	Sceptics	Compliants	Reactionaries
Czech Republic	58	15	17	9
Poland	58	16	18	8
Romania	44	28	16	11
Slovenia	41	23	26	11
Bulgaria	31	10	34	24
Slovakia	30	18	31	22
Hungary	22	21	27	29
Belarus	11	12	24	53
Russia	10	30	18	41
Ukraine	10	14	23	52

Sources: see Table 18.4.

cases (Hungary, Russia, Ukraine, and Belarus) the current system was viewed less favourably than the old system, and in three cases (Russia, Ukraine, and Belarus) also the future system was viewed less favourably than the old system.

If attitudes towards the old political system are combined with those towards the current political system, it is possible to distinguish four categories of respondents. These categories, the distribution of which is presented in Table 18.5, are:

1. the democrats, characterized by a non-positive evaluation of the old régime and a positive evaluation of the current régime;
2. the sceptics, characterized by a non-positive evaluation of the old régime and a non-positive evaluation of the current régime;
3. the compliants, characterized by a positive evaluation of the old régime and a positive evaluation of the current régime; and
4. the reactionaries, characterized by a positive evaluation of the old régime and a non-positive evaluation of the current régime.

The main alternatives to democracy were military rule, communist rule, and a strong leader (conceived either as a dictator or as an effective government). Of the three main alternatives mentioned, support for communist rule and a strong leader exceeded that for military rule. By the end of 1995, the highest support for communist rule and a strong leader was to be found in Russia, Ukraine, and Belarus. Of Russian respondents, for instance, in January 1996 39 per cent favoured return to communist rule, 34 per cent a tough dictatorship, and 10 per cent military rule.[15]

Everywhere, it should be added, a sizeable majority of respondents (between 60 and 80 per cent) wanted the most important decisions about the economy to be made by experts, not by the government and parliament. That is to say, they endorsed technocracy which, obviously, raises the question of its compatibility with democracy.

18.5 POLITICS

Generally, public opinion is affected by memory of the past (which, however, may be distorted), perception of the present (which too need not correspond to reality), and expectation of the future (which may be based on wishful thinking). Moreover, it may be inconsistent and volatile. The same applies to public opinion in post-communist countries. In each of them it is affected by the country's history, experience, and tradition, pre-communist as well as communist; by the progress of political and economic transformation and the costs it imposes and the benefits it brings; and by prospective developments, desired or dreaded.

Concerning specifically the impact of the collapse of communism on people's expectations, it met some of them, thwarted others, and triggered off still others. However, the subsequent transformation failed to realize quite a few of the last-mentioned, partly because many of them were unrealistic. Thus, it did not do away with a tension between expectations and reality which, of course, existed under communism too.

Since the collapse of communism gave rise to political pluralism and competition for power, a gap perceived by people between their expectations and reality could manifest itself not only in public opinion as ascertained by sample surveys, but also in voting behaviour. In a number of cases, whereas in the first post-communist elections the voters tended to elect free-market political parties, in the second post-communist elections they tended to elect more interventionist political parties. *Inter alia*, the former communists and their allies were returned to power in Lithuania in October–November 1992, in Poland in September 1993,[16] in Hungary in May 1994, and in Bulgaria in December 1994.[17] A swing to the former communists and other left-leaning political parties also took place in Ukraine (March–April 1994), Slovakia (September–October 1994), Estonia (March 1995), Latvia (autumn 1995), Russia (December 1995), and the Czech Republic (May–June 1996).[18] Yet, between mid-1996 and April 1997 the former communists were voted out of office in Lithuania, Romania, and Bulgaria. And in Mongolia, where the former communists won the first free election in 1992, they lost the second held on 30 June 1996.

Various factors contributed to these shifts in voting preferences, including opposition to transformation in principle; dissatisfaction with the speed of transformation, particular policies, and the economic and social consequences of transformation; and the desire for greater political stability. However, the main factor was most probably a wish on the part of many voters to have a government that, while upholding political and economic freedom, would guarantee economic security via state-provided welfare.[19]

As to the impact of the speed of transformation on voting behaviour, a 1996 study rejected the conventional wisdom that radical reformers lose elections. Its authors concluded that gradual reform was very unpopular, and that whoever was responsible was likely to lose any election. In contrast, radical reform did not necessarily prevent the re-election of the government pursuing it.[20]

CONCLUSION

Surveys of public opinion in post-communist societies abound. However, their findings (some of which have been discussed in the present chapter) should be taken with caution because, *inter alia*, everywhere public opinion tends to be amorphous and contradictory and to undergo change (temporary or permanent). Moreover, it does not guarantee that people behave or would behave in conformity with the opinions expressed by them.

Be that as it may, in democratic political systems governments are not able to ignore public opinion and, therefore, must make decisions about when to follow it and when to lead it. If they were responsive to any whim of public opinion, they would be weak governments prone to frequent U-turns and unable to pursue coherent policies, thus creating instability and putting the economy, the polity, and society at risk. In contrast, if they want to mould public opinion, their options are to try to change people's expectations, people's perception of reality, or the reality itself.

Also opposition parties are not able to ignore public opinion. Hence, in their search for power they attempt to raise people's expectations and to undermine the sitting government's credibility.

Yet, they too face the problem of credibility: it is more than likely that their credibility as an alternative government would be weakened or lost if the electorate felt that they could not (or in fact did not intend to) fulfil their promises.

Obviously, in democratic political systems public opinion is affected not only by the behaviour of the government and the opposition but also by the behaviour of pressure groups and the mass media. That is to say, pressure groups and the mass media (albeit usually in combination with other factors, such as one-off events) have an impact on the mood of the time, mood swings, and voting behaviour. Simultaneously, though, public opinion influences the behaviour of pressure groups and the mass media, just as it influences the behaviour of the government and the opposition.

Concerning specifically post-communist countries, the available sample surveys demonstrate that between the collapse of communism and the mid-1990s public opinion varied considerably from one post-communist country to another and, within the same country, from one year to another. On top of that, within each country it was divided over a number of issues, not unanimous.

During this period, it follows from these surveys as well as from voting behaviour, support for free-market policies declined and that for interventionist policies increased. Although on the whole a political system based on political pluralism and competition for power continued to be preferred to authoritarianism, there occurred a shift away from belief in self-reliance (which means that the individual is expected to be responsible for his or her own welfare) towards belief in dependency (which means that the state is expected to be responsible for individual welfare).[21]

Part V
Finale

An inherent and, hence, universal feature of both traditional and modern societies is a tension between spontaneity (individual freedom) and control (regulation). Consequently economies, as a subsystem of society concerned with the production and distribution of goods and services, also experience it. More specifically, economies experience a tension between economic individualism and economic collectivism, which in modern economies revolves around the role of the state in the economy.

It is not surprising, then, that although currently economic and political liberalization is under way, not only in post-communist societies but throughout the world, this tension remains very much in evidence. At the same time, its outcome is far from certain. That is to say, there is no guarantee that the ongoing process of economic and political liberalization will continue to assert itself and will not come to a standstill or undergo a reversal.

Since economic liberalization is an important dimension of the ongoing global change, the two chapters that make up Part V inquire into the factors that on the one hand contribute to it and on the other hinder it. Technological, demographic, economic, political, social, and cultural factors are identified as being of relevance, and special attention is paid to the questions of self-interest, the constraints that governments face, and contemporary socialism.

19 The Individual, the Market, and the State

Economic development in the sense of economic growth accompanied by a substantial structural or organizational change in the economy is characterized by the decline of traditional economies and the emergence and diffusion of modern ones. It is an uneven, protracted, and open-ended process, which entails a tension between spontaneity (economic freedom) and control (economic regulation) or, in other words, between economic individualism and economic collectivism.

19.1 MODERN ECONOMIC SYSTEMS

In modern economies, economic activity can be marketed or non-marketed, legal or illegal, and recorded or unrecorded. As a result, five sectors may be distinguished in these economies, namely, the first or official eonomy, the second or unofficial economy, the government economy, the household economy, and the voluntary economy. On top of that, the so-called mutual-help economy is also to be found.

Depending on the predominating type of coordinating mechanism (market or command) and the predominating type of ownership of the means of production (private or public), in modern economies the first or official economy is always a variant of one of the four theoretically possible pure types of modern economic system. The four pure types are market capitalism, command capitalism, market socialism, and command socialism.

Each type of modern economic system is based on certain values. In turn, it has a distinct impact on the structure of economic power and economic decision-making, the flow and nature of information, the character of economic institutions, the structure and values of society, the behaviour and attitudes of economic actors, the legal system, the political system, and the role the state plays in the economy.

The performance of an established modern economic system is determined jointly by its nature, the individuals who operate it, and the intrasocietal (domestic) and extrasocietal (international) environment in which it functions. On the other hand, its performance affects its legitimacy. If it loses legitimacy because it does not meet people's expectations, it either has to be maintained by coercion or undergoes transformation.

For the individuals who operate the established modern economic system, its nature simultaneously constitutes constraints and provides opportunities. These imposed constraints and these available opportunities have an effect on the operating individuals' performance within (and even outside) the system in question. However, their performance within (as well as outside) the system in question also depends on their abilities, qualifications, skills, and motivation, one component of which is self-interest.

19.2 SELF-INTEREST

In analyses of human motivation, the role of self-interest has been recognized by, *inter alia*, Thomas Hobbes (1588–1679), John Locke (1632–1704), David Hume (1711–76), and Adam Smith. The last-mentioned postulated in 1776 that individuals were motivated by self-interest and that, being led in the pursuit of self-interest by an invisible hand, they unintentionally contributed to the general welfare. Actually, '[b]y pursuing his own interest he [the individual] frequently promotes that of the society more effectually than when he really intends to promote it.'[1]

In contrast, the critics of the *laissez-faire* variant of market capitalism, as well as of the free-market variant of market capitalism, argue that market capitalism is based on, or at least encourages, selfish (egoistic, materialistic, acquisitive, greedy) motivation and behaviour on the part of economic actors, and that, if left alone, it will not generate socially desirable results. Hence, selfish and similar motivation and behaviour on the part of economic actors should be harnessed to socially beneficial ends.

Two questions arise in connection with Adam Smith's invisible hand theorem and its criticism, namely, that of the occurrence of self-interest and that of its consequences. More specifically, is the pursuit of self-interest confined exclusively to market capitalism, or is it to be found in any economic system irrespective of its type? Secondly, on the assumption that the consequences of the pursuit of self-interest can be both beneficial and harmful, for whom are they beneficial and for whom are they harmful?

Concerning the first question, it follows from the available empirical evidence that in practice the pursuit of self-interest is not confined to a particular economic system, i.e., to market capitalism. It is to be found in any established economic system irrespective of its type. No established economic system (including command socialism) and no established political system (including totalist authoritarianism) can eradicate it. Attempts to eradicate it are futile.

Support for this view comes from Stephen K. Sanderson who argues, in his book presenting an outline of a general theory of social evolution, that most human behaviour is motivated by the pursuit of self-interest and that virtually all human behaviour is egoistic at the genotypic level. As put by him, '[h]uman individuals are egoistic beings who are highly motivated to satisfy their own needs and wants. They seek to behave adaptively by maximizing the benefits and minimizing the costs of any course of action (or at least generating more benefits than costs).'

One further proposition of Sanderson's deserves mentioning, due to its obvious (albeit often ignored) significance. It states that individuals acting in their own interests create social structures and systems that are frequently (indeed, perhaps usually) constituted in ways that individuals never intended. Thus, individually purposive or intended human action leads to many unintended and even unwanted consequences.[2]

Another support for the view expressed above comes from Graeme Donald Snooks' economic model concerned with forces determining the way societies change. According to this model, designed to explain the dynamics of human society, the driving force in human society is a dynamic version of economic man called materialist man, who is a decision-maker attempting to survive and, with survival, to maximize material advantage over his lifetime.[3]

It seems irrefutable, then, that in any society individuals in their role of economic actors (which nobody is able to escape) are motivated by self-interest, stemming from the desire to maximize the probability of survival and the achievement of material advantage (prosperity). Both dimensions of this desire are interlinked and one cannot be attained without the other.

Being motivated by self-interest, individuals have to adapt their behaviour to the natural, political, economic, social, and cultural environment in which they operate, and to changes therein. Thus, the pursuit of self-interest may induce – *inter alia* – effort, initiative, risk-taking, and responsibility as well as passivity, rent-seeking, risk-avoidance, change-aversion, and dependency; competitiveness as well as cooperation; aggressiveness as well as submissiveness; compliance as well as deviance; restraint as well as fervour; and secretiveness as well as openness.

Yet, although individuals are undoubtedly motivated by self-interest, they are not motivated exclusively by it. In addition, they are motivated by sympathy, compassion, affection, love, loyalty, sense of (moral) duty, feelings of guilt, ideas, ideals, identification with a cause, envy, anger, hatred, and the like.

Obviously, the pursuit of self-interest is not confined to individuals. Other economic actors too have to pursue their own economic interests if they want to survive economically and to maximize material advantage, the examples being households, firms, trade unions, local communities, and nations. Moreover, political actors (such as politicians, political parties, pressure groups, and states) have to pursue their own political interests if they want to survive politically and to maximize political power or influence.

As follows from the foregoing, the terms 'self-interest', 'selfishness', and 'egoism' may be used interchangeably and without any derogatory meaning. However, they may also be used to denote reprehensible behaviour, behaviour that for one reason or another is viewed as improper, distasteful, callous, harmful, unacceptable. In this case, the pursuit of self-interest (selfishness, egoism) is contrasted with altruism and the latter is regarded as superior to the former.

The emphasis on altruism raises a number of questions, though. One is that of its definition: altruism has been defined, for instance, as regard or concern for others, as acting knowingly in other people's interests, and as caring or doing good for others without expecting reward or reciprocation. Another is that of the impact of altruistic behaviour on others: it can make them better off or worse off, elicit gratitude or scorn, and encourage reciprocation or exploitation of the altruistic actor. Still another is that of the motivation underlying apparently altruistic behaviour: does it stem from genuine altruism or from self-interest?

Concerning the relationship between altruism and self-interest, both Stephen K. Sanderson and Graeme Donald Snooks argue that self-interest precedes altruism. According to the former, 'the very behavior that is phenotypically altruistic is almost always genotypically selfish, that is, it is driven by motives that are purely egoistic. Human behavior includes large amounts of both phenotypic egoism and phenotypic altruism, but virtually all human behavior is egoistic at the genotypic level.'[4] According to the latter, 'mankind's nature has been genetically determined, and...what is taken to be altruism is merely the strategy of maximizing individual material well-being through the well-being of the group to which they belong. And it will not change in the future because in a competitive world the struggle for survival and prosperity will be with us always.'[5]

Snooks also touches upon the question of self-sacrifice. In a relatively small number of cases, he admits, self-sacrifice can and does exist. However, 'if man were motivated primarily by self-sacrifice, the human race long ago would have lost the battle for survival...one must survive in order to reproduce.'[6]

In sum, the motives underlying the behaviour of individuals are economic as well as non-economic.[7] While on the one hand the latter can reinforce, dilute, or frustrate the former, on the other hand the former can override the latter. Thus, individuals experience a tension between economic and non-economic motives which implies a tension between self-interest and altruism.

The tension between self-interest and altruism would not disappear with the elimination of private ownership of the means of production. According to Joseph E. Stiglitz, a misconceived objection to private ownership of the means of production is that private firms pursue their objectives at the expense of public objectives. A corresponding myth is that 'state enterprises pursue "social" objectives.... [In fact,] state enterprises are frequently more interested in improving the welfare of their workers (and managers) than in pursuing national objectives (however those might be defined).'[8]

Moreover, the tension between self-interest and altruism gives rise to the question of the nexus between economic variables and voting behaviour. As recalled by Timothy J. Colton, political scientists distinguish between pocketbook or egocentric voting and sociotropic or sociocentric voting. The former is based on private well-being, on microeconomic and personal considerations, the latter on the health of the economy as a whole, on macroeconomic and general considerations.[9] The latter, it may safely be assumed, is not devoid of self-interest, but it is self-interest guided by a wider and longer perspective rather than by an expectation of immediate gratification.

19.3   THE STATE

An inherent and, hence, universal feature of societies, whether traditional or modern, is a tension between spontaneity (individual freedom) and control (regulation), the latter being needed to maintain a system of ordered relationships. The difference between traditional and modern societies is that while in the case of traditional societies control (regulation) is exerted by custom and tradition, in the case of modern societies it is exerted by the law of the state.

Yet, although in modern societies control (regulation) is exerted by the law of the state, custom and tradition do not cease to play an important role. As a set of procedures (rules of conduct) inherited from the past, tradition defines the actors' rights, duties, and responsibilities, and provides guidelines for the solution of recurrent problems. Thus, it enables predictability and contributes to stability. At the same time, being inimical to change, particularly to rapid change, it puts a check on political power.

Since societies experience a tension between spontaneity (individual freedom) and control (regulation), economies as a subsystem of society also experience it. More specifically, they experience a tension between economic individualism and economic collectivism, which in modern economies revolves around the role of the state in the economy and has five main interrelated dimensions, concerning the coordinating mechanism, the ownership of the means of production, the criteria applied to economic activity, the perceived sources of individual welfare, and the distribution of income and wealth.

Under economic individualism, the state is means-orientated in the sense of being concerned with process or procedure. Consequently, government intervention in property rights, the operation of the market, and the outcome of economic activity aims at preserving and expanding economic freedom and competition. In contrast, under economic collectivism the state is goal-orientated in the sense of being concerned with an end-state or final outcome. Consequently, government intervention in property rights, the operation of the market, and the outcome of economic activity aims at restraining or suppressing economic freedom and competition.

Naturally, in practice neither pure economic individualism (which separates economic power and economic decision-making from political power and political decision-making) nor pure economic collectivism (which fuses economic power and economic decision-making with political power and political decision-making) is to be found. There are only degrees of economic individualism and economic collectivism, with one of them predominating. If anarcho-capitalism is disregarded, the *laissez-faire* variant of market capitalism is the extreme case of economic individualism and command socialism is the extreme form of economic collectivism.

19.4 CONSTRAINTS

The role the state plays in modern economies depends on the established type of modern economic system and on the policies pursued by the sitting government. It can range from a minimal one (confined to national defence and the maintenance of law and order, including the protection of private property and the enforcement of contracts) to an all-embracing one (amounting to comprehensive public ownership of the means of production and central direction of entire economic activity).

In modern history, the role of the state in the economy has been expanding as well as contracting. More precisely, there have been periods favouring big government and periods favouring limited or minimal government. Yet, none of these periods suppressed national differences and put an end to the scope of political power as a theoretical and political issue. In the 1990s, for instance, although command socialism was discredited, a tension between the free-market variant of market capitalism and its interventionist variant did not disappear, and even the dawn of the post-market era was announced.

When the role of the state in the economy is discussed, the question of its constraints cannot be avoided. Whatever politicians and the public at large might believe or pretend to believe, governments (just as economic actors in general) are not omnipotent. They face a number of constraints, of which three are of fundamental importance, because they are inherent in the nature of things.

The first of these three constraints is the pervasive economic phenomenon of scarcity, due to which the basic economic problem is the allocation of scarce means (resources) among competing ends for the achievement of maximum results. Scarcity gives rise to the need for efficiency, allocative as well as productive; at the same time, though, efficiency requires private ownership of the means of production combined with a competitive market. Besides, scarcity implies that in surplus-producing economies the extent of surplus-producing economic activity and the extent of surplus-consuming economic activity are inversely related (in capitalist market economies, for instance, this applies to the relation between the size of the surplus-producing market sector and the size of the surplus-consuming non-market sector).

Closely connected with this constraint is another one, namely, the cost-benefit nexus, arising from the fact that there are no benefits without costs. Since there is no free lunch and since resources are scarce, costs (which include time and the opportunities foregone) and benefits must be carefully weighed against each other, bearing in mind that long-term benefits usually require short-term costs (i.e., deferred gratification), that short-term benefits can be costly in the long run, and that benefits may be apparent, not real.

Finally, the last of these three constraints is the risk factor. No purposeful activity, whether economic or non-economic, is without a risk. Since economic, political, and other actors do not have complete control over events, situations, and developments, any purposeful activity of theirs contains a possibility of unintended consequences.[10] Although some risks may be reduced or avoided if foreseen and if appropriate precautions are taken, it is not possible to eliminate risks altogether, risk-free existence is an illusion.

In sum, inasmuch as governments face these three constraints, their extractive, allocative, distributive, and regulative capabilities are circumscribed. They are resource-constrained, are not able to put out of operation universally valid economic laws, and can fail, i.e., need not achieve their objectives. To give a few examples, under command socialism the bureaucratization of the economy gives rise to covert non-compliance with those formal norms and administrative orders which impede economic actors' activities and goal-attainment, and chronic shortages affecting producers and consumers alike give rise to illegal second economy activities which, obviously, are a specific manifestation of covert non-compliance. Under market capitalism, excessive taxation encourages tax evasion and capital flight and depresses saving; exessive regulation brings about inflexibility and induces non-observance of laws, by-laws, and directives; both excessive taxation and excessive regulation discourage foreign direct investment; and a high or rising size of the surplus-consuming non-market sector has an adverse impact on the size of the surplus-producing market sector.

Besides the three constraints specified above, governments are constrained by the nature of the established economic system and its logic. That is to say, as long as they want to maintain the established economic system, they have to pursue policies that are compatible with its nature and to refrain from pursuing policies that would undermine it because they are incompatible with its nature.

At the same time, governments face not only economic constraints, but also political constraints (which in democratic political systems include the opposition, pressure groups, and the electorate), social constraints (e.g., the age composition and the occupational structure of the population), and cultural constraints (e.g., a dependency culture). These constraints either prevent governments from pursuing certain policies or force them to adopt others.

CONCLUSION

Of the four types of modern economic system distinguished in the present study, three (command capitalism, market socialism, and command socialism) are by their nature transitory. The only economically viable type of modern economic system is market capitalism, a pluralistic, competitive, horizontally organized, spontaneous, and open economic system, based on private ownership of the means of production and market coordination.

Market capitalism puts a check on the scope of political power. Nevertheless, the role the state plays in capitalist market economies varies from one capitalist market economy to another and, within the same capitalist market economy, over time, giving rise to three variants of market capitalism, namely, the *laissez-faire* variant, the free-market variant, and the interventionist variant. The first two, it should be added, tend to be misunderstood and/or misrepresented, being frequently treated as identical and as amounting to anarcho-capitalism.

Currently, capitalist market economies experience a tension between the free-market variant of market capitalism and its interventionist variant. Under the former, government (the visible hand) has a limited, albeit important, role to play in the economy. The role consists of setting a stable legal framework defining economic actors' rights and responsibilities, i.e., the rules of conduct, and of correcting market failures (such as monopolies, anti-competitive practices, externalities, and lack of private initiative) with a view to improving allocative efficiency. Under the latter, government intervenes directly or indirectly in property rights, the operation of the market, and/or the outcome of economic activity with a view to attaining specific economic or non-economic objectives other than allocative efficiency.

In choosing between these two variants of market capitalism it ought to be remembered that government intervention in the economy can improve as well as obstruct the operation of the market, enhance as well as curb economic freedom. Since market forces cannot forever be denied and since economic freedom contributes to economic growth and prosperity, less government intervention in the economy is preferable to more government intervention in the economy.[11]

Yet, although less government intervention in the economy is preferable to more government intervention in the economy, democratic political systems create conditions for the emergence and operation of forces competing for rents and trying to divert resources from investment to consumption. This means, so runs one argument, that democracy is bad for investment and economic growth, and that in order to stimulate economic growth, it is necessary to have an authoritarian political system or at least to hold political participation down.[12]

20 The World in Transition

As the clock is unstoppably ticking, bringing the end of the twentieth century nearer and nearer, the world continues to undergo change. The change is taking place in, as well as between, developed, developing, and post-communist countries; it is not only economic, but also political, social, and cultural; on the one hand it reflects and on the other creates tensions in, as well as between, individual economies, polities, societies, and cultures.

20.1 ECONOMIC LIBERALIZATION

One important dimension of the ongoing global change has been economic liberalization. It started around 1980 and has meant either change *within* the system or change *of* the system. In the former case it has amounted to privatization and deregulation within the confines of a predominantly capitalist market economy (the examples being Britain, the United States, New Zealand, and Chile), while in the latter case it has amounted to the transformation of the established variant of command socialism (the examples being China, Vietnam, and the post-communist countries).

Economic liberalization has been launched by governments in both democratic and authoritarian political systems. Simultaneously, though, in authoritarian political systems political liberalization has been in evidence, with pressure for it arising sometimes from poor economic performance (e.g., in a number of Latin American countries), sometimes from increasing affluence (e.g., in South Korea, Singapore, and Chile).[1] This is not to say, of course, that in authoritarian political systems pressure for political liberalization arises exclusively from economic factors.

Although a worldwide process, economic liberalization (and, similarly, political liberalization) has been neither uniform nor synchronized. Moreover, by the end of 1997 it was still far from complete. Not surprisingly, the same applied to economic transformation in the post-communist countries. In these countries, most of which used to belong to the Soviet block, the extent and pace of economic transformation have varied considerably from one country to another. Nevertheless, these countries could be grouped into those which adopted fast and comprehensive economic transformation and those where economic transformation has been slow and piecemeal.[2] This had an impact on their economic performance: the former have performed better than the latter, turning the initial recession into recovery in a relatively short time.

While on the one hand the extent and pace of economic transformation affected economic performance, on the other hand the progress of economic transformation was affected by the domestic political situation, arising from political pluralism and competition for power. In brief, while a weak and/or unstable government was likely to retard the progress of economic transformation, a strong and stable government (one committed to economic transformation and having the political will and capability to see it through) was likely to accelerate it.

Be that as it may, by the end of 1997 the post-communist countries continued to face a number of problems. They concerned, *inter alia*, economic growth, open inflation, open unemployment, unfinished privatization and restructuring,[3] inadequate infrastructure, bad debts,[4] corporate governance, excessive regulation, second economy activity, relatively low saving and investment rates, overextended social security systems, high government spending, budget deficits, foreign debts, export opportunities, and ageing populations.

For some of these countries, an additional problem was to gain full membership of the European Union (EU). However, the integration of Central and Eastern Europe into the EU was not high on the latter's agenda.[5] Although making promises, the EU was dragging its feet on enlargement, for at least three reasons: deepening of the EU was taking precedence over its widening (after all, the Maastricht treaty of 1991 marked 'a new stage in the process of creating an ever closer union among the peoples of Europe'); it was feared that, due to subsidies from the Common Agricultural Policy and the structural funds for poorer regions, full and rapid integration of Central and Eastern Europe into the EU would be too costly because it would involve massive hand-outs; and the EU was preoccupied with the issue of the introduction of a single currency.

On the part of the applicants, a barrier to their full integration into the EU was the still incomplete harmonization of their legal and other institutional standards with those prevailing in the EU countries. The advantage of this harmonization process is that it keeps up the momentum of transformation and builds up investors' confidence in the applicants. Its danger is that the applicants could fall into the EU's rigidity trap that erodes competitiveness and stifles economic growth.

Thus, bringing Central and Eastern European countries into the EU will be no easy task. The obstacles include the national interests of the EU members and the cost of integration. However, the latter could be reduced if the existing system of EU subsidies were reformed and if, for a long transition period, the new members were willing to make concessions, i.e., to accept lower and/or fewer benefits than the present EU members enjoy.

In sum, economic transformation in the post-communist countries may be, and most probably is, an irreversible process. Yet, by the end of 1997 it was still far from complete everywhere, even in those post-communist countries where it was most advanced. Not surprisingly, the same applied to political transformation, i.e., to democratization. It too was still far from complete everywhere, despite the existence in these countries of political pluralism and competition for power.

Some Western views deserve to be mentioned in this connection. According to John Mueller, most of the post-communist countries of Central and Eastern Europe have essentially completed their transition to democracy and capitalism. They are democratic, if democracy is understood to mean a political system in which the government can be overthrown non-violently, and they are capitalist, if capitalism is understood to mean an economic system in which it is possible to make a profit legally.[6] In contrast, Charles Gati argued that in the mid-1990s most post-communist countries were facing the prospect of neither democracy nor totalitarianism, that the transition was producing a group of semi-authoritarian (and, therefore, semi-democratic), nationalist, populist régimes. Only in the Czech Republic, Poland, Hungary, and Slovenia, and to a lesser extent in Estonia, Latvia, and Lithuania, were the democratic prospects promising.[7]

While Gati contended that in most post-communist countries the transition to democracy had lost its early popular appeal and, hence, its early momentum, Mary Kaldor and Ivan Vejvoda suggested that in the search for democratic institutions, rules, and procedures the main internal obstacle facing the countries of Central and Eastern Europe remained the absence of a democratic political culture.[8] However, Mueller was of a different opinion. He held that pre-existing negative attitudes (cultural legacies) need not necessarily be a notable hindrance to the establishment of democracy or capitalism, that minds were not permanently deformed by the communist experience.

All in all, by the end of 1997 there continued to exist different assessments not only of the progress of political and economic transformation in the post-communist countries, but also of the prospects for its successful completion, i.e., for the establishment of a stable and well-functioning political and economic system. At the same time, some post-communist countries were better placed than others successfully to complete their political and economic transformation.

Since economic transformation is expected noticeably to improve economic performance, it is not futile to insert a brief note on what leads to high rates of economic growth. Although they differ about the details, most economists agree that open trade, relatively few market distortions, small government, and high saving and investment rates have been crucial to the performance of the fastest-growing developing countries. Accordingly, if the post-communist countries adopted this course, they could catch up with their EU neighbours faster than if they persisted in their current policies and copied EU labour and social legislation.[9]

20.2   UNDERLYING CAUSES

Although since around 1980 economic liberalization has been an important dimension of the ongoing global change, hitherto free-market economics has not triumphed. Governments continue to intervene in the economy, and government intervention in the economy continues to be advocated. In the European Union, for instance, interventionist, corporatist, welfarist, and protectionist strivings have not ceased to assert themselves.[10] Consequently, it is hardly possible to avoid inquiring into the factors that currently contribute to economic liberalization, as well as into those that stand in its way.[11] Obviously, the impact of these factors is not exclusively economic; it is political too, affecting both policy-making and the nature of the political system.

One of these factors is the third crucial revolution in the economic development of mankind, namely, the information revolution, a product of the new information technology. It helps to disperse economic (and other) information, economic decision-making, and economic power. It also increases the role of applied knowledge in the organization of production, the enhancement of productivity, and the creation of wealth. This trend towards a more knowledge-based economy is reflected in the shift from material production to information-processing (symbolic-analytic) activities, as measured in terms of the proportion in GDP of such activities and in terms of the proportion of the population engaged in such activities.

In combination with improvements in transportation, the information revolution is contributing to the globalization of the world economy, to global economic and financial integration. Capital, technology, knowledge, information, management, labour, production, and markets are increasingly organized across national boundaries, with companies physically or electronically relocating to where the profit is greatest and the regulation least. Thus, the days of segmented markets, of relatively independent national economies free to pursue their own economic policies in response to domestic concerns and problems, are numbered: a new international division of labour is emerging, and competition is increasingly played out globally.

Globalization, it follows, imposes additional constraints on government intervention in the economy. Additional, because governments have never been omnipotent, i.e., they have never been able to buck the market, to subdue impersonal economic forces. On the whole, markets take power away from governments that do the wrong things and, thereby, force governments to pursue policies that benefit their economies and their citizens.

However, globalization is hindered by regionalization, a tendency towards the formation of transnational regional trade blocs, such as the European Union (EU), the North American Free Trade Agreement (NAFTA), the Association of South East Asian Nations (ASEAN), the Latin American Free Trade Area (LAFTA), and the Central American Common Market (CACM). This means that there is a tension between free trade at the global level and protectionism at the regional level.

As a process of transnationalization of financial and productive activities, both globalization and regionalization give rise to a tension between themselves on the one hand and the nation-state and nationalism on the other. Hitherto, though, they have led neither to the end of the nation-state, nor to the demise of nationalism. Nationalism is still very much alive (as evinced, *inter alia*, by the disintegration in the early 1990s of three federal states, namely, the Soviet Union, Yugoslavia, and Czechoslovakia), and so are national interests (as evinced, *inter alia*, by the behaviour of the individual EU members). Moreover, neither a homogenization of cultures nor the emergence of a supranational identity is in sight.

In search of the factors that on the one hand contribute to and on the other stand in the way of economic liberalization, demography cannot be disregarded. World population is growing rapidly: it reached about one billion in 1800, slightly over 2.5 billion in 1950, and approximately 5.6 billion in 1994. By 2050, the world will probably have at least 7.9 billion people, but might well have even more, perhaps as many as 12 billion. However, these figures conceal that in many developed countries, due to low birth rates and higher life expectancy, the population is ageing. This has an effect not only on welfare spending, but also on economic growth, labour force participation, labour adaptability and mobility, income distribution, consumption patterns, the propensity to save, and voting behaviour.

Besides, the figures on world population growth conceal changes in the family structure. Under the impact of industrialization, urbanization, women's entry into the labour force, social policies, and permissive values, the trend has been from the traditional extended family (which was both a productive and a cradle-to-grave welfare unit) through the one-earner nuclear family to the two-earner nuclear family and the post-nuclear (incomplete, i.e., lone-parent or single-parent) family. Its implications include high divorce rates, high rates of out-of-wedlock childbearing, and calls for (improvements in) state-provided welfare.

Accordingly, population ageing and changes in the family structure (as well as open unemployment) raise the question of the existence and future of the welfare state. Since it consists of non-marketed activities, it must be financed through taxation. While providing the population with benefits in cash and kind, it has a number of drawbacks: in particular, it is centralized, bureaucratic, and inefficient; gives priority to consumption and the redistribution of income and wealth over wealth creation; demotivates (e.g., blunts the work ethic); and helps to bring about a dependency culture. At the same time, it generates vested interests in its maintenance and expansion on the part of both welfare recipients and welfare producers and bureaucrats. These interests lead to demands for higher welfare spending and to opposition and resistance to welfare cuts and welfare privatization. As a result, where the welfare state is established, elected governments find it difficult to reduce welfare spending, although high welfare spending adversely affects the market sector and the country's long-term prosperity.

Thus, the welfare role of the state is in need of redefinition. Despite enjoying widespread popular support, the welfare state is under pressure because of the cost of state-provided welfare and limits to welfare spending. Expressed differently, there is a tension between public provision paid for out of taxes and private provision paid for out of self-insurance and personal savings.

20.3 SOCIALISM

An important factor contributing to economic liberalization has been the worldwide resurgence of belief in market capitalism. It holds that governments, facing constraints and being unable forever to defy the laws of economics, are not omnipotent, and is wary of public owner-ship of the means of production, interventionism, corporatism, pro-tectionism, and welfare statism. It is based not only on theoretical arguments, but also on empirical evidence: socialist command econom-ies proved to be permeated by covert non-compliance and illegal second economy activities and to have economic performance vastly inferior to that of market capitalism; in capitalist market economies, suffocating and unpopular regulation and taxation lead to exit into the second economy and even from the country. On the whole, economic freedom has a positive impact on economic growth and prosperity.

Nevertheless, mistrust of market forces and belief in the indispen-sable and intrinsically beneficial role of the state in the economy has not disappeared. Since market forces cannot be left to themselves, it is argued, the state should guide the market, protect domestic producers against foreign competition, provide economic security, and under-take a desirable redistribution of income and wealth. This implies that socialism (a form of economic collectivism) is far from dead. Although in the 1980s it was in retreat and disarray, in the early 1990s it started to reinvent itself, to rethink its aims and policies. In a word, it started to change its spots.[12]

Contemporary Western socialism lacks a theoretical framework and a clear vision, is driven by moral and other sentiments, focuses on particular issues, and advocates or pursues policies that tend to be populist and paternalistic. At the same time, its standard-bearers (intellectuals, educators, opinion makers, and left-wing politicians) frequently shy away from left-speak and from using the term 'social-ism', and are to be found even among the self-proclaimed liberals.

In principle, contemporary Western socialism may be divided into two main strands. One, market socialism, accepts that the market is desirable but argues for democratization of the economy and/or the redistribution of wealth.[13] The other strand, called here neo-socialism, accepts market capitalism, albeit with the proviso that both the market and private ownership of the means of production would be regulated by the state which, simultaneously, would pursue redistributive and welfarist policies.

Regarding the latter strand, one of its features is its interventionist orientation. While it distances itself from traditional interventionism which replaces the market, it advocates 'new interventionism' which seeks creatively to guide (use and shape) the market. According to Robert Wade, for instance, 'new interventionism' is characterized by the fact that it 'uses price and non-price methods to channel investment away from unproductive uses, expand technological capacity, strengthen links with foreign firms and give a directional thrust to selected industries.'[14]

Another feature of neo-socialism is its protectionist orientation.[15] Although it is not averse to tariffs on imports, import quotas, and import controls in order to offset international cost differences, promote infant industries, and/or safeguard jobs, it also calls for equalization of labour costs in the countries of origin. On the surface, the call for 'fair labour practices' in exporting countries is compatible with free trade. In fact, if put into effect, it would stifle foreign competition by increasing labour costs in countries with lower labour costs.

The last (and, in the final analysis, central) feature of neo-socialism is its welfarist and distributionist orientation. Its language is that of equality, social justice, fairness, solidarity, cooperation, partnership, collective responsibility, stakeholding, communitarianism, economic and social rights, entitlements, social inclusion, the poor-rich (disadvantaged-privileged, loser-winner) dichotomy, compassion, caring, positive discrimination, affirmative action, and the like. Yet, these words are often only vaguely defined, thus allowing (and at least sometimes intended to allow) different interpretations.

Obviously, welfarist policies require resources. However, there are limits to welfare spending, because governments' extractive capabilities are circumscribed both economically and politically. Therefore, neo-socialism tries to shift the cost of its social objectives to private firms. That is to say, in its view private firms' primary responsibility should be to stakeholders, such as employees and the community, not to shareholders.[16] As a result, private firms' costs would be forced up, but the share in GDP of government spending would be kept down.

In sum, command socialism is currently out of fashion in the West, and so are theories predicting the imminent downfall of capitalism and the inevitable rise of socialism, i.e., theories based on the principle of socio-economic determinism and a linear definition of history. What is alive, though, is socialism in the sense of calls for a redistribution of economic power, wealth, and income by means of activist government.[17]

At this juncture, a brief note on pressure groups is appropriate. Pressure groups defend the status quo or seek change by demanding government intervention or non-intervention. Those demanding government intervention may then be divided into the gain-seeking ones and the norm-setting ones. The former confine themselves to demanding government intervention in the economy in order to protect their vested interests or gain an advantage for themselves and/or their clients. In contrast, the latter demand government intervention in the economy *and* society in order to impose their values and standards on the population at large. Expressed differently, they want an activist government engaged in social engineering of the kind determined by them.

Pressure group activity is likely to increase if the government is a highly responsive (and, hence, a weak) government. As intervention-demanding pressure groups proliferate and succeed in bringing about desired policy outcomes, the scope of political power expands. Thus, successful intervention-demanding pressure groups, and particularly those of the norm-setting sort, intentionally or unintentionally pave the way for the erosion of freedom, totalism and, ultimately, totalist authoritarianism.

CONCLUSION

Over the last fifteen years or so, the world has been moving towards liberal democracy, conceived as democratic politics and free-market economics. This does not mean, though, that liberal democracy has triumphed. In theory, the idea of liberal democracy continues to be widely challenged. In practice, the future of liberal democracy is far from assured.

Although economic liberalization has reduced the scope of political power, it has put an end neither to interventionism, corporatism, welfare statism, and protectionism, nor to calls for a redistribution within market capitalism of economic power, wealth, and income by means of activist government. The role the state plays in the economy remains considerable and, at the same time, there is a danger that governments will adopt the active-but-lean tactic. That is to say, to create an impression of being socially-minded without imposing an additional burden on the taxpayers, they may resort to taxation in disguise by shifting the cost of their social objectives to private firms.

Besides economic liberalization, political liberalization (democratization) has been taking place. However, *per se* political liberalization does not amount to the establishment of a stable democratic political system. Such a system can be established only if certain conditions are fulfilled. They are:

1. the rule of law;
2. a limited government, i.e., one with a limited scope of political power;
3. a strong government, i.e., one that does not incessantly yield to every and any opposition and pressure group demand;
4. the existence of a well-trained bureaucracy; and
5. the exercise of political self-restraint by the electorate.[18]

Social structure too has been undergoing change. *Inter alia*, while both the agricultural sector and the industrial sector have been contracting, the service sector has been expanding; as the importance of knowledge and skills and their continual updating has been increasing, the proportion of the population engaged in information-processing (symbolic-analytic) activities has been rising; the availability of jobs for life has been shrinking; and mobility (occupational and geographical, upward and downward, intergenerational and intragenerational) has been gaining in significance.

Also cultural deregulation has been noticeable. Broadly speaking, it has manifested itself by declining respect for traditions, conventions, and customs, as well as for law, an example of the latter being second economy activities. More specifically, albeit not exhaustively, there has been a tendency towards a rights-without-duties-and-responsibility culture, towards self-assertion of sectional interests and unconventional lifestyles, towards redefinition of morality and normality, towards imposition on society of particularistic values and norms, towards intolerance, sophistry, and emotiveness, and towards weakening of familial ties.

Finally, one dimension of the globalization of the world economy has been the formation of transnational regional trade blocs. These blocs provide large internal markets which, by reducing or eliminating barriers to internal flows, offer scope for considerable economies of scale and for greater efficiency. At the same time, though, they might turn into fortress economies by erecting barriers against goods and services produced in other trade blocs. Moreover, they do not exclude the possibility of their disintegration if they begin to be seen as harming the national interests of at least some of their members.

To conclude, although economic liberalization is taking place world-wide, the multidimensional tension between economic individualism and economic collectivism, inherent in modern economies and revolving around the role of the state in the economy, has not disappeared. However, it is not between market capitalism and command socialism any more. It is between two variants of market capitalism, namely, the free-market variant and the interventionist variant.

Despite political liberalization in most parts of the world, stable democratic political systems have not been established everywhere. On top of that, even long-established democracies are vulnerable to unrepresentative but determined and ruthless pressure groups, whether gain-seeking or norm-setting ones, and to a lack of political self-restraint on the part of the electorate. Intentionally or unintentionally, pressure groups and the electorate can undermine market capitalism, the fabric of society and, ultimately, democracy itself.

Of course, economic and political tensions manifest themselves not only within individual countries, large or small. They manifest themselves between individual countries too, arising from the issue of national sovereignty and from divergent national interests. Consequently, they do not cease to manifest themselves by the creation of transnational regional trade blocs and would not cease to manifest themselves even by the creation of supranational states.

In sum, economic and political tensions persist and, presumably, will persist in the future. At the same time, their outcome is never predetermined. Currently, throughout the world economies, polities, societies, and cultures may be in transition. Despite that, the end of history is not in sight.

Notes

1 AN HISTORICAL OVERVIEW

1. Three major forms of the division of labour may be distinguished: the technical (referring to the disaggregation of a given production process into discrete stages, and the consequent specialization of workers in each of these stages), the social (referring to the specialization of roles played by individuals and other economic actors in society), and the spatial (referring to the specialization of production by geographic zones and manifesting itself at various spatial levels).
2. Andrew M. Kamarck, *Economics and the Real World*, Oxford, Basil Blackwell, 1983, pp. 51–2, and Philip Mattera, *Off the Books*, London, Pluto Press, 1985, p. 12.
3. A model of relations among the characteristics of hunting-gathering societies is to be found in Gerhard Lenski and Jean Lenski, *Human Societies: An Introduction to Macrosociology*, New York, McGraw-Hill Book Company, 1989 (fifth edition, second printing), p. 126, Figure 5.11.
4. In hunting-gathering societies, even the role of leader (headman) and that of shaman (medicine man) were part-time specialities. (Gerhard E. Lenski, *Power and Privilege: A Theory of Social Stratification*, New York, McGraw-Hill Book Company, 1966, pp. 99–100.)
5. Slavery appears when the slave can produce more than he consumes, i.e., a surplus. (Bronislaw Malinowski, *Freedom and Civilization*, London, George Allen & Unwin Ltd, 1947, pp. 301–2.)
6. On the secularized city-state as an ancient form of polity see Gabriel A. Almond and G. Bingham Powell, Jr, *Comparative Politics: A Developmental Approach*, Boston, Little, Brown and Company, 1966, pp. 255–9.
7. J.M. Roberts, *The Pelican History of the World*, Harmondsworth, Penguin Books, 1980, pp. 55 and 58.
8. Rondo Cameron, *A Concise Economic History of the World*, Oxford, Oxford University Press, 1993 (second edition), p. 32.
9. Rondo Cameron, op. cit., p. 44.
10. Angus Maddison, *Phases of Capitalist Development*, Oxford, Oxford University Press, 1982, pp. 4–5.
11. Although advancing agrarianism was still predominantly rural and agricultural, by the beginning of the eighteenth century there existed in Western Europe urban handicraft production, rural cottage industry, and a commercial sector.
12. The dates of take-off, maturity, and high mass- consumption in selected countries are to be found in W.W. Rostow, *The Stages of Economic Growth*, Cambridge, Cambridge University Press, 1960 (reprinted), pp. xii and 38, and W.W. Rostow, *The World Economy*, London, Macmillan, 1978, p. 51, Chart II-2.

13. Cf. William Ashworth, *A Short History of the International Economy since 1850*, London, Longmans, Green and Co., 1967 (second edition, reprinted), Chapter V.

14. According to T.G. Williams, 'Carthage [before its destruction by the Romans in the second century B.C.] affords a remarkable example of an early state consciously pursuing mercantile ends, that is to say, the regulation of commerce in the interests of political power, involving the regulation of industry, the reservation of markets, and the exclusion of competition, wherever by so doing national ends would be served. The colonies of Carthage were never allowed to grow out of economic dependence,...' (*The History of Commerce*, London, Sir Isaac Pitman & Sons, Ltd, 1926, p. 29.)

15. E. Lipson, *A Planned Economy or Free Enterprise*, London, Adam & Charles Black, 1946 (second edition), p. 48.

16. On the reaction against free trade see T.G. Williams, op. cit., Chapter XIV.

17. The emergence between 1870 and 1914 of socialism as a major force in European history is discussed by Albert S. Lindemann, *A History of European Socialism*, New Haven, Yale University Press, 1983, Chapter 4.

18. Cf. George N. Halm, *Economic Systems*, New York, Holt, Rinehart and Winston, Inc., 1968 (third edition), Chapter 23.

19. On indicative planning see *Journal of Comparative Economics*, vol. 14, no. 4 (1990).

20. An analysis of successful and failed communist take-overs since 1917 is to be found in Thomas T. Hammond (ed.), *The Anatomy of Communist Takeovers*, New Haven, Yale University Press, 1975. See also Bogdan Szajkowski, *The Establishment of Marxist Regimes*, London, Butterworth Scientific, 1982.

21. Anne O. Krueger, *Political Economy of Policy Reform in Developing Countries*, Cambridge, Massachusetts, The MIT Press, 1993, p. 39.

22. According to Peter N. Stearns, '[t]he biggest jolt the industrial revolution administered to the Western family was the progressive removal of work from the home.' (*The Industrial Revolution in World History*, Boulder, Colorado, Westview Press, 1993, p. 59.)

23. See, for example, Gerhard E. Lenski, *Power and Privilege*, op. cit. Major changes in the class structure of European society since 1750 are summarized by Peter N. Stearns and Herrick Chapman, *European Society in Upheaval. Social History Since 1750*, New York, Macmillan Publishing Company, 1992 (third edition), p. 417, Appendix.

24. The world population was put at about 7.5 million in 8000 B.C., 14 million in 3000 B.C., 252 million in A.D. 200, 206 million in A.D. 500, 442 million in A.D. 1500, 1,668 million in A.D. 1900, and 2,516 million in A.D. 1950. (Graeme Donald Snooks, *The Dynamic Society: Exploring the sources of global change*, London, Routledge, 1996, p. 49, Table 3.1.)

25. J.L. Porket, 'The Visible Versus the Invisible Hand: A Tension Inherent in Modern Economies', a paper presented at the 17th World Congress of the Czechoslovak Society of Arts and Sciences, Prague, 26–29 June 1994.

2 TYPES OF MODERN ECONOMIC SYSTEM

1. J.L. Porket, *Work, Employment and Unemployment in the Soviet Union*, London, Macmillan, 1989, Chapter 1.

2. The organic-mechanistic distinction is usually applied to the analysis of formal organizations, such as industrial firms. Mechanistic systems are characterized by centralization of authority, a precise division of tasks, and procedural rigidity. Initiative is in the hands of administrative leaders, and information flows along vertical lines. In contrast, organic systems are based on a limited number of rules that are consistent but far from comprehensive, have a loosely defined internal division of labour, and depend on lateral communication and spontaneous co-operation. (T.H. Rigby, *Lenin's Government: Sovnarkom 1917–1922*, Cambridge, Cambridge University Press, 1979, pp. 22–3, and Bruce Parrott, *Politics and Technology in the Soviet Union*, Cambridge, Massachusetts, The MIT Press, 1983, pp. 14–16.)

3. The basic assumptions underlying perfect market economies and absolute command economies are summarized in a simplified way by Oleg Zinam, 'The Economics of Command Economies', in Jan S. Prybyla (ed.), *Comparative Economic Systems*, New York, Appleton-Century-Crofts, 1969, pp. 30–1, Table 2.3.

4. Robert L. Heilbroner, *The Making of Economic Society*, Englewood Cliffs, New Jersey, Prentice Hall, 1989 (eighth edition), Chapter 1.

5. Karel Englis, *An Essay on Economic Systems. A Teleological Approach*, Boulder, East European Monographs, 1986, pp. 56–7.

6. Alfred G. Meyer, 'Theories of Convergence', in Chalmers Johnson (ed.), *Change in Communist Systems*, Stanford, California, Stanford University Press, 1970, pp. 313–41; David Lane, *The Socialist Industrial State*, London, George Allen & Unwin Ltd., 1976, pp. 54–62; Bruno Dallago, Horst Brezinski and Wladimir Andreff (eds), *Convergence and System Change*, Aldershot, Dartmouth Publishing Company Limited, 1991.

7. John Kenneth Galbraith, *The New Industrial State*, London, André Deutsch, 1972 (second edition), p. 392.

8. Ralf Dahrendorf, *Reflections on the Revolution in Europe*, London, Chatto & Windus, 1990, pp. 37ff.

9. Jan S. Prybyla, 'The Road From Socialism: Why, Where, What, and How', *Problems of Communism*, vol. XL, nos. 1–2 (January-April 1991), pp. 1–17.

10. János Kornai, *The Socialist System: The Political Economy of Communism*, Oxford, Oxford University Press, 1992, p. 504.

11. J.L. Porket, 'Tensions in Post-Communist Economies', a paper presented at the conference on International Privatization: Strategies and Practices, University of St. Andrews, Scotland, 12–14 September 1991, and J.L. Porket, 'Post-Communist Societies and the Tension Between Economic Individualism and Economic Collectivism', a paper presented at the First European Conference of Sociology, University of Vienna (Austria), 26–29 August 1992.

12. Procedural justice is based on general abstract rules of conduct referring to yet unknown cases and equally to all persons in the objective circumstances described by the rules, irrespective of the effects which observance of the rules will produce in a particular situation. The concepts of procedural and social justice were discussed by Norman P. Barry, *An Introduction to Modern Political Theory*, London, Macmillan, 1989 (second edition), Chapter 6.

13. See e.g. F.A. Hayek, *The Constitution of Liberty*, London, Routledge & Kegan Paul, 1960, p. 93. Hayek's procedural justice was criticized by David Miller, *Market, State, and Community*, Oxford, Clarendon Press, 1989, Chapter 2. The aim of his criticism was 'to destroy the view that procedural justice can stand independently as an alternative to social or distributive justice' (p. 70).

14. Carl J. Friedrich, *Limited Government. A Comparison*, Englewood Cliffs, N.J., Prentice-Hall, Inc. 1974, p. 69. The author also recalls that Marx and Engels had little use for the tradition of natural or any other rights.

15. Equality as an issue was discussed by Walter D. Connor, *Socialism, Politics, and Equality*, New York, Columbia University Press, 1979, Chapter 1, and Norman P. Barry, op. cit., Chapter 7.

16. According to Milton and Rose Friedman, 'A society that puts equality – in the sense of equality of outcome – ahead of freedom will end up with neither equality nor freedom.... On the other hand, a society that puts freedom first will, as a happy by-product, end up with both greater freedom and greater equality.' (*Free to Choose*, New York, Harcourt Brace Jovanovich, 1980, p. 148.)

17. Peter Self, *Government by the Market? The Politics of Public Choice*, Basingstoke, Macmillan, 1993, p. 251.

18. Norman Barry, *Welfare*, Milton Keynes, Open University Press, 1994 (reprinted), p. 95.

19. Oleg Zinam, op. cit., pp. 20–4, and Lee D. Badgett, *Defeated by a Maze: The Soviet Economy and Its Defense–Industrial Sector*, Santa Monica, CA, The RAND Corporation, 1988, pp. 1 and 5–7.

20. Igor Birman,'Rosefielde and My Cumulative Disequilibrium Hypothesis: A Comment', *Soviet Studies*, vol. XLI, no. 1 (January 1989), pp. 141–8.

21. *The New Palgrave: A Dictionary of Economics*, London, Macmillan, 1987, pp. 904–7.

22. Adam Smith's definition of political economy is to be found at the start of Book IV of his *An Inquiry into the Nature and Causes of the Wealth of Nations*, London, J.M. Dent & Sons Ltd, 1929 (reprinted).

23. Lionel Robbins, *An Essay on the Nature and Significance of Economic Science*, London, Macmillan, 1932, p. 15.

24. Ernesto Screpanti and Stefano Zamagni, *An Outline of the History of Economic Thought*, Oxford, Clarendon Press, 1993, p. 383.

25. Kurt W. Rothschild, 'Political Economy or Economics?', *European Journal of Political Economy*, vol. 5, no. 1 (1989), pp. 1–12.

26. Friedrich Schneider, 'Political Economy or Economics? A Comment', *European Journal of Political Economy*, vol. 5, no. 1 (1989), pp. 13–19.

27. Richard Swedberg and Mark Granovetter, 'Introduction', in Mark Granovetter and Richard Swedberg (eds), *The Sociology of Economic Life*, Boulder, Westview Press, 1992.
28. One of the advocates of socio-economics is Amitai Etzioni, *The Moral Dimension: Toward a New Economics*, New York, The Free Press, 1988.

3 ENVIRONMENT OF MODERN ECONOMIC SYSTEMS

1. David Easton, *A Framework for Political Analysis*, Englewood Cliffs, N.J., Prentice-Hall, Inc., 1965, Chapter 5. In his classification of the environment of political systems, Easton does not specify technology as a separate component.
2. Karl W. Deutsch, *Politics and Government*, Boston, Houghton Mifflin Company, 1970, p. 198.
3. On the distinction between the processes of change *within* the system and those *of* the system see Talcott Parsons, *The Social System*, The Free Press of Glencoe, 1964 (fifth printing), Chapter XI.
4. On parapolitical systems and the differences between them and political systems see David Easton, op. cit., pp. 50–6.
5. Variants of democracy are discussed by David Held, *Models of Democracy*, Cambridge, Polity Press, 1989 (reprinted).
6. A similar view was held by Joseph A. Schumpeter, *Capitalism, Socialism, and Democracy*, New York, Harper & Brothers Publishers, 1947 (second edition), Chapter XXII. According to him, the role of the people in a democracy is to produce a government.
7. On the growth in the number of democracies between 1790 and 1990 see Francis Fukuyama, *The End of History and the Last Man*, London, Penguin Books, 1992, pp. 49–50. On the coming of democracy see R.M. MacIver, *The Web of Government*, New York, The Macmillan Company, 1947 (second printing), pp. 175–92.
8. See e.g. David Held (ed.), *Prospects for Democracy*, Cambridge, Polity Press, 1993, Chapter 3 and Chapter 6; *The Economist*, 17 September 1994, pp. 29–30; ibid., 17 June 1995, pp. 21–23.
9. See also J.L. Porket, *Authority in Communist Czechoslovakia Prior to 1968*, an unpublished Ph.D. thesis, London School of Economics and Political Science, 1973, Chapter 10.
10. On the relationship between modern political and economic systems see e.g. Karel Englis, *An Essay on Economic Systems. A Teleological Approach*, Boulder, East European Monographs, 1986, Chapter XIV; Peter L. Berger, *The Capitalist Revolution*, Aldershot, Wildwood House, 1987, Chapters 4 and 8; J.L. Porket, *Work, Employment and Unemployment in the Soviet Union*, London, Macmillan, 1989, pp. 4–6; Gerhard Schwarz, 'Limitations to the Interdependence of Systems', in Kurt Dopfer and Karl-F. Raible (eds), *The Evolution of Economic Systems*, London, Macmillan, 1990, Chapter 3.
11. Milton Friedman, *Capitalism and Freedom*, Chicago, The University of Chicago Press, 1982 (reissued), p. 8.

12. The distinction between private pressure groups and public ones was discussed by Maurice Duverger, *Party Politics and Pressure Groups*, London, Thomas Nelson and Sons Ltd, 1972, pp. 106–7.
13. Robert A. Dahl, *Polyarchy: Participation and Opposition*, New Haven, Yale University Press, 1971, p. 1.
14. Cf. Graham K. Wilson, *Interest Groups*, Oxford, Basil Blackwell, 1990, pp. 2–4, and Joan M. Nelson, 'Labor and Business Roles in Dual Transitions: Building Blocks or Stumbling Blocks?' in Joan M. Nelson et al., *Intricate Links: Democratization and Market Reforms in Latin America and Eastern Europe*, New Brunswick, Transaction Publishers, 1994, pp. 148–51.
15. Robert Moss wrote in 1975 that in Britain it was argued that the state owed everyone a 'suitable' standard of living, regardless of labour. (*The Collapse of Democracy*, London, Temple Smith, 1975, p. 53.) In the opinion of Friedrich August Hayek, '[s]ocialism has taught many people that they possess claims irrespective of performance, irrespective of participation'. (*The Fatal Conceit: The Errors of Socialism*, London, Routledge, 1988, p. 153.)
16. According to Amitai Etzioni, tribalism 'in both its primitive and modern forms tends to handle non-members not just as means...but as consumable, perishable objects.' (*The Active Society*, London, Collier-Macmillan Limited, 1968 (second printing), p. 11.) See also Stephen Amidon, 'The closing of the liberal mind', *The Sunday Times*, 6 November 1994, pp. 10.10–10.12.
17. The use of linguistic subversion by the Economic Collectivists is discussed by Richard M. Ebeling, 'Liberalism and Collectivism in the 20th Century', *Political Studies*, vol. XLI, special issue (1993), pp. 66–77.
18. Michael Novak, *The Spirit of Democratic Capitalism*, New York, Touchstone, 1983, p. 14.
19. The argument that democracy entrenches economic freedoms and, in doing so, underpins growth, was discussed by *The Economist*, 27 August 1994, pp. 17–19.

4 MARKET CAPITALISM

1. F.A. Hayek, 'The Moral Imperative of the Market', in Martin J. Anderson (ed.), *The Unfinished Agenda*, London, The Institute of Economic Affairs, 1986, pp. 143–9.
2. On externalities see e.g. Andrew Schotter, *Free Market Economics: A Critical Appraisal*, Oxford, Basil Blackwell, 1990 (second edition), pp. 28 and 54–7.
3. Jan S. Prybyla, 'Meaning and Classification of Economic Systems: An Outline', in Jan S. Prybyla (ed.), *Comparative Economic Systems*, New York, Appleton-Century-Crofts, 1969, pp. 12–14.
4. See e.g. Harvey W. Peck, *Economic Thought and Its Institutional Background*, London, George Allen & Unwin Ltd, 1935, Chapter V, and

Eric Roll, *A History of Economic Thought*, London, Faber and Faber, 1992 (fifth edition), pp. 111–20.

5. William Doyle, *The Oxford History of the French Revolution*, Oxford, Oxford University Press, 1989 (reprinted), p. 57.

6. Adam Smith, *An Inquiry into the Nature and Causes of the Wealth of Nations*, London, J.M. Dent & Sons, 1929 (reprinted), Book V, Chapter 1.

7. On competition policy see *Oxford Review of Economic Policy*, vol. 9, no. 2 (summer 1993). It should be remembered, of course, that monopolies can be threatened by imported goods and by substitute products.

8. Wilhelm Röpke, *International Economic Disintegration*, London, William Hodge and Company, Limited, 1942, p. 5.

9. For comparison, in Milton Friedman's view the role of government in a free society is to maintain law and order, define property rights, serve as a means whereby property rights and other rules of the economic game can be modified, adjudicate disputes about the interpretation of the rules, enforce contracts, promote competition, provide a monetary framework, engage in activities to counter technical monopolies and overcome neighbourhood effects widely regarded as sufficiently important to justify government intervention, and on paternalistic grounds supplement private charity and the private family in protecting the irresponsible, whether madman or child. (*Capitalism and Freedom*, Chicago, The University of Chicago Press, 1982 (reissued), Chapter II.)

10. Roger Scruton, *A Dictionary of Political Thought*, London, Pan Books, 1983, p. 156.

11. John Kenneth Galbraith, *The Affluent Society*, London, André Deutsch, 1985 (fourth edition).

12. Ernesto Screpanti and Stefano Zamagni, *An Outline of the History of Economic Thought*, Oxford, Oxford University Press, 1993, pp. 419–20.

13. Peter A. Hall, 'Introduction', in Peter A. Hall (ed.), *The Political Power of Economic Ideas: Keynesianism across Nations*, Princeton, New Jersey, Princeton University Press, 1989, p. 4.

14. Angus Maddison, *Phases of Capitalist Development*, Oxford, Oxford University Press, 1982. The characteristics of the 'Golden Age' are given on p. 92, Table 4.11, and pp. 126ff. See also Angus Maddison, *The World Economy in the 20th Century*, Paris, OECD, 1989, pp. 34–7.

15. Robert O. Keohane, 'The World Political Economy and the Crisis of Embedded Liberalism', in John H. Goldthorpe (ed.), *Order and Conflict in Contemporary Capitalism*, Oxford, Oxford University Press, 1988 (reprinted), p. 19. According to the author, in European societies after the Second World War '[l]iberalism was "embedded" in the acceptance of an extensive role for the state, both in the steering of the economy and in assuring a decent life to citizens. Internationally, the form of liberalism agreed to after World War II had to be consistent with the welfare state rather than in conflict with it.'

16. Angus Maddison's explanation for the breakdown of the 'Golden Age' system, which was followed by growth deceleration and accelerated inflation, is given on pp. 136ff of *Phases of Capitalist Development*, op. cit.

17. *The Economist*, 2 October 1993, pp. 73–4. In more detail see Jozef M. van Brabant, *Industrial Policy in Eastern Europe: Governing the Transition*, Dordrecht, Kluwer Academic Publishers, 1993, pp. 207–19.
18. Cf. John Mueller, 'Democracy, Capitalism, and the End of Transition', in Michael Mandelbaum (ed.), *Postcommunism: Four Perspectives*, New York, Council on Foreign Relations, 1996, pp. 122–30.
19. On typologies of total economic activity under market capitalism see Jiri Skolka, 'The Parallel Economy in Austria', in Wulf Gaertner and Alois Wenig (eds), *The Economics of the Shadow Economy*, Berlin, Springer-Verlag, 1985, pp. 60–3, and Stephen Smith, *Britain's Shadow Economy*, Oxford, Clarendon Press, 1986, Chapter 2.
20. Dieter Cassel and Ulrich Cichy, 'The Shadow Economy and Economic Policy in East and West: A Comparative System Approach', in Sergio Alessandrini and Bruno Dallago (eds), *The Unofficial Economy*, Aldershot, Gower, 1987, pp. 139–40.
21. Quoted by Dieter Cassel and E. Ulrich Cichy, 'Explaining the Growing Shadow Economy in East and West: A Comparative Systems Approach', *Comparative Economic Studies*, vol. XXVIII, no. 1 (spring 1986), pp. 20–41. As to Italy see also Philip Mattera, *Off the Books*, London, Pluto Press, 1985, Chapter 7.
22. *The Economist*, 14 August 1993, p. 25, and *The Economist*, 12 February 1994, p. 81.
23. Besides not being identical with anarcho-capitalism in the sense of a free-for-all, the *laissez-faire* variant of market capitalism is not identical with anarchism which opposes the state in all its forms and insists that the economy must be run by voluntary autonomous groups.

5   COMMAND CAPITALISM

1. On the Nazi economy see e.g. Avraham Barkai, *Nazi Economics: Ideology, Theory, and Policy*, Oxford, Berg Publishers Limited, 1990, and R.J. Overy, *War and Economy in the Third Reich*, Oxford, Oxford University Press, 1994.
2. Charles E. Lindblom, *Politics and Markets: The World's Political-Economic Systems*, New York, Basic Books, 1977, pp. 98–100.
3. R.E. Pahl and J.T. Winkler, 'The Coming Corporatism', *New Society*, 10 October 1974, pp. 72–6.
4. A survey of the various meanings of corporatism is to be found in Frederic L. Pryor, 'Corporatism as an Economic System: A Review Essay', *Journal of Comparative Economics*, vol. 12, no. 3 (September 1988), pp. 317–44.
5. On the levels of corporatism see Peter J. Williamson, *Corporatism in Perspective*, London, SAGE Publications, 1989, Chapter 7.
6. As to France see Matthew H. Elbow, *French Corporative Theory: 1789–1948*, New York, Octagon Books, 1966 (reprinted).

7. The motives of the advocates of the corporate state were discussed by Carl Landauer, *Contemporary Economic Systems*, Philadelphia, J.B. Lippincott Company, 1964, pp. 200–7.

8. Philippe C. Schmitter, 'Still the Century of Corporatism?' in Philippe C. Schmitter and Gerhard Lehmbruch (eds), *Trends Toward Corporatist Intermediation*, London, SAGE Publications, 1979, pp. 25–7.

9. See e.g. Ilja Scholten (ed.), *Political Stability and Neo-Corporatism*, London, SAGE Publications, 1987.

10. Valerie Bunce and John M. Echols III, 'Soviet Politics in the Brezhnev Era: "Pluralism" or "Corporatism"?', in Donald R. Kelly (ed.), *Soviet Politics in the Brezhnev Era*, New York, Praeger, 1980, Chapter 1. The corporatist conceptualization of the Soviet system was rejected by Archie Brown, 'Political Power and the Soviet State: Western and Soviet Perspectives', in Neil Harding (ed.), *The State in Socialist Society*, London, Macmillan, 1984, p. 87.

11. Alex Pravda and Blair A. Ruble, 'Communist Trade Unions: Varieties of Dualism', in Alex Pravda and Blair A. Ruble (eds.), *Trade Unions in Communist States*, London, Allen & Unwin, 1986, p. 12.

12. Philippe C. Schmitter, op. cit., pp. 13–17.

13. Michael Bruno and Jeffrey D. Sachs, *Economics of Worldwide Stagflation*, Oxford, Basil Blackwell, 1985, p. 226, Table 11.3; Gerhard Lehmbruch, 'Concertation and the Structure of Corporatist Networks', in John H. Goldthorpe (ed.), *Order and Conflict in Contemporary Capitalism*, Oxford, Oxford University Press, 1988 (reprinted), p. 66, Table 3.1; Frederic L. Pryor, op. cit., p. 326, Table 1; Peter J. Williamson, op. cit, p. 150, Table 7.1.

14. Austrian corporatism (social partnership) is discussed by Günter Bischof and Anton Pelinka (eds), *Austro-Corporatism: Past – Present – Future*, New Brunswick, Transaction Publishers, 1996. According to the editors, '[c]orporatism has been one of the most significant aspects of Austrian political culture after World War II' (p. 1).

15. On corporatism without labour see Graham K. Wilson, *Interest Groups*, Oxford, Basil Blackwell, 1990, pp. 125–33.

16. Gerhard Lehmbruch, op. cit., p. 62.

17. Philippe C. Schmitter, 'Corporatism is Dead! Long Live Corporatism!' *Government and Opposition*, vol. 24, no. 1 (winter 1989), pp. 54–73.

18. It should be added that some political theorists, arguing from Marxist premises, invoked neo-corporatism to explain how, through successful manipulation, crises did not come to a head and class struggles were not exacerbated. Others, arguing from pluralist premises, embraced neo-corporatism as a solution to what was termed the problem of 'ungovernability', thought to be a consequence of the overloading of the system of communication.

19. The 1906 Trade Disputes Act granted trade unions total immunity for torts alleged to have been committed by or on behalf of them, it turned trade unions into privileged bodies exempted from the ordinary law of the land. The tension between voluntarism and regulation in British industrial relations is discussed by Robert Taylor, 'Industrial Relations: Regulation Against Voluntarism', in David Marquand and Anthony

Seldon (eds), *The Ideas that Shaped Post-War Britain*, London, Fontana Books, 1996, Chapter 5.

20. J. Wil Foppen, 'The Netherlands and the Crisis as a Policy Challenge: Integration or Ideological Manoeuvres?' in E. Damgaard, P. Gerlich and J.J. Richardson (eds), *The Politics of Economic Crisis*, Aldershot, Avebury, 1989, pp. 102–3.

21. See e.g. Alice Brown and Desmond S. King, 'Economic Change and Labour Market Policy: Corporatist and Dualist Tendencies in Britain and Sweden', *West European Politics*, vol. 11, no. 3 (July 1988), pp. 75–91.

22. Pam Woodall, 'The Swedish Economy', *The Economist*, 3 March 1990, Survey. Between 1973 and 1982, employment in the public sector went up by 45 per cent, while that in the private sector fell by three per cent. (Quoted by Carlo Dell'Aringa, 'Industrial Relations and the Role of the State in the EEC Countries', in David Marsden (ed.), *Pay and Employment in the New Europe*, Aldershot, Edward Elgar, 1992, p. 190, Table 6.)

23. J.L. Porket, *Unemployment in Capitalist, Communist and Post-Communist Economies*, Basingstoke, Macmillan, 1995, p. 181, Table 18.1.

24. Klaus von Beyme, *Challenge to Power*, London, SAGE Publications, 1980, pp. 75–6, Table 6; Michael Bruno and Jeffrey D. Sachs, op. cit., p. 169, Table 8.13 and p. 225, Table 11.2; Richard Layard, Stephen Nickell and Richard Jackman, *Unemployment*, Oxford, Oxford University Press, 1991, p. 88, Table 1.

25. *The Economist*, 23 July 1994, p. 112.

26. *The Economist*, 29 January 1994, p. 118. See also Richard Layard, Stephen Nickell and Richard Jackman, op. cit., pp. 96–9.

27. Hugh Compston, 'Union Participation in Economic Policy-Making in Austria, Switzerland, The Netherlands, Belgium and Ireland, 1970–1992', *West European Politics*, vol. 17, no. 1 (January 1994), pp. 123–45.

28. Andrei S. Markovits, 'Austrian Corporatism in Comparative Perspective', in Günter Bischof and Anton Pelinka (eds), op. cit., p. 6.

29. Will Hutton, 'The Stakeholder Society', in David Marquand and Anthony Seldon (eds), op. cit., Chapter 12.

6 MARKET SOCIALISM

1. The English translation of von Mises' article is to be found in F.A. Hayek (ed.), *Collectivist Economic Planning*, London, George Routledge & Sons, 1935.

2. Also Barone's article, translated as 'The Ministry of Production in the Collectivist State', is to be found in F.A. Hayek (ed.), op. cit.

3. Oskar Lange, 'On the Economic Theory of Socialism', *Review of Economic Studies*, vol. 4, No. 1 (October 1936), pp. 53–71, and vol. 4, no. 2 (February 1937), pp. 123–42. Reprinted in Oskar Lange and Fred M. Taylor, *On the Economic Theory of Socialism*, ed. Benjamin E. Lippincott, New York, McGraw-Hill Book Company, 1964, pp. 57–142.

4. According to Lange, '[a]ctually the process of trial and error would, of course, proceed on the basis of the prices *historically given.*' (Oskar Lange and Fred M. Taylor, op. cit., p. 86.)

5. Oskar Lange and Fred M. Taylor, op. cit., pp. 109.

6. Oskar Lange and Fred M. Taylor, op. cit., pp. 82–3.

7. Abba P. Lerner, *The Economics of Control*, New York, Macmillan, 1944.

8. Abba P. Lerner, op. cit., pp. 84–5.

9. Don Lavoie, *Rivalry and central planning*, Cambridge, Cambridge University Press, 1985.

10. Don Lavoie, 'Computation, Incentives, and Discovery: The Cognitive Function of Markets in Market Socialism', *The Annals of The American Academy of Political and Social Science*, vol. 507 (January 1990), pp. 72–9.

11. Joseph E. Stiglitz, *Whither Socialism?* Cambridge, Massachusetts, The MIT Press, 1994, pp. 195–6.

12. Joze Mencinger, 'From a Capitalist to a Capitalist Economy?' in James Simmie and Joze Dekleva (eds), *Yugoslavia in Turmoil: After Self-Management?* London, Pinter, 1991, Chapter 5.

13. Gertrude E. Schroeder, 'Property Rights Issues in Economic Reforms in Socialist Countries', *Studies in Comparative Communism*, vol. XXI, no. 2 (summer 1988), pp. 175–88.

14. Wlodzimierz Brus, 'The "March into Socialism"', in Henryk Flakierski and Thomas T. Sekine (eds), *Socialist Dilemmas: East and West*, Armonk, New York, M.E. Sharpe, Inc., 1990, pp. 28–38.

15. Marc Fleurbaey, 'Economic Democracy and Equality: A Proposal', in Pranab K. Bardhan and John E. Roemer (eds), *Market Socialism: The Current Debate*, Oxford, Oxford University Press, 1993, Chapter 16.

16. David Schweickart, *Against Capitalism*, Cambridge University Press, 1993, p. ix.

17. John E. Roemer, 'Can there be Socialism after Communism?' in Pranab K. Bardhan and John E. Roemer (eds), op. cit., p. 89, and John E. Roemer, *A Future for Socialism*, London, Verso, 1994, p. 6.

18. David Miller, *Market, State, and Community*, Oxford, Clarendon Press, 1989, pp. 9–11.

19. David Miller, op. cit., p. 321.

20. James A. Yunker, 'Ludwig von Mises on the "Artificial Market"', *Comparative Economic Studies*, vol. XXXII, no. 1 (spring 1990), pp. 108–40.

21. Pranab Bardhan and John E. Roemer, 'Market Socialism: A Case for Rejuvenation', *Journal of Economic Perspectives*, vol. 6, no. 3 (summer 1992), pp. 101–16. It should be added that the authors advocated market socialism for post-communist Eastern Europe too.

22. One advocate of market socialism was Alec Nove, *The Economics of Feasible Socialism Revisited*, London, HarperCollins *Academic*, 1991 (second edition). The main features of a feasible form of socialism are summarized on pp. 245–7. The original version was published in 1983.

23. John Gray, *Beyond the New Right*, London, Routledge, 1993, p. 98.

24. John E. Roemer, *A Future for Socialism*, op. cit., pp. 51–3.

25. In this connection see also Paul Hirst, 'Associational Democracy', in David Held (ed.), *Prospects for Democracy*, Cambridge, Polity Press, 1993, Chapter 5.

7 COMMAND SOCIALISM

1. The main characteristics of an absolute command economy were summarized and compared with those of a perfect market economy by Oleg Zinam, 'The Economics of Command Economies', in Jan S. Prybyla (ed.), *Comparative Economic Systems*, New York, Appleton-Century-Crofts, 1969, pp. 30–1, Table 2.3.
2. On the logical incompatibility of a planned economy and freedom for the individual see John Jewkes, *Ordeal by Planning*, London, Macmillan, 1949 (reprinted), Chapter X, and John Jewkes, *The New Ordeal by Planning*, London, Macmillan, 1968, Chapter VIII.
3. The contrasting features of capitalism and socialism were summarized by J. Wilczynski, *Comparative Industrial Relations*, London, Macmillan, 1983, pp. 2–3, Figure 1.1.
4. On soft and hard budget constraint see János Kornai, *The Socialist System*, Oxford, Clarendon Press, 1992, pp. 140–5.
5. For example, in 1978–80 the Soviet-bloc economies consumed on average nearly twice as much energy relative to gross domestic product and capital as the market economies. Despite that, aggregate output per worker in the former averaged only 60 per cent of that in the latter. (John R. Moroney, 'Energy Consumption, Capital and Real Output: A Comparison of Market and Planned Economies', *Journal of Comparative Economics*, vol. 14, no. 2 (June 1990), pp. 199–220.)
6. Cf. J.L. Porket, *Unemployment in Capitalist, Communist and Post-Communist Economies*, Basingstoke, Macmillan, 1995, pp. 39–42 and 151–4.
7. According to János Kornai, a socialist command economy is a shortage economy, and shortages make production inefficient by leading to interruptions in production, forced substitutions, the weakening of workers' discipline and morale, and the quantity drive. (*Growth, Shortage and Efficiency*, Oxford, Basil Blackwell, 1982, pp. 95–102.)
8. Gregory Grossman, 'What Was – Is, Will Be – The Command Economy?' *MOCT-MOST*, vol. 4, no. 1 (1994), pp. 5–22.
9. Some aspects of the Soviet-bloc countries' relative economic performance are discussed by J.L. Porket, op. cit., Chapter 7.
10. On the pre-1978 Chinese economy see Jan Deleyne, *The Chinese Economy*, London, André Deutsch, 1973, and Alexander Eckstein, *China's Economic Revolution*, Cambridge, Cambridge University Press, 1977. On the first decade of the economic reform see Dwight Heald Perkins, 'Reforming China's Economic System', *Journal of Economic Literature*, vol. XXVI, no. 2 (June 1988), pp. 601–45, and Dorothy J. Solinger, 'Capitalist Measures With Chinese Characteristics', *Problems of Communism*, vol. XXXVIII, no. 1 (January-February 1989), pp. 19–33.

11. On the evolution of views on planning and market in Czechoslovakia, Hungary, Poland, and the Soviet Union see Jan Adam, *Planning and Market in Soviet and East European Thought, 1960s–1992*, Basingstoke, Macmillan, 1993.

12. The main actors promoting or inhibiting economic reform in a Soviet-type society include the government (in effect, the party leadership), the state and party bureaucracy, knowledge specialists, enterprise directors, and blue-collar workers.

13. János Kornai, *The Socialist System*, op. cit., p. XXV.

14. Dieter Cassel and Ulrich Cichy, 'The Shadow Economy and Economic Policy in East and West: A Comparative System Approach', in Sergio Alessandrini and Bruno Dallago (eds), *The Unofficial Economy*, Aldershot, Gower, 1987, pp. 140–1. See also Steven L. Sampson, 'The Second Economy of the Soviet Union and Eastern Europe', *The Annals of The American Academy of Political and Social Sciences*, vol. 493 (September 1987), pp. 120–136. According to him, in socialist centrally planned economies the second economy has a lubricating function, a mollifying one, and a corrosive one, with the first two being offset by the last-mentioned.

15. J.L. Porket, 'Private Plots – One Dimension of the Soviet Second Economy', *Economic Affairs*, vol. 10, no. 4 (April-May 1990), pp. 28–32.

16. Private plot output, it should be added, was partly consumed by the private plot holders themselves, partly put on the market by them. Only its marketed part fell under the second economy, while its non-marketed part fell under the household economy.

17. Karin Plokker, 'The Development of Individual and Cooperative Labour Activity in the Soviet Union', *Soviet Studies*, vol. 42, no. 3 (July 1990), pp. 403–28, and Darrell Slider, 'Embattled Entrepreneurs: Soviet Cooperatives in an Unreformed Economy', *Soviet Studies*, vol. 43, no. 5 (1991), pp. 797–821.

18. Bogdan Mroz, 'Poland's Economy in Transition to Private Ownership', *Soviet Studies*, vol. 43, no. 4 (1991), pp. 677–88.

19. Thomas B. Gold, 'Urban Private Business in China', *Studies in Comparative Communism*, vol. XXII, nos. 2–3 (summer-autumn 1989), pp. 187–201.

20. On informal property rights in the Soviet Union see Gregory Grossman, 'The Second Economy: Boon or Bane for the Reform of the First Economy?', in Stanislaw Gomulka, Yong-Chool Ha, and Cae-One Kim (eds), *Economic Reforms in the Socialist World*, Basingstoke, Macmillan, 1989, pp. 79–83.

21. Quoted by Dieter Cassel and E. Ulrich Cichy, 'Explaining the Growing Shadow Economy in East and West: A Comparative Systems Approach', *Comparative Economic Studies*, vol. XXVIII, no. 1 (spring 1986), pp. 20–41.

22. T. Koryagina, 'Tenevaya ekonomika v SSSR', *Voprosy ekonomiki*, no. 3 (March 1990), pp. 110–20. For comparison, the gross national product amounted to 875 thousand million roubles in 1988 and to 924 thousand million roubles in 1989. (*Narodnoe khozyaistvo SSSR*, 1989, p. 6.)

23. Marian Wisniewski, 'The Sources and Dimensions of the Second Economy in Poland', *Oeconomica Polona*, vol. XIII, no. 2 (1986), p. 273, Table 3.
24. Stefan Taigner, 'Polands Second Economy', *Osteuropa-Wirtschaft*, vol. 32, no. 2 (June 1987), pp. 107–21.
25. Bogdan Mroz, op. cit., pp. 678–9.
26. István R. Gábor, 'Second Economy in State Socialism: Past Experience and Future Prospects', *European Economic Review*, vol. 33, nos. 2–3 (March 1989), pp. 597–604.
27. Horst Brezinski and Paul Peterson, 'Die Parallelwirtschaft in Rumänien – ein dynamischer Sektor', *Südosteuropa*, vol. 36, no. 5 (1987), pp. 227–44.
28. Horst Brezinski, 'The Second Economy in the GDR – Pragmatism is Gaining Ground', *Studies in Comparative Communism*, vol. XX, no. 1 (spring 1987), pp. 85–101. See also Günter Manz, ' "Schattenwirtschaft" in der DDR', *Wirtschaftswissenschaft*, vol. 38, no. 2 (1990), pp. 219–29. According to some estimates, in 1987 the East German legal agricultural private sector accounted for 24 per cent of total agricultural output.
29. One form of non-compliance is formalism, a purely nominal compliance witth centrally promulgated formal norms and a purely nominal implementation of administrative orders.
30. On the formal and informal dimensions of state enterprises and their informal culture see J.L. Porket, *Podnik jako sociální systém*, Bratislava, Ústav ekonomiky a organizácie stavebníctva, 1967, pp. 16–30, and J.L. Porket, *Work, Employment and Unemployment in the Soviet Union*, London, Macmillan, 1989, pp. 122–3.

8   THE GOVERNMENT ECONOMY

1. Cf. Peter Self, *Government by the Market?* Basingstoke, Macmillan, 1993, pp. 36–44.
2. See also Spencer J. Pack, *Capitalism as a Moral System*, Aldershot, Edward Elgar, 1991. According to him, Adam Smith was not 'a proponent of an extreme, dogmatic version of laissez-faire capitalism. There are a fair number of tasks which Smith feels the government can and/or ought to do in a capitalist society' (p. 69).
3. A third characteristic of public goods which is sometimes mentioned is non-rejectability. (Nicholas Barr, *The Economics of the Welfare State*, London, Weidenfeld and Nicolson, 1993 (second edition), pp. 81–2 and 106–7.)
4. See e.g. Andrew Schotter, *Free Market Economics*, Oxford, Basil Blackwell, 1990, pp. 57–63 and 100–101.
5. See e.g. Holger Bonus, 'Öffentliche Güter: Verführung und Gefangenendilemma', in Wolfgang Stützel, Christian Watrin, Hans Willgerodt and Karl Höhmann (eds), *Grundtexte zur Sozialen Marktwirtschaft*, Stuttgart, Gustav Fischer Verlag, 1981, pp. 283–305, and Arthur Seldon, *Capitalism*, Oxford, Basil Blackwell, 1990, pp. 167–74.

6. Milton and Rose Friedman, *Free to Choose*, London, Secker & Warburg, 1980, pp. 116–17.

7. David W. Conklin, *Comparative Economic Systems*, Cambridge, Cambridge University Press, 1991, pp. 167–70.

8. *The Economist*, 11 June 1994, p. 131, and ibid., 20 August 1994, pp. 15–16. See also David W. Conklin, op. cit., pp. 172–7.

9. David W. Conklin, op. cit., pp. 164–6 and 190–211.

10. E.F. Schumacher, 'Public Finance – Its Relation to Full Employment', in The Oxford University Institute of Statistics, *The Economics of Full Employment*, Oxford, Basil Blackwell, 1948 (reprinted), Part IV. To the five principles of orthodox public finance mentioned in the text, the author added a sixth one, namely, to pay off the national debt as fast as possible.

11. Peter A. Hall, 'Introduction', in Peter A. Hall (ed.), *The Political Power of Economic Ideas: Keynesianism across Nations*, Princeton, New Jersey, Princeton University Press, 1989, p. 4.

12. W.W. Rostow, *The World Economy*, London, Macmillan, 1978, p. 60. Higher shares were to be found in the poorer countries of southern and eastern Europe, such as Spain, Italy, and Russia. In the Balkan nations it ranged from 20 to 30 per cent in the early 1900s. (Rondo Cameron, *A Concise Economic History of the World*, Oxford, Oxford University Press, 1993 (second edition), p. 320.)

13. Angus Maddison, *The World Economy in the 20th Century*, Paris, OECD, 1989, p. 71, Table 6.3.

14. As to OECD countries between 1965 and 1986 see OECD, *Revenue Statistics of OECD Member Countries 1965–1987*, Paris, OECD, 1987, p. 83, Table 3.

15. Government saving, household saving, and corporate saving make up national saving. On changes in gross national saving ratios in OECD countries between 1976 and 1992 see *OECD Economic Outlook*, no. 55 (June 1994), p. A28, Annex Table 25. See also *The Economist*, 14 October 1989, p. 113.

16. For 1978–93 see *OECD Economic Outlook*, no. 55 (June 1994), p. A31, Annex Table 28.

17. *OECD Economic Outlook*, no. 55 (June 1994), p. A35, Annex Table 32.

18. In the socialist command economies established in the Soviet-bloc countries, the measure of national income was net material product (NMP), which was confined to the so-called material production and excluded public administration, health, and education. GDP in national currency began to be calculated in Hungary in 1970, in Poland in 1986, and in the Soviet Union in 1988.

19. Calculated from the estimates of Soviet GNP by Genadii Zoteev, 'Ob otsenke natsional'nogo produkta', *Ekonomicheskaya gazeta*, no. 42 (October 1987), and *Narodnoe khozyaistvo SSSR za 70 let*, Moskva, 1987, p. 629.

20. G. Zoteev and E. Kh'yuitt, 'Protsess ekonomicheskikh reform i ego katalizatory', *Kommunist*, no. 13 (September 1989), p. 59, Table 2.

21. Food subsidies went up from 2.1 per cent of government expenditure in 1960 through 7.8 per cent in 1970 and 8.1 per cent in 1980 to 14.5 per

cent in 1985 and 18.2 per cent in 1989. (Karen M. Brooks, 'Soviet Agriculture's Halting Reform', *Problems of Communism*, vol. XXXIX, no. 2 (March-April 1990), p. 37, Table 7, and own calculations.) On subsidies to consumers and state enterprises in Bulgaria, Czechoslovakia, Hungary, and Poland see Paul J.J. Welfens, 'The Socialist Shadow Economy: Causes, Characteristics, and Role for Systemic Reforms', *Economic Systems*, vol. 16, no. 1 (April 1992), pp. 113–47.

22. For 1971–83 see Charles Wolf, Jr., 'The Costs and Benefits of the Soviet Empire', in Henry S. Rowen and Charles Wolf, Jr. (eds), *The Future of the Soviet Empire*, London, Macmillan, 1988, Chapter 7.

23. See e.g. R.T. Maddock, *The Political Economy of Soviet Defence Spending*, London, Macmillan, 1988; Steven Rosefielde, 'Soviet Defence Spending: The Contribution to the New Accountancy', *Soviet Studies*, vol. 42, no. 1 (January 1990), pp. 59–80; Dmitri Steinberg, 'Trends in Soviet Military Expenditure', *Soviet Studies*, vol. 42, no. 4 (October 1990), pp. 675–99.

24. *Narodnoe khozyaistvo SSSR*, 1989, pp. 11 and 612. It should be added that the USSR Ministry of Internal Affairs (MVD) and the KGB had their own budgets that were separate from those of the USSR Ministry of Defence. (Cf. Dmitri Steinberg, op. cit., p. 678.)

25. R.T. Maddock, op. cit., Chapter 6.

26. Keith Crane, 'The Determinants of Spending in Eastern Europe: Defence Expenditure in the Non-Soviet Warsaw Pact', in Christopher Coker (ed.), *Drifting Apart? The Superpowers and Their European Allies*, London, Brassey's Defence Publishers, 1989, Chapter 4.

27. Mario I. Blejer and Gyorgy Szapary, 'The Evolving Role of Tax Policy in China', *Journal of Comparative Economics*, vol. 14, no. 3 (September 1990), pp. 452–72.

28. Cf. Robert Bacon and Walter Eltis, *Britain's Economic Problem Revisited*, Basingstoke, Macmillan, 1996 (third edition). The authors emphasized that 'the distinction between the market and non-market sectors of the economy is not the same as the distinction between the public and private sectors. A profit-making nationalised industry is in the public sector but its entire output is marketed. Council houses, if they are let at rents which cover all costs, also provide much-desired marketed output. It is only in so far as nationalised industries make losses and houses are let at rents which fail to cover costs that they are part of the non-market sector which has to draw on the market sector for its consumption and investment requirements' (p. 31).

29. Robert Skidelsky, *The World After Communism: A Polemic For Our Time*, London, Macmillan, 1995, p. 192.

9 THE WELFARE STATE

1. Welfare pluralism was discussed by Norman Johnson, *The Welfare State in Transition: The Theory and Practice of Welfare Pluralism*, Brighton, Wheatsheaf Books, 1987. The term 'welfare mix' was used by Richard

Rose, 'Common Goals but Different Roles: The State's Contribution to the Welfare Mix', in Richard Rose and Rei Shiratori (eds), *The Welfare State East and West*, Oxford, Oxford University Press, 1986, Chapter 1.

2. Alessandro Cigno, *Economics of the Family*, Oxford, Clarendon Press, 1991, pp. 41–2.

3. On welfare as one of the ends of the state see Charles E. Merriam, *Systematic Politics*, Chicago, University of Chicago Press, 1946 (second impression), pp. 50–4 and 297. On the general-welfare functions of the state see R.M. McIver, *The Web of Government*, New York, Macmillan, 1947 (second printing), pp. 331–40.

4. A distinction between the needs model and the [social] insurance model was made by Brian Barry, 'The Continuing Relevance of Socialism', in Robert Skidelsky (ed.), *Thatcherism*, London, Chatto & Windus, 1988, Chapter 8. Some other typologies of welfare state regimes were summarized by Christopher Pierson, *Beyond the Welfare State? The New Political Economy of Welfare*, Cambridge, Polity Press, 1991, pp. 184–7.

5. See e.g. Erik Allardt, 'The Civic Conception of the Welfare State in Scandinavia', in Richard Rose and Rei Shiratori (eds), op.cit., Chapter 5.

6. On differences in the state provision of welfare among industrial countries see e.g. P.R. Kaim-Caudle, *Comparative Social Policy and Social Security*, London, Martin Robertson, 1973, and Margaret S. Gordon, *Social Security Policies in Industrial Countries*, Cambridge, Cambridge University Press, 1988.

7. An overview of social security benefits available in the United Kingdom by the end of the 1980s is to be found in Thomas and Dorothy Wilson (eds), *The State and Social Welfare*, London, Longman, 1991, Appendix. These benefits fell into three groups, namely, (1) national insurance benefits; (2) non-contributory, non-means-tested benefits; and (3) means-tested benefits.

8. The question of welfare rights is discussed by Norman Barry, *Welfare*, Milton Keynes, Open University Press, 1994 (reprinted), pp. 78–85.

9. On sources of revenue for social security programmes in OECD countries in 1979–80 see Margaret S. Gordon, op. cit., p. 30, Table 2.3.

10. Cf. Margaret S. Gordon, op.cit., pp. 203–5; John Peet, 'Health Care', *The Economist*, 6 July 1991, Survey; Nicholas Barr, *The Economics of the Welfare State*, London, Weidenfeld and Nicolson, 1993 (second edition), pp. 305–9.

11. Anatole Kaletsky, 'The National Health Service can Survive as it is, Thank You', *The Times*, 21 September 1995, p. 27.

12. Milton Friedman, *Capitalism and Freedom*, Chicago, The University of Chicago Press, 1982 (reissued), pp. 10–11.

13. Howard Glennerster, 'Social Policy since the Second World War', in Nicholas Barr et al., *The State of Welfare*, Oxford, Clarendon Press, 1990, p. 21, Fig. 2.1.

14. Howard Glennerster, op. cit., p. 22, Table 2.2, and Edwin Bell, 'Social Policy and Economic Reality', *The OECD Observer*, no. 183 (August/September 1993), pp. 14–15.

15. John Creedy and Richard Disney, 'Can We Afford to Grow Older?' *European Economic Review*, vol. 33, nos. 2–3 (March 1989), pp. 367–76.

16. *OECD Economic Outlook*, no. 57 (June 1995), p. 33. See also Barbara Beck, 'The Economics of Ageing', *The Economist*, 27 January 1996, Survey.

17. See e.g. Helmut Reisen, 'On the Weath of Nations and Retirees', in Richard O'Brien (ed.), *Finance and the International Economy: 8*, Oxford University Press, 1994, Chapter 5. He argues that private funded pension schemes have to be phased in now because the cost of publicly provided pensions will become unsustainable; that they should seek maximum returns on pension fund assets; and that the need for high returns on pension fund assets implies a need for global diversification.

18. OECD, *Future Global Capital Shortages: Real Threat or Pure Fiction?* Paris, OECD, 1996, p. 3.

19. A criticism of the British welfare state is to be found in Paul Einzig, *Decline and Fall? Britain's Crisis in the Sixties*. London, Macmillan, 1969, Chapter 10.

20. Theodore Geiger, *Welfare and Efficiency*, London, Macmillan, 1979, pp. 12–13.

21. As to Britain between 1983 and 1993 see David Lipsey, 'Do We Really Want More Public Spending?', in Roger Jowell et al. (eds), *British Social Attitudes: the 11th report*, Aldershot, Dartmouth Publishing Company, 1994, Chapter 1. See also the results of an opinion poll conducted by MORI in June 1988, as presented by Ivor Crewe, 'Values: The Crusade that Failed', in Dennis Kavanagh and Anthony Seldon (eds), *The Thatcher Effect*, Oxford, Clarendon Press, 1989, pp. 241–3.

22. On the relationship between welfare statism and international competitiveness see Alfred Pfaller et al., 'The Issue', in Alfred Pfaller, Ian Gough, and Göran Therborn (eds), *Can the Welfare State Compete?*, Basingstoke, Macmillan, 1991, Chapter 1. The ambiguity of the notion of international competitiveness is emphasized by Harald Trabold, who defines it as the capacity to combine the ability to sell, the ability to attract, and the ability to adjust with knowledge in such a way that the result is the highest possible real income. ('Die internationale Wettbewerbsfähigkeit einer Volkswirtschaft', *DIW Vierteljahrsheft*, vol. 64, no. 2 (1995), pp. 169–85.

23. On a voucher plan for elementary and secondary schooling and for higher education see Milton and Rose Friedman, *Free to Choose*, London, Secker & Warburg, 1980, pp. 158–75 and 185–7.

24. OECD, *Progress in Structural Reform: Supplement to OECD Economic Outlook 47*, Paris, 1990, p. 14. See also Christopher Pierson, op. cit., pp. 174–6, Table 5.3.

25. *The Economist*, 26 August 1995, pp. 33–4.

26. Some problematic aspects and contradictions of the welfare state are discussed by Anthony Giddens, *Beyond Left and Right: The Future of Radical Politics*, Cambridge, Polity Press, 1994, pp. 17–18, 74–7 and 134–50. His thesis is that 'the current problems of the welfare state should not be seen as a fiscal crisis (nor are they the result of the need

of the Western societies to compete more fiercely than before on world markets), but one of the management of risk' (p. 180).

10 WELFARE UNDER COMMAND SOCIALISM

1. The term 'administered mass organizations' was used by Gregory J. Kasza 'to describe formal organizations structured and managed by the state's ruling apparatus to shape mass social action for the purpose of implementing public policy.' ('Weapons of the Strong: Organization and Terror', in H.E. Chehabi and Alfred Stepan (eds), *Politics, Society, and Democracy: Comparative Studies*, Boulder, Westview Press, 1995, p. 218.)

2. On social welfare prior to the October Revolution see Bernice Q. Madison, *Social Welfare in the Soviet Union*, Stanford, California, Stanford University Press, 1968, Chapter I, and Gaston V. Rimlinger, *Welfare Policy and Industrialization in Europe, America, and Russia*, London, John Wiley & Sons, Inc., 1971, pp. 245–52.

3. A detailed survey of the development of social security between the October Revolution and the mid-1960s is to be found in Gaston V. Rimlinger, op. cit., pp. 252–301.

4. See e.g. J.L. Porket, *Main Features of Social Security in Eastern Europe*, Centre for Soviet and East European Studies, St. Antony's College, Oxford, Papers in East European Economics, Paper No. 51 (1977). In this study, the term 'social security' denoted curative and preventive medical care, income maintenance in case of involuntary loss of earnings or of an important part of earnings, and a supplementary income in case of family responsibilities.

5. As to Czechoslovakia see Zdenek Deyl, *Sociální vývoj Ceskoslovenska 1918–1938*, Praha, Academia, 1985, especially pp. 179–89.

6. In Hungary, social insurance covered some 31 per cent of the population in 1938. (The Chief Administration of Social Insurance of the Central Council of the Hungarian Trade Unions, *The Development of Social Insurance in Hungary over Three Decades*, Budapest, 1975, p. 33.)

7. This attempt was briefly discussed by J.L. Porket, 'The Economic Lot of Polish Retired Workers', *Osteuropa-Wirtschaft*, vol. 26, no. 4 (1981), pp. 294–303.

8. For example, in Hungary 41 per cent of the population were covered by social insurance in 1949, 72 per cent in 1959, 97 per cent in 1963, and 99 per cent in 1972. (The Chief Administration of Social Insurance of the Central Council of the Hungarian Trade Unions, op. cit., p.110.)

9. Zsuzsa Ferge, *A Society in the Making*, Harmondsworth, Penguin Books, 1979, pp. 61–6; Martin McCauley, *The German Democratic Republic since 1945*, London, Macmillan, 1983, p. 178; Karel Pinc, *Sociální politika a socialistické hospodárství*, Praha, Univerzita Karlova, 1983, pp. 45–9.

10. Yu.E. Volkov and V.Z. Rogovin, *Voprosy sotsial'noi politiki KPSS*, Moskva, Izdatel'stvo politicheskoi literatury, 1981, p. 29.

11. Helga Michalsky, 'Social Policy and the Transformation of Society', in Klaus von Beyme and Hartmut Zimmerman (eds), *Policymaking in the German Democratic Republic*, Aldershot, Gower, 1984, p. 242.
12. Helga Michalsky, op. cit., p. 246.
13. *Bol'shaya Sovetskaya Entsiklopediya*, Moskva, Izdatel'stvo Sovetskaya Entsiklopediya, 1972 (third edition), vol. 7, p. 151.
14. E.M. Primakov and A.I. Vlasov (eds), *What's What in World Politics*, Moscow, Progress Publishers, 1987, pp. 447–8.
15. The concept of social consumption funds can be traced back to Karl Marx, 'Marginal Notes to the Program of the German Workers' Party', in Karl Marx and Frederick Engels, *Selected Works*, Moscow, Foreign Languages Publishing House, 1949, vol. II, pp. 20–1.
16. J.L. Porket, *Unemployment in Capitalist, Communist and Post-Communist Economies*, Basingstoke, Macmillan, 1995, pp. 39–42.
17. J.L. Porket, *Work, Employment and Unemployment in the Soviet Union*, London, Macmillan, 1989, pp. 87 and 190.
18. Phillip J. Bryson and Philip J. Perry, '*Sozialpolitik*: East German Social Welfare Policies', *Comparative Economic Studies*, vol. XXVIII, no. 2 (summer 1986), p. 16, Table 10.
19. Calculated from K. Janácek and H. Zelenková, *K rovnováze vnitrního spotrebitelského trhu*, Praha, Ekonomický ústav CSAV, 1988, p. 42, n. 4, and *Statistická rocenka Ceskoslovenské socialistické republiky*, 1986, p. 144.
20. Josef Brcák and Hana Brydlová, *Mzdy v soudobém kapitalismu*. Praha, Horizont, 1976, p. 62.
21. Calculated from *Narodnoe khozyaistvo SSSR*, 1989, pp. 6 and 82. The increase was mainly due to growing outlays for pensions.
22. J.L. Porket, 'Old Age Pension Schemes in the Soviet Union and Eastern Europe', *Social Policy & Administration*, vol. 13, no. 1 (spring 1979), pp. 22–36.
23. J.L. Porket, *Inequalities in Eastern Europe: The Case of Old-Age Pensioners*, Russian and East European Centre, St. Antony's College, Oxford, Papers in East European Economics, Paper no. 64 (August 1980), and J.L. Porket, 'Retired Workers under Soviet-Type Socialism', *Social Policy & Administration*, vol. 16, no. 3 (autumn 1982), pp. 253–69.
24. On the strengths, weaknesses, and perennial problems of the health care systems in Soviet-controlled Eastern Europe see Alexander S. Preker and Richard G.A. Feachem, 'Health and Health Care', in Nicholas Barr (ed.), *Labor Markets and Social Policy in Central and Eastern Europe*, New York, Oxford University Press, 1994, pp. 288–97. As to the Soviet Union see Michael Ryan, *Doctors and the State in the Soviet Union*, London, Macmillan, 1989.
25. See e.g. *Narodnoe khozyaistvo SSSR*, 1989, pp. 677–8.
26. Walter D. Connor, *Socialism, Politics, and Equality*, New York, Columbia University Press, 1979, pp. 277–87; Gregory D. Andrusz, *Housing and Urban Development in the USSR*, London, Macmillan, 1984; Kazimierz J. Zaniewski, 'Housing Inequalities Under Socialism: A Geographic Perspective', *Studies in Comparative Communism*, vol. XXII, no. 4 (winter 1989), pp. 291–306.

27. In more detail see Anthony B. Atkinson and John Micklewright, *Economic Transformation in Eastern Europe and the Distribution of Income*, Cambridge, Cambridge University Press, 1992, Chapter 8.
28. On the Chinese welfare system see John Dixon, 'China', in John Dixon and David Macarov (eds), *Social Welfare in Socialist Countries*, London, Routledge, 1992, Chapter 2.
29. Cf. *The Economist*, 16 September 1995, pp. 87–8.

11 ECONOMIC TRANSFORMATION

1. R. Kanbur and J. McIntosh, 'Dual Economies', in John Eatwell, Murray Milgate, and Peter Newman (eds), *Economic Development*, London, Macmillan, 1991 (reprinted), pp. 114ff. The notion of dualism was originally outlined by Thomas Robert Malthus (1766–1834).
2. Angus Maddison, *Phases of Capitalist Development*, Oxford, Oxford University Press, 1982, Chapter 1.
3. W.W. Rostow, *The Stages of Economic Growth: A Non- Communist Manifesto*, Cambridge, Cambridge University Press, 1960 (reprinted).
4. Raymond Aron, *Main Currents in Sociological Thought: Vol.1*, Harmondsworth, Penguin, 1969 (reprinted), pp. 118–25; Ernest Gellner, 'Economic Interpretation of History', in John Eatwell, Murray Milgate, and Peter Newman (eds), *Marxian Economics*, London, Macmillan, 1990, pp. 148ff; R. Jessop, 'Mode of Production', in *ibid.*, pp. 289ff.
5. Stephen K. Sanderson, *Social Transformations: A General Theory of Historical Development*, Oxford, Blackwell, 1995, pp. 8–9 and 389–91.
6. Stephen K. Sanderson, op. cit., p. 374.
7. Angus Maddison, *Dynamic Forces in Capitalist Development: A Long-Run Comparative View*, Oxford, Oxford University Press, 1991, p. 26.
8. See e.g. David Drakakis-Smith, 'Less Developed Economies and Dependence', in P.W. Daniels and W.F. Lever (eds), *The Global Economy in Transition*, London, Longman, 1996, Chapter 11.
9. Keith Griffin, *Alternative Strategies for Economic Development*, Basingstoke, Macmillan, 1989.
10. Anne O. Krueger, *Political Economy of Policy Reform in Developing Countries*, London, The MIT Press, 1993.
11. There are many different definitions of values. According to Maurice Duverger, for instance, 'values are beliefs relative to good and evil, right and wrong, to what ought to be and what ought not to be.' (*The Study of Politics*, London, Thomas Nelson and Sons Ltd, 1972, p. 9.)
12. Cf. Robert Skidelsky, *The World After Communism*, London, Macmillan, 1995, pp. 124–7. It is worth recalling in this connection that in the 1970s it was believed in the Soviet-bloc countries that the application of advanced mathematical methods and computers would modernize central planning and management, enable a more rational allocation and utilization of scarce resources, and stimulate economic growth.
13. Pam Woodall, 'The World Economy', *The Economist*, 7 October 1995, Survey.

14. On the relationship between political and economic systems see also Leszek Balcerowicz, *Socialism, Capitalism, Transformation*, Budapest, Central European University Press, 1995, Chapter 8.

15. Felipe Fernández-Armesto, *Millennium*, London, Bantam Press, 1995, p. 707. On the role of technology and technological innovation in the life of human societies see also Gerhard Lenski and Jean Lenski, *Human Societies: An Introduction to Macrosociology*, New York, McGraw-Hill Book Company, 1989 (fifth edition), pp. 92–3.

12 POST-COMMUNIST TRANSFORMATION

1. See e.g. J.L. Porket, *Unemployment in Capitalist, Communist and Post-Communist Economies*, Basingstoke, Macmillan, 1995, Chapter 7.

2. For a similar reason, command capitalism too has a short-term advantage over market capitalism.

3. A comparison of the Soviet-bloc countries' per capita GDP in 1960, 1970, 1980, and 1986, expressed as a percentage of that of the United States, is to be found in Eva Ehrlich, 'Contest between Countries: 1937–1986', *Soviet Studies*, vol. 43, no. 5 (1991), p. 887, Table 7. For 1985 see also Hans Aage, 'Sustainable Transition', in Robert W. Campbell (ed.), *The Postcommunist Economic Transformation*, Boulder, Westview Press, 1994, pp. 28–30, Table 2.2.

4. On economic growth in the Soviet-bloc countries between 1961 and 1989 see János Kornai, *The Socialist System*, Oxford, Clarendon Press, 1992, pp. 194–5, Table 9.10, and p. 200, Table 9.11. See also Marie Lavigne, *The Economics of Transition: From Socialist Economy to Market Economy*, Basingstoke, Macmillan, 1995, p. 58, Table 4.4, which covers the years 1951—90.

5. Ivan Sujan et al., 'Inflácia a nerovnováha na trhu spotrebného tovaru v cs. ekonomike', *Politická ekonomie*, nos. 9–10 (1991), pp. 757–73.

6. On open, hidden, and repressed inflation in Poland between 1945 and 1982 see Batara Simatupang, *The Polish Economic Crisis*, London, Routledge, 1994, Chapter 3.

7. The various relevant comparisons include that by Kazimierz Laski, 'An Economic Comparison of Poland and Spain', in Henryk Flakierski and Thomas T. Sekine (eds), *Socialist Dilemmas: East and West*, Armonk, M.E. Sharpe Inc., 1990, pp. 78–87, and that by Jan Ake Dellenbrant, 'Estonia's economic development 1940–1990 in comparison with Finland's', in Anders Åslund (ed.), *Market socialism or the restoration of capitalism?* Cambridge, Cambridge University Press, 1992, Chapter 10.

8. Alexander Dallin, 'Causes of the Collapse of the USSR', *Post-Soviet Affairs*, vol. 8, no. 4 (October-December 1992), pp. 279–302.

9. Cf. Michael Ellman, 'Multiple Causes of the Collapse', *RFE/RL Research Report*, vol. 2, no. 23 (4 June 1993), pp. 55–8.

10. According to Hannes Adomeit, the theories put forward by Western scholars and Soviet decision-makers to explain Gorbachev's role in the demise of the Soviet bloc can be said to lie on a continuum ranging

from 'complete control' to 'complete loss of control', or from 'perfect planning' to 'utter subjectivism and spontaneity'. ('Gorbachev, German Unification and the Collapse of Empire', *Post-Soviet Affairs*, vol. 10, no. 3 (July-September 1994), pp. 197–230.)

11. On the causes of the collapse of communism see also George Schöpflin, 'The End of Communism in Eastern Europe', *International Affairs*, vol. 66, no. 1 (1990), pp. 3–16; Vladimir G. Treml, 'Two Schools of Thought', *RFE/RL Research Report*, vol.2, no. 23 (4 June 1993), pp. 53–5; Barbara A. Misztal, 'Understanding Political Change in Eastern Europe: A Sociological Perspective', *Sociology*, vol. 27, no. 3 (August 1993), pp. 451–70; Robert Skidelsky, *The World After Communism*, London, Macmillan, 1995, Chapter 6.

12. J.L. Porket, *Work, Employment and Unemployment in the Soviet Union*, Basingstoke, 1989, p. 186.

13. Marie Lavigne, op. cit., p. 29.

14. Zbigniew Brzezinski, *The Grand Failure: The Birth and Death of Communism in the Twentieth Century*, London, Macdonald, 1990, pp. 1–2 and 232.

15. These four dimensions of the crisis of communism are based on Jürgen Habermas, *Legitimation Crisis*, Cambridge, Polity Press, 1992 (reprinted). In Part II of this book, the German original of which was published in 1973, the author offered a classification of possible crisis tendencies specific to advanced capitalism.

16. Barry W. Ickes and Randi Ryterman, 'From Enterprise to Firm: Notes for a Theory of the Enterprise in Transition', in Robert W. Campbell (ed.), *The Postcommunist Economic Transformation*, Boulder, Westview Press, 1994, pp. 87 and 100.

17. See e.g. Christopher G.A. Bryant and Edmund Mokrzycki, 'Introduction', in Christopher G.A. Bryant and Edmund Mokrzycki (eds), *The New Great Transformation?* London, Routledge, 1994, Chapter 1.

18. See e.g. Bernard Chavance, *The Transformation of Communist Systems*, Boulder, Westview Press, 1994, p. 212.

19. According to Michael Mandelbaum, '[c]ommunist economies were not, strictly speaking, *under*developed; they were *mis*developed. The transition from communism therefore involves not only building new structures but also destroying existing ones.' ('Introduction', in Michael Mandelbaum (ed.), *Postcommunism: Four Perspectives*, New York, A Council on Foreign Relations Book, 1996, p. 11.)

13 MODELS FOR TRANSFORMATION

1. Francis Fukuyama, *The End of History and the Last Man*, London, Penguin Books, 1992, p. xi.

2. Francis Fukuyama, op. cit., Chapter 20.

3. Pat Devine, 'Alternative Possibilities for Post-Communist Economies', in Paul Cook and Frederick Nixson (eds), *The Move to the Market?* Basingstoke, Macmillan, 1995, Chapter 2.

4. Pat Devine, op.cit., p. 40.
5. Hans van Zon, *Alternative Scenarios for Central Europe*, Aldershot, Avebury, 1994, pp. 71–7.
6. Hans van Zon, op.cit., p. 77.
7. J.L. Porket, 'Transforming Command Socialism', *The Slavonic and East European Review*, vol. 74, no. 2 (April 1996), pp. 252–8.
8. See e.g. Robert Skidelsky (ed.), *Thatcherism*, London, Chatto & Windus, 1988; Dennis Kavanagh and Anthony Seldon (eds), *The Thatcher Effect*, Oxford, Clarendon Press, 1989; Shirley Robin Letwin, *The Anatomy of Thatcherism*, London, Fontana, 1992. According to Samuel Brittan, 'Mrs Thatcher clearly learned the lesson of not biting off more than she could chew. Patrick Minford reminds us that the Thatcherite ministers initially concentrated on three limited economic objectives – mastering inflation, union reform and privatization – in carefully selected and cautious order.' (*Capitalism with a Human Face*, Aldershot, Edward Elgar, 1995, p. 185.)
9. See e.g. John Keane and John Owens, *After Full Employment*, London, Hutchinson, 1986, Chapter 7, and Robert Skidelsky, *The World After Communism: A Polemic For Our Time*, London, Macmillan, 1995, pp. 127–32 and 135–6.
10. See e.g. *The Economist*, 23 March 1991, pp. 103–4, and Donald T. Brash, *New Zealand's Remarkable Reforms*, London, The Institute of Economic Affairs, 1996.
11. Brian Girvin, 'Introduction: Varieties of Conservatism', in Brian Girvin (ed.), *The Transformation of Contemporary Conservatism*, London, SAGE, 1988, Chapter 1.
12. Barbara Krug, 'Blood, Sweat, or Cheating: Politics and the Transformation of Socialist Economies in China, the USSR, and Eastern Europe', *Studies in Comparative Communism*, vol. XXIV, no. 2 (June 1991), pp.137–50.
13. Alan Peacock and Hans Willgerodt (eds), *Germany's Social Market Economy: Origins and Evolution*, London, Macmillan 1989; Alan Peacock and Hans Willgerodt (eds), *German Neo-Liberals and the Social Market Economy*, London, Macmillan, 1989; Philipp von Bismarck, *Soziale Marktwirtschaft*, Freiburg, Herder, 1992.
14. Cf. W.R. Smyser, *The Economy of United Germany*, London, Hurst & Company, 1992, Chapters 2 and 6, and Norman Barry, 'The Social Market Economy', in Ellen Frankel Paul, Fred D. Miller, Jr., and Jeffrey Paul, *Liberalism and the Economic Order*, Cambridge, Cambridge University Press, 1993, pp. 1–25.
15. According to Christopher S. Allen, in West Germany 'Keynesian policies were popular only for a brief period during the Grand Coalition (1966–1969) and the early years of center-left government (1969–1974) under Willy Brandt.' ('The Underdevelopment of Keynesianism in the Federal Republic of Germany', in Peter A. Hall (ed.), *The Political Power of Economic Ideas: Keynesianism across Nations*, Princeton, New Jersey, Princeton University Press, 1989, p. 263.)
16. On co-determination see e.g. Svetozar Pejovich, 'Codetermination in the West: The Case of Germany', in Svetozar Pejovich (ed.), *Philo-*

sophical and Economic Foundations of Capitalism, Lexington, Massachusetts, D.C. Heath and Company, 1983, Chapter 8.
17. DIW, *Wochenbericht*, nos 22–23 (30 May 1996), p. 392.
18. Ingemar Ståhl, 'Sweden at the End of the Middle Way', in Svetozar Pejovich (ed.), op. cit., p. 127, Table 9.4. See also Palle Schelde Anderson and Johnny Akerholm, 'Scandinavia', in Andrea Boltho (ed.), *The European Economy*, Oxford, Oxford University Press, 1982, p. 613, Table 21.3.
19. Pekka Kosonen, 'The Scandinavian Welfare Model in the New Europe', in Thomas P. Boje and Sven E. Olsson Hort (eds), *Scandinavia in a New Europe*, Oslo, Scandinavian University Press, 1993, pp. 46 and 58, Table 1.
20. Pam Woodall, 'The Swedish Economy', *The Economist*, 3 March 1990, Survey.
21. Michel Albert, *Capitalism against Capitalism*, London, Whurr Publishers, 1993. The book is discussed by Peter Saundres, *Capitalism*, Buckingham, Open University Press, 1995, pp. 107–15.
22. See e.g. Dwight Heald Perkins, 'Reforming China's Economic System', *Journal of Economic Literature*, vol. XXVI, no. 2 (June 1988), pp. 601–45; Richard Pomfret, 'Chinese Economic Reform, 1978–1994', *MOCT-MOST*, vol. 5, no. 1 (1995), pp. 13–27; *The China Quarterly*, no. 144 (December 1995); Dominic Ziegler, 'China: Ready to Face the World?' *The Economist*, 8 March 1997, Survey.
23. Joseph S. Berliner, 'Perestroika and the Chinese Model', in Robert W. Campbell, *The Postcommunist Economic Transformation*, Boulder, Westview Press, 1994, Chapter 11.
24. Patrick Bolton, 'Privatization and the Separation of Ownership and Control: Lessons from Chinese Enterprise Reform', *Economics of Transition*, vol. 3, no. 1 (March 1995), pp. 1–12.
25. Louis Emmerij, 'Eastern Europe in a Developmental Perspective', in Jacques Hersh and Johannes Dragsbaek Schmidt (eds), *The Aftermath of 'Real Existing Socialism' in Eastern Europe: Volume 1: Between Western Europe and East Asia*, Basingstoke, Macmillan, 1996, p. 82.
26. Richard Pomfret, *Asian Economies in Transition: Reforming Centrally Planned Economies*, Cheltenham, Edward Elgar, 1996, p. 144.
27. A summary of some Western views on the relevance of the Chinese model to other post-communist countries is to be found in Ian Jeffries, *A Guide to the Economies in Transition*, London, Routledge, 1996, pp. 35–41.
28. The market-friendly view falls in the middle ground between the neoclassical and revisionist views. In the neoclassical interpretation of East Asia's success, the market takes centre stage in economic life and governments play a minor role. In contrast, the revisionist view sees market failures as pervasive and a justification for governments to lead the market in critical ways. In the market-friendly strategy, rapid growth is associated with effective but carefully delimited government activism, the appropriate role of government being to ensure adequate investments in people, provision of a competitive climate for enterprise, openness to international trade, and stable macroeconomic management.

(The World Bank, *The East Asian Miracle: Economic Growth and Public Policy*, New York, Oxford University Press, 1993, pp. 81–7.)

29. Paul Krugman, 'The Myth of Asia's Miracle', *Foreign Affairs*, vol. 73, no. 6 (November-December 1994), pp. 62–78.

30. Kyoko Sheridan, *Governing the Japanese Economy*, Cambridge, Polity Press, 1994, p. 209. The author sees government not as intervening in Japan's economy from outside the economic system, but as an integral element in the system (p. 3).

31. Brian Reading, *Japan: The Coming Collapse*, London, Weidenfeld and Nicolson, 1992, p. 5.

32. Some dimensions of Latin America's market revolution are discussed by Joan M. Nelson and contributors, *Intricate Links: Democratization and Market Reforms in Latin America and Eastern Europe*, New Brunswick, Transaction Publishers, 1994, and Gary McMahon (ed.), *Lessons in Economic Policy for Eastern Europe from Latin America*, Basingstoke, Macmillan, 1996.

14 COMPONENTS AND DYNAMICS OF ECONOMIC TRANS-FORMATION

1. See e.g. Shafiqul Islam, 'Conclusion: Problems of Planning a Market Economy', in Shafiqul Islam and Michael Mandelbaum (eds), *Making Markets*, New York, Council on Foreign Relations Press, 1993, pp. 182–3, and Jozef M. Van Brabant, 'Lessons from the Wholesale Transformations in the East', *Comparative Economic Studies*, vol. 35, no. 4 (winter 1993), pp. 73ff.

2. See e.g. Tony Killick and Christopher Stevens, 'Economic Adjustment in Eastern Europe: Lessons from the Third World', in Graham Bird (ed.), *Economic Reform in Eastern Europe*, Aldershot, Edward Elgar, 1992, pp. 121–3.

3. See e.g. Peter Murrell, 'What is Shock Therapy? What Did it Do in Poland and Russia?' *Post-Soviet Affairs*, vol. 9, no. 2 (April-June 1993), pp. 111–40; Gerard Roland, 'The Role of Political Constraints in Transition Strategies', *Economics of Transition*, vol. 2, no. 1 (March 1994), pp. 27–41; Herman W. Hoen, 'Theoretically Underpinning the Transition in Eastern Europe: An Austrian View', *Economic Systems*, vol. 19, no. 1 (March 1995), pp. 59–77, who surveys neoclassical, post-Keynesian, and Austrian approaches to the transition; Ian Jeffries, *A Guide to the Economies in Transition*, London, Routledge, 1996, pp. 17–28.

4. Andreas Pickel, 'Jump-starting a Market Economy: A Critique of the Radical Strategy for Economic Reform in Light of the East German Experience', *Studies in Comparative Communism*, vol. XXV, no. 2 (June 1992), pp. 177–91.

5. On economic transformation in eastern Germany, which was a result of German unification, see Daniel Gros and Alfred Steinherr, *Winds of Change: Economic Transition in Central and Eastern Europe*, London,

Longman, 1995, Chapter 10, and J.L. Porket, *Unemployment in Capitalist, Communist and Post-Communist Economies*, Basingstoke, Macmillan, 1995, Chapter 12.

6. Gabor Bakos, 'Hungarian Transition after Three Years', *Europe-Asia Studies*, vol. 46, no. 7 (1994), pp. 1189–214.

7. On the relevance to post-communist societies of China's experience see John McMillan and Barry Naughton, 'How to Reform a Planned Economy: Lessons from China', *Oxford Review of Economic Policy*, vol. 8, no. 1 (spring 1992), pp. 130–43, and Mark Knell and Wenyan Yang, 'Lessons from China on a Strategy for the Socialist Economies in Transition', in Mark Knell and Christine Rider, *Socialist Economies in Transition: Appraisals of the Market Mechanism*, Aldershot, Edward Elgar, 1992, Chapter 11.

8. A stylized phasing of various transformation measures with the premise that the transformation will take ten years is to be found in Shafiqul Islam, op. cit., p 190, Figure 1.

9. L. Haddad, 'On the Rational Sequencing of Enterprise Reform', *The Journal of Communist Studies and Transition Politics*, vol. 11, no. 1 (March 1995), pp. 91–109.

10. Jozef M. van Brabant, *Industrial Policy in Eastern Europe: Governing the Transition*, London, Kluwer Academic Publishers, 1993, p. 170.

11. Jeffrey Sachs, *Understanding 'Shock Therapy'*, London, The Social Market Foundation, 1994, p. 31.

12. Peter Murrell, 'Evolution in Economics and in the Economic Reform of the Centrally Planned Economies', in Christopher Clague and Gordon C. Rausser (eds), *The Emergence of Market Economies in Eastern Europe*, Oxford, Blackwell, 1992, p. 40.

13. Gerard Roland, op. cit., pp. 34–5.

14. Michael A. Landesmann, 'Industrial Policy and the Transition in East-Central Europe', in Gábor Hunya (ed.), *Economic Transformation in East-Central Europe and in the Newly Independent States*, Boulder, Westview Press, 1994, pp. 136 and 153.

15. Janos Fath, 'Industrial Policies for Countries in Transition?' in Gábor Hunya (ed.), op. cit., Chapter 6.

16. On the role of the state during economic transformation see also Christopher Clague, 'The Journey to a Market Economy', in Christopher Clague and Gordon C. Rausser (eds), op. cit., Chapter 1; Jerald Hage and Z. Jeffrey Shi, 'Alternative Strategies for the Reconstruction of the State During Economic Reform', *Governance: An International Journal of Policy and Administration*, vol. 6, n. 4 (October 1993), pp. 463–91; Bruno Dallago, 'The Market and The State: The Paradox of Transition', *MOCT-MOST*, vol. 6, no. 4 (1996), pp. 1–29.

17. The importance of liberalization and stabilization for economic transformation was also emphasized by The World Bank, *World Development Report 1996: From Plan to Market*, New York, Oxford University Press, 1996. According to it, '[t]he two are intricately linked and can and should be initiated early. In the longer term, institutional reforms – establishing clear property rights, sound legal and financial infrastructure, and effective government – will be needed to make markets work

efficiently and support growth. But liberalization and stabilization are essential first steps, and they can achieve a great deal even when other key features of an effective market are lacking' (p. 22).

18. Robert Skidelsky, *The World After Communism: A Polemic For Our Time*, London, Macmillan, 1995, pp. 162–3, and Robert Skidelsky, 'The State and Economy: Reflections on the Transition from Communism to Capitalism in Russia', in Michael Mandelbaum (ed.), *Post-communism: Four Perspectives*, New York, A Council on Foreign Relations Book, 1996, pp. 78–9.

15 ECONOMIC TRANSFORMATION IN PRACTICE

1. On Mongolia see Richard Pomfret, *Asian Economies in Transition: Reforming Centrally Planned Economies*, Cheltenham, Edward Elgar, 1996, Chapter 6.
2. Domenico Mario Nuti, 'Lessons from the Stabilisation Programmes of Central and Eastern European Countries, 1989–1991', in Laszlo Somogyi (ed.), *The Political Economy of the Transition Process in Eastern Europe*, Aldershot, Edward Elgar, 1993, pp. 40–9.
3. See e.g. M. Donald Hancock and Helga A. Welsh (eds), *German Unification: Process and Outcomes*, Boulder, Westview Press, 1994.
4. According to Nicholas Eberstadt, under the impact of unification and systemic transformation eastern Germany experienced an upswing in mortality and a collapse of births and new marriages. ('Demographic Shocks in Eastern Germany, 1989–93', *Europe-Asia Studies*, vol. 46, no. 3 (1994), pp. 519–33.)
5. Janusz Beksiak et al., *The Polish Transformation: Programme and Progress*, London, The Centre for Research into Communist Economies, 1990.
6. Kemal Dervis and Timothy Condon, 'Hungary – Partial Successes and Remaining Challenges: The Emergence of a "Gradualist" Success Story?' in Olivier Jean Blanchard, Kenneth A. Froot, and Jeffrey D. Sachs (eds), *The Transition in Eastern Europe: Vol. 1*, Chicago, The University of Chicago Press, 1994, p. 125, Table 4.2
7. United Nations, *World Economic and Social Survey 1995*, New York, 1995, p. 20.
8. IMF, *World Economic Outlook*, October 1994, p. 74.
9. *The Economist*, 7 October 1995, p. 127; EIU, *Country Report: Russia*, 1st quarter 1996, p. 25; Vincent Koen, 'Russian Macroeconomic Data: Existence, Access, Interpretation', *Communist Economies & Economic Transformation*, vol. 8, no. 3 (1996), pp. 321–33.
10. Jan Winiecki, 'The Inevitability of a Fall in Output in the Early Stages of Transition to the Market: Theoretical Underpinnings', *Soviet Studies*, vol. 43, no. 4 (1991), pp. 669–76.
11. John Williamson, 'Why Did Output Fall in Eastern Europe?' in Laszlo Somogyi (ed.), op. cit., Chapter 2.

12. See also Dariusz K. Rosati, 'Output Decline during Transition from Plan to Market: A Reconsideration', *Economics of Transition*, vol. 2, no. 4 (1994), pp. 419–441, and Ian Jeffries, *A Guide to the Economies in Transition*, London, Routledge, 1996, pp. 41–7.

13. On changes in employment between 1990 and 1994 see ILO, *World employment 1995*, Geneva, 1995, p. 109, Table 16.

14. *Russian Economic Trends*, various issues.

15. Cf. Richard Layard and Andrea Richter, 'How Much Unemployment is Needed for Restructuring: The Russian Experience', *Economics of Transition*, vol. 3, no. 1 (March 1995), pp. 39–58.

16. For 1992 see J.L. Porket, *Unemployment in Capitalist, Communist and Post-Communist Economies*, Basingstoke, Macmillan, 1995, p. 118, and for 1995 see OECD, *OECD Surveys 1995–1996: Germany*, Paris, 1996, p. 107, Table 25.

17. OECD, *OECD Economic Surveys: Hungary 1993*, Paris, 1993, p. 22, Table 3.

18. Maurice Ernst, Michael Alexeev, and Paul Marer, *Transforming the Core: Restructuring Industrial Enterprises in Russia and Central Europe*, Boulder, Westview Press, 1996, pp. 97–8.

19. For 1990–92 see United Nations, *World Economic and Social Survey 1994*, New York, 1994, p. 192, Table VI.10.

20. János Köllo, 'Unemployment and the prospects for employment policy in Hungary', in Marvin Jackson, Jenö Koltay and Wouter Biesbrouck, *Unemployment and Evolving Labor Markets in Central and Eastern Europe*, Aldershot, Avebury, 1995, p. 202. As to Poland see Maurice Ernst, Michael Alexeev, and Paul Marer, op. cit., p. 86.

21. IMF, *World Economic Outlook*, op. cit., pp. 74–9.

22. On the factors responsible for weakening tax revenue/GDP ratios between 1988 and 1993 see also Staff of European I, IMF, 'Eastern Europe – Factors Underlying the Weakening Performance of Tax Revenues', *Economic Systems*, vol. 19, no. 2 (June 1995), pp. 101–24.

23. See e.g. International Social Security Association, *Restructuring social security in Central and Eastern Europe: A guide to recent development, policy issues and options*, Geneva, 1994.

24. *The Economist*, 16 July 1994, pp. 41 and 44. See also Mikhail Delyagin and Lev Freinkman, 'Extrabudgetary Funds in Russian Public Finance', *RFE/RL Research Report*, vol. 2, no. 48, 3 December 1993, pp.49–54.

25. Horst Brezinski and Michael Fritsch, 'Transformation: The Shocking German Way', *MOCT-MOST*, vol. 5, no. 4 (1995), pp. 1–25. Net public sector transfers from western Germany to eastern Germany amounted to 52 per cent of eastern German GDP in 1991, to 44 per cent in 1992, to 42 per cent in 1993, to 36 per cent in 1994, and to 37 per cent in 1995. (OECD, *OECD Surveys 1995–1996: Germany*, op. cit., p. 28, Table 8.)

26. Salvatore Zecchini, 'Transition Approaches In Retrospect', *MOCT-MOST*, vol. 5, no. 2 (1995), pp. 1–44. See also J.L. Porket, 'Transforming Command Socialism', *The Slavonic and East European Review*, vol. 74, no. 2 (April 1996), pp. 252–8.

16 PRIVATIZATION

1. Cf. David W. Conklin, *Comparative economic systems*, Cambridge, Cambridge University Press, 1991, pp. 294–9.
2. John Keegan, *A History of Warfare*, London, PIMLICO, 1994, pp. 306–7.
3. Michael Klein and Neil Roger, 'Back to the Future: The Potential *in* Infrastructure Privatisation', in Richard O'Brien (ed.), *Finance and the International Economy: 8*, Oxford University Press, 1994, pp. 47–8,
4. Branko Milanovic, 'Privatisation in Post-communist Societies', *Communist Economies and Economic Transformation*, vol. 3, no. 1 (1991), pp. 5–39. See also David W. Conklin, op. cit., p. 302, Table 9.1, and Bela Balassa, 'Public Enterprise in Developing Countries: Issues of Privatization', in *Public Finance and Performance of Enterprises*, Proceedings of the 43rd Congress of the International Institute of Public Finance, Paris, 1987, pp. 417–33.
5. On nationalization and privatization in France between 1981 and 1993 see Serge Halimi, Jonathan Michie and Seumas Milne, 'The Mitterrand Experience', in Jonathan Michie and John Grieve Smith (eds), *Unemployment in Europe*, London, Academic Press, 1994, Chapter 6.
6. *The Economist*, 19 June 1993, p. 130, and *ibid*., 21 August 1993, pp. 18–20.
7. *The Economist*, 22 March 1997, p. 155.
8. János Kornai, *The Socialist System*, Oxford, Clarendon Press, 1992, p. 72, Table 5.1. According to Branko Milanovic, though, in Hungary the share in total value added (or output) of the public sector was only 65.2 per cent (op. cit., p. 8, Table 3).
9. János Kornai, op. cit., pp. 399–403.
10. Peter L. Berger, *The Capitalist Revolution*, Aldershot, Wildwood House Limited, 1987, p. 190.
11. Some views on privatization were summarized by Ian Jeffries, *A Guide to the Economies in Transition*, London, Routledge, 1996, pp. 48–56.
12. Joseph E. Stiglitz, *Whither Socialism?* London, The MIT Press, 1994, p. 192.
13. Peter Murrell, 'Evolution in Economics and in the Economic Reform of the Centrally Planned Economies', in Christopher Clague and Gordon C. Rausser (eds), *The Emergence of Market Economies in Eastern Europe*, Oxford, Blackwell, 1992, Chapter 3.
14. L. Haddad, 'On the Rational Sequencing of Enterprise Reform', *The Journal of Communist Studies and Transition Politics*, vol. 11, no. 1 (March 1995), pp. 91–109.
15. The distinction between top-down transformation and bottom-up transformation was made by Horst Brezinski and Michael Fritsch (eds), *The Economic Impact of New Firms in Post-Socialist Countries: Bottom-up Transformation in Eastern Europe*, Cheltenham, Edward Elgar, 1996, p. 1.
16. J.L. Porket in his review of the book by John S. Earle, Roman Frydman and Andrzej Rapaczynski (eds), *Privatization in the Transition to a*

Market Economy: Studies of Preconditions and Policies in Eastern Europe, London, Pinter, 1993, in *The Slavonic and East European Review*, vol. 72, no. 3 (July 1994), pp. 581–3.

17. Squatter sovereignty was regarded as probably the best single principle of initial property distribution by Martin L. Weitzman, 'How Not to Privatize', in Mario Baldassarri, Luigi Paganetto and Edmund S. Phelps (eds), *Privatization Processes in Eastern Europe*, Basingstoke. Macmillan, 1993, p. 256.

18. A comparison of give-away privatization proposals is to be found in Daniel Gros and Alfred Steinherr, *Winds of Change: Economic Transition in Central and Eastern Europe*, London, Longman, 1995, p. 189, Table 8.1.

19. Cf. John P. Bonin and István P. Székely (eds), *The Development and Reform of Financial Systems in Central and Eastern Europe*, Aldershot, Edward Elgar, 1994.

20. Joseph E. Stiglitz, op. cit., p. 209.

21. On privatization in eastern Germany see Eric Owen Smith, *The German Economy*, London, Routledge, 1994, pp. 475–90, and Herbert Brücker, 'Selling Eastern Germany: On the Economic Rationale of the Treuhandanstalt's Privatisation and Restructuring Strategy', *MOCT-MOST*, vol. 5, no. 4 (1995), pp. 55–77.

22. United Nations, *World Economic and Social Survey 1995*, New York, 1995, p. 97, Table VI.1.

23. On small-scale privatization in the Czech Republic, Hungary, and Poland see John S. Earle, Roman Frydman, Andrzej Rapaczynski and Joel Turkewitz, *Small Privatization*, Budapest, Central European University Press, 1994. In eastern Germany, small-scale privatization had been completed by the end of 1991.

24. European Bank for Reconstruction and Development, *Transition report 1996*, p. 11, Table 2.1.

25. Legally, opportunities for the appropriation of state enterprises' productive assets by state enterprise managers were already created in Poland and Hungary before the collapse of communism, giving rise to the so-called spontaneous privatization.

26. A model of the survival-oriented enterprise was developed by Barry W. Ickes and Randi Ryterman, 'From Enterprise to Firm: Notes for a Theory of the Enterprise in Transition', in Robert W. Campbell (ed.), *The Postcommunist Economic Transformation*, Boulder, Westview Press, 1994, Chapter 5.

27. On bankruptcy law and policy in some post-communist countries see OECD, *OECD Economic Surveys: Hungary 1993*, Paris, 1993, pp. 80–7, and *OECD Economic Outlook*, no. 55 (June 1994), pp. 116–17.

17 HOUSEHOLDS

1. See also Bartlomiej Kaminski, 'The Legacy of Communism', in John P. Hardt and Richard F. Kaufman (eds), *East-Central European*

Economies in Transition, Armonk, M.E. Sharpe, 1995, p. 17, Table 1. The table compares per capita GNP in Czechoslovakia, Bulgaria, Hungary, Poland, and Romania with that in Austria, Finland, Greece, Italy, Portugal, Spain, and Turkey in 1938 and 1990. It shows, *inter alia*, that while in 1938 Austria, Czechoslovakia, and Finland had similar levels of per capita GNP, namely, US$ 1800, in 1990 per capita GNP was US$ 19200 in Austria and US$ 26100 in Finland, but only US$ 3100 in Czechoslovakia. The figures for 1938 have been adjusted to 1990 prices with the US GDP deflator.

2. *Russian Economic Trends*, vol. 4, no. 4 (1995), p. 49, Table 41. According to the official statistics, in 1996 real wages rose by 13 per cent on their 1995 average. However, because wage arrears grew markedly, real wages actually paid were only some seven per cent higher on average in 1996 than in 1995. (Ibid., vol. 6, no. 1 (1997), p. 69.)
3. DIW, *Wochenbericht*, no. 8 (23 February 1995), p. 191, Table 4; *The Economics of Transition*, vol. 3, no. 4 (1995), p. 524, Table 2, and ibid., vol. 4, no. 2 (October 1996), pp. 535–6, Table A; EBRD, *Transition report update*, April 1996, pp. 16–17.
4. Horst Brezinski and Michael Fritsch, 'Transformation: The Shocking German Way', *MOCT-MOST*, vol. 5, No. 4 (1995), p. 20, Table A.5.
5. Daniel Gros and Alfred Steinherr, *Winds of Change*, London, Longman, 1995, p. 460, Table 15.2 and p. 463, Table 15.3.
6. See also OCDE/CCET, *Short-Term Economic Indicators: Transition Economies*, no. 1 (1996), pp. 146–7.
7. *The Economist*, 9 December 1995, p. 138.
8. Branko Milanovic, 'Poverty in Eastern Europe in the Years of Crisis, 1978 to 1987: Poland, Hungary, and Yugoslavia', *The World Bank Economic Review*, vol. 5, no. 2 (May 1991), pp. 187–205; Anthony B. Atkinson and John Micklewright, *Economic transformation in Eastern Europe and the distribution of income*, Cambridge, Cambridge University Press, 1992; Sándor Sipos, 'Income Transfers: Family Support and Poverty Relief', in Nicholas Barr (ed.), *Labor Markets and Social Policy in Central and Eastern Europe*, New York, Oxford University Press, 1994, pp. 232–4.
9. UN Economic Commission for Europe, *Trends in Europe and North America – 1995*, New York, United Nations, 1995, p. 93, Table 5.6. The figure for Hungary is for 1991.
10. *Russian Economic Trends*, vol. 6, no. 1 (1997), p. 78, Table 65. See also Alastair McAuley, 'Russia and the Baltics: Poverty and Poverty Research in a Changing World', in Else Oyen, S.M. Miller and Syed Abdus Samad (eds), *Poverty: A Global Review*, Oslo, Scandinavian University Press, 1996, Chapter 17.
11. *The Economist*, 16 December 1995, p. 52. Pension indicators for selected post-communist countries in 1992 are to be found in IMF, *World Economic Outlook*, May 1996, p. 85, Table 22.
12. Branko Milanovic, 'Income, Inequality and Poverty During the Transition: A Survey of the Evidence', *MOCT-MOST*, vol. 6, no. 1 (1996), pp. 131–47. The countries studied were Bulgaria, the Czech Republic, Hungary, Poland, Romania, Slovakia, and Slovenia.

13. Adam Smith, *An Inquiry into the Nature and Causes of the Wealth of Nations*, Book V, Chapter II, Part II, Article IV.
14. The incidence of subjective poverty tends to be higher than the incidence of objective poverty. See e.g. Zdenek Pavlík (ed.), *Human Development Report: Czech Republic 1996*, Prague, Faculty of Science, Charles University, 1996, p. 51, Table 4.7.
15. *The Economist*, 24 February 1996, pp. 30 and 32, and Office for National Statistics, *Social Trends 27*, London, The Stationery Office, 1997, p. 112, Table 6.10.
16. Cf. Anthony B. Atkinson, 'Comparing Poverty Rates Internationally: Lessons from Recent Studies in Developed Countries', *The World Bank Economic Review*, vol. 5, no. 1 (January 1991), pp. 3–21.
17. Some examples are to be found in Björn Halleröd, 'The Truly Poor: Direct and Indirect Consensual Measurement of Poverty in Sweden', *Journal of European Social Policy*, vol. 5, no. 2 (1995), pp. 111–29, and David G. Green, *Community Without Politics*, London, IEA Health and Welfare Unit, 1996, pp. 57–62.
18. See Giovanni Andrea Cornia et al., 'Policy, Poverty and Capabilities in the Economies in Transition', *MOCT-MOST*, vol. 6, no. 1 (1996), pp. 149–72.
19. Ian Jeffries, *A Guide to the Economies in Transition*, London, Routledge, 1996, p. 265.
20. *Ekonom*, no. 51 (1994), pp. 17–19, and ibid., no. 1 (1995), p. 14.
21. Ian Jeffries, op. cit., p. 504.
22. Ian Jeffries, op. cit., p. 473.
23. Ian Jeffries, op. cit., p. 223.
24. In the United States, for example, prohibition created the potential for an illegal market in alcohol and was a major impetus for the growth of organized crime.
25. See e.g. Gianluca Fiorentini and Sam Peltzman (eds), *The economics of organized crime*, Cambridge, Cambridge University Press, 1995.
26. Mancur Olson, 'The Devolution of Power in Post-Communist Societies: Therapies for Corruption, Fragmentation and Economic Retardation', in Robert Skidelsky (ed.), *Russia's Stormy Path to Reform*, London, The Social Market Foundation, 1995, pp. 12–13.
27. There is also the so-called consensual poverty. While subjective poverty means that people regard themselves as poor, consensual poverty is to a large degree based on public opinion. That is to say, the poverty line is ascertained by sample surveys in which the respondents define whom they regard as poor.
28. Milton Friedman, *Capitalism and Freedom*, Chicago, The University of Chicago Press, 1982 (reissued), Chapter 12, and Milton and Rose Friedman, *Free to Choose: A Personal Statement*, London, Secker & Warburg, 1980, pp. 119–26.
29. Samuel Brittan, *Capitalism with a Human Face*, Aldershot, Edward Elgar, 1995, Chapter 13.
30. Four income support strategies and two labour market strategies were discussed by Robert Haveman, 'Reducing Poverty while Increasing Employment: A Primer on Alternative Strategies, and a Blueprint', *OECD Economic Studies*, no. 26 (1996/I), pp. 7–42.

31. Cf. Peter Abrahamson, 'Social Exclusion in Europe: Old Wine in New Bottles?' and Jos Berghman, 'Conceptualising Social Exclusion', papers presented at the European Science Foundation Conference on 'European Societies or European Society? Social Exclusion and Social Integration in Europe: Theoretical and Policy Perspectives on Poverty and Inequality', Blarney, Ireland, 26–31 March 1996.

18   ATTITUDES AND POLITICS

1. Cf. Ted Robert Gurr, *Why Men Rebel*, Princeton, New Jersey, Princeton University Press, 1971 (third printing), p. 24.
2. According to F.A. Hayek, the 'invisible hand' of Adam Smith had perhaps better have been described as an invisible or unsurveyable pattern. (*The Fatal Conceit: The Errors of Socialism*, London, Routledge, 1992 (reprinted), p. 14.)
3. Calculated from European Commission, *Central and Eastern Eurobarometer*, no. 6 (March 1996), Annex figure 4.
4. Jirí Vecerník, 'Economic and Political Man', *Czech Sociological Review*, vol. III (Fall 1995), no. 2, p. 163.
5. According to one survey, in 1993 and 1994 between 50 and 61 per cent of Hungarian, Polish, Czech, and Slovak respondents favoured neo-corporatism of the kind existing in Austria or Sweden, while the remaining respondents favoured either a minimal state or a planned economy. (Fritz Plasser and Peter Ulram, 'Measuring Political Culture in East Central Europe: Political Trust and System Support', in Fritz Plasser and Andreas Pribersky (eds), *Political Culture in East Central Europe*, Aldershot, Avebury, 1996, pp. 14–15.)
6. Richard Rose et al., *Germans in Comparative Perspective*, Centre for the Study of Public Policy, University of Strathclyde, Studies in Public Policy No. 218 (1993), and Richard Rose and Christian Haerpfer, *The Impact of a Ready-Made State: Advantages of East Germans*, Centre for the Study of Public Policy, University of Strathclyde, Studies in Public Policy No. 268 (1996).
7. For selected post-communist countries, the share of food in household consumption between 1989 and 1993 is given in IMF, *World Economic Outlook*, October 1994, p. 84, Table 16.
8. Richard Rose and Christian Haerpfer, *New Democracies Barometer IV: A 10-Nation Survey*, Centre for the Study of Public Policy, University of Strathclyde, Studies in Public Policy No. 262 (1996), p. 57.
9. Richard Rose and Christian Haerpfer, *New Democracies Barometer IV: A 10-Nation Survey*, op. cit., p. 60, and Richard Rose, *New Russia Barometer V: Between Two Elections*, Centre for the Study of Public Policy, University of Strathclyde, Studies in Public Policy No. 260 (1996), p. 34.
10. Richard Rose and Christian Haerpfer, *New Democracies Barometer IV: A 10-Nation Survey*, op. cit., pp. 68–70.

11. Jirí Vecerník, 'Staré a nové ekonomické nerovnosti: prípad ceskych zemí', *Sociologický casopis*, vol. 31, no. 3 (1995), p. 329, Table 1.

12. Richard Rose, *New Russia Barometer V: Between Two Elections*, op. cit., pp. 19–20.

13. The World Bank, *World Development Report, 1996: From Plan to Market*, Washington, Oxford University Press, 1996, p. 172, Table A.1, and IMF, *World Economic Outlook*, October 1996, p. 88, Table 23.

14. Calculated from European Commission, *Central and Eastern Eurobarometer*, no. 6 (March 1996), Annex figure 6.

15. Richard Rose, *New Russia Barometer V: Between Two Elections*, op. cit., p. 58, Figure 8.

16. Subsequently, in November 1995, Poland elected a former communist to the post of president.

17. The Bulgarian government elected in December 1994 argued for a greater engagement of the state in economic life based on a regulated market. (Jean M. Due and Stephen C. Schmidt, 'Progress on Privatization in Bulgaria', *Comparative Economic Studies*, vol. 37, no. 1 (spring 1995), pp. 55–77.)

18. Of 200 parliamentary seats, the Czech Social Democratic Party won in the 1996 parliamentary elections 61 seats (compared with 16 in 1992), and the Communist Party of Bohemia and Moravia 22.

19. According to Janos Simon, sample survey findings suggest that in postcommunist countries quite a few people identify democracy with economic and social welfare. (*Popular Conceptions of Democracy in Post-Communist Europe*, Centre for the Study of Public Policy, University of Strathclyde, Studies in Public Policy No. 273, 1996.)

20. Anders Åslund, Peter Boone and Simon Johnson, 'How to Stabilize: Lessons from Post-communist Countries', *Brookings Papers on Economic Activity*, no. 1 (1996), pp. 217–91.

21. On a shift in attitudes towards the locus of responsibility in Russia between 1989 and 1995 see also Robert J. Brym, 'Re-evaluating Mass Support for Political and Economic Change in Russia', *EUROPE-ASIA STUDIES*, Vol. 48, no. 5 (1996), pp. 751–66.

19 THE INDIVIDUAL, THE MARKET, AND THE STATE

1. Adam Smith, *An Inquiry into the Nature and Causes of the Wealth of Nations*, London, J.M. Dent, 1929 (reprinted), Vol. I, Book IV, Chapter II. On Adam Smith's invisible hand doctrine see also Samuel Brittan, *Capitalism with a Human Face*, Aldershot, Edward Elgar, 1995, Chapters 1, 2 and 14.

2. Stephen K. Sanderson, *Social Transformations: A General Theory of Historical Development*, Oxford, Blackwell, 1995, pp. 12–13 and 397–9.

3. Graeme Donald Snooks, *The Dynamic Society: Exploring the sources of global change*, London, Routledge, 1996, pp. 4–5, 8, 171–201 and 437.

4. Stephen K. Sanderson, op. cit., p. 13.

5. Graeme Donald Snooks, op. cit., p. 13.

6. Graeme Donald Snooks, op. cit., p. 220.
7. According to W.W. Rostow, '[David] Hume and [Adam] Smith exhibited a lively sense that the economic behavior of individuals was often governed by noneconomic human motives and objectives; and they also understood that the weaving of such elements into economic analysis had to be quite precise if it were to be useful.' (*Theorists of Economic Growth from David Hume to the Present: With a Perspective on the Next Century*, New York, Oxford University Press, 1990, p. 481.)
8. Joseph E. Stiglitz, *Whither Socialism?* Cambridge, Massachusetts, The MIT Press, 1994, p. 250.
9. Timothy J. Colton, 'Economics and Voting in Russia', *Post-Soviet Affairs*, vol. 12, no. 4 (October-December 1996), pp. 289–317.
10. Unintended consequences may be divided into those which are harmful and those which are beneficial for the respective actor, other actors, and the established system, and into those which are recognized as such and those which are not. (Cf. Robert K. Merton, *Social Theory and Social Structure*, Glencoe, Illinois, The Free Press, 1958 (second printing of revised edition), p. 51.)
11. See also James Gwartney, Robert Lawson and Walter Bloc, *Economic Freedom of the World: 1975–1995*, London, The Institute of Economic Affairs, 1996, pp. 107–8.
12. On the relation between economic development and democracy see Adam Przeworski and Fernando Limongi, 'Modernization: Theories and Facts', *World Politics*, vol. 49, no. 2 (January 1997), pp. 155–83.

20 THE WORLD IN TRANSITION

1. On the relation between fundamental political and economic structures in various regions of the world see John D. Sullivan, 'Democracy and Global Economic Growth', in Brad Roberts (ed.), *New Forces in the World Economy*, Cambridge, Massachusetts, The MIT Press, 1996, pp. 67ff.
2. A more detailed classification was made by Martha de Melo, Cevdet Denizer, and Alan Gelb, 'Patterns of Transition from Plan to Market', *The World Bank Economic Review*, vol. 10, no. 3 (September 1996), pp. 397–424. Measuring post-communist transformation primarily in terms of the cumulative liberalization of internal prices, external markets, and private sector entry, they distinguished four reform groups: advanced reformers (Slovenia, Poland, Hungary, the Czech Republic, Slovakia), high-intermediate reformers (Estonia, Bulgaria, Lithuania, Latvia, Albania, Romania, Mongolia), low-intermediate reformers (Russia, Kyrgyzstan, Moldova, Kazakhstan), and slow reformers (Uzbekistan, Belarus, Ukraine, Turkmenistan).
3. On restructuring see Maurice Ernst, Michael Alexeev, and Paul Marer, *Transforming the Core: Restructuring Industrial Enterprises in Russia and Central Europe*, Boulder, Westview Press, 1996.
4. The bad-debt problem is discussed in *MOCT-MOST*, vol 4, no. 3 (1994).

5. Relations between the EU and Central and Eastern Europe are examined in Rumen Dobrinsky and Michael Landesmann (eds), *Transforming Economies and European Integration*, Aldershot, Edward Elgar, 1995.

6. John Mueller, 'Democracy, Capitalism, and the End of Transition', in Michael Mandelbaum (ed.), *Postcommunism: Four Perspectives*, New York, A Council on Foreign Relations Book, 1996, Chapter 3.

7. Charles Gati, 'If Not Democracy, What? Leaders, Laggards, and Losers in the Postcommunist World', in Michael Mandelbaum (ed.), op. cit., Chapter 4.

8. Mary Kaldor and Ivan Vejvoda, 'Democratization in central and east European countries', *International Affairs*, vol. 73, no. 1 (January 1997), pp. 59–82.

9. Two paradoxes of economic transformation, identified by Martha de Melo, Cevdet Denizer, and Alan Gelb in their above-quoted article, deserve mentioning in this connection. First, the attempt to maintain output by subsidizing enterprises results in larger declines in output than occur under a policy of reducing subsidies. Second, price liberalization results in lower inflation than occurs under a policy of continued price controls.

10. Vincent Cable formulated three scenarios for the EU's future: fortress (mercantilist) Europe, wider (multi-speed) Europe, and fragmented Europe or the return to nationalism. ('Key Trends in the European Economy and Future Scenarios', in Hugh Miall (ed.), *Redefining Europe: New Patterns of Conflict and Cooperation*, London, Pinter, 1994, Chapter 6.)

11. For a preliminary version see J.L. Porket, 'The Individual and the State.' A paper presented at the 18th World Congress of the Czechoslovak Society of Arts and Sciences, Brno, the Czech Republic, 25–29 August 1996.

12. J.L. Porket, 'Socialism on the Retreat, but not Dead', *The Slavonic and East European Review*, vol. 71, no. 1 (January 1993), pp. 133–6, and J.L. Porket, 'The Visible versus the Invisible Hand: A Tension Inherent in Post-Communist Economies.' A paper prepared for the V. ICSEES World Congress, Warsaw, 6–11 August 1995.

13. The recent advocacy for, and in, the West of a new form of market socialism is discussed by Christopher Pierson, *Socialism after Communism: The New Market Socialism*, Cambridge, Polity Press, 1995.

14. *The Economist*, 4 April 1992, p. 91.

15. In John Gray's view, new protectionism is needed because unfettered global free trade makes people economically insecure and poses the threat of social and political upheavals. ('Into the Abyss?' *The Sunday Times*, 30 October 1994, p. 2.6.) See also Colin Hines, 'The "New Protectionism",' *Economic Affairs*, vol. 16, no. 5 (winter 1996), pp. 29–32. According to him, the New Protectionism is an alternative to free markets and global free trade. 'Its essence is to allow nations and communities to retake control over their local economies and to make them as diverse as possible. It uses policies which ensure that over a period of time there is a transition from the present situation where all

economies are trying to compete with each other, to one where goods and servicies are provided locally wherever possible.'

16. According to a statement by the Catholic Bishops' Conference of England & Wales, for instance, '[p]rofits should not be regarded as solely of interest to managers or shareholders, but as a source of a social dividend in which others have a right to benefit.' (*The Common Good and the Catholic Church's Social Teaching*, London, 1996, p. 21.)

17. On the neo-revisionism of the 1980s and 1990s see Donald Sassoon, *One Hundred Years of Socialism: The West European Left in the Twentieth Century*, London, I.B. Tauris, 1996, Chapter 24.

18. Of these five main conditions, the second, fourth, and fifth were mentioned by Samuel Brittan, *Capitalism with a Human Face*, Aldershot, Edward Elgar, 1995, Chapter 5.

Select Bibliography

ADAM, Jan. *Planning and Market in Soviet and East European Thought, 1960s–1992.* (Basingstoke: Macmillan, 1993.)

ALBERT, Michel. *Capitalism against Capitalism.* (London: Whurr Publishers, 1993.)

ALESSANDRINI, Sergio and DALLAGO, Bruno (eds). *The Unofficial Economy.* (Aldershot: Gower, 1987.)

ALLARDT, Erik and ROKKAN, Stein (eds). *Mass Politics: Studies in Political Sociology.* (New York: The Free Press, 1970.)

ALMOND, Gabriel A. and POWELL, Jr., G. Bingham. *Comparative Politics: A Developmental Approach.* (Boston: Little, Brown and Company, 1966.)

ANDERSON, Martin J. (ed.). *The Unfinished Agenda.* (London: The Institute of Economic Affairs, 1986.)

ANDRUSZ, Gregory D. *Housing and Urban Development in the USSR.* (London: Macmillan, 1984.)

ASHWORTH, William. *A Short History of The International Economy since 1850.* (London: Longmans, Green and Co., 1967, second edition, reprinted.)

ÅSLUND, Anders. *Private Enterprise in Eastern Europe.* (London: Macmillan, 1985.)

ÅSLUND, Anders (ed.). *Market Socialism or the Restoration of Capitalism?* (Cambridge: Cambridge University Press, 1992.)

ÅSLUND, Anders and LAYARD, Richard (eds). *Changing the Economic System in Russia.* (London: Pinter Publishers, 1993.)

ATKINSON, Anthony B. and MICKLEWRIGHT, John. *Economic Transformation in Eastern Europe and the Distribution of Income.* (Cambridge: Cambridge University Press, 1992.)

BACON, Robert and ELTIS, Walter. *Britain's Economic Problem Revisited.* (Basingstoke: Macmillan, 1996, third edition.)

BALCEROWICZ, Leszek. *Socialism, Capitalism, Transformation.* (Budapest: Central European University Press, 1995.)

BALDASSARRI, Mario, PAGANETTO, Luigi, and PHELPS, Edmund S. (eds). *Privatization Process in Eastern Europe: Theoretical Foundations and Empirical Results.* (Basingstoke: Macmillan, 1993.)

BALFOUR, Campbell. *Industrial Relations in the Common Market.* (London: Routledge & Kegan Paul, 1972.)

BARDHAN, Pranab and ROEMER, John E. 'Market Socialism: A Case for Rejuvenation.' *Journal of Economic Perspectives,* vol. 6, no. 3 (summer 1992), pp. 101–116.

BARDHAN, Pranab K. and ROEMER, John E. (eds). *Market Socialism: The Current Debate.* (Oxford: Oxford University Press, 1993.)

BARKAI, Avraham. *Nazi Economics: Ideology, Theory, and Policy.* (Oxford: Berg Publishers Limited, 1990.)

BARR, Nicholas et al, *The State of Welfare.* (Oxford: Clarendon Press, 1990.)

BARR, Nicholas. *The Economics of the Welfare State*. (London: Weidenfeld and Nicolson, 1993, second edition.)

BARR, Nicholas (ed.). *Labor Markets and Social Policy in Central and Eastern Europe*. (New York: Oxford University Press, 1994.)

BARRACLOUGH, Geoffrey (ed.). *The Times Atlas of World History*. (London: Book Club Associates, 1979, reprinted.)

BARRY, Norman P. *An Introduction to Modern Political Theory*. (London: Macmillan, 1989, second edition.)

BARRY, Norman. *Welfare*. (Milton Keynes: Open University Press, 1994, reprinted.)

BARTH, Richard C., ROE, Alan R., and WONG, Chorng-Huey (eds). *Coordinating Stablilization and Structural Reform*. (Washington, D.C.: IMF, 1994.)

BELL, Daniel. *The End of Ideology: On the Exhaustion of Political Ideas in the Fifties*. (New York: The Free Press, 1965, revised edition.)

BERGER, Peter L. *The Capitalist Revolution*. (Aldershot: Wildwood House, 1987.)

BEYME, Klaus von. *Challenge to Power*. (London: SAGE Publications, 1980.)

BEYME, Klaus von and ZIMMERMAN, Hartmut (eds). *Policymaking in the German Democratic Republic*. (Aldershot: Gower, 1984.)

BIRD, Graham (ed.). *Economic Reform in Eastern Europe*. (Aldershot: Edward Elgar, 1992.)

BISCHOF, Günter and PELINKA, Anton (eds). *Austro-Corporatism: Past – Present – Future*. (New Brunswick: Transaction Publishers, 1996.)

BISMARCK, Philipp von. *Soziale Marktwirtschaft*. (Freiburg: Herder, 1992.)

BLANCHARD, Olivier Jean, FROOT, Kenneth A., and SACHS, Jeffrey D. (eds). *The Transition in Eastern Europe: Vol. 1*. (Chicago: The University of Chicago Press, 1994.)

BLOMMESTEIN, Hans and MARRESE, Michael (eds). *Transformation of Planned Economies: Property Rights Reform and Macroeconomic Stability*. (Paris: OECD, 1991.)

BLONDEL, Jean. *An Introduction to Comparative Government*. (London: Weidenfeld and Nicolson, 1969.)

BOJE, Thomas P. and HORT, Sven E. Olsson (eds). *Scandinavia in a New Europe*. (Oslo: Scandinavian University Press, 1993.)

BOLTHO, Andrea (ed.). *The European Economy: Growth and Crisis*. (Oxford: Oxford University Press, 1982.)

BONIN, John P. and SZÉKELY, István P. (eds). *The Development and Reform of Financial Systems in Central and Eastern Europe*. (Aldershot: Edward Elgar, 1994.)

BORNSTEIN, Morris. *Plan and Market*. (New Haven: Yale University Press, 1973.)

BRABANT, Jozef M. van. *Industrial Policy in Eastern Europe: Governing the Transition*. (Dordrecht: Kluwer Academic Publishers, 1993.)

BRADA, Josef C. 'The Transformation from Communism to Capitalism: How Far? How Fast?' *Post-Soviet Affairs*, vol. 9, no. 2 (April-June 1993), pp. 87–110.

BRASH, Donald T. *New Zealand's Remarkable Reforms*. (London: The Institute of Economic Affairs, 1996.)

BREZINSKI, Horst and FRITSCH, Michael (eds). *The Economic Impact of New Firms in Post-Socialist Countries: Bottom-up Transformation in Eastern Europe.* (Cheltenham: Edward Elgar, 1996.)

BRITTAN, Samuel. *Capitalism with a Human Face.* (Aldershot: Edward Elgar, 1995.)

BRÜCK, Gerhard W. *Allgemeine Sozialpolitik.* (Köln: Bund-Verlag, 1976.)

BRUNO, Michael and SACHS, Jeffrey D. *Economics of Worldwide Stagflation.* (Oxford: Basil Blackwell, 1985.)

BRYANT, Christopher G.A. and MOKRZYCKI, Edmund (eds), *The New Great Transformation?* (London: Routledge, 1994.).

BRZEZINSKI, Zbigniew. *The Grand Failure: The Birth and Death of Communism in the Twentieth Century.* (London: Macdonald, 1990.)

CAMERON, Rondo. *A Concise Economic History of the World.* (Oxford: Oxford University Press, 1993, second edition.)

CAMPBELL, Robert W. (ed.). *The Postcommunist Economic Transformation.* (Boulder: Westview Press, 1994.)

CARSON, Richard L. *Comparative Economic Systems.* (Armong, New York: M.E. Sharpe, 1990.)

CAVE, Martin and HARE, Paul. *Alternative Approaches to Economic Planning.* (London: Macmillan, 1981.)

CHAVANCE, Bernard. *The Transformation of Communist Systems: Economic Reform Since the 1950s.* (Boulder: Westview Press, 1994.)

CHEHABI, H.E. and STEPAN, Alfred (eds). *Politics, Society, and Democracy: Comparative Studies.* (Boulder: Westview Press, 1995.)

CHILDE, Gordon. *What Happened in History.* (Harmondsworth: Penguin Books, 1986, reprinted.)

CIGNO, Alessandro. *Economics of the Family.* (Oxford: Clarendon Press, 1991.)

CLAGUE, Christopher and RAUSSER, Gordon C. (eds). *The Emergence of Market Economies in Eastern Europe.* (Oxford: Blackwell, 1992.)

COHN, Stanley H. *Economic Development in the Soviet Union.* (Lexington, Massachusetts: D.C. Heath and Company, 1970.)

COKER, Christopher (ed.). *Drifting Apart? The Superpowers and Their European Allies.* (London: Brassey's Defence Publishers, 1989.)

COMPSTON, Hugh. 'Union Participation in Economic Policy-Making in Austria, Switzerland, The Netherlands, Belgium and Ireland, 1970–1992.' *West European Politics,* vol. 17, no. 1 (January 1994), pp. 123–145.

CONKLIN, David W. *Comparative Economic Systems: Objectives, Decision Modes, and the Process of Choice.* (Cambridge: Cambridge University Press, 1991.)

CONNOR, Walter D. *Socialism, Politics, and Equality.* (New York: Columbia University Press, 1979.)

COOK, Paul and NIXSON, Frederick (eds). *The Move to the Market?* (Basingstoke: Macmillan, 1995.)

CREEDY, John and DISNEY, Richard. 'Can We Afford to Grow Older? Population Aging and Social Security.' *European Economic Review,* vol. 33, nos. 2–3 (March 1989), pp. 367–376.

CRICK, Bernard. *Socialism.* (Milton Keynes: Open University Press, 1987.)

CURWEN, Peter (ed.). *Understanding the UK Economy*. (Basingstoke: Macmillan, 1990.)

DAHL, Robert A. *Polyarchy: Participation and Opposition*. (New Haven: Yale University Press, 1971.)

DAHRENDORF, Ralf. *Reflections on the Revolution in Europe*. (London: Chatto & Windus, 1990.)

DALLAGO, Bruno, BREZINSKI, Horst, and ANDREFF, Wladimir (eds). *Convergence and System Change*. (Aldershot: Dartmouth, 1991.)

DALLIN, Alexander. 'Causes of the Collapse of the USSR.' *Post-Soviet Affairs*, vol. 8, no. 4 (October-December 1992), pp. 279–302.

DAMGAARD, E., GERLICH, P., and RICHARDSON, J.J. (eds). *The Politics of Economic Crisis*. (Aldershot: Avebury, 1989.)

DANIELS, P.W. and LEVER, W.F. (eds). *The Global Economy in Transition*. (London: Longman, 1996.)

DELEYNE, Jan. *The Chinese Economy*. (London: André Deutsch, 1973.)

DESAI, Padma. *The Soviet Economy: Problems and Prospects*. (Oxford: Basil Blackwell, 1987.)

DEUTSCH, Karl W. *Politics and Government*. (Boston: Houghton Mifflin Company, 1970.)

DEYL, Zdenek. *Sociální vývoj Ceskoslovenska 1918–1938*. (Praha: Academia, 1985.)

DIXON, John and MACAROV, David (eds). *Social Welfare in Socialist Countries*. (London: Routledge, 1992.)

DOBRINSKY, Rumen and LANDESMANN, Michael (eds). *Transforming Economies and European Integration*. (Aldershot: Edward Elgar, 1995.)

DOPFER, Kurt and RAIBLE, Karl-F. (eds). *The Evolution of Economic Systems*. (Basingstoke: Macmillan, 1990.)

DOYLE, William. *The Oxford History of the French Revolution*. (Oxford: Oxford University Press, 1989, reprinted.)

DUVERGER, Maurice. *Party Politics and Pressure Groups*. (London: Thomas Nelson and Sons Ltd, 1972.)

DUVERGER, Maurice. *The Study of Politics*. (London: Thomas Nelson and Sons Ltd, 1972.)

EARLE, John S. et al. *Small Privatization*. (Budapest: Central European University Press, 1994.)

EASTON, David. *A Framework for Political Analysis*. (Englewood Cliffs, N.J.: Prentice-Hall, Inc., 1965.)

EATWELL, John, MILGATE, Murray, and NEWMAN, Peter (eds). *Marxian Economics*. (London: Macmillan, 1990.)

EATWELL, John, MILGATE, Murray, and NEWMAN, Peter (eds). *Economic Development*. (London: Macmillan, 1991, reprinted.)

EBRD. *Transition Report 1996*.

EBRD. *Transition Report Update*. (April 1996.)

ECKSTEIN, Alexander. *China's Economic Revolution*. (Cambridge: Cambridge University Press, 1977.)

EINZIG, Paul. *Decline and Fall? Britain's Crisis in the Sixties*. (London: Macmillan, 1969.)

ELBOW, Matthew H. *French Corporative Theory: 1789–1948*. (New York: Octagon Books, 1966, reprinted.)

ENGLIS, Karel. *An Essay on Economic Systems: A Teleological Approach.* (Boulder: East European Monographs, 1986.)

ERNST, Maurice, ALEXEEV, Michael, and MARER, Paul. *Transforming the Core: Restructuring Industrial Enterprises in Russia and Central Europe.* (Boulder: Westview Press, 1996.)

ETZIONI, Amitai. *The Active Society: A Theory of Societal and Political Processes.* (London: Collier-Macmillan Limited, 1968, second printing.)

ETZIONI, Amitai. *The Moral Dimension: Toward a New Economics.* (New York: The Free Press, 1988.)

FERGE, ZSUZSA. *A Society in the Making.* (Harmondsworth: Penguin Books, 1979.)

FERNÁNDEZ-ARMESTO, Felipe. *Millennium.* (London: Bantam Press, 1995.)

FISCHER, George. *The Soviet System and Modern Society.* (New York: Atherton Press, 1968.)

FLAKIERSKI, Henryk and SEKINE, Thomas T. (eds). *Socialist Dilemmas: East and West.* (Armonk, New York: M.E. Sharpe, 1990.)

FRIEDGUT, Theodore H. *Political Participation In the USSR.* (Princeton, New Jersey: Princeton University Press, 1979.)

FRIEDMAN, Milton. *Capitalism and Freedom.* (Chicago: The University of Chicago Press, 1982, reissued.)

FRIEDMAN, Milton and FRIEDMAN, Rose. *Free to Choose: A Personal Statement.* (New York: Harcourt Brace Janovich, 1980.)

FRIEDRICH, Carl J. *Limited Government: A Comparison.* (Englewood Cliffs, N.J.: Prentice-Hall, Inc., 1974.)

FUKUYAMA, Francis. *The End of History and the Last Man.* (London: Penguin Books, 1992.)

GAERTNER, Wulf and WENIG, Alois (eds). *The Economics of the Shadow Economy.* (Berlin: Springer-Verlag, 1985.)

GALBRAITH, John Kenneth. *The New Industrial State.* (London: Andre Deutsch, 1972, second edition.)

GALBRAITH, John Kenneth. *The Affluent Society.* (London: André Deutsch, 1985, fourth edition.)

GALBRAITH, John Kenneth. *A History of Economics: The Past as the Present.* (London: Penguin Books, 1991, reprinted.)

GATI, Charles (ed.). *The Politics of Modernization in Eastern Europe.* (New York: Praeger Publishers, 1974.)

GEIGER, Theodore. *Welfare and Efficiency.* (London: Macmillan, 1979.)

GIDDENS, Anthony. *Beyond Left and Right: The Future of Radical Politics.* (Cambridge: Polity Press, 1994.)

GIRVIN, Brian (ed.). *The Transformation of Contemporary Conservatism.* (London: SAGE Publications, 1988.)

GOLDTHORPE, John H. (ed.). *Order and Conflict in Contemporary Capitalism.* (Oxford: Clarendon Press, 1988, reprinted.)

GORDON, Margaret S. *Social Security Policies in Industrial Countries.* (Cambridge: Cambridge University Press, 1988,)

GOWLAND, D.H. (ed.). *Finance in Eastern Europe.* (Aldershot: Dartmouth, 1992.)

GRAHAM, Andrew and SELDON, Anthony (eds). *Government and Economies in the Postwar World*. (London: Routledge, 1990.)

GRAHAM, Carol. *Safety Nets, Politics, and the Poor: Transitions to Market Economies*. (Washington, D.C.: The Brookings Institution, 1994.)

GRANOVETTER, Mark and SWEDBERG, Richard (eds). *The Sociology of Economic Life*. (Boulder: Westview Press, 1992.)

GRAY, John. *Beyond the New Right*. (London: Routledge, 1993.)

GRIFFIN, Keith. *Alternative Strategies for Economic Development*. (Basingstoke: Macmillan, 1989.)

GRIFFITHS, Brian. *Morality and the Market Place*. (London: Hodder & Stoughton, 1982.

GROS, Daniel and STEINHERR, Alfred. *Winds of Change: Economic Transition in Central and Eastern Europe*. (London: Longman, 1995.)

GROSSMAN, Gregory. *Economic Systems*. (Englewood Cliffs, New Jersey: Prentice-Hall, 1974, second edition.)

GROSSMAN, Gregory. 'What Was – Is, Will Be – The Command Economy.' *MOCT-MOST*, vol. 4, no. 1 (1994), pp. 5–22.

GURR, Ted Robert. *Why Men Rebel*. (Princeton, New Jersey: Princeton University Press, 1971, third printing.)

GWARTNEY, James, LAWSON, Robert, and BLOC, Walter. *Economic Freedom of the World: 1975–1995*. (London: The Institute of Economic Affairs, 1996.)

HABERMAS, Jürgen. *Legitimation Crisis*. (Cambridge: Polity Press, 1992, reprinted.)

HALL, Peter A. (ed.). *The Political Power of Economic Ideas: Keynesianism across Nations*. (Princeton, New Jersey: Princeton University Press, 1989.)

HALM, George N. *Economic Systems*. (New York: Holt, Rinehart and Winston, Inc., 1968, third edition.)

HAMMOND, Thomas T. (ed.). *The Anatomy of Communist Takeovers*. (New Haven: Yale University Press, 1975.)

HANCOCK, M. Donald and WELSH, Helga A. (eds). *German Unification: Process and Outcomes*. (Boulder: Westview Press, 1994.)

HARDING, Neil (ed.). *The State in Socialist Society*. (London: Macmillan, 1984.)

HARDT, John P. and KAUFMAN, Richard F. (eds). *East-Central European Economies in Transition*. (Armonk, New York: M.E. Sharpe, 1995.)

HAUSNER, Jerzy, JESSOP, Bob, and NIELSEN, Klaus (eds). *Strategic Choice and Path-Dependency in Post-Socialism: Institutional Dynamics in the Transformation Process*. (Aldershot: Edward Elgar, 1995.)

HAYEK, F.A. (ed.). *Collectivist Economic Planning*. (London: George Routledge & Sons, 1935.)

HAYEK, F.A. *The Constitution of Liberty*. (London: Routledge & Kegan Paul, 1960.)

HAYEK, F.A. *The Fatal Conceit: The Errors of Socialism*. (London: Routledge, 1988.)

HEILBRONER, Robert L. *The Making of Economic Society*. (Englewood Cliffs, New Jersey: Prentice Hall, 1989, eighth edition.)

HELD, David. *Models of Democracy*. (Cambridge: Polity Press, 1989, reprinted.)

HELD, David (ed.). *Prospects for Democracy.* (Cambridge: Polity Press, 1993.)

HERSH, Jacques and SCHMIDT, Johannes Dragsbaek (eds). *The Aftermath of 'Real Existing Socialism' in Eastern Europe: Volume 1: Between Western Europe and East Asia.* (Basingstoke: Macmillan, 1996.)

HEWETT, Ed. A. *Reforming the Soviet Economy: Equality versus Efficiency.* (Washington, D.C.: The Brookings Institution, 1988.)

HEWETT, Ed. A. and WINSTON, Victor H. (eds). *Milestones in Glasnost and Perestroyka: Politics and People.* (Washington, D.C.: The Brookings Institution, 1991.)

HIGGINS, Joan. *States of Welfare.* (Oxford: Basil Blackwell and Martin Robertson, 1981.)

HOFFMANN, Erik P. and LAIRD, Robbin F. *The Politics of Economic Modernization in the Soviet Union.* (London: Cornell University Press, 1982.)

HOLMES, Leslie. *The End of Communist Power: Anti-Corruption Campaigns and Legitimation Crisis.* (Cambridge: Polity Press, 1993.)

HOUGH, Jerry F. *The Soviet Prefects: The Local Party Organs in Industrial Decision-making.* (Cambridge, Massachusetts: Harvard University Press, 1969).

HOWARD, Michael. *The Lessons of History.* (Oxford: Clarendon Press, 1991.)

HUNT, Diana. *Economic Theories of Development: An Analysis of Competing Paradigms.* (New York: Harvester Wheatsheaf, 1989.)

HUNTFORD, Roland. *The New Totalitarians.* (London: Allen Lane The Penguin Press, 1971.)

HUNYA, Gábor (ed.). *Economic Transformation in East-Central Europe and in the Newly Independent States.* (Boulder: Westview Press, 1994.)

ILO. *World employment 1995.* (Geneva: 1995.)

INTERNATIONAL SOCIAL SECURITY ASSOCIATION. *Restructuring Social Security in Central and Eastern Europe: A Guide to Recent Development, Policy Issues and Options.* (Geneva: 1994.)

ISLAM, Shafiqul and MANDELBAUM, Michael (eds). *Making Markets: Economic Transformation in Eastern Europe and the Post-Soviet States.* (New York: Council on Foreign Relations Press, 1993.)

JACKSON, Marvin, KOLTAY, Jenö, and BIESBROUCK, Wouter. *Unemployment and Evolving Labor Market in Central and Eastern Europe.* (Aldershot: Avebury, 1995.)

JEFFRIES, Ian. *A Guide to the Economies in Transition.* (London: Routledge, 1996.)

JEWKES, John. *Ordeal by Planning.* (London: Macmillan, 1949, reprinted.)

JEWKES, John. *The New Ordeal by Planning.* (London: Macmillan, 1968.)

JOHNSON, Chalmers (ed.). *Change in Communist Systems.* (Stanford, California: Stanford University Press, 1970.)

JOHNSON, Norman. *The Welfare State in Transition: The Theory and Practice of Welfare Pluralism.* (Brighton: Wheatsheaf Books, 1987.)

KAIM-CAUDLE, P.R. *Comparative Social Policy and Social Security.* (London: Martin Robertson, 1973.)

KAMARCK, Andrew M. *Economics and the Real World.* (Oxford: Basil Blackwell, 1983.)

KASSOF, Allen. *Prospects for Soviet Society*. (London: Pall Mall Press, 1968.)
KAVANAGH, Dennis and SELDON, Anthony (eds). *The Thatcher Effect*. (Oxford: Clarendon Press, 1989.)
KEEGAN, John. *A History of Warfare*. (London: PIMLICO, 1994.)
KELLY, Donald R. (ed.). *Soviet Politics in the Brezhnev Era*. (New York: Praeger, 1980.)
KNELL, Mark and RIDER, Christine (eds). *Socialist Economies in Transition: Appraisals of the Market Mechanism*. (Aldershot: Edward Elgar, 1992.)
KORNAI, János. *Economics of Shortage*. (Amsterdam: North-Holland Publishing Company, 1980.)
KORNAI, János. *Growth, Shortage and Efficiency*. (Oxford: Basil Blackwell, 1982.)
KORNAI, János. *The Socialist System: The Political Economy of Communism*. (Oxford: Oxford University Press, 1992.)
KREJCÍ, Jaroslav and MACHONIN, Pavel. *Czechoslovakia, 1918–92: A Laboratory for Social Change*. (Basingstoke: Macmillan, 1996.)
KRUEGER, Anne O. *Political Economy of Policy Reform in Developing Countries*. (Cambridge, Massachusetts: The MIT Press, 1993.)
KURZ, Heinz D. (ed.). *United Germany and the New Europe*. (Aldershot: Edward Elgar, 1993.)
LANDAUER, Carl. *Contemporary Economic Systems*. (Philadelphia: J.B. Lippincott Company, 1964.)
LANE, David. *The Socialist Industrial State*. (London: George Allen & Unwin Ltd., 1976.)
LANGE, Oskar and TAYLOR, Fred M. *On the Economic Theory of Socialism*: ed. Benjamin E. Lippincott. (New York: McGraw-Hill Book Company, 1964.)
LANGE, Peter and REGINI, Marino (eds). *State, Market, and Social Regulation: New Perspectives on Italy*. (Cambridge: Cambridge University Press, 1989.)
LAVIGNE, Marie. *The Economics of Transition: From Socialist Economy to Market Economy*. (Basingstoke: Macmillan, 1995.)
LAVOIE, Don. *Rivalry and Central Planning*. (Cambridge: Cambridge University Press, 1985.)
LENSKI, Gerhard E. *Power and Privilege. A Theory of Social Stratification*. (New York: McGraw-Hill Book Company, 1966.)
LENSKI, Gerhard and LENSKI, Jean. *Human Societies: An Introduction to Macrosociology*. (New York: McGraw-Hill Book Company, 1989, fifth edition, second printing.)
LERNER, Abba P. *The Economics of Control*. (New York: Macmillan, 1944.)
LETWIN, Shirley Robin. *The Anatomy of Thatcherism*. (London: Fontana, 1992.)
LINDBLOM, Charles E. *Politics and Market: The World's Political-Economic Systems*. (New York: Basic Books, 1977.)
LINDBLOM, Charles E. *Democracy and Market System*. (Oslo: Norwegian University Press, 1988.)
LINDEMANN, Albert S. *A History of European Socialism*. (New Haven: Yale University Press, 1983.)

LIPSON, E. *A Planned Economy or Free Enterprise.* (London; Adam & Charles Black, 1946, second edition.)

MACFARLANE, L.J. *The Theory and Practice of Human Rights.* (London: Maurice Temple Smith, 1985.)

MacIVER, R.M. *The Web of Government.* (New York: The Macmillan Company, 1947, second printing.)

MADDISON, Angus. *Phases of Capitalist Development.* (Oxford: Oxford University Press, 1982.)

MADDISON, Angus. *The World Economy in the 20th Century.* (Paris: OECD, 1989.)

MADDISON, Angus. *Dynamic Forces in Capitalist Development: A Long-Run Comparative View.* (Oxford: Oxford University Press, 1991.)

MADDOCK, R.T. *The Political Economy of Soviet Defence Spending.* (London: Macmillan, 1988.)

MADISON, Bernice Q. *Social Welfare in the Soviet Union.* (Stanford, California: Stanford University Press, 1968.)

MALINOWSKI, Bronislaw. *Freedom and Civilization.* (London: George Allen & Unwin Ltd., 1947.)

MANDELBAUM, Michael (ed.). *Postcommunism: Four Perspectives.* (New York: A Council on Foreign Relations Book, 1996.)

MANKIW, N. Gregory and ROMER, David (eds). *New Keynesian Economics.* (Cambridge, Massachusetts: The MIT Press, 1991.)

MARQUAND, David and SELDON, Anthony (eds). *The Ideas that Shaped Post-War Britain.* (London: Fontana Press, 1996.)

MARSDEN, David (ed.). *Pay and Employment in the New Europe.* (Aldershot: Edward Elgar, 1992.)

MARSHALL, G.P. *Social Goals and Economic Perspectives.* (Harmondsworth: Penguin Books, 1980.)

MATTERA, Philip. *Off the Books.* (London: Pluto Press, 1985.)

McCAULEY, Martin. *The German Democratic Republic since 1945.* (London: Macmillan, 1983.)

McMAHON, Gary (ed.). *Lessons in Economic Policy for Eastern Europe from Latin America.* (Basingstoke; Macmillan, 1996.)

MEJSTRÍK, Michal (ed.). *The Privatization Process in East-Central Europe: Evolutionary Process in Czech Privatization.* (Dordrecht: Kluwer Academic Publishers, 1997.)

MERRIAM, Charles E. *Systematic Politics.* (Chicago: University of Chicago Press, 1946, second impression.)

MERTON, Robert K. *Social Theory and Social Structure.* (Glencoe, Illinois: The Free Press, 1958, second printing of revised edition.)

MIALL, Hugh (ed.). *Redefining Europe: New Patterns of Conflict and Cooperation.* (London: Pinter, 1994.)

MICHIE, Jonathan and SMITH, John Grieve (eds). *Unemployment in Europe.* (London: Academic Press, 1994.)

MILLER, David. *Market, State, and Community.* (Oxford: Clarendon Press, 1989.)

MILLER, R.F., MILLER, J.H., and RIGBY, T.H. *Gorbachev at the Helm: A New Era in Soviet Politics?* (London: Croom Helm, 1987.

MOORE, Barrington, Jr. *Social Origins of Dictatorship and Democracy: Lord and Peasant in the Making of the Modern World.* (London: Allen Lane The Penguin Press, 1967.)

MORONEY, John R. 'Energy Consumption, Capital and Real Output: A Comparison of Market and Planned Economies.' *Journal of Comparative Economics*, vol. 14, no. 2 (June 1990), pp. 199–220.

MOSS, Robert. *The Collapse of Democracy.* (London: Maurice Temple Smith, 1975.)

NELL, Edward. *Prosperity and Public Spending.* (Boston: Unwin Hyman, 1988.)

NELSON, Joan M. et al. *Intricate Links: Democratization and Market Reforms in Latin America and Eastern Europe.* (New Brunswick; Transaction Publishers, 1994.)

NEW PALGRAVE, THE: *A Dictionary of Economics.* (London: Macmillan, 1987.)

NISBET, Robert. *Twilight of Authority.* (London: Heinemann, 1976.)

NOVAK, Michael. *The Spirit of Democratic Capitalism.* (New York: Touchstone, 1983.)

NOVE, Alec. *The Economics of Feasible Socialism Revisited.* (London: HarperCollinsAcademic, 1991, second edition.)

NOVE, Alec and THATCHER, Ian D. (eds). *Markets and Socialism.* (Aldershot: Edward Elgar, 1994.)

NOZICK, Robert. *Anarchy, State, and Utopia.* (Oxford: Basil Blackwell, 1974.)

NUGENT, Neill (ed.). *The European Union 1995: Annual Review of Activities.* (Oxford: Blackwell, 1996.)

O'BRIEN, Richard (ed.). *Finance and the International Economy: 8.* (Oxford University Press, 1994.)

OECD. *Revenue Statistics of OECD Member Countries 1965–1987.* (Paris: OECD, 1987.)

OECD. *OECD Economic Surveys: Hungary 1993.* (Paris: 1993.)

OECD. *OECD Surveys 1995–1996: Germany.* (Paris: 1996.)

OECD. *Future Global Capital Shortages: Real Threat or Pure Fiction?* (Paris: OECD, 1996.)

OLSON, David M. and NORTON, Philip (eds). *The New Parliaments of Central and Eastern Europe.* (London: Frank Cass, 1996.)

OLŠOVSKÝ, Rudolf, PRUCHA, Václav, and URBANOVÁ, Zora. *Strucné dejiny svetového hospodárství.* (Praha: Státní pedagogické nakladatelství, 1978.)

OVERY, R.J. *War and Economy in the Third Reich.* (Oxford: Oxford University Press, 1994.)

OXFORD UNIVERSITY INSTITUTE OF STATISTICS, THE. *The Economics of Full Employment.* (Oxford: Basil Blackwell, 1948.)

ØYEN, Else, MILLER, S.M., and SAMAD, Syed Abdus (eds). *Poverty: A Global Review.* (Oslo: Scandinavian University Press, 1996.)

PACK, Spencer J. *Capitalism as a Moral System: Adam Smith's Critique of the Free Market Economy.* (Aldershot: Edward Elgar, 1991.)

PARKIN, Frank. *Class Inequality and Political Order.* (London: MacGibbon & Kee, 1971.)

PARROTT, Bruce. *Politics and Technology in the Soviet Union*. (Cambridge, Massachusetts: The MIT Press, 1983.)

PARSONS, Talcott. *The Social System*. (The Free Press of Glencoe, 1964, fifth printing.)

PAUL, Ellen Frankel, MILLER, Jr., Fred D., and PAUL, Jeffrey (eds). *Liberalism and the Economic Order*. (Cambridge: Cambridge University Press, 1993.)

PAVLÍK, Zdenek (ed.). *Human Development Report: Czech Republic 1996*. (Prague: Faculty of Science, Charles University, 1996.)

PEACOCK, Alan and WILLGERODT, Hans (eds). *Germany's Social Market Economy: Origins and Evolution*. (London: Macmillan, 1989.)

PEACOCK, Alan and WILLGERODT, Hans (eds). *German Neo-Liberals and the Social Market Economy*. (London: Macmillan, 1989.)

PECK, Harvey W. *Economic Thought and Its Institutional Background*. (London: George Allen & Unwin Ltd., 1935.)

PEJOVICH, Svetozar (ed.). *Philosophical and Economic Foundations of Capitalism*. (Lexington, Massachusetts: D.C. Heath and Company, 1983.)

PFALLER, Alfred, GOUGH, Ian, and THERBORN, Göran (eds). *Can the Welfare State Compete?* (Basingstoke: Macmillan, 1991.)

PIERSON, Christopher. *Beyond the Welfare State? The New Political Economy of Welfare*. (Cambridge: Polity Press, 1991.)

PIERSON, Christopher. *Socialism after Communism: The New Market Socialism*. (Cambridge: Polity Press, 1995.)

PINC, Karel. *Sociální politika a socialistické hospodárství*. (Praha: Univerzita Karlova, 1983.)

PLASSER, Fritz and PRIBERSKY, Andreas (eds). *Political Culture in East Central Europe*. (Aldershot: Avebury, 1996.)

POLANYI, Karl. *The Livelihood of Man*. (New York: Academic Press, 1977.)

POMFRET, Richard. *Asian Economies in Transition: Reforming Centrally Planned Economies*. (Cheltenham: Edward Elgar, 1996.)

PORKET, J.L. *Podnik jako sociální systém*. (Bratislava: Ústav ekonomiky a organizácie stavebníctva, 1967.)

PORKET, J.L. *Authority in Communist Czechoslovakia Prior to 1968*. An unpublished Ph.D. thesis, London School of Economic and Political Science, 1973.

PORKET, J.L. *Main Features of Social Security in Eastern Europe*, Centre for Soviet and East European Studies, St. Antony's College, Oxford, Papers in East European Economics, Paper No. 51, 1977.

PORKET, J.L. 'Old Age Pension Schemes in the Soviet Union and Eastern Europe.' *Social Policy & Administration*, vol. 13, no. 1 (spring 1979), pp. 22–36.

PORKET, J.L. 'Inequalities in Eastern Europe: The Case of Old-Age Pensioners', Russian and East European Centre, St. Antony's College, Oxford, Papers in East European Economics, Paper No. 64, 1980.

PORKET, J.L. 'The Economic Lot of Polish Retired Workers.' *Osteuropa-Wirtschaft*, vol. 26, no. 4 (1981), pp. 294–303.

PORKET, J.L. 'Retired Workers under Soviet-Type Socialism', *Social Policy & Administration*, vol. 16, no. 3 (autumn 1982), pp. 253–69.

PORKET, J.L. *Work, Employment and Unemployment in the Soviet Union.* (London: Macmillan, 1989.)

PORKET, J.L. 'Private Plots – One Dimension of the Soviet Second Economy.' *Economic Affairs*, vol. 10, no. 4 (April- May 1990), pp. 28–32.

PORKET, J.L. 'Tensions in Post-Communist Economies.' A paper presented at the conference on International Privatization: Strategies and Practices, University of St. Andrews, Scotland, 12–14 September 1991.

PORKET, J.L. 'Post-Communist Societies and the Tension Between Economic Individualism and Economic Collectivism.' A paper presented at the First European Conference of Sociology, University of Vienna (Austria), 26–29 August 1992.

PORKET, J.L. 'Socialism on the Retreat, but not Dead.' *The Slavonic and East European Review*, vol. 71, no. 1 (January 1993), pp. 133–6.

PORKET, J.L. 'The Visible Versus the Invisible Hand: A Tension Inherent in Modern Economies.' A paper presented at the 17th World Congress of the Czechoslovak Society of Arts and Sciences, Prague, 26–29 June 1994.

PORKET, J.L. *Unemployment in Capitalist, Communist and Post- Communist Economies.* (Basingstoke: Macmillan, 1995.)

PORKET, J.L. 'The Visible Versus the Invisible Hand: A Tension Inherent in Post-Communist Economies.' A paper prepared for the V. ICSEES World Congress, Warsaw, 6–11 August 1995.

PORKET, J.L. 'From Reform to Transformation: the Case of Poland.' *The Slavonic and East European Review*, vol. 74, no. 1 (January 1996), pp. 90–4.

PORKET, J.L. 'Transforming Command Socialism'. *The Slavonic and East Europen Review*, vol. 74, no. 2 (April 1996), pp. 252–8.

PORKET, J.L. 'The Individual and the State.' A paper presented at the 18th World Congress of the Czechoslovak Society of Arts and Sciences, Brno, the Czech Republic, 25–29 August 1996.

PORTES, Richard (ed.). *Economic Transformation in Central Europe: A Progress Report.* (London: Centre for Economic Policy Research, 1993.)

PRAVDA, Alex and RUBLE, Blair A. (eds). *Trade Unions in Communist States.* (London: Allen & Unwin, 1986.)

PRYBYLA, Jan S. (ed.). *Comparative Economic Systems.* (New York: Appleton-Century-Crofts, 1969.)

PRYBYLA, Jan S. 'The Road From Socialism: Why, Where, What, and How.' *Problems of Communism*, vol. XL, nos. 1–2 (January-April 1991), pp. 1–17.

PRYOR, Frederic L. *Public Expenditures in Communist and Capitalist Nations.* (London: George Allen and Unwin Ltd, 1968.)

PRYOR, Frederic L. 'Corporatism as an Economic System: A Review Essay.' *Journal of Comparative Economics*, vol. 12, no. 3 (September 1988), pp. 317–44.

READING, Brian. *Japan: The Coming Collapse.* (London: Weidenfeld and Nicolson, 1992.)

RIGBY, T.H. *Lenin's Government: Sovnarkom 1917–1922.* (Cambridge: Cambridge University Press, 1979.)

RIMLINGER, Gaston V. *Welfare Policy and Industrialization in Europe, America, and Russia.* (New York: John Wiley & Sons, 1971.)

ROBBINS, Lionel. *An Essay on the Nature & Significance of Economic Science.* (London: Macmillan, 1932.)

ROBERTS, Brad (ed.). *New Forces in the World Economy.* (Cambridge, Massachusetts: The MIT Press, 1996.)

ROBERTS, J.M. *The Pelican History of the World.* (Harmondsworth: Penguin Books, 1980.)

ROBERTS, Paul Craig. *Alienation and the Soviet Economy: Toward a General Theory of Marxian Alienation, Organizational Principles, and the Soviet Economy.* (Albuquerque: University of New Mexico Press, 1971.)

ROEMER, John E. *A Future for Socialism.* (London: Verso, 1994.)

ROLL, Eric. *A History of Economic Thought.* (London: Faber and Faber, 1992, fifth edition.)

RÖPKE, Wilhelm. *International Economic Disintegration.* (London: William Hodge and Company, Limited, 1942.)

ROSE, Richard and SHIRATORI, Rei (eds). *The Welfare State East and West.* (Oxford: Oxford University Press, 1986.)

ROSTOW, W.W. *The Stages of Economic Growth: A Non-Communist Manifesto.* (Cambridge: Cambridge University Press, 1960, reprinted.)

ROSTOW, W.W. *The World Economy.* (London: Macmillan, 1978.)

ROSTOW, W.W. *Theorists of Economic Growth from David Hume to the Present: With a Perspective on the Next Century.* (New York: Oxford University Press, 1990.)

ROTH, Gabriel. *The Private Provision of Public Services in Developing Countries.* (New York: Oxford University Press, 1987.)

ROTHSCHILD, Kurt W. 'Political Economy or Economics?' *European Journal of Political Economy,* vol. 5, no. 1 (1989), pp. 1–12.

ROWEN, Henry S. and Wolf, Jr., Charles (eds). *The Future of the Soviet Empire.* (London: Macmillan, 1988.)

ROWLEY, Charles K. and PEACOCK, Alan T. *Welfare Economics.* (London: Martin Robertson, 1975.)

RYAN, Michael. *Doctors and the State in the Soviet Union.* (London: Macmillan, 1989.)

SACHS, Jeffrey. *Understanding 'Shock Therapy'.* (London: The Social Market Foundation, 1994.)

SANDERSON, Stephen K. *Social Transformations: A General Theory of Historical Development.* (Oxford: Blackwell, 1995.)

SASSOON, Donald. *One Hundred Years of Socialism: The West European Left in the Twentieth Century.* (London: I.B. Tauris, 1996.)

SAUNDERS, Peter. *Capitalism. A Social Audit.* (Buckingham: Open University Press, 1995.)

SCHMITTER, Philippe C. and LEHMBRUCH, Gerhard (eds). *Trends Toward Corporatist Intermediation.* (London: SAGE Publications, 1979.)

SCHOLTEN, Ilja (ed.). *Political Stability and Neo-Corporatism.* (London: SAGE Publications, 1987.)

SCHOTTER, Andrew. *Free Market Economics: A Critical Appraisal.* (Oxford: Basil Blackwell, 1990, second edition.)

SCHUMPETER, Joseph A. *Capitalism, Socialism, and Democracy.* (New York: Harper & Brothers Publishers, 1947, second edition.)

SCHWEICKART, David. *Against Capitalism.* (Cambridge University Press, 1993.)

SCREPANTI, Ernesto and ZAMAGNI, Stefano. *An Outline of the History of Economic Thought*. (Oxford: Clarendon Press, 1993.)

SCRUTON, Roger. *A Dictionary of Political Thought*. (London: Pan Books, 1983.)

SELDON, Arthur. *Capitalism*. (Oxford: Basil Blackwell, 1990.)

SELF, Peter. *Government by the Market? The Politics of Public Choice*. (Basingstoke: Macmillan, 1993.)

SHAPIRO, Jane P. and POTICHNYJ, Peter J. (eds). *Change and Adaptation in Soviet and East European Politics*. (New York: Praeger Publishers, 1976.)

SHERIDAN, Kyoko. *Governing the Japanese Economy*. (Cambridge: Polity Press, 1994.)

SIMATUPANG, Batara. *The Polish Economic Crisis*. (London: Routledge, 1994.)

SIMMIE, James and DEKLEVA, Joze (eds). *Yugoslavia in Turmoil: After Self-Management?* (London: Pinter, 1991.)

SKIDELSKY, Robert (ed.). *Thatcherism*. (London: Chatto & Windus, 1988.)

SKIDELSKY, Robert. *The World After Communism: A Polemic For Our Time*. (London: Macmillan, 1995.)

SKIDELSKY, Robert (ed.). *Russia's Stormy Path to Reform*. (London: The Social Market Foundation, 1995.)

SLAY, Ben. *The Polish Economy: Crisis, Reform, and Transformation*. (Princeton, New Jersey: Princeton University Press, 1994.)

SMELSER, Neil J. *The Sociology of Economic Life*. (London: Prentice-Hall International, Inc., 1976, second edition.)

SMIT, Hans and PECHOTA, Vratislav (eds). *Privatization in Eastern Europe: Legal, Economic, and Social Aspects*. (Dordrecht, The Netherlands: Martinus Nijhoff Publishers, 1994.)

SMITH, Adam. *An Inquiry into the Nature and Causes of the Wealth of Nations*. (London: J.M. Dent & Sons Ltd., 1929, reprinted.)

SMITH, Eric Owen. *The German Economy*. (London: Routledge, 1994.)

SMITH, Stephen. *Britain's Shadow Economy*. (Oxford: Clarendon Press, 1986.)

SMYSER, W.R. *The Economy of United Germany: Colossus at the Crossroads*. (London: Hurst & Company, 1992.)

SNOOKS, Graeme Donald. *The Dynamic Society: Exploring the Sources of Global Change*. (London: Routledge, 1996.)

SOMOGYI, Laszlo (ed.). *The Political Economy of the Transition Process in Eastern Europe*. (Aldershot: Edward Elgar, 1993.)

SOROS, George. *Soros on Soros: Staying Ahead of the Curve*. (New York: John Wiley & Sons, 1995.)

STANDFEST, Erich. *Sozialpolitik als Reformpolitik*. (Köln: Bund-Verlag, 1979.)

STEARNS, Peter N. *The Industrial Revolution in World History*. (Boulder, Colorado: Westview Press, 1993.)

STEARNS, Peter N. (ed.). *Encyclopedia of Social History*. (New York: Garland Publishing, 1994.)

STEARNS, Peter N. and CHAPMAN, Herrick. *European Society in Upheaval. Social History Since 1750*. (New York: Macmillan Publishing Company, 1992, third edition.)

STIGLITZ, Joseph E. *Whither Socialism?* (Cambridge, Massachusetts: The MIT Press, 1994.)

STUBBS, Richard and UNDERHILL, Geoffrey R.D. (eds). *Political Economy and the Changing Global Order.* (Basingstoke: Macmillan, 1994.)

STÜTZEL, Wolfgang, WATRIN, Christian, WILLGERODT, Hans, and HÖHMANN Karl (eds), *Grundtexte zur Sozialen Marktwirtschaft.* (Stuttgart: Gustav Fischer Verlag, 1981.)

SZACKI, Jerzy. *Liberalism after Communism.* (Budapest: Central European University Press, 1995.)

SZAJKOWSKI, Bogdan. *The Establishment of Marxist Regimes.* (London: Butterworth Scientific, 1982.)

THANE, Pat. *Foundations of the Welfare State.* (London: Longman, 1994, eleventh impression.)

UEBE, Götz. *World of Economic Models: A catalogue of typical specifications of economic models.* (Aldershot: Avebury, 1995.)

UN ECONOMIC COMMISSION FOR EUROPE. *Trends in Europe and North America – 1995.* (New York: United Nations, 1995.)

UNITED NATIONS. *World Economic and Social Survey 1994.* (New York: 1994.)

UNITED NATIONS. *World Economic and Social Survey 1995: Current Trends and Policies in the World Economy.* (New York: 1995.)

UNITED NATIONS. *World Economic and Social Survey 1996: Trends and Policies in the World Economy.* (New York: 1996.)

VANDAMME, Jacques (ed.). *New Dimensions in European Social Policy.* (London; Croom Helm, 1985.)

VICKERS, Geoffrey. *Human Systems are Different.* (London: Harper & Row, Publishers, 1983.)

VILJOEN, Stephan. *Economic Systems in World History.* (London: Longman, 1974.)

VOLTEN, Peter M.E. (ed.). *Bound to Change: Consolidating Democracy in East Central Europe.* (New York: Institute for East West Studies, 1992.)

VOSLENSKY, Michael. *Nomenklatura.* (London: The Bodley Head, 1984.)

WELFENS, Maria J. 'Das Phänomen der Schattenwirtschaft im Sozialismus,' *Osteuropa-Wirtschaft,* vol. 33, no. 1 (March 1988), pp. 1–15.

WILCZYNSKI, J. *Comparative Industrial Relations.* (London: Macmillan, 1983.)

WILLIAMS, T.G. *The History of Commerce.* (London: Sir Isaac Pitman & Sons, Ltd., 1926.)

WILLIAMSON, Peter J. *Corporatism in Perspective.* (London: SAGE, 1989.)

WILSON, Graham K. *Interest Groups.* (Oxford: Basil Blackwell, 1990.)

WILSON, Thomas and WILSON, Dorothy J. *The Political Economy of the Welfare State.* (London: George Allen & Unwin, 1982.

WILSON, Thomas and WILSON, Dorothy (eds). *The State and Social Welfare.* (London: Longman, 1991.)

WITT, Peter-Christian (ed.). *Wealth and Taxation in Central Europe.* (Leamington Spa: Berg, 1987.)

WORLD BANK, THE. *The East Asian Miracle: Economic Growth and Public Policy.* (New York: Oxford University Press, 1993.)

WORLD BANK, THE. *World Development Report 1996: From Plan to Market.* (New York: Oxford University Press, 1996.)

YASIN, E.G. *Khozyaistvennye sistemy i radikal'naya reforma.* (Moskva: Ekonomika, 1989.)

YUNKER, James A. 'Ludwig von Mises on the "Artificial Market".' *Comparative Economic Studies,* vol. XXXII, no. 1 (Spring 1990), pp. 108–40.

ZON, Hans van. *Alternative Scenarios for Central Europe: Poland, Czech Republic, Slovakia and Hungary.* (Aldershot: Avebury, 1994.)

ZWASS, Adam. *From Failed Communism to Underdeveloped Capitalism.* (Armonk, New York: M.E. Sharpe, 1995.)

Subject Index

Name Index